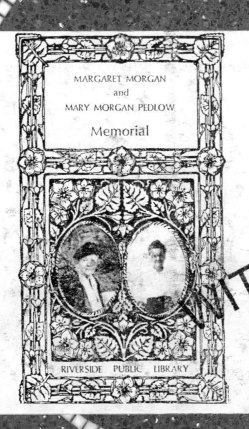

MARGARET MORGAN
and
MARY MORGAN PEDLOW

Memorial

RIVERSIDE PUBLIC LIBRARY

The Getty Villa

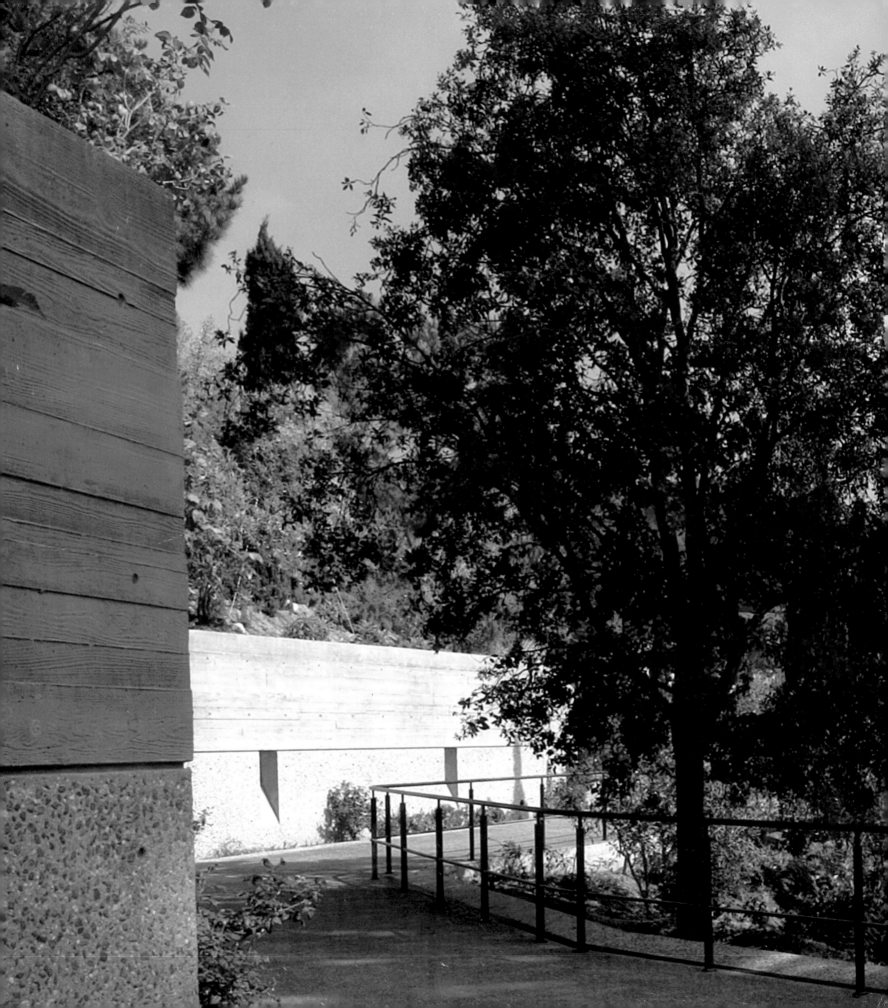

The Getty Villa

Marion True and Jorge Silvetti

WITH AN INTRODUCTION BY
Salvatore Settis

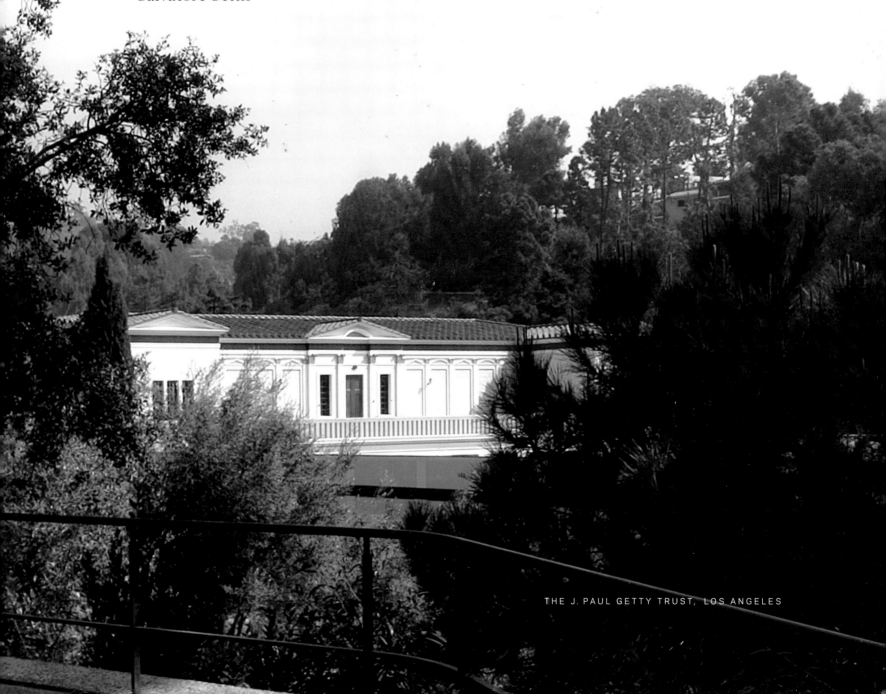

THE J. PAUL GETTY TRUST, LOS ANGELES

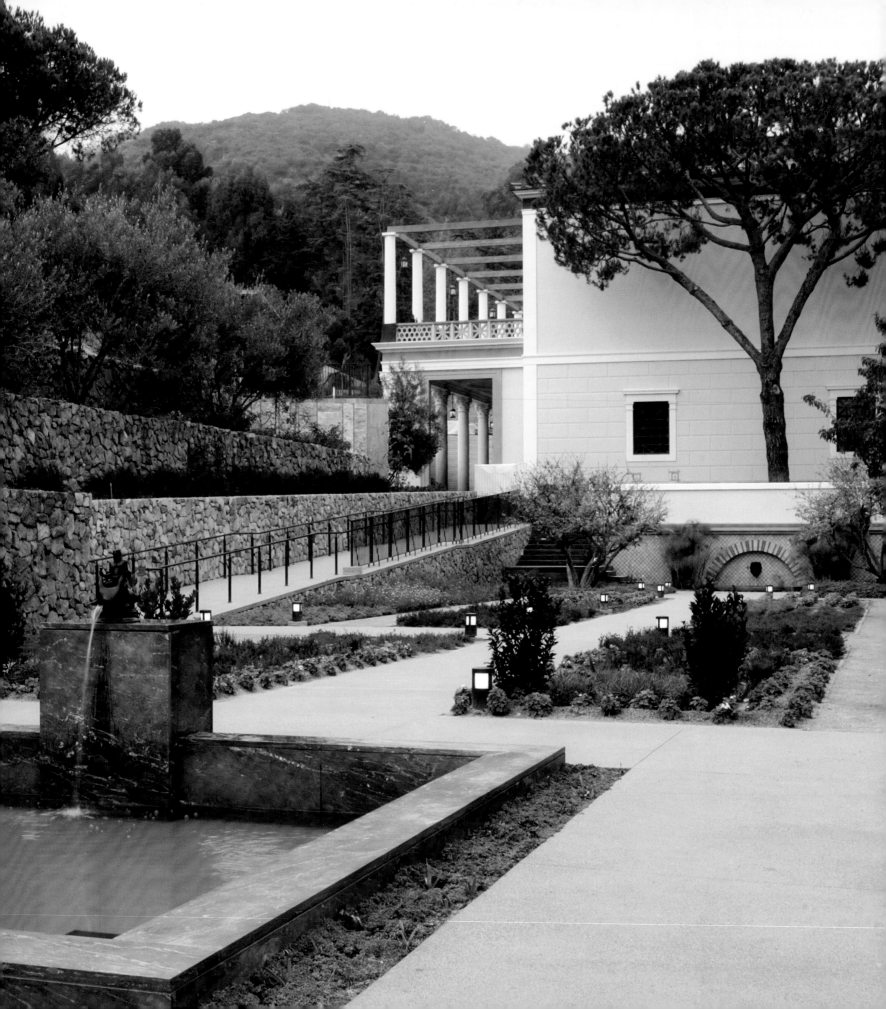

Contents

Foreword   ix
BARRY MUNITZ

Introduction   xi
SALVATORE SETTIS

PART I   The Getty Villa   1

MARION TRUE

1   A Collection Comes to Malibu   3

2   Reconstructing the Villa dei Papiri   13

3   The Villa Renovation Project   59

4   A New Beginning   93

PART II   The Getty Villa Reimagined   97

JORGE SILVETTI

1   Prologue   99

2   Staking Out the Field   107

3   Deciphering the Language—Interpreting the Site   117

4   Tectonic Shifts and the Unearthing of the Villa   129

5   Systematic Exploration and Extraordinary New Findings   145

6   The Museum Restored   173

7   Epilogue   201

Acknowledgments   213

Illustration Credits   219

Index   223

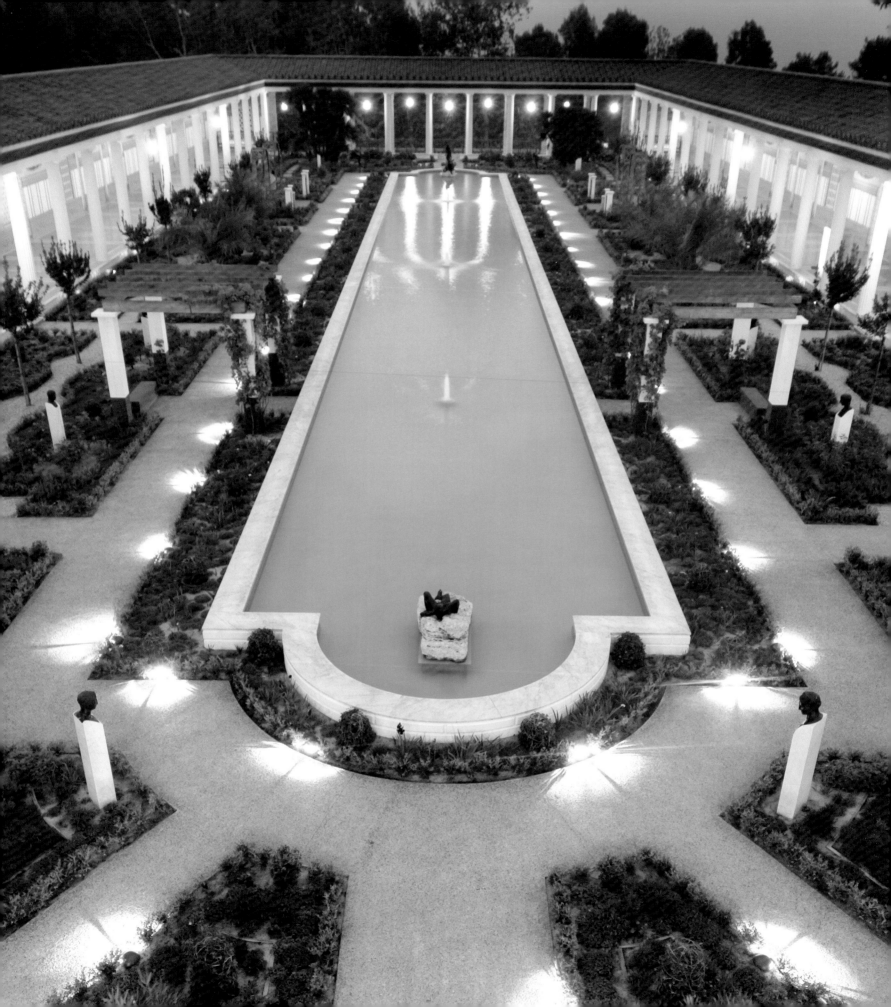

Foreword

For the Board and the administration of the J. Paul Getty Trust, the decision to transform its founder's visionary creation—the Getty Villa—into a center for the study and appreciation of classical arts and culture was both realistic and imaginative. An appropriate and productive use had to be found for the original buildings and the magnificent properties surrounding them, and what more suitable purpose could they serve than to house the works of ancient art and the conservation and research activities that these collections inspire? Although the decision was relatively straightforward, its realization was not so easy to achieve. Mr. Getty's replica of the Villa dei Papiri was a complex, controversial facility located deep within a steep-sided canyon. This canyon, and a carefully regulated coastal zone, was surrounded by residential neighborhoods whose inhabitants were understandably concerned about the level of noise and traffic in the area. The only public access to the site was from the overburdened Pacific Coast Highway, and the predictable interest in this unique complex presented extraordinary hurdles for all of our constituencies.

Fortunately, the team charged with overseeing this renovation and expansion project was up to all of these challenges. The architects, led by Rodolfo Machado and Jorge Silvetti, great specialists in site planning, immediately grasped the difficulty of accommodating additional activities on the site without destroying the lush, natural beauty of the setting. The professional staff of the Getty, led creatively by Marion True, knew well what should be preserved and what needed to be changed after many years of experience working on that site. Laboring together, they created and refined the Master Plan.

Everyone understood that one of the plan's principal objectives had to be integrating aspects of all the Getty Trust programs on the site. Since the interest and expertise of the Museum, the Conservation Institute, the Research Institute, and the Foundation naturally intersect around the arts and cultures of the ancient Mediterranean, the close working quarters were quickly recognized as facilitators for natural collaboration in thoughtful and meaningful ways.

The transformation of this site has now been accomplished. The Getty Villa has been enhanced with additional spaces and programs that respect and amplify its benefactor's original vision. It has taken eight years and the dedication of many people who never lost enthusiasm for the project and its objectives. I hope that all of those visiting the site and reading this book will agree that Mr. Getty would have been pleased with the spectacular results.

BARRY MUNITZ
President and Chief Executive Officer
The J. Paul Getty Trust

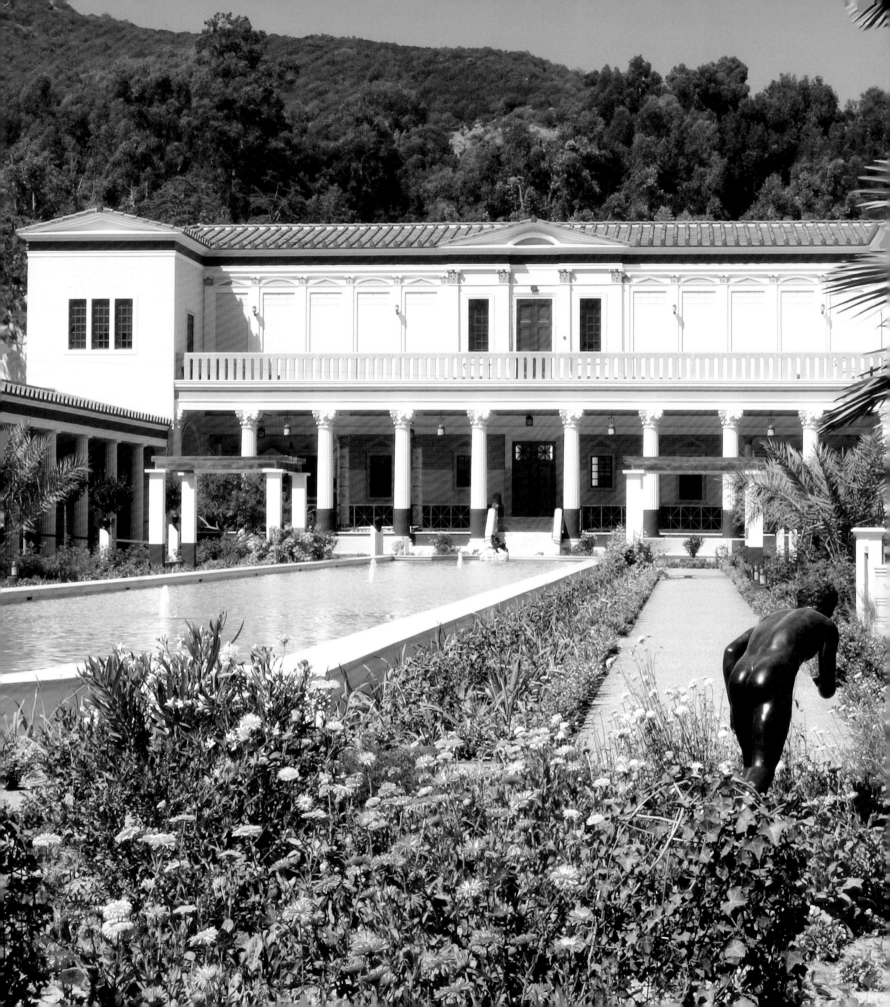

Introduction

SALVATORE SETTIS

Museum design has unexpectedly emerged, in the past few decades, as one of the principal subjects of contemporary architecture. The new wings designed for such venerated museums as those in Stuttgart, London, and Washington, for instance, have had to vie with the functionality and renown of the preexisting structures in order to distinguish themselves. Architects have conceived, and continue to conceive, the designs for new museum additions in marked competition with the preexisting structures, either by appropriating elements from the original design that are then reinterpreted through new vocabularies, or by creating designs that break radically with the past.

More and more frequently the architectonic forms of new museums have become a strongly identifying element. In certain cases iconic design has become the principal factor in attracting visitors, as if the museum itself were a work of art, a kind of giant "sculpture," independent of the collections housed within.

Two relatively contemporary projects, Richard Meier's Getty Center in Los Angeles and Frank Gehry's experimental design for the Bilbao Guggenheim, have played a large role in this debate, by rethinking traditions and adopting radically contrasting strategies vis-à-vis the use of space and forms, as well as by rethinking the relationship between the "envelopes" and the contents of each museum. Other newly created museums, particularly in Europe, have utilized preexisting, historic structures, whose forms are presumed to transmit a message of continuity with the past, thereby creating a kind of contextual environment for the exhibited works, as if they were the "historic" contents and furnishings of equally "historic" buildings.

These developments are taking place in a context of profound evolution, as a result not only of the often uncontrolled growth of cities but also of the unanticipated, unrestrainable growth of the museum-going public. This has created an opportunity for museums to cast themselves in the role of collectors of memories and keepers of traditions in new urban environments that have "no history" or traditions of their own, such as in projects now in development in Hong Kong. This trend has also provided a justification, a kind of cultural alibi, for operations of large-scale real-estate construction ventures.

Museums must come to terms with a public that, as it has continued to grow, has also become less and less cultivated. This compels museums to diversify their offerings and to identify strategies that will attract a segment of the population that has been traditionally resistant to crossing a museum threshold. The quality of a collection, how it is installed, and how it is presented is clearly of paramount importance in this twofold context. But the choice of an architectural style that is not only functional but also captivating is becoming no less important; museum architecture is itself becoming an element of value, independent of its function as a space that houses a collection of works of art. If a museum's architecture, or interior design, can attract more attention than its collections, it is a subject that increasingly merits our careful consideration.

As the Getty Villa reopens on the original site of the J. Paul Getty Museum, the lush Cañon de Sentimiento in Malibu, California, what are the questions it raises? What was the significance of J. Paul Getty's decision, in 1968, to build a museum whose form replicates an ancient Roman structure? And what is the significance as that same architecture is reintroduced in the changed context of 2005, revisited, renovated, and enriched with new contents?

As Marion True and Jorge Silvetti recount in their essays in this book, the initial nucleus of the Getty Museum was the Ranch House, which was constructed in the 1920s in the Spanish Colonial style, then readapted several times. Getty purchased that property in 1945 to use as a museum in which to display his collection of art and antiquities. It opened to the public for a few hours a week in 1954, and the works were displayed in a way that Getty himself described as "modest and unpretentious."

As Getty acquired new works and his collection expanded, it necessitated the addition of new spaces to the Ranch House until finally, in 1968, he decided to commission a new structure to serve as his museum. After rejecting other proposals, he selected a design for a copy of a Roman villa, the Villa dei Papiri in Herculaneum, which had been buried by the eruption of Mount Vesuvius in A.D. 79, then partially excavated in the eighteenth century.

This exercise in "reconstruction," which required a compromise between architectural fidelity and functional demands, was guided by archaeologist Norman Neuerburg and supervised by architect Edward Genter. It opened to the public in January 1974 and, until the inauguration of the new Getty Center in 1997, served the exhibition needs of not only Getty's Greek and Roman collection (which was more in keeping with the Villa's architectonic form) but his other collections as well, including Renaissance painting and sculpture and eighteenth-century furniture and tapestries.

With the opening of the new museum at the Getty Center, the Getty Trust made the strategic decision to utilize the Villa as a separate section of the museum, dedicated exclusively to its collection of ancient art and antiquities. Architects Jorge Silvetti and Rodolfo Machado were selected to renovate the Villa and to rethink radically its uses and functions.

Using the form of an ancient villa as a museum space was a choice that, in 1968, was far from obvious and that generated a great deal of controversy. There had, however, been significant precedents in California, most prominent among them the Hearst Castle in San Simeon (1919–37) and the Huntington Art Gallery in San Marino (1908–11). Other precedents, of a different sort, may be traced back to Europe.

The Hearst Castle was begun in 1919, when William Randolph Hearst enlisted architect Julia Morgan to design in the San Simeon hills a showy residence in a style that was then known as "The San Diego Look." The San Diego Look had been created by New York architect Bertram Goodhue several years earlier for his buildings at the 1915 Panama-California Exposition in San Diego and paid homage to California's Spanish Colonial past, adopting the Late Baroque vocabulary of Spanish architect and sculptor José Benito de Churriguera (1665–1725).

Although Churriguera, who was known after his death as "The Michelangelo of Spain," never worked in the New World, the architecture of the Spanish colonies, and especially Mexico's, was highly influenced by his work.

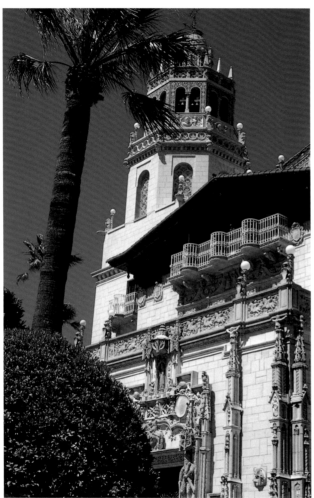

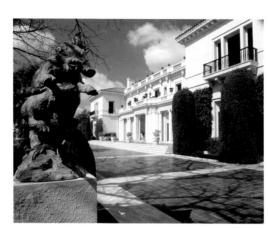

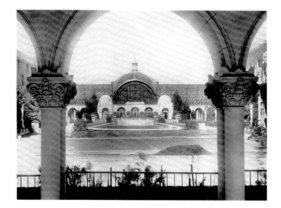

The Churrigueresque style, which was based on his imaginative combinations of Mannerist and Baroque models from both the Spanish and Italian traditions, was deplored, however, by critics of the Neoclassical age as extravagant and capricious.

In this context, the initial idea for Hearst Castle can be seen as an exercise in historic eclecticism, not that different from a German *Rathaus* built in the Italian Renaissance style, for instance, or many of the Neo-Byzantine,

Neo-Gothic, or Neo-Baroque structures that proliferated in Europe in the second half of the nineteenth century.

The inherently eclectic character of the exercise was magnified, however, by a California sensibility; Hearst and his architect industriously multiplied the references and quotations, making ample use of the international arts and antiquities markets to incorporate numerous architectural elements (including portals, floors, and ceilings) salvaged from

clockwise from left
Hearst Castle in San Simeon, California; the Huntington Art Gallery in San Marino, California; the Panama-California Exposition in San Diego, California

European palaces, churches, and monasteries. The two towers that distinguish the Hearst Castle's profile against the perpetually blue California sky were taken—literally—from a Spanish monastery, the Colegiata de Santa María la Mayor, in Ronda; the Gothic-style portal includes original Spanish and French sculpture from the thirteenth through fifteenth centuries; the windows are Venetian, both original and replicas; the floor of the vestibule is an ancient Roman mosaic; the portal is attributed to Sansovino; and the Assembly Room has an original ceiling from the Italian Renaissance, a large sixteenth-century French fireplace, tapestries by Rubens and Giulio Romano, and sculpture by Thorvaldsen and Canova. On the edge of the Neptune Pool stands a Roman temple, whose columns, entablature, and pediment, although they date from different times, all come from Italy. Eight replicas of classical statues, in Carrara marble, were expressly commissioned from Carlo Freter of Pietrasanta, Italy.

The aesthetic can be characterized as a generous eclecticism that, while setting out to create an improbable, "virtual" Spanish past, brings together, through accumulation and an element of chance, a kind of visionary recapitulation of much of the history of European art, resulting in a kind of compromise between romantic nostalgia and an antiquities shop.

A contrasting principle guided the Huntington Art Gallery, in San Marino, California, which was originally designed by architects Myron Hunt and Elmer Grey to be Henry E. Huntington's residence. At the same time that the project was being designed and executed (1908–11), Huntington was getting his start as a collector, cultivating a highly selective and confident eye.

Initially drawn to books and manuscripts about English and American history and literature, Huntington then went on to acquire an excellent series of English paintings from the eighteenth and early nineteenth centuries as well as French paintings, furniture, decorative objects, and sculpture from the same period. His taste was so clearly defined that even important acquisitions from other periods (a painting by Rogier van der Weyden, for example), did not alter the overall tone of his collection. The cohesive effect was also enhanced by a careful attention to the interior décor, such as in the use of important antique French and English fabrics.

The design Huntington selected for the home that was later to house his collection was in the Beaux Arts style. This was hardly surprising, given that the Beaux Arts aesthetic was considered very much in keeping with the academic tradition and therefore the fitting architectural counterpart to a collection centered on Gainsborough, Reynolds, Constable, Lawrence, and Turner. (Not everyone was equally enthusiastic: that was the same year—1908—that Frank Lloyd Wright referred to the Beaux Arts style as "Frenchite pastry.")

At the time, architect Myron Hunt was utilizing a wide variety of idioms, including the Churrigueresque style, which he used in 1913 for the First Congregational Church of Riverside, California. His choice of a Beaux Arts style for Huntington's house, and again later for the gallery he designed for Huntington, was therefore clearly made based on the idea of congruence with the collections and the owner's taste.

Huntington transformed the Huntington Art Gallery into a public collection in 1927. The Hearst Castle was opened to the public in 1958, seven years after Hearst's death and after it became the property of the State of California. While ostensibly divergent, these two important precedents shared a common principle: that the architecture of the museum-home of a California magnate should reflect the character of the art collection, omnivorous and eclectic in Hearst's case, selective and focused in Huntington's.

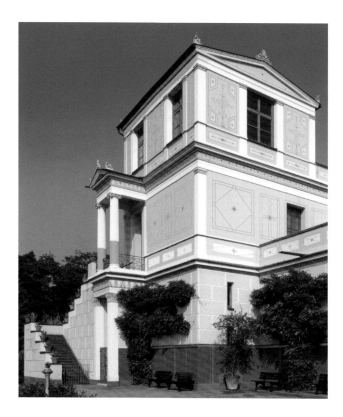

J. Paul Getty's decision, in 1968, to build a
Roman-style villa to house his collections was,
nevertheless, not an obvious one. He was not
as indiscriminate a collector as Hearst, nor as
selective as Huntington. His collections focused
on three fundamental areas: eighteenth-century
French furniture and decorative arts, paintings
by European old masters, and classical Greek
and Roman works.

If he had wanted to respect congruence
with the California landscape, a new museum
structure could have been conceived as an
extension of the Ranch House in the Spanish
Colonial style. If instead he had chosen to adopt
a principle of congruence with his collections,
he could have chosen a design in the Beaux
Arts style, to complement his French decorative
arts; in a Neo-Renaissance style, to complement his painting collection; or in a Neoclassical
style, to better "frame" his antiquities. In fact,
the alternative designs the architectural firm of
Langdon Wilson presented to Getty included
a design in the Spanish Colonial style; one in
the Palladian style, introducing both Italian and
English elements; and one using modernist
vocabulary reminiscent of the 1930s and 1940s.
Getty, however, chose to go in another direction.

The California homes built by Huntington
and Hearst were not the only precedents
informing the Getty Villa, however. Equally
significant was the architectural challenge
of reconstructing, and assigning new functions
to, forms and decorative styles from classical
antiquity. While, as a result of the excavations
of Pompeii and Herculaneum, there are countless rooms, furniture, and decorative motifs
"in the ancient style" in buildings and homes
all over Europe, two buildings are particularly
worth noting. The Pompejanum, in Aschaffenburg, Germany, and the Maison Grecque,
in Cap-Ferrat, France, are important examples
of a creative and functional re-adaptation of
ancient architectural structures.

The Pompejanum, a summer residence built
in 1840–48 by architect Friedrich von Gärtner
for King Ludwig I of Bavaria, was an adaptation
of Pompeian houses that Ludwig had visited,
and in particular of the House of the Dioskouri,
which was unearthed between 1828 and 1829.
The building's architecture, mosaic floors, wall
paintings, and design and furnishing elements
were all borrowed from Pompeii, and it is
surrounded by a Mediterranean-style garden
with lemon, almond, and fig trees (as the Getty
Villa would be too).

The Pompejanum was severely damaged
by Allied bombing raids in 1945 and was not
restored until the 1980s, although its restoration
and how best to use the structure had been
under discussion since the 1960s. Conceived as
a royal residence (or perhaps as a royal caprice),
it was a more or less faithful copy of a Pompeian
house but, at the same time, seemed naturally
destined for a museum function, to display (as it
does today) paintings, mosaics, and sculpture
from the Roman era. It also invoked Bavaria's
Roman past, situated as it was near Limes,
the fortified frontier of the Roman Empire (of

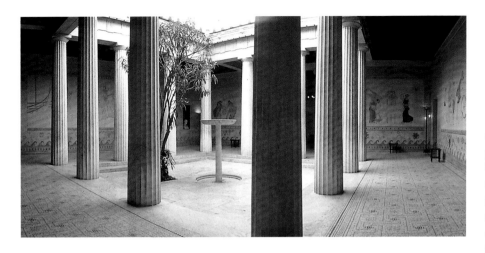

The courtyard of the Villa
Kerylos in Cap-Ferrat, France

which, however, Aschaffenburg was never actually part).

The Villa Kerylos, in Cap-Ferrat, was,
instead, the archaeological dream of a Hellenic
scholar, Théodore Reinach, made possible
through his encounter with a like-minded
architect, Emmanuel Pontremoli. Built between
1902 and 1908, it was intended to be a faithful
reconstruction of one of the peristyle houses
from the second to first century b.c. on the
island of Delos, which had been excavated by the
French School of Archaeology, beginning in
1872 and most intensely between 1904 and 1914.

The Villa Kerylos was a celebration of the
glories of French Mediterranean archaeology,
but also an allusion to the Greek colonization
of the French Mediterranean coast (the architect was from Nice, the ancient Nikaia). Indeed,
the villa was christened "Kerylos," or "halcyon,"
a seabird thought by the ancient Greeks to
have been a bearer of good omens. The main
rooms were given Greek names as well. While
some names are relatively familiar, such as
Bibliotheca (for the library), others, such as
Thyroreion (for the atrium) and *Amphityros* (for
the vestibule), indicated a more sophisticated
level of erudition and alluded to the fact that the
Hellenistic model had been the archetype for
Roman villas in the Vesuvian region.

Materials were chosen very carefully, from
the Carrara marble to the alabaster. Chosen
equally carefully were the muralists, Gustave-
Louis Jaulmes and Adrien Karbowsky, who
painted the walls with mythological scenes

chosen by Reinach and often copied from Attic
pottery, and the sculptor, Jean-Paul-Baptiste
Gasq, who created stucco reliefs in the ancient
style. Everything, from furniture, to fabrics,
to vases, was carefully designed in the Greek
style, and a gallery was added that contained
casts of ancient sculptural masterpieces such as
the *Discobolos* and the Apollo Belvedere. Other
reproductions of ancient sculpture included
the bust of Polycletus's *Doryphoros* and the
so-called *Sappho,* bronze reproductions of works
found in the Villa dei Papiri in Herculaneum.
Like the identical ones that decorated the Outer
Peristyle of the Getty Villa many years later,
they were likely cast at the Chiurazzi foundry
that was established by Gennaro Chiurazzi
in 1840 in Naples, and which gained notoriety
during the St. Louis World's Fair of 1904.

With the precedents of the Pompejanum
and Kerylos, the unacknowledged influences of
Hearst Castle and the Huntington Art Gallery,
and the proposals that he himself had commissioned, Getty's choice for his villa-museum
was idiosyncratic, but carefully considered (see
part 1 of this book for other important details).
Not only did he elect to build a villa (a private
residence, whose tone and dimensions, therefore, reflect the wealth and culture of its owner),
but an *ancient* villa, as if choosing to favor one
of his three collections above the others for its
"classical" nature. The design of the Villa could
almost be seen as an attempt to translate the
Ranch House into ancient Roman vocabulary.

While Getty never spent much time at the
Ranch House and never actually saw the Malibu
Villa in person, what was significant was the
Villa's use of a typology that recalled the Roman
aristocracy's aesthetic, i.e., their desires to emu-
late the Greek style of living and to display their
own cultivation both through the architectural
form itself and the collections assembled within.
And in fact Getty styled himself as the last in
a chain of wealthy collectors: in his early 1950s

novella, *A Journey from Corinth*, the Lands-
downe Herakles, then the most significant piece
in Getty's hands, features as originally from
Corinth, then sold to the owner of the Villa dei
Papiri, and finally moved to Hadrian's Villa
near Tivoli, where it was actually found in 1790.

The selection of the Villa dei Papiri as
the specific model for the Villa was most likely
due not just to the fact that it is particularly
spacious and sumptuous, but that its owners'
cultivation is evidenced by the rich library of
papyrus scrolls it contained, which were partially
destroyed by the eruption of Vesuvius but are
still partially legible. Further evidence of that
sophistication was the lavish sculpture decoration in the Villa dei Papiri, some of which
was copied from Greek originals and which
was reproduced at the Getty Villa, again by the
Chiurazzi foundry.

A museum based on the design of an
ancient villa should presumably communicate
to visitors the idea of an ancient style of
sophisticated living that implies not so much a
repudiation of urban life as a wise and temporary distancing from it. The decision to construct a faithful copy of a particular ancient villa
was probably based on the desire to suggest,
through the accuracy of the reconstruction, that
a visitor there is the guest not only of J. Paul
Getty but of a distant and remote world as well,
whose site could be the shores of the Tyrrhenian
Sea as easily as the Pacific coast.

What, then, is the significance of proposing
the same villa again in 2005 in a form that has
been radically renovated? How does it now dif-
fer from the idea and the premises of the original 1968 project? These questions bring to mind
a celebrated story by Jorge Luis Borges, "Pierre
Menard, Author of Don Quixote," likely a
tribute to Miguel de Unamuno's *Vida de don
Quijote y Sancho* (1895).

In that story, written in 1939, Borges nar-
rates that Pierre Menard, a fictional French

writer, decided in 1918 to rewrite *Don Quixote*.
He was not content, however, simply to retell
Cervantes's immortal story, but instead aspired
to write the very same book, word for word,
not by copying it, but rather by generating
the same story himself, through an intimate
identification with the author, because he had
"...contracted the mysterious duty of reconstructing literally his spontaneous work."
"The initial method he conceived was relatively
simple," writes Borges. It was "...to know
Spanish well, to re-embrace the Catholic faith,
fight against Moors or Turks [and] forget
European history between 1602 and 1918...but
[he] rejected it as too easy."

Finally, after years of toiling, Menard writes
several pages of *Don Quixote*. It is identical
to Cervantes's *Don Quixote*, word for word, but
what a difference! Consider the following
passage from *Don Quixote*: "...la verdad, cuya
madre es la historia, émula del tiempo, depósito
de las acciones, testigo de lo pasado, ejemplo y
aviso de lo presente, advertencia de lo por venir"
[...truth, whose mother is history, who is the
rival of time, depository of deeds, witness of
the past, example and lesson to the present, and
warning to the future.] "Written in the seven-
teenth century," writes Borges, "...this enumer-
ation is a mere rhetorical eulogy of history."
But reflecting on Menard's version, Borges
continues, "History, *mother* of truth: the idea is
astounding. Menard, a contemporary of William
James, does not define history as an investigation
of reality, but as its origin. Historical truth, for
him, is not what took place; it is what we think
took place. The final clauses—*example and
lesson to the present, and warning to the future*—
are shamelessly pragmatic." As Borges suggests,
a text (as well as an architecture) changes its
meaning (as well as its sign) when it is proposed
again, even identically, at a later time.

Three hundred years passed between
the "first" and the "second" *Don Quixote*. Only

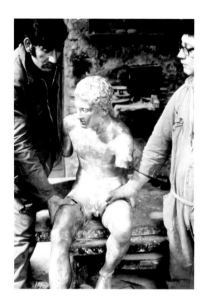

The Chiurazzi foundry
in Naples

thirty have passed between the first and the second Villa, but a rereading of J. Paul Getty's design choice today is no less remote from the interpretations it may have aroused back in 1968. This is due not just to the sudden acceleration and compression that history seems to have undergone in the last few generations. It is also due, more specifically, to the rise and fall of postmodern architecture, with its vast baggage of borrowed elements from ancient idioms.

The most influential declaration of a poetics of modernism in the United States was perhaps that of Robert Venturi (*Complexity and Contradiction in Architecture*, 1966). He exalted vitality, hybridization, and quotation as antidotes to the rigors of modernist tradition. While Mies van der Rohe famously remarked that "Less is more," Venturi's response was that "Less is a bore." In fact, the inclusion of elements or sections taken directly from classical and Neoclassical models (such as capitals, columns, and facades) was a particularly insistent characteristic of postmodern architecture.

This grafting of obvious quotations from the Greco-Roman vocabulary (but also from the "once removed" Renaissance and Neoclassical vocabularies), both eclectic and representational, was a polemical reaction against the modernist idiom and its repudiation of the decorative (as when Adolf Loos declared, "Ornament is a crime," in 1910).

The postmodernist use of a classical vocabulary is an indulgent reintroduction of the ornamental lexicon, often with an irony that is deliberately irreverent. The insistent use of these classical elements does not in any way signify a return to a classical style after the modernist period, but rather implies a fairly simplified historic model, a kind of binary opposition between the modern and what preceded it (seen as a whole), playfully regrouped, as if it were not a historic legacy, but rather a kind of virtual reality. It was, however, this distinctive quota-

tion of a classical vocabulary that played a crucial role in signaling the sharp separation of the postmodern from the modern idiom.

The Getty Villa, while more or less contemporary to the initial phase of postmodern architecture, was not at all in step with the poetics Venturi and others, in America and elsewhere, were proposing. Unlike postmodern structures, the Villa did not present fragmentary classical quotations grafted onto the surface of a clearly modernist framework, unless the Villa itself is read as a single, gigantic citation of the Villa dei Papiri in Herculaneum.

Getty's choice of idiom and style was completely independent of the development of postmodernism and the ideas that characterized it. It was, in fact, so discordant with them (as well as with the entire modernist tradition) that the Villa received highly critical reviews in the press. Yet at the time the Villa was, perhaps inadvertently, in its own way fairly original. While it implies precedents such as the villas constructed for Ludwig I and Théodore Reinach, those designs represented the convergence of multiple original models (various houses in Pompeii and Delos). The Getty Villa, instead, was based on a closer adherence to a single model. Indeed, the very fact that the Villa dei Papiri had not been (and still has not been) completely excavated worked in its favor, in a way; its design was based on the meticulous plans archaeologist Karl Weber drew of the Villa dei Papiri while it was first being excavated in the mid-eighteenth century.

Through the good offices of archaeologist Norman Neuerburg, the Villa therefore signified something different from the fantastical architecture of a Bavarian king or a French scholar. It was, rather, the "philological" reconstruction of an ancient monument, not that different from the many reconstructions of lost paintings by Greek artists, compiled first by Renaissance painters (such as Apelles' *Calumny*,

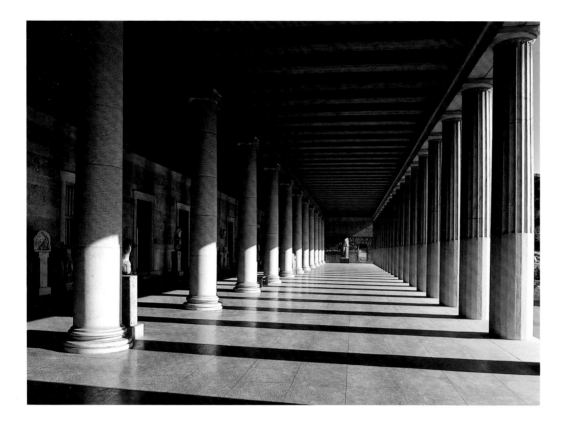

by Botticelli), then later by the nineteenth- and twentieth-century archaeologists (such as the frescoes of Polygnotus in Delphi).

A few years before ground was broken for the Getty Villa, work began in Athens for the reconstruction of the Stoa of Attalos, which was destined to house the Museum of the Agora. The project had been conceived, originally, as a museum to display artifacts unearthed in the American excavations in the Agora area. The plans for the new structure, which claimed to be an exact reproduction of the ancient original, were based on extremely limited archaeological remains that had, nonetheless, been very carefully collected, numbered, and interpreted. The work, which continued from 1953 to 1956, was financed through a fund-raising campaign aimed at private American donors, including John D. Rockefeller, who contributed nearly half of the funds.

If the Hearst Castle and the Huntington Art Gallery set important precedents in California and the Pompejanum and the Villa Kerylos established precedents for the re-creation of luxurious living spaces from the ancient world, the reconstruction of the Stoa of Attalos helped legitimize the idea that it is possible to reconstruct ancient edifices based on limited archaeological remains and only partial knowledge of the original structure, and that that very reconstruction is an appropriate space in which to house a museum.

In this sense, too, the Getty Villa, while contemporary with a great deal of postmodern architecture, was conceived with a very different set of premises. Yet its use of classical typology and decoration distinguished it as well from the San Marino and San Simeon precedents. It is not a Beaux Arts design, but it could, in a sense, be called pre-postmodern.

•

Thirty years later, now that the momentum of postmodernism in architecture seems to have peaked, we have to see the renovated Getty Villa as post-postmodern. While nothing could better illuminate the project than the essays in this

The Stoa of Attalos in Athens

book written by Marion True and Jorge Silvetti, a few brief observations can be made.

First, it is tempting to think that this new version of the Villa best interprets Getty's original intentions, that it best achieves that "appropriateness" of which he boasted. The decision to use the Villa to house the archaeological collections, which are the most harmonious with the Villa's architectonic form, may actually be seen as consistent with those intentions. It is no less true, however, that such a focused and "purist" use of the structure was something that Getty himself never considered.

Machado and Silvetti approached the renovation projects with a more detached point of view. On the one hand, they were very aware, as Silvetti notes in his essay in this volume, of the "referential properties" of the Villa's architecture. They were also very aware, on the other hand, that creating a perfect replica of an original whose design is only known in part is an impossible task and that they would therefore only be able to aspire to "re-create character at the Villa not through imitation, but through evocation."

Machado and Silvetti's "new Old Villa" is, in fact, doubly evocative: not only does it quote the presumed architecture of a Roman villa near Naples but the Getty Museum's Malibu structure has now itself been historicized, in part due to the eight years it was closed (1997–2005) for restoration. The "scientific-archaeological" character of the reconstruction of a Roman villa, which was the project's declared intention in the years between 1968 and 1974, has given way to respect for the Villa today as a historical object from those very years. Consistent with this approach was the decision to conserve the Ranch House, even while modifying its function, and to connect that facility, the original home of the Getty Museum, with the Villa by means of a new partially subterranean auditorium.

One of the chief challenges Silvetti and Machado faced was a reevaluation of the uses of the Villa's spaces. They were charged not only with transforming the space into a museum devoted exclusively to antiquities but also with relocating certain functions into new facilities (such as the Auditorium). That created the need to rethink the relationship between the Villa's form and its overall function, something which had always been fairly problematic, not only due to program requirements (such as parking) but also to the fact that the Villa was never, as a matter of fact, a "villa": it was never inhabited by J. Paul Getty or anyone else. The Getty Villa was conceived using an architectonic typology that is fundamentally and exquisitely private (the villa) to serve as a public museum space, thereby creating a radical dislocation of scope.

One could view the addition of a theater in 2005, for instance, beyond the obvious program goals that determined it, as a kind of reunification of form and function. Thanks to the mild California climate, an ancient-style theater, i.e., an open-air theater, could be re-created and used *as such* (the same form used for the same function, although in a notably transformed context).

The vocabulary adopted by Machado and Silvetti is consistent with the fact that the Villa can be "read" on two levels. Guided by the principle of an "unprecedented realism," that makes awareness of the relationship between form, function, and society a fundamental element in the practice of architecture, Machado and Silvetti have refused to take a simple historicist approach, borrowing "classical elements or icons as those coming from the classical orders and ornaments." Instead, they have understood contemporary materials and elements to be the structural supports of their vocabulary. By doing so, they have shifted the significance of historic and thematic references to "…the way this contemporary vocabulary is deployed and relates to the original buildings, to the landscape, and to each other."

The layering of building materials, including a kind of travertine that recalls both the ample use of that stone by Richard Meier at the Getty Center as well as the symbolic stature that its use has already acquired, is the result of a narrative intent that is exquisite in its precision. The modifications "frame" the way in which the Getty Villa should be seen, and reseen, by its visitors. The "original" Villa therefore assumes the status of an *objet trouvé*, of a "site of discovery and exploration," as if it were, itself, an archaeological artifact, which in turn recalls another archaeological artifact, the original villa in Herculaneum that, by virtue of still being buried, is unreachable.

Machado and Silvetti's design, almost as a *gradus ad Parnassum*, becomes an informed and discreet guide to the revisited and re-created structure, conceived through a lexicon that is from time to time referential and functional. The architecture, understood as form but also as space for social functions, is reformulated according to a spirit that is not at all nostalgic, but instead animated by an experimental tension, magnified rather than restrained by the poetics of reuse.

When it opened in 1974, the Getty Villa was met with an onslaught of criticism. It quickly became, however, enormously popular not only with Southern Californians but with everyone who visited it. J. Paul Getty's original idea was, therefore, much more in tune with the curiosity and the expectations of the public than his critics had imagined. As an exercise in archaeological reconstruction, the Villa grad-

ually earned a place, as well, in the specialized literature of scholars of Roman villas.

The Getty Villa is not a substitute for the original Roman villa, nor can it claim the richness of meaning of an original classical building in ruins, and yet it has its own value, both didactic and for the experience of volumes and spaces, that guarantees its uniqueness.

In the interim, the restored Pompejanum has been reopened to the public and, like the Villa Kerylos (which has become public property), it has assumed museum status. Nonetheless, the Getty Villa, which was conceived from the beginning as a museum and which has now become the only museum of classical archaeology in the United States, remains an unparalleled experiment.

J. Paul Getty's original project implied a conjecture about public reaction that time has vindicated. The "new version" of the Villa does not confirm or negate the idea that a classical villa is a particularly appropriate design for a museum, but rather transfers that idea of "appropriateness" from a copy of the Villa dei Papiri to the Getty Villa. This is achieved through an extremely careful study of access paths and visitor circulation, a new equilibrium between the site itself and the structures, and the use of an elegant and careful vocabulary, rich with historic meaning and urbanistic erudition.

Like Pierre Menard's *Quixote*, the Villa is the same, but at the same time completely renovated, its meaning altered. Framed by Rodolfo Machado and Jorge Silvetti's imaginative vision, the Getty Villa makes an important contribution to contemporary debate over what form a museum should take and what meaning that form confers.

Note: Quotes from "Pierre Menard, Author of Don Quixote," in Jorge Luis Borges, *Ficciones*, ed. Anthony Kerrigan (New York, Grove Press, 1962).

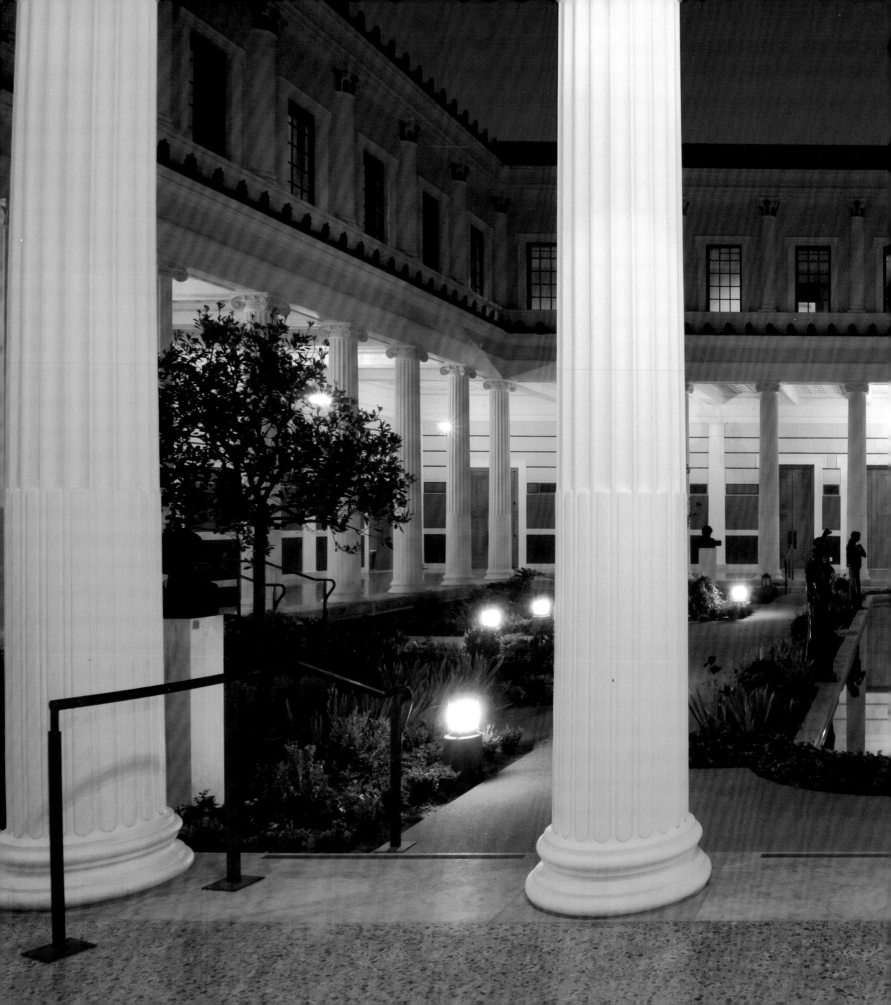

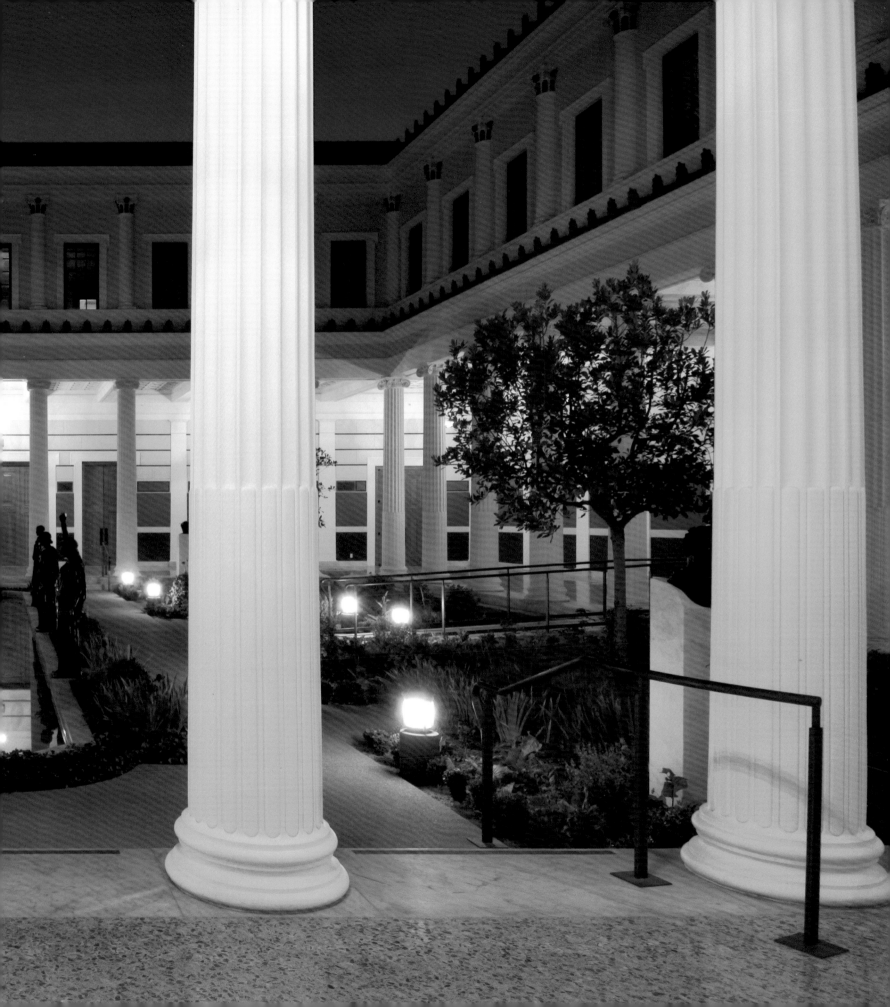

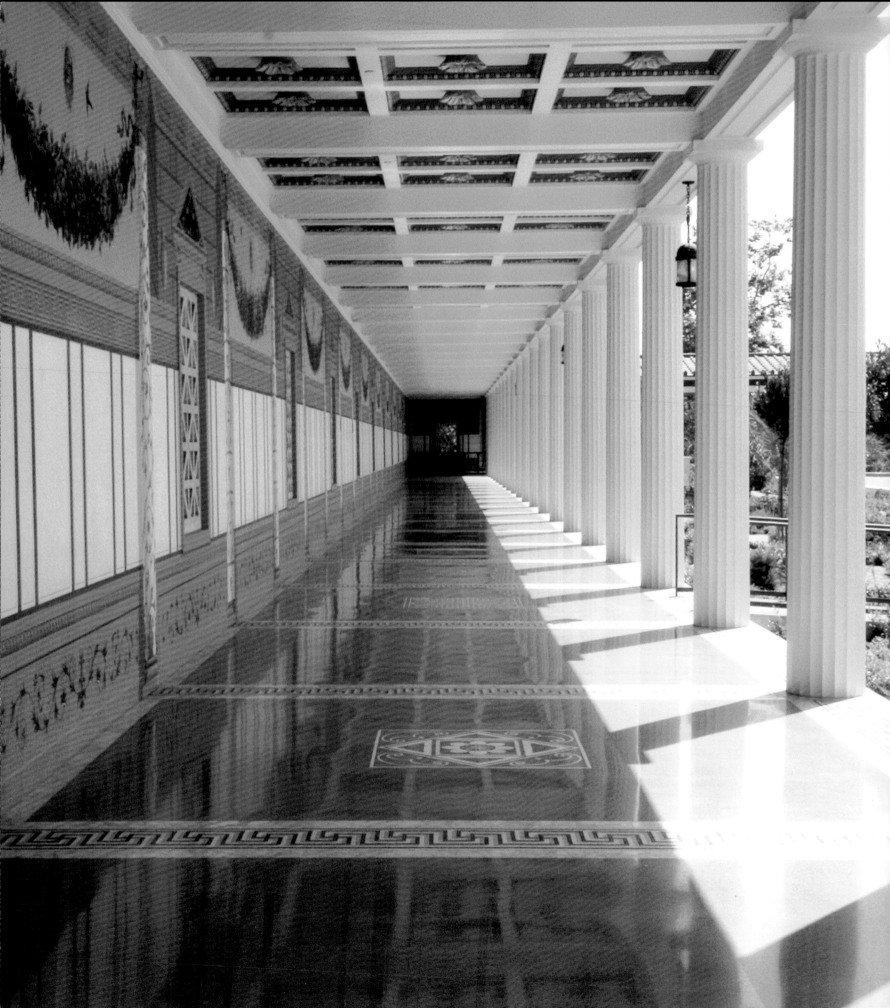

The Getty Villa

MARION TRUE

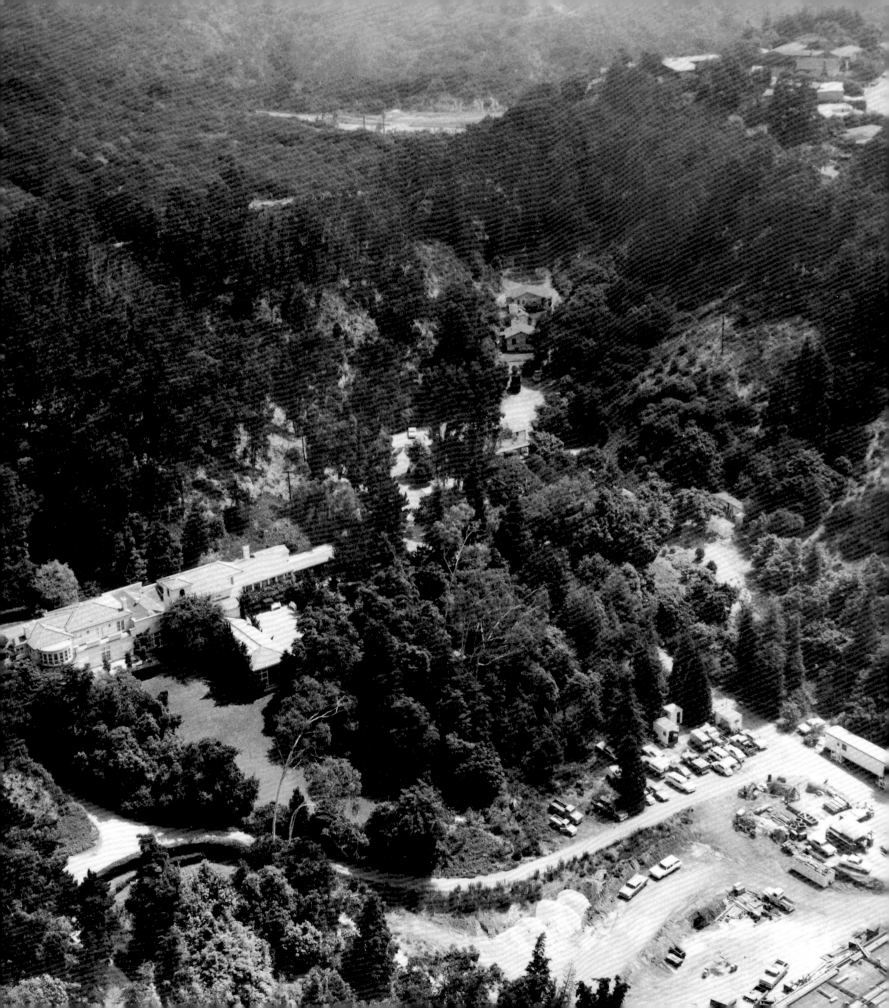

A Collection Comes to Malibu

I

THE MALIBU PROPERTY

The lush, secluded Cañon de Sentimiento that houses the Getty Villa runs down to the Pacific coast just at the border between Los Angeles and Malibu. Originally part of Rancho Boca de Santa Monica, a Mexican land grant given in 1839 to Francisco Marquez and Ysidro Reyes, the canyon had become by 1921 the home of Judge Claude I. Parker, a Los Angeles tax and estate attorney (fig. 1). Renaming the property Cañada Sentimienta, he built a large, gracious Spanish Colonial–style house deep within the canyon, looking out to the sea. Parker and his wife used the western part of the property to grow lemons and avocados, but in the area around the house they planted beautiful formal gardens and ornamental trees. The house had been changed through various additions by the time that J. Paul Getty bought the sixty-four-acre canyon in 1945, but it retained much of its original casual charm (fig. 2).

Getty already owned a large house in the Hancock Park area of Los Angeles and a beach house in Santa Monica, so it is not clear just how much time he spent at the property, now called the Getty Ranch, before he left the United States for good in 1951. But if one can trust Ethel Le Vane's effusive descriptions in the book *Collector's Choice*, which she coauthored with Getty in 1955, he clearly enjoyed the property and used it to entertain and to showcase parts of his growing art collection.

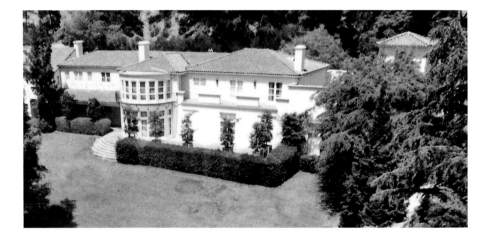

MR. GETTY'S MUSEUM

By this time, Getty had become a notable but sporadic collector of three kinds of art: French furniture of the eighteenth century, Greek and Roman antiquities, and old master paintings. His highly regarded furniture, qualitatively the best of his three collections, included a rolltop desk by Bernard Molitor (1755–1833), a double desk (fig. 3) by Bernard II van Risenburgh (after 1696–ca. 1766), a *bureau plat* (desk) by Charles Cressent (1685–1768) from the Josse Collection, and two Sèvres mounted *secrétaires* by Martin Carlin (ca. 1730–1785) and Adam Weisweiler (1744–1820). Getty's most important antiquities included famous Roman statues of Herakles and Leda, both from the Lansdowne Collection;

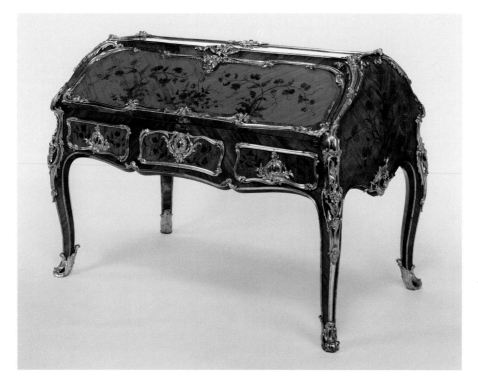

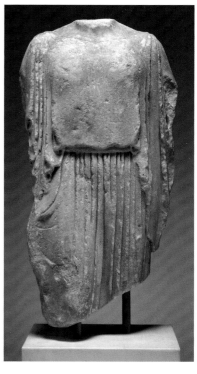

Figure 3. Double desk
by Bernard II van Risenburgh,
ca. 1750

Figure 4. The Elgin Kore,
Greek, ca. 470 B.C.

the statue of a kore from the Elgin Collection (fig. 4); and marble portraits of the Roman empresses Agrippina and Sabina. Though paintings were the weakest area of the collection (figs. 5, 6), they did include *Portrait of James Christie* by Thomas Gainsborough (1727–1788); *Portrait of Marten Looten* by Rembrandt (1606–1669); *The Penitent Magdalene* by Titian (ca. 1488–1576), and *The Death of Dido*, then attributed to Peter Paul Rubens (1577–1640). Not all the paintings that he bought stood up very well over years of study, with some of the most notable (including the Rubens *Dido*) later reattributed and downgraded to copies or workshop pieces, but a number of the antiquities and pieces of French furniture purchased early in Getty's collecting career remain highlights of the Museum's collections to this day.

J. Paul Getty also bought a number of fine tapestries and carpets. After he donated the most famous of these—the splendid sixteenth-century Persian textile known as the Ardabil carpet—as well as a suite of tapestries designed by François Boucher (1703–1770) and Rembrandt's *Portrait of Marten Looten* to the Los Angeles County Museum of Art in 1953, his advisers and, perhaps most importantly, his dedicated assistant, Norris Bramlett, suggested to Getty that he should establish his own museum instead of dividing his now-substantial collection among various institutions around the world. The ranch in Pacific Palisades offered the perfect setting for a private gallery, and making the collection accessible to the public would bring with it certain tax benefits that appealed to the wealthy but thrifty collector.

In 1953, a trust for "the diffusion of artistic and general knowledge" was created, and parts of the main Getty Ranch House were renovated so that the J. Paul Getty Museum could open its doors to the public there in May 1954 (fig. 7). Getty himself was in Kuwait when the facility was inaugurated, but he sent the following message: "I hope this museum, modest and unpretentious as it is, will nevertheless give pleasure to the many people in and around Los Angeles who are interested in the periods of art represented here" (quoted in J. Walsh and D. Gribbon, *The J. Paul Getty Museum and Its Collections* [Los Angeles, 1997], p. 29).

According to the accounts of those who worked at the Museum in those early days, the atmosphere was relaxed and the schedule far from demanding. Public hours were restricted to two afternoons a week, on Wednesdays and Saturdays from three until five o'clock, and visitors had to make appointments in advance. On a third, flexible, day, the Museum was available for group visits, but only for two hours. Most of the art was installed in the house's theater and in galleries on both levels of an addition that had been built at the east end of the house in 1946. From 1970 to 1974, art was also displayed in the library, the adjacent corridor, and in two small dressing rooms. The largest pieces of ancient sculpture were displayed outside around the walled courtyard on the east side of the house (fig. 8) until 1957, when a special gallery was built beside the courtyard to accommodate them (fig. 9). Because this courtyard served as the entrance for the public, early Museum visitors were greeted by some of the highlights of the collection, including Getty's most prized antiquity, the Lansdowne Herakles (fig. 10), as well as the Mazarin Venus (a Roman statue formerly in the Cook Collection in Richmond, England, and once thought to have been in the seventeenth-century collection of Cardinal Mazarin) and the portrait statue of

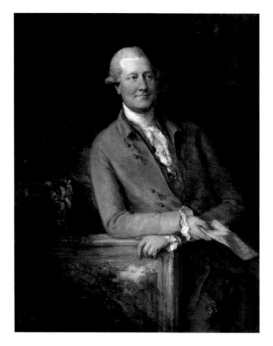

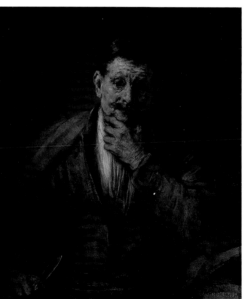

Figure 5. *James Christie* by Thomas Gainsborough, 1778

Figure 6. *St. Bartholomew* by Rembrandt, 1661

Faustina (formerly in the Earl of Pembroke's collection at Wilton House, in Salisbury, England). At the center of this outdoor gallery was a large Italianate fountain whose base was decorated with three bronze monkeys that eventually gave the Monkey Court its name.

Before establishing the Museum, Getty had considered ending his collecting of furniture and paintings in order to concentrate exclusively

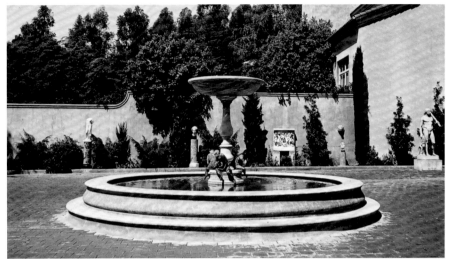

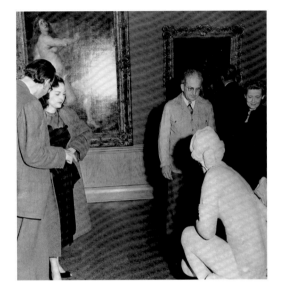

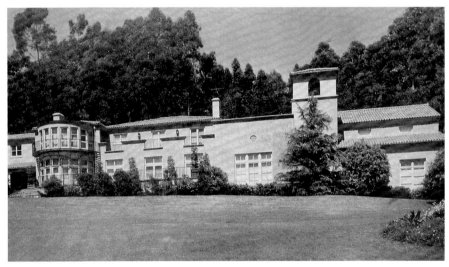

Figure 7. Visitors looking at the collections (including the *Dido* then attributed to Rubens and the *Crouching Aphrodite* from the Cook Collection) in the newly opened Getty Museum in the Ranch House, 1954

Figure 8. Ancient sculpture displayed around the Monkey Fountain in the courtyard to the east of the Ranch House, 1954

Figure 9. The Getty Ranch House in 1957

on acquiring antiquities. As he wrote in his diary in 1951, "I am disinclined to buy any more French furniture since I now have all I need. I believe my buying of art objects, except Graeco-Roman, is about finished" (quoted in G. Wilson, unpublished manuscript, p. 17; included in "J. Paul Getty as a Collector," unpublished essays compiled in 1982). Interestingly, Getty's decision to display publicly the results of his collecting activities seems to have actually spurred him on to pursue more acquisitions (fig. 11). Of course, as the Museum and his interest in art became more widely known, Getty was often the object of pursuit as well, a fact of life he complained about bitterly. As he wrote

to Norris Bramlett early in 1958, "I wish to go on record right here that it is very burdensome to me to be pestered by art dealers and to give up my time inspecting art objects, getting expertises, conducting negotiations, etc." (quoted in Walsh and Gribbon, *The J. Paul Getty Museum and Its Collections*, p. 37). In spite of Getty's annoyance, his collections, especially of antiquities, continued to expand, and they eventually outgrew the available gallery space in the Ranch House (fig. 12).

Once he established the Museum in Malibu, Getty decided to forgo any further purchases of antiquities for himself, preferring to acquire only for the Museum. In 1954, the Mazarin

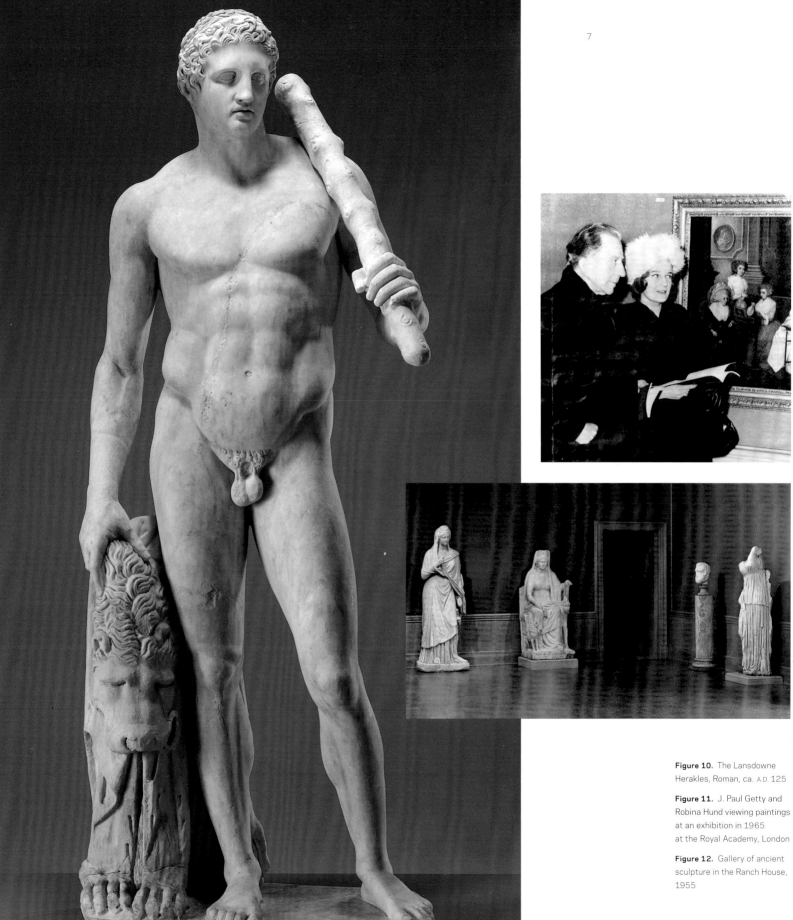

7

Figure 10. The Lansdowne
Herakles, Roman, ca. A.D. 125

Figure 11. J. Paul Getty and
Robina Hund viewing paintings
at an exhibition in 1965
at the Royal Academy, London

Figure 12. Gallery of ancient
sculpture in the Ranch House,
1955

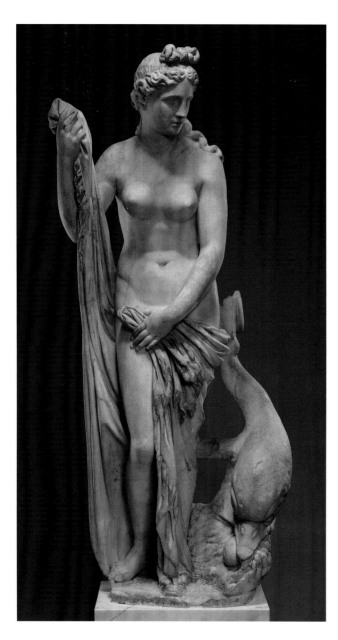

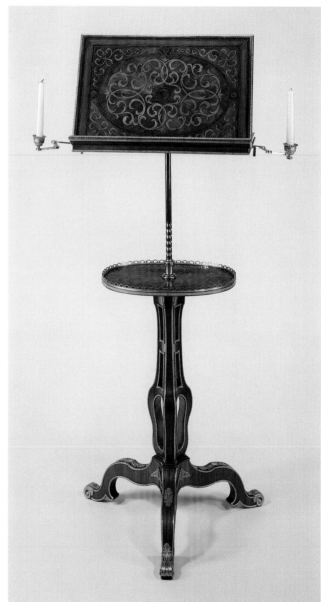

Venus was the first antiquity acquired specifically for the new museum (fig. 13). Among the
most notable pieces of ancient art added during
the next few years were a Roman portrait statue
of a woman as Cybele (formerly in the Mattei
Collection in Rome), a portrait head of Julia
Titi, and two large Greek marble funerary lions.
Getty was also attracted to smaller objects, and
his purchases during this time included such
fine small bronzes as the Etruscan statuette of
Tinia (Zeus to the Greeks) from Piombino and
some Roman glass.

Getty temporarily showed the same
restraint in collecting decorative arts, acquiring
a number of objects for the Museum between
1953 and 1955. He augmented his already
distinguished collection of French furniture by
purchasing several important pieces from the
Chester Beatty Collection, including a commode
by Gilles Joubert (1689–1775), a music stand by
Carlin (fig. 14), and yet another *bureau plat*
by Cressent. After these purchases, however,
he bought nothing more of importance for
the Museum's French furniture collection until
1971. When he began to buy furniture once
again, in 1967, it was for his home at Sutton
Place rather than for the Museum.

Oddly enough, Getty did not adopt any
policy of detachment with respect to the
Museum's paintings collection. Though he
made almost no notable additions to either the
Museum or his personal collection for nearly
a decade, Getty did finally buy some significant
paintings—including Gainsborough's *Portrait
of Anne, Countess of Chesterfield*; Rembrandt's
St. Bartholomew; and one of his most expensive
purchases, *Diana and Her Nymphs on the Hunt*,
which was thought at the time to be by Rubens
but is now attributed to his workshop. These
remained in England, however, either at Getty's
home at Sutton Place or on loan to the National
Gallery in London, and did not come to
the Malibu museum until several years later.

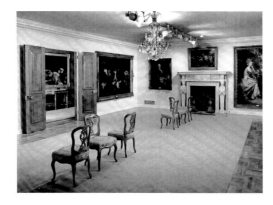

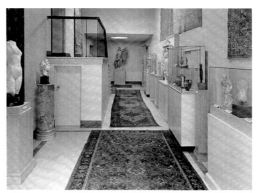

The addition of a new antiquities gallery
in 1957 provided some temporary relief for the
overcrowding in the Ranch House, but eventually even the living room, the dressing rooms,
and the narrow hallways were adapted to
become exhibition areas (figs. 15, 16). Finally,
sometime in 1968, Getty made a very personal
and ultimately controversial decision about
a new building for his museum in Malibu. The
idea that he needed to build a proper museum
for the collections was itself not the least bit
controversial—there was every good reason
to expand in order to accommodate the works
of art more appropriately and safely, and
the sixty-four-acre canyon still offered plenty of
empty space. At first, his intention was only
to add a wing to the existing building. In April

opposite
Figure 13. The Mazarin Venus,
Roman, A.D. 100–200

Figure 14. Music stand
attributed to Martin Carlin,
French, ca. 1770–75

Figure 15. Gallery of old
master paintings in the living
room of the Ranch House,
ca. 1955

Figure 16. Hallway in the
Ranch House used to
display ancient sculpture
and oriental carpets

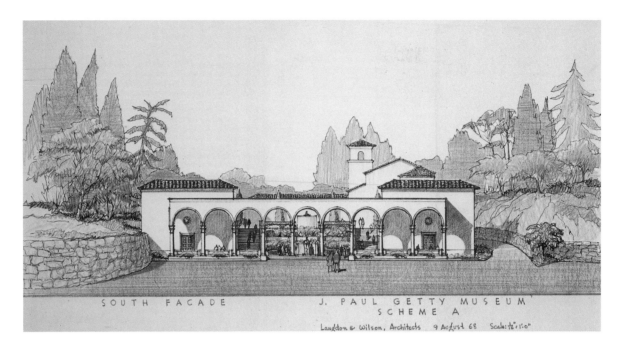

SOUTH FACADE   J. PAUL GETTY MUSEUM
                                      SCHEME A
                              Langdon & Wilson, Architects   9 August 68   Scale: ½"=1'·0"

Figure 17. One of three designs by the architectural firm Langdon Wilson for the extension of the Getty Museum. This one would have enclosed the courtyard on the east side with structures in the same Spanish Colonial style as the Ranch House.

opposite
Figure 18. The ground plan, north and south facades, and cross-sections of spacious galleries and vaulted colonnades proposed in another Langdon Wilson extension design recall eighteenth-century Palladian architecture.

Figure 19. Plan of upper galleries and courtyard

1968, his secretary Carole Tier wrote to Norris Bramlett: "As [Mr. Getty] mentioned to you on the telephone yesterday, he would recommend that the museum build an addition to its present premises which are too crowded. He thinks the addition should be in keeping with, and actually enhance the present premises. An expenditure of say one million would be appropriate. . . . A good architect should be employed" (quoted in G. Wilson, unpublished manuscript, p. 26). Working with these instructions, Getty's staff in Los Angeles engaged the Los Angeles–based architectural firm of Langdon Wilson early in 1968 to explore some possible strategies for extending the Ranch House and enclosing the walled courtyard at the public entrance.

The three solutions proposed were fairly predictable: the first in the Spanish Colonial style of the Ranch House itself; the second in the more severe modernist style reminiscent of the Italian architecture that emerged under fascism; and the third in an arcaded Palladian vocabu-

lary that recalled the elegant eighteenth-century country villas of Italy (figs. 17–19). None of these concepts pleased Getty, and he made that clear. He also made it clear that he would not entertain the possibility of a very contemporary building: "I refuse to pay for one of those concrete-bunker type structures that are the fad among museum architects—nor for some tinted-glass and stainless-steel monstrosity" (quoted in *Handbook of the J. Paul Getty Museum* [Malibu, 1986], p. 18).

What ultimately generated controversy was Getty's highly original decision, discussed with no one—not even his British architect and adviser, Stephen Garrett—that the new building would re-create a celebrated, though largely unexcavated, luxurious Roman seaside villa from the first century B.C.: the so-called Villa dei Papiri. Located just outside the ancient site of Herculaneum, the villa had been covered by the eruption of Mount Vesuvius in A.D. 79 that had also destroyed Pompeii.

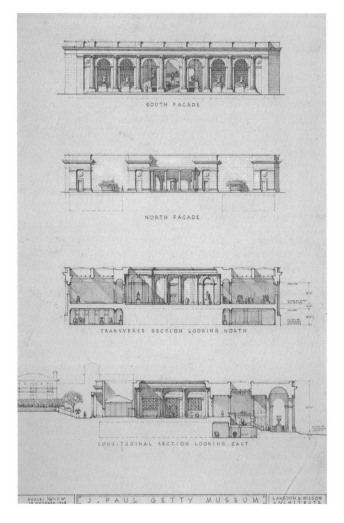

SOUTH FACADE

NORTH FACADE

TRANSVERSE SECTION LOOKING NORTH

LONGITUDINAL SECTION LOOKING EAST

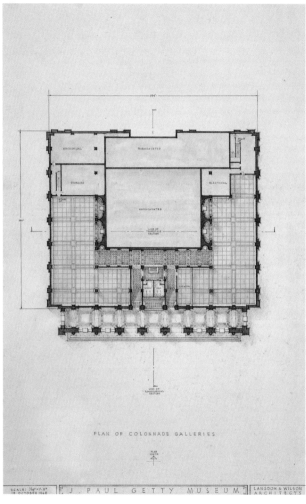

PLAN OF COLONNADE GALLERIES

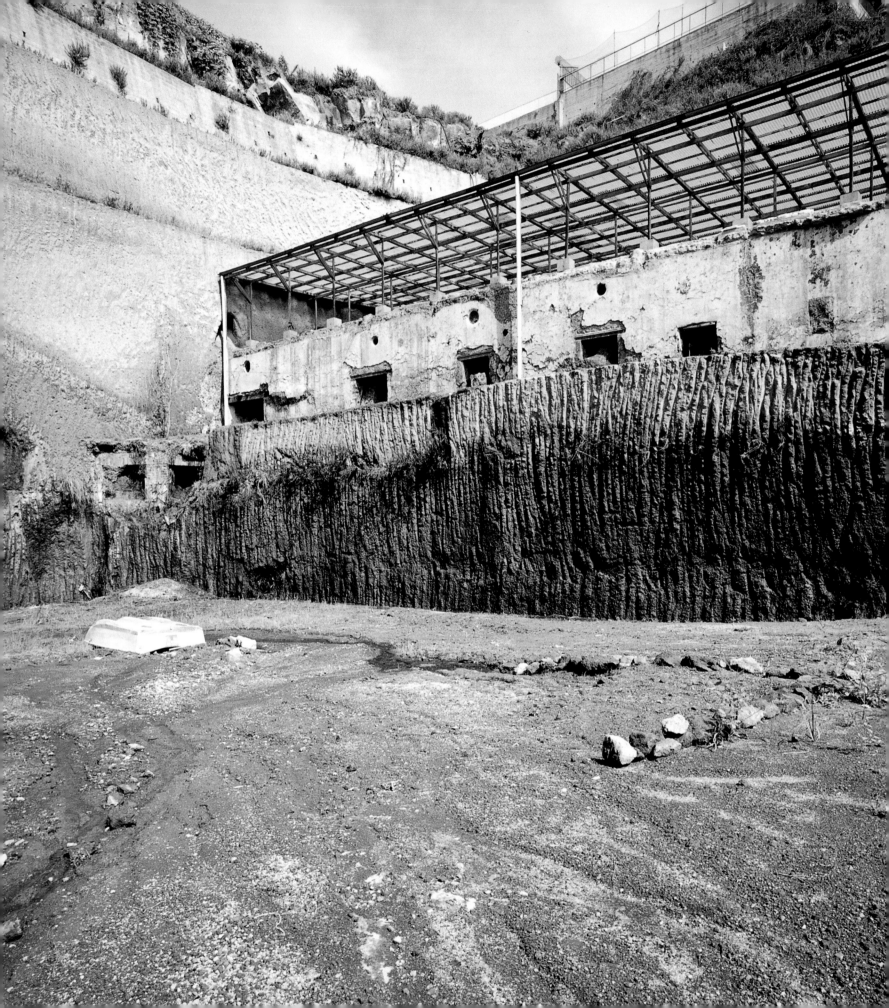

2 Reconstructing the Villa dei Papiri

Discovered by accident in 1750 when farmers were digging a well, the Villa dei Papiri was the largest and most luxuriously furnished seaside villa found during the early excavations at Herculaneum (fig. 20). This grand estate, located about one hundred meters from the theater at the outskirts of the ancient city, was originally situated on the coastline, which has now moved nearly three kilometers farther out. It remained completely covered by volcanic debris until the end of the twentieth century. Extensive excavations conducted between 1986 and 1993 finally laid open the remains of the villa's atrium and its high podium as well as terraces that led down to the shore. (Exposed sections of the villa and other buildings uncovered during the course of the excavation were opened to the public in spring 2003.)

In the eighteenth century, however, the still-buried villa had been systematically explored by means of a network of tunnels dug through the hardened mud and volcanic material. These first explorations were directed by the Swiss engineer Karl Weber, working under Roque Joaquín de Alcubierre for the Spanish Bourbon king, Charles III. Though conducted under the most difficult conditions, Weber's subterranean excavations yielded the largest collection of bronze and marble sculptures ever found in a private residence around the Bay of Naples, as well as the remains of fine wall paintings and many small vessels and precious objects. All of the recovered objects were immediately taken to the royal palace in nearby Portici, where Charles III had established a museum. Since he controlled the region around both Pompeii and Herculaneum and he paid for the excavations, Charles considered that anything found at the sites belonged to him, and he closely guarded access to the newly retrieved treasures. The news of the rediscovery of the ancient cities covered by Vesuvius in A.D. 79 quickly seized the attention of European nobility as well as intellectuals like Johann Wolfgang von Goethe and Johann Joachim Winckelmann, who made the long and difficult journey to Portici to see both the sites and the rare works of art uncovered with the buildings.

In addition to the building and its works of art, Weber's workers discovered a unique cache of blackened materials that were recognized fairly quickly, fortunately, as carbonized papyrus book rolls (fig. 21). Approximately eleven hundred of these fragile rolls, complete or fragmentary, have been preserved. Work began immediately on the painstaking and agonizingly slow process of trying to unroll and decipher the ancient texts. Regrettably, many were destroyed in this process, and by 1800 only some one hundred rolls had been transcribed. The task continues to this day, and only a little more than half have been read. Those that have been opened and deciphered are primarily texts related to Epicurean philosophy, with the largest number being works by the Greek philosopher Philodemos of Gadara.

opposite
Figure 20. The south side of the excavated section of the original Villa dei Papiri just outside of Herculaneum (uncovered between 1986 and 1993) shows that the building was originally set on a high podium. Interior stairs and a series of terraces originally led down to the seashore, which was just in front of this facade of the building.

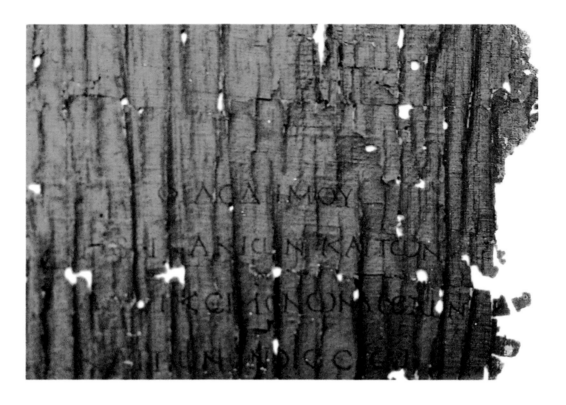

Figure 21. Fragmentary carbonized papyrus roll found at the Villa dei Papiri. The text is by Philodemos, and the scroll is housed at the Officina dei Papiri in Naples.

Classical scholars have long believed that Philodemos, who lived in the Bay of Naples region in the later first century B.C., enjoyed the patronage of Lucius Calpurnius Piso Caesoninus, to whom he dedicated a poem and a philosophical treatise. Piso, who was the wealthy father-in-law of Julius Caesar, is known from other ancient texts to have owned a house in the region and would have been an appropriate owner for a residence as magnificent as the one we now call the Villa dei Papiri. Thus the blackened papyrus book rolls not only lent the villa its modern-day name but also helped suggest the identity of its original owner.

The exploratory tunnels, dug in the hopes of finding and removing statues, mosaics, or other archaeological treasures, also permitted the villa to be mapped. Weber managed to draw a fairly detailed ground plan of the massive structure, carefully noting the findspots of the major sculptures before they were removed (fig. 22). Weber's plan, now preserved in the National Archaeological Museum of Naples, would become the basis for J. Paul Getty's new museum.

Though Getty's decision to re-create an ancient Roman villa to house his collection took his advisers by surprise, it was hardly out of character and might even be considered predictable. Getty had a lifelong fascination with ancient history and artifacts. At various times, he had owned houses in Italy—one on the sea, just north of Rome, in Palo (fig. 23), and one on the Bay of Naples, in Posillipo, on the Isle of Gaiola. Both were built over ancient Roman villas, and he took great care in the renovations of these homes to expose what remained of the original antique structures, including mosaic

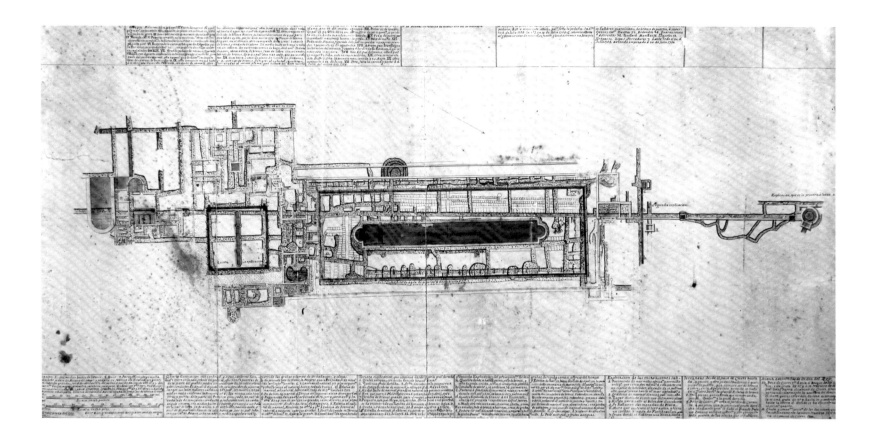

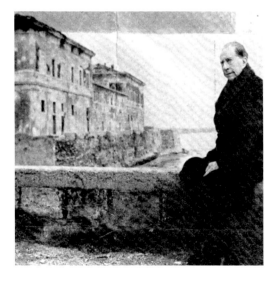

floors and fragmentary wall paintings. In his collection of ancient art, Getty favored pieces with interesting historical connections. He even went so far as to create fictional histories for some of his objects, placing them in the possession of important personalities from antiquity.

One of these stories featured his most prized antiquity, the statue of Herakles that had come from the distinguished collection assembled by the Marquess of Lansdowne in London. Found at Hadrian's Villa near Tivoli by amateur excavators in 1790 and restored in Rome, the monumental marble image was celebrated for its beauty and for its embodiment of the ideal hero. In the nineteenth century, the Lansdowne Herakles became more famous than the Apollo Belvedere, but by the middle of the twentieth century few collectors were interested in ancient art. When the Lansdowne marbles were

Figure 22. Ground plan of the Villa dei Papiri drawn by Karl Weber in 1758

Figure 23. J. Paul Getty in front of his seaside castle in Palo on the Tyrrhenian Sea. Though the castle was constructed during the Middle Ages, its foundations date back some twenty-five hundred years, and local legend has it that the original building once hosted Rome's emperors.

auctioned at Christie's in London on March 5, 1930 (lot 34), the Herakles failed to sell, and in 1951 Getty was able to purchase it through Spink in London for the modest sum of £6,600 (roughly $18,500 at the time). The bargain price only enhanced Getty's enthusiasm for the piece, and in 1955 he gave it a major role in *A Journey from Corinth*, his romantic novella set in ancient Herculaneum in the second century B.C.

A Journey from Corinth tells the story of a young Greek landscape architect, Glaucus, and his wife, who want to leave their native Corinth to find work and a better life in the colonies of southern Italy before the Roman army invades the city. One of the sacred images in the agora of Corinth is a statue of the youthful hero-god Herakles. Before departing, Glaucus stops beneath the statue to make an oath of devotion to his love. After arriving in the city of Neapolis (present-day Naples) in Campania, Glaucus finds work planning the gardens of a magnificent seaside villa just outside Herculaneum, a popular summer resort for rich Romans. The owner of the villa is none other than the historical figure Lucius Calpurnius Piso, mentioned above as the patron of Philodemos and the presumed owner of the Villa dei Papiri. Getty describes Piso as "a wealthy Roman owning a large villa and estate at Herculaneum, . . . a pleasant-looking Roman in his late thirties, although a trifle pompous in manner" (*A Journey from Corinth*, p. 311). From the accounts of those who knew J. Paul Getty, his description of Piso bears a remarkable resemblance to the rich oilman himself.

Later, when Glaucus has successfully established himself in Piso's employment, he learns that the Romans have conquered Corinth. Many of the city's treasures are brought to Neapolis and sold at auction. Among them is, of course, the statue of Herakles, witness to Glaucus's oath. Glaucus persuades Piso to buy the sculp-

ture as a work of art worthy to adorn his great villa. The young Greek lovers find themselves once again under the protection of their divine Corinthian hero. As Getty writes it, the end of the story reflects the modern history of the piece, for the statue later leaves Herculaneum. First, the descendants of Piso offer it to the emperor Nero as a gift. After passing through the hands of various Roman emperors, the marble finally ends up in the possession of the great philhellene Hadrian (fig. 24) at his residence near Tivoli—where it was found during excavations in the early 1790s. Getty later noted that the statue eventually "followed the sun westward to the New World" (E. Le Vane and J. P. Getty, *Collector's Choice* [London, 1955], p. 329).

Getty was a great admirer of Hadrian, and the idea that the Lansdowne Herakles could have once been in the emperor's possession greatly enhanced the statue's value in Getty's eyes. In his diary of 1962 (J. Frel, unpublished manuscript, "J. Paul Getty as a Collector" [1982], p. 17), he compared himself to two other great collectors of ancient art: William Randolph Hearst, the publishing magnate of northern California (who inspired a certain jealousy in Getty), and the Roman emperor Hadrian. Getty ultimately decided that he was superior to Hearst, noting that his own taste was "more classical and discerning" and that he preferred "quality to quantity." Decidedly competitive with Hearst, who was buying on a scale that was unprecedented for an American collector, Getty chafed at the idea that Hearst "lived like a Roman emperor" at San Simeon, his hilltop castle in Cambria, California (fig. 25), while Getty himself worked hard and lived modestly. (However, Getty did note, somewhat smugly, that in 1950 he was twice as rich as Hearst.) Comparing San Simeon with Hadrian's Villa, Getty concluded that Hearst's two pools

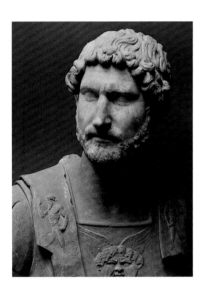

Figure 24. Portrait bust of the emperor Hadrian, Roman, ca. A.D. 120, in the Musei Capitolini, Rome

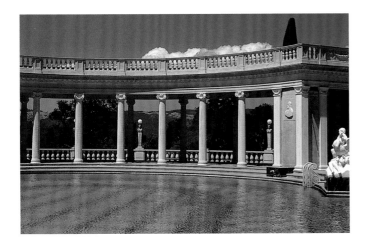

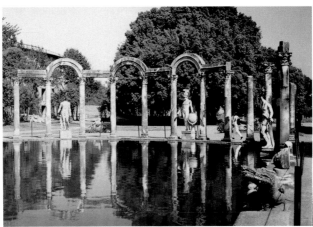

were even more impressive than Hadrian's (fig. 26). In some fundamental way, Getty's decision to re-create the extravagant Villa dei Papiri, with its great outer peristyle and connections to imperial Rome, was surely fueled by his envy of Hearst.

While the fulfillment of an old fantasy and the desire to eclipse a competing collector played some part in Getty's selection of the model for his museum, the decision was also based on personal taste and a strong sense of the "appropriateness" of a Roman villa as a place to display his collections, especially his antiquities. Writing later about his reasons for building the Villa, Getty explained his thinking very clearly:

> The public should know that what they will finally see wasn't done on a mere whim or chosen by a committee delegated for such a task. It will simply be what I felt a good museum should be, and it will have the character of a building I would like to visit myself.... The principal reason concerns the collection of Greek and Roman art which the museum has managed to acquire ... and what could be more logical than to display it in a classical building where it might originally have been seen? There is, I believe, no other place in the world where one can see such a building in any state except ruins, as one sees them now in Pompeii. There are replicas and imitations of ancient public buildings but none of a private structure—so this one should provide a unique experience.

Quoted in "Getty Says Museum No Mere Whim."

> This idea lies close to my heart, and the reason is that I like a museum to be intimate and friendly. I do not get much pleasure from a series of neutral galleries in which one sees a row of paintings or a row of statues as I do when they are placed in an appropriate setting. I would like every visitor at Malibu to feel as if I had invited him to come and look about and feel at home.

Quoted in H. Seldis, "The Getty Museum Rises in Splendor," IHT September 25, 1973; originally in an article by J. Paul Getty, "Getty Museum Invitation from the Collector," USC archives New Museum Malibu 2—28-1-74.

Figure 25. The Neptune Pool, the outdoor swimming pool at Hearst Castle

Figure 26. View of the north end of the Canopus at Hadrian's Villa at Tivoli

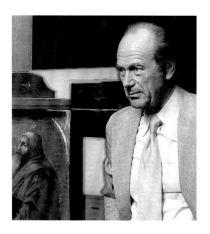

Figure 27. Stephen Garrett, J. Paul Getty's architectural adviser, oversaw the building of the Getty Villa and became its director in 1976.

opposite
Figure 28. View of the atrium of the Villa San Marco, Stabiae

RE-CREATING A ROMAN *VILLA MARITTIMA*

Getty seems to have made the decision to re-create the Villa dei Papiri by himself and over the objections of his friends and architectural advisers. (For instance, architect Stephen Garrett [fig. 27], Getty's overseer for the project and the Villa's first director after Getty himself, has acknowledged in personal conversation that he would have preferred a modern building.) In many ways, this grand example of an ancient Roman *villa marittima* (seaside retreat), was an ideal model for a small museum, especially one that was rich in ancient art and located on the site of a former lemon and avocado ranch. According to descriptions found in the writings of three ancient Romans—Cicero, Pliny the Younger, and Horace—a villa was a country estate where busy Romans sought to escape the turmoil and squalor of city life, especially during the summer months (figs. 28–30). Such an estate usually included fairly extensive property for agricultural production, and the ancient authors often referred with pride to the quality of the wines and oils from their gardens.

Though its plan evolved, probably over three centuries, the Villa dei Papiri seems to have begun as a typical Roman house built around a central hall, or atrium. At the heart of the house, the large atrium served as the public area where guests were received and commerce or business was transacted. Some of the Villa dei Papiri's rooms and spaces opened directly onto the atrium, such as large niches (*alae*) and the extended living room space (*tablinum*) at the south end that also opened onto a west-facing portico overlooking the sea. On its north side, the atrium opened onto an inner peristyle—an intimate garden courtyard surrounded by a graceful colonnade. Other private areas, including the baths and libraries, were arranged along the sides of a second colonnaded garden court-

yard to the east. As was typical of a Roman country house, the Villa dei Papiri allowed for the interplay between interior and exterior spaces, alternating between light and shaded areas. A larger, more extravagant peristyle garden, or *viridarium*, was added later to the northwest side of the original complex. It ran parallel to the seashore and was joined to the inner peristyle by an elaborate open *tablinum*. This garden had a magnificent central pool (*euripus*) and was lavishly adorned with sculptures in bronze and marble, as was the connecting *tablinum*. The sculptures—depicting animals, mythological subjects (such as the Greek god Hermes and drunken satyrs), athletes, Greek philosophers, and political notables—were intended to inspire thoughtful reflection as one walked along the shaded colonnade, admiring the views across the Bay of Naples.

Although reconstructing such a building would fulfill Getty's personal concept of the ideal space for his collection of ancient art, it was clear that adapting an ancient personal residence for use as a modern public museum would present major logistical challenges. Obviously, Getty could not realize the project without collaborating with experts. The eighteenth-century ground plan of Karl Weber was, after all, only a two-dimensional representation that mapped the layout of what seemed to be one level of the building. (It should be noted that the excavations conducted by the Italians from 1986 to 1993 have made it clear that even this ground plan did not really reflect a single level, but in fact included elements distributed over three different levels of the original structure; in addition, the discovery of pipes leading to an upper level as well as structural beams proves that the area around the atrium of the Villa dei Papiri had a second floor.) Because no documents existed to provide details of the

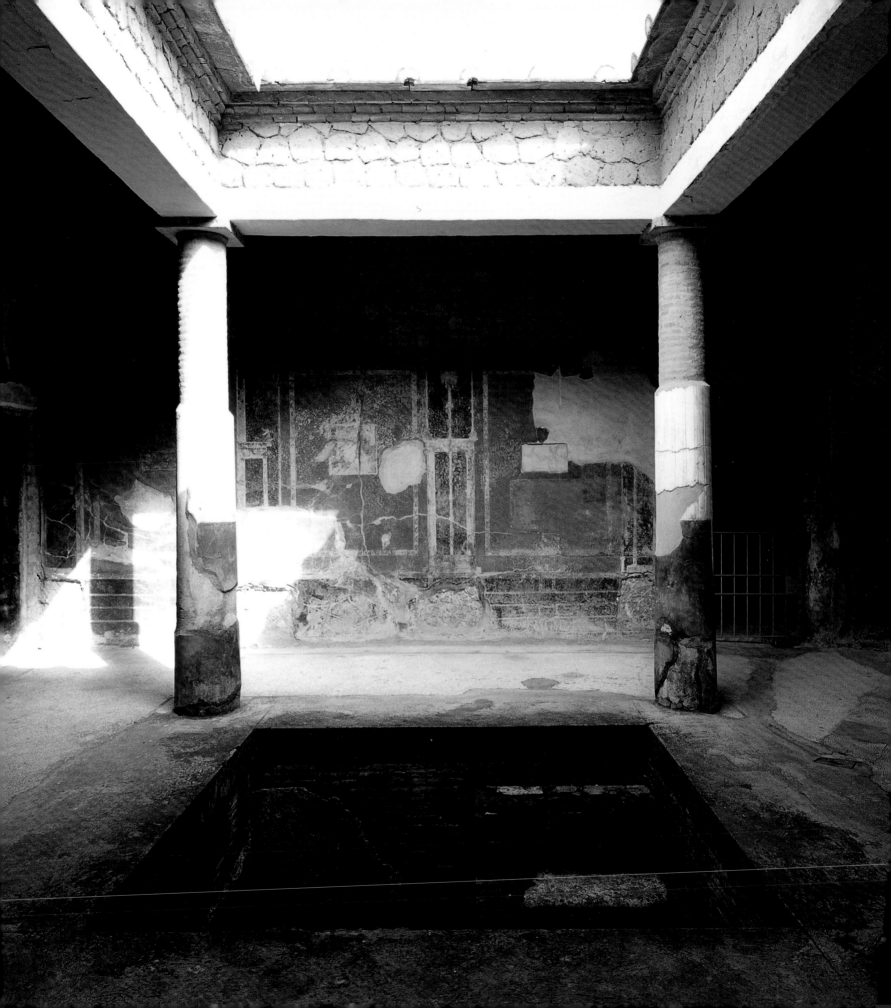

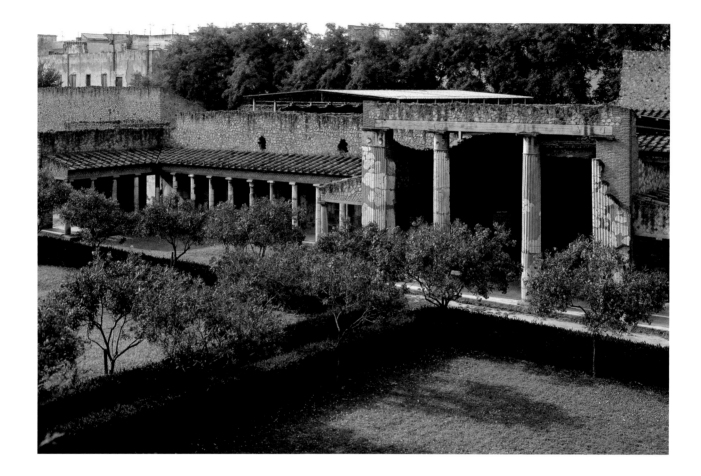

Figure 29. View of the
peristyle and gardens of the
Imperial Villa at Oplontis,
thought to be the residence
of the empress Poppaea,
wife of Nero

opposite
Figure 30. View of the atrium
of the Casa di Cei, Pompeii

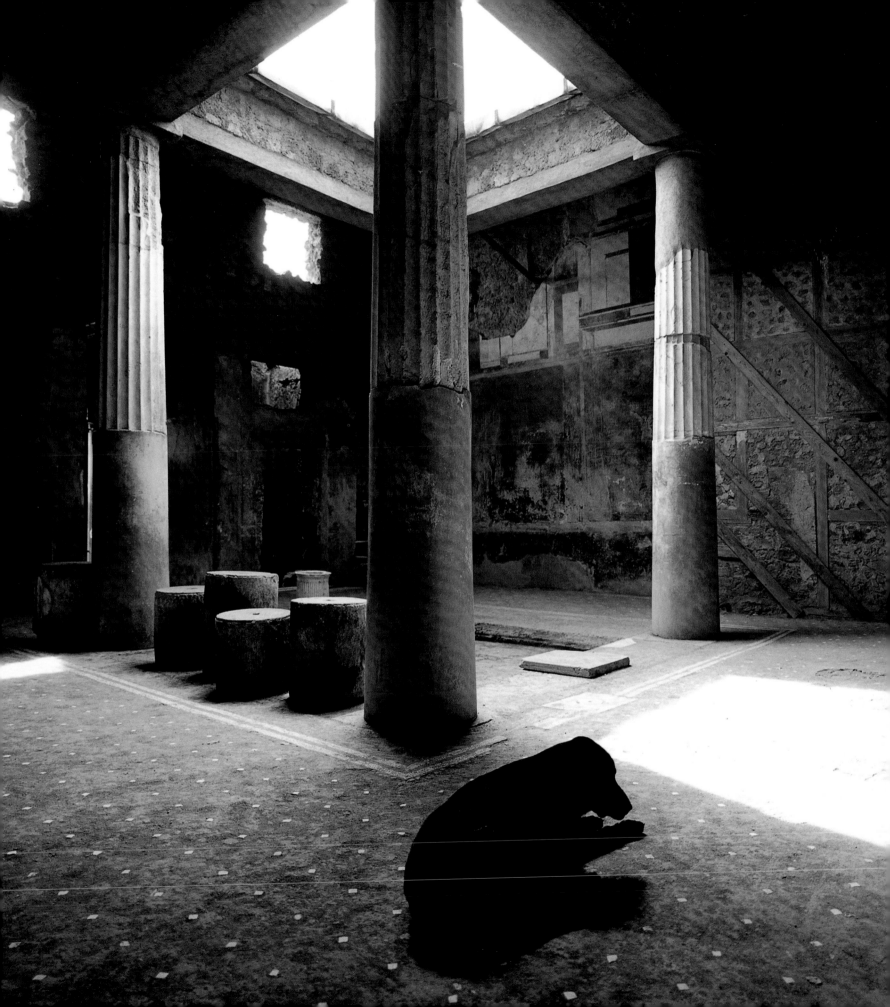

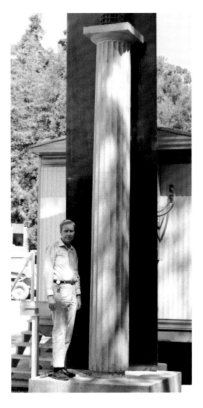

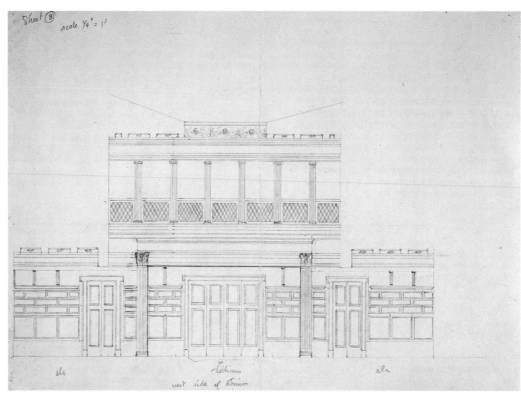

Figure 31. Norman Neuerburg, a historian of Roman architecture, brought his extensive knowledge of similar ancient structures to Getty's re-creation of the Villa dei Papiri.

Figure 32. The House of the Samnites in Herculaneum served as the inspiration for Neuerburg's elevation drawings of the Museum's Atrium.

building's elevations or superstructures, Getty's overseer, Stephen Garrett, was advised by Burton Fredericksen, Curator of Paintings, to enlist the services of Norman Neuerburg (fig. 31), a respected historian of ancient architecture, to help design a fairly accurate re-creation of what the villa may have looked like.

Trained at the Institute of Fine Arts in New York and at the American Academy in Rome, Neuerburg had done his graduate work on Roman fountain houses (public buildings that enclosed the all-important source of fresh water in Roman cities). Through his research, he had become intimately familiar with the sites of Pompeii and Herculaneum, and especially with the preserved domestic architecture there. Starting with the Weber ground plan, he first

made one major alteration to accommodate the villa to the Malibu site—he shifted the orientation of the great outer peristyle so that it would run down the canyon perpendicular to the sea instead of running parallel to it as it did in Herculaneum (figs. 32–35). He also opened the south end of the peristyle to take full advantage of the view out to the sea (fig. 36).

Neuerburg then drew upon his knowledge of houses, public buildings, and even tombs from various Roman sites for the myriad architectural details that would make the re-created building believable (figs. 37–40). He used mosaic floors from the Villa dei Papiri itself for the Museum's Temple of Herakles and Basilica and incorporated a two-story atrium based on one in the House of the Samnites at

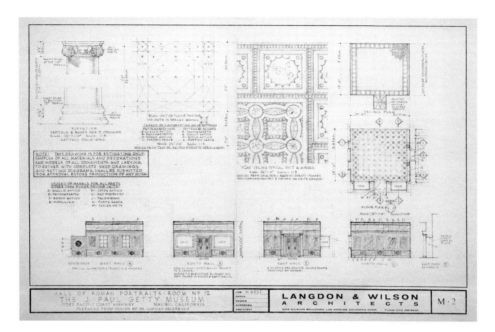

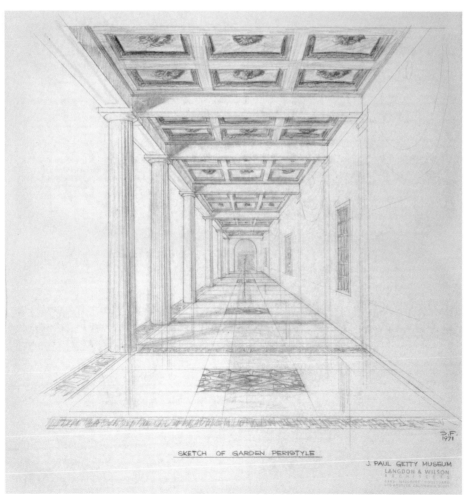

SKETCH OF GARDEN PERISTYLE

Figure 33. Neuerburg's meticulously researched plans for the elaborate decoration in the Room of Colored Marbles included a floor influenced by one in the House of the Relief of Orestes at Pompeii.

Figure 34. The drawing for the shaded Doric colonnade of the Outer Peristyle garden included a coffered ceiling and terrazzo floor with inset patterns.

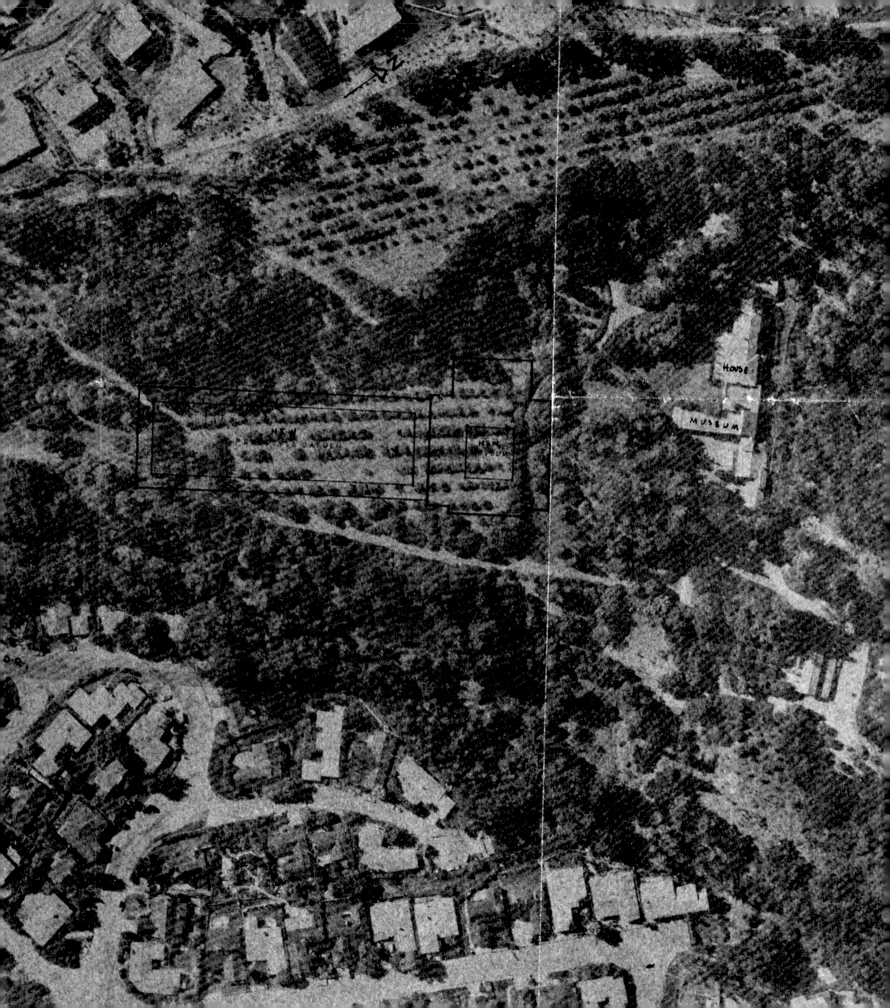

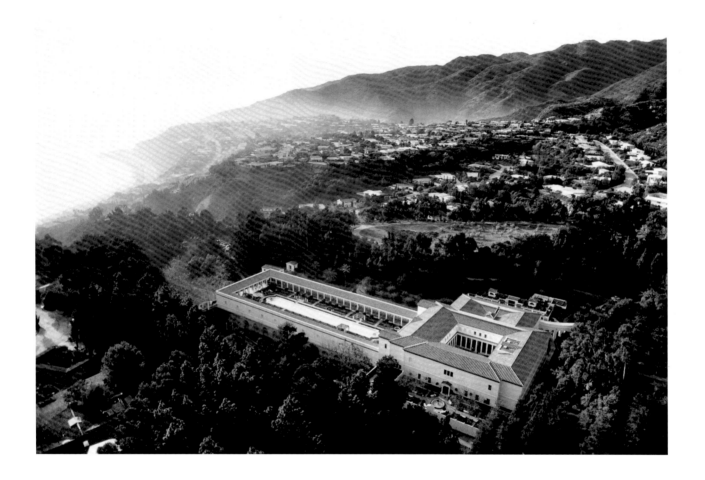

opposite

Figure 35. Aerial photo of the secluded Cañon de Sentimiento, including the Ranch House with the outline of the Villa superimposed

Figure 36. Aerial photo of the Museum, the surrounding residential neighborhood, and the Pacific coast

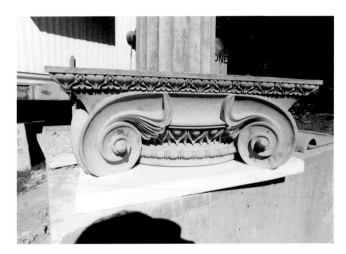

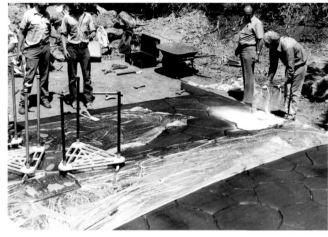

Figures 37–40. Images of ancient details being painstakingly reconstructed (counterclockwise from top left): Fig. 37. The newly cast Ionic capitals for the columns of the Inner Peristyle. Fig. 38. One of the cast laurel wreaths that decorate the east and west corners of the Outer Peristyle's south facade. Fig. 39. Cast pieces of the architectural moldings used throughout the building. Fig. 40. The outlines of the "stones" in the pseudo-Roman road being pressed into the fresh tar.

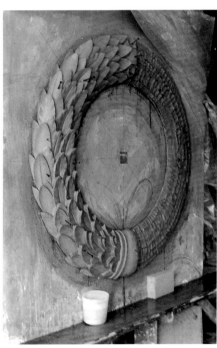

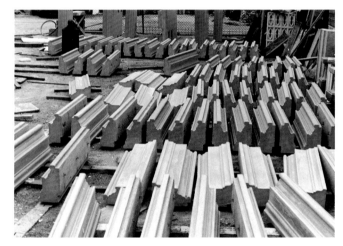

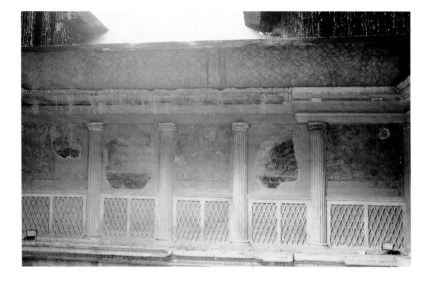

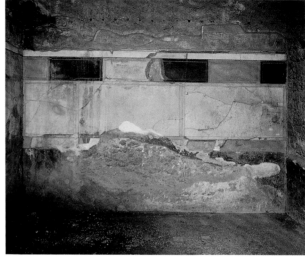

Herculaneum (fig. 41). The restrained wall decoration in the Museum's Atrium and Inner Peristyle (executed in the manner of Roman First Style wall paintings), as well as the "tumbling blocks" pattern in the *tablinum* of the Atrium, came from the House of the Faun in Pompeii (figs. 42, 43). The black and white mosaic of city walls around the Atrium's *impluvium* (collecting pool) came from the House of Diomedes in Pompeii. Indeed, decorative features in the Museum come from many other ancient buildings at Pompeii (fig. 44).

However, Getty's objective was more complex than making a simple re-creation of a Roman seaside villa. Working with the architectural firm Langdon Wilson, and in particular with project architect Edward Genter, Neuerburg had to create a building that would look like a Roman villa but could function as a modern museum. The building needed to accommodate all of the amenities expected by visitors as well as the security requirements and climate controls necessary to protect the collec-

tions. Many modifications had to be made to adjust the ancient model to fit its new purpose. Rooms that would have been living quarters in antiquity had to become galleries, and additional space had to be made for parking, an elevator, restrooms, offices, an auditorium, conservation labs, and preparations workshops.

The building's adaptation was done very skillfully—in fact, from the time it opened to the public, many visitors never realized that the Museum was not an accurate replica of the Villa dei Papiri in all its details—but it did present some anomalies, such as the way one entered the Museum. Most visitors arrived by car, and because the parking garage was tucked beneath the Outer Peristyle, there was no real entrance to the Museum (fig. 45). Visitors ascended to the building by a small, dark set of stairs in the corner of the parking structure or by an elevator; neither route was appropriate to the experience that awaited them (fig. 46). But once within the garden walls, most visitors forgot this awkward introduction.

Figure 41. The upper story of the atrium of the House of the Samnites in Herculaneum, showing the pseudo-colonnade and lattice railing that inspired Neuerburg's treatment of the second level of the Museum's Atrium

Figure 42. A wall in the House of the Faun in Pompeii painted in what is known as the First Style of Pompeian wall painting

overleaf
Figure 43. View of the tumbling-blocks mosaic and inner peristyle in the House of the Faun, Pompeii

Figure 44. Inner peristyle garden in the Villa San Marco, Stabiae

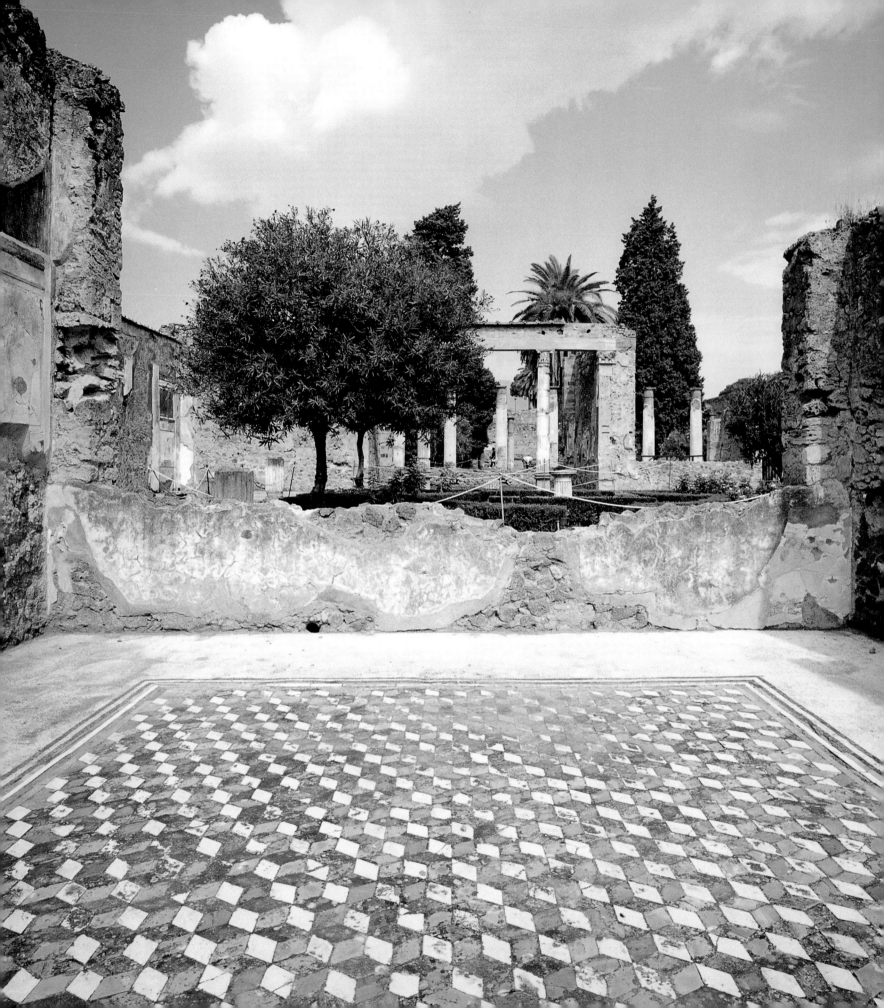

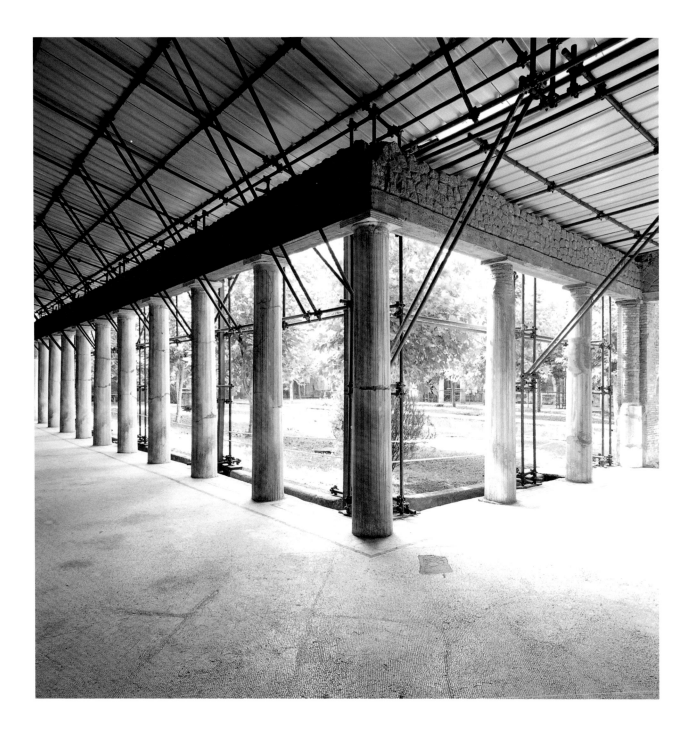

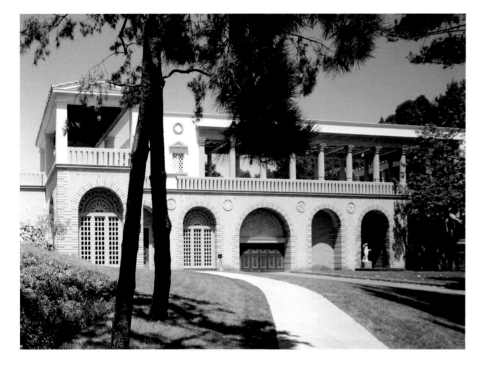

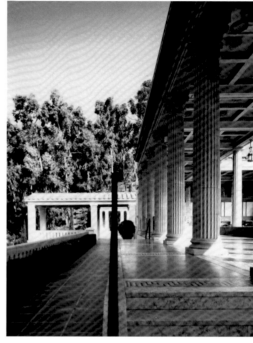

Figure 45. South elevation of
the completed Getty Museum,
showing the open colonnade
at the end of the Outer
Peristyle above the arched
facade of the garage

Figure 46. View toward the
West Belvedere showing the
open Corinthian colonnade at
the south end of the Outer
Peristyle

opposite
Figure 47. Perspective down
the west side of the Outer
Peristyle showing the completed wall paintings, coffered
ceiling, and Doric columns

The polished red terrazzo floors of the long open porticoes (fig. 47), the fountains in the large reflecting pool, and the bronze sculptures arranged in the lush Outer Peristyle (fig. 48) brought to life the images of villas around the Bay of Naples known from excavations and from representations in ancient wall paintings. One small modification that had to be made to the original plan was the depth of the 210-foot-long pool. It was approximately 6 feet deep in the ancient villa, but it had to be restricted to 18 inches in the re-created garden to avoid having a lifeguard on duty around the clock.

The bronzes displayed among the plants and along the colonnades were replicas of famous originals found in the eighteenth century in the Villa dei Papiri. The Chiurazzi foundry in Naples, which had received permission in the nineteenth century to make molds of the best-known masterpieces of the National Archaeological Museum of Naples as well as other famous Italian collections, was fortunately still in business and provided the patinated cast-bronze figures that decorated both the Inner and Outer Peristyles. In many cases, however, the placement of the bronzes in the gardens did not correspond with their original findspots. Rather, the statues were artfully dispersed among the arbors and flower beds. Some were situated in fanciful juxtapositions that distorted what they actually represented. A pair of runners, for example, were positioned as wrestlers in a face-off.

For the decoration of the Outer Peristyle's walls, the ceiling and walls of the West Porch (now called the Entrance Porch), and the ceiling of the entrance vestibule (adapted from a second *tablinum*) between the Outer and Inner

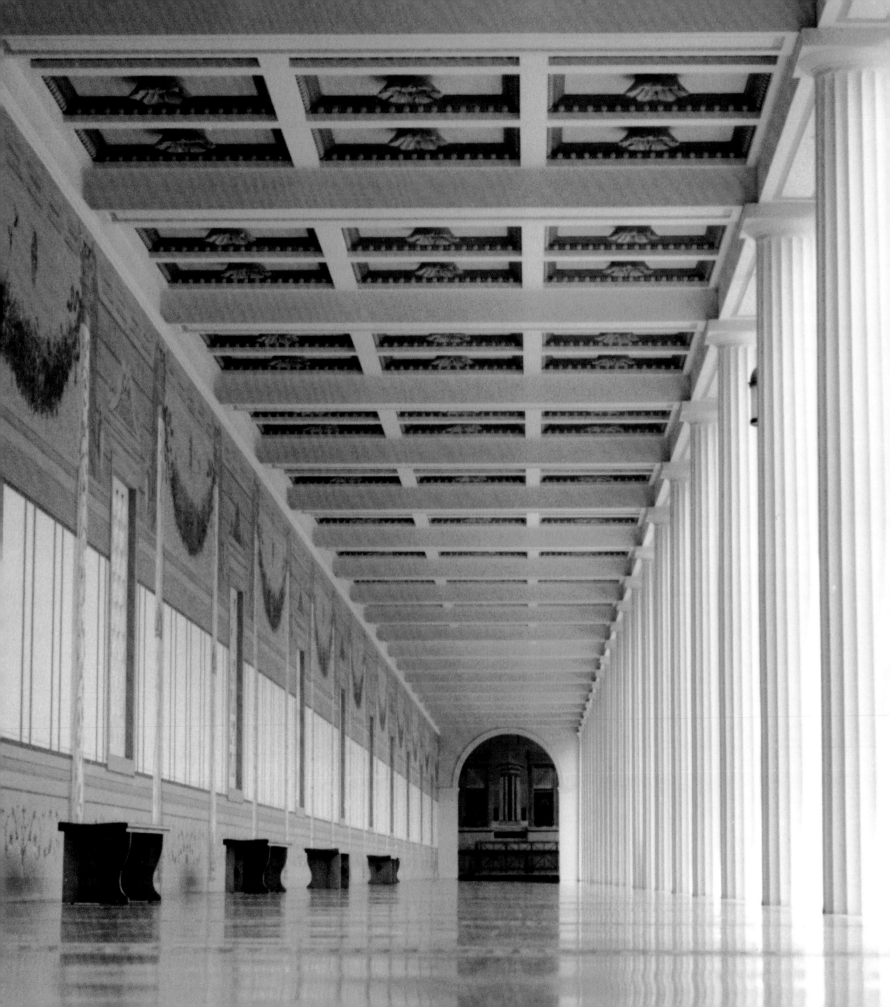

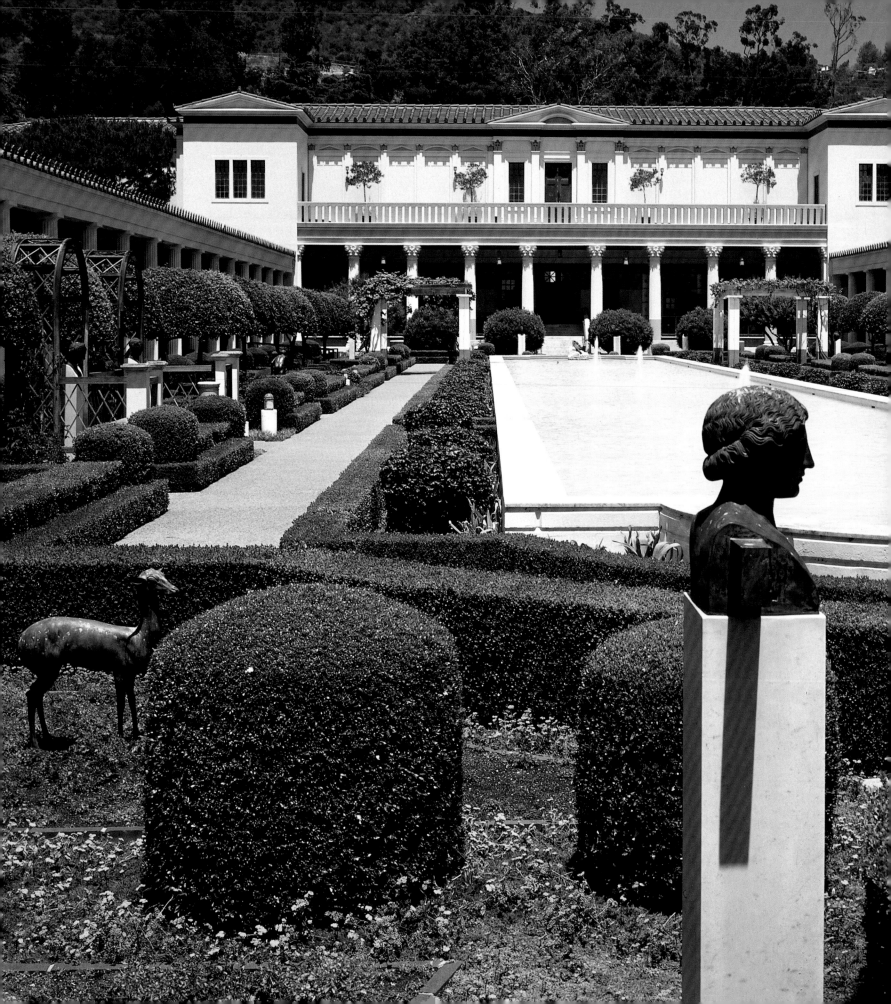

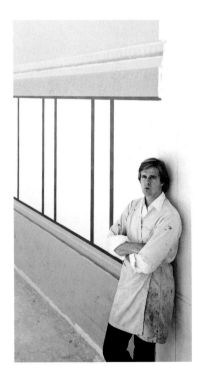

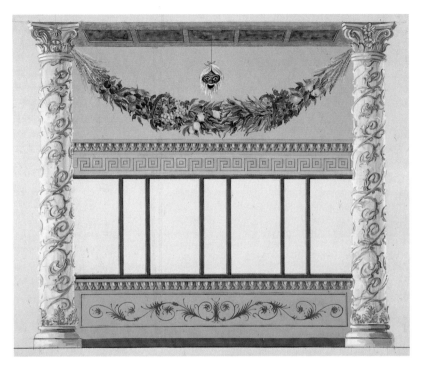

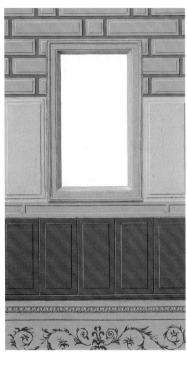

Peristyles, Neuerburg found a talented young artist, Garth Benton (fig. 49), who created designs that both copied and adapted Second Style Roman wall paintings (figs. 50, 51), an illusionistic style dating to the first century B.C. The scheme for the Outer Peristyle was derived from many sources (figs. 52, 53): the still lifes of ducks and deer were taken directly from fragmentary wall paintings discovered in the Villa dei Papiri; the garlands between the columns along the side walls were taken from the Villa of P. Fannius Synistor in Pompeii; the illusionistic architectural framework for the doors leading to the Herb Garden and the East Belvedere came from the House of the Griffins on the Palatine; and the baskets and glass vessels of fruit were from a villa recently excavated at Oplontis, near Torre Annunziata. Evoking the impression of opulence and peace, the completed Getty Museum was exactly the retreat

for reflection and *otium* (leisure) advocated by ancient writers.

Inside, the building maintained this illusion of ancient magnificence in a small number of splendid public spaces: the grand, two-story Atrium with its pseudo-*compluvium* (a fake skylight made from a bronze grille set against faux alabaster and illuminated from behind by electric lights) and a real *impluvium*, complete with a small fountain at one end; the Room of Colored Marbles; the *tablinum*, at the end of the Atrium by the West Porch; the Basilica; and the Temple of Herakles. The walls and floor of the entrance vestibule (the space between the Inner and Outer Peristyles) were copied from various sources (figs. 54, 55): the twisted columns from the House of the Relief of Orestes at Herculaneum, the floor from the House of the Deer at Herculaneum. The vine arbor motif of the ceiling paintings in recessed niches was

Figure 48. Outer Peristyle looking north to the Museum. Replicas of the bronze sculpture found in the Villa dei Papiri were placed in the garden without consideration for their original findspots.

Figures 49-51. Garth Benton (fig. 49) modeled the designs for the paintings in the Outer Peristyle from ancient sources. The motif of the garlands (fig. 50) was inspired by Second Style wall paintings once in the Villa of P. Fannius Synistor at Boscoreale and others from the House of Livia in Rome. A more restrained First Style design (fig. 51), a composite of different sources, was used on either side of the bronze doors that open to the Inner Peristyle.

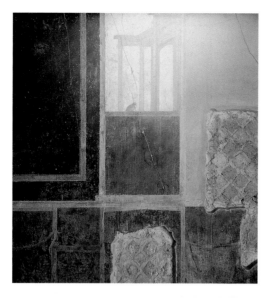

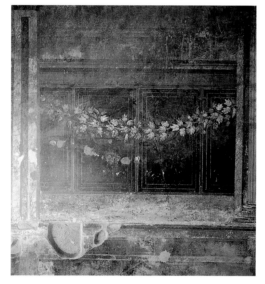

Figure 52. Detail of a painted wall in the Villa San Marco, Stabiae

Figure 53. Detail from a painted wall in the *tablinum* of the Villa of the Mysteries near Pompeii

inspired by originals in the House of the Fruit Orchard and the House of Diomedes in Pompeii.

In the Room of Colored Marbles (figs. 56, 57) (conceived by Neuerburg as the Hall of Roman Portraits, as if it were a kind of family shrine for ancestors), wall designs were derived from a number of sources, but the floor was based on a design from the House of the Relief of Orestes. The adjoining Basilica (fig. 58)— originally called the Temple of Cybele and designed as the setting for Getty's portrait statue of a woman as a priestess of Cybele—was revetted with colored stones laid in intricate patterns meant to echo the schemes of rooms discovered on the Palatine Hill in Rome in the eighteenth century (according to Neuerburg's unpublished notes). The elaborate vaulted plaster ceiling, with its coffered panels and splendid acanthus scrolls, was adapted from two different Pompeian sources: the coffers from the House of the Cryptoporticus, and the scrolls from the Forum Baths. The acanthus motifs in the domed ceiling over the apse came from the House of Menander at Pompeii. The floor copied an original in the Villa dei Papiri (fig. 59).

The most elaborate floor in the building was in the Temple of Herakles, the room created to house the Lansdowne Herakles (figs. 60–62). This floor also reproduced a marble pavement found in the Villa dei Papiri—in this case in the belvedere, the first place struck by the farmers who made the original discovery while digging a well. The glorious geometric design incorporating yellow *giallo antico* and dark gray *africano* marble was combined with an impressive travertine niche and a domed ceiling designed by Neuerburg, who found the inspiration for this fantastic space in a small underground temple dedicated to Herakles that had been excavated near Tivoli.

Other galleries had simpler decoration, but all included marble or terrazzo floors, classical

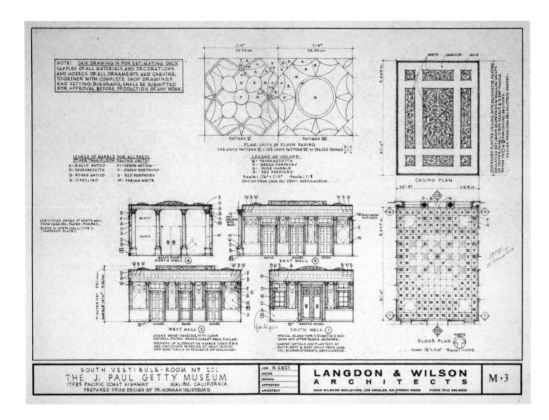

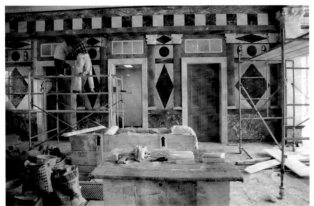

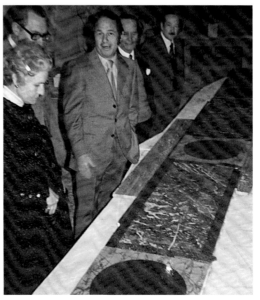

SOUTH VESTIBULE · ROOM Nº 101
THE J. PAUL GETTY MUSEUM
17985 PACIFIC COAST HIGHWAY   MALIBU, CALIFORNIA
PREPARED FROM DESIGN BY DR. NORMAN NEUERBURG

LANGDON & WILSON
ARCHITECTS

Figures 54, 55. Langdon Wilson's large drawing (fig. 54) shows the elevations and floor design of the south vestibule of the Museum, a space completely revetted in colored marbles (fig. 55).

Figure 56. Before the stonework for the Room of Colored Marbles was set in the walls, a section was presented to some of the Getty staff.

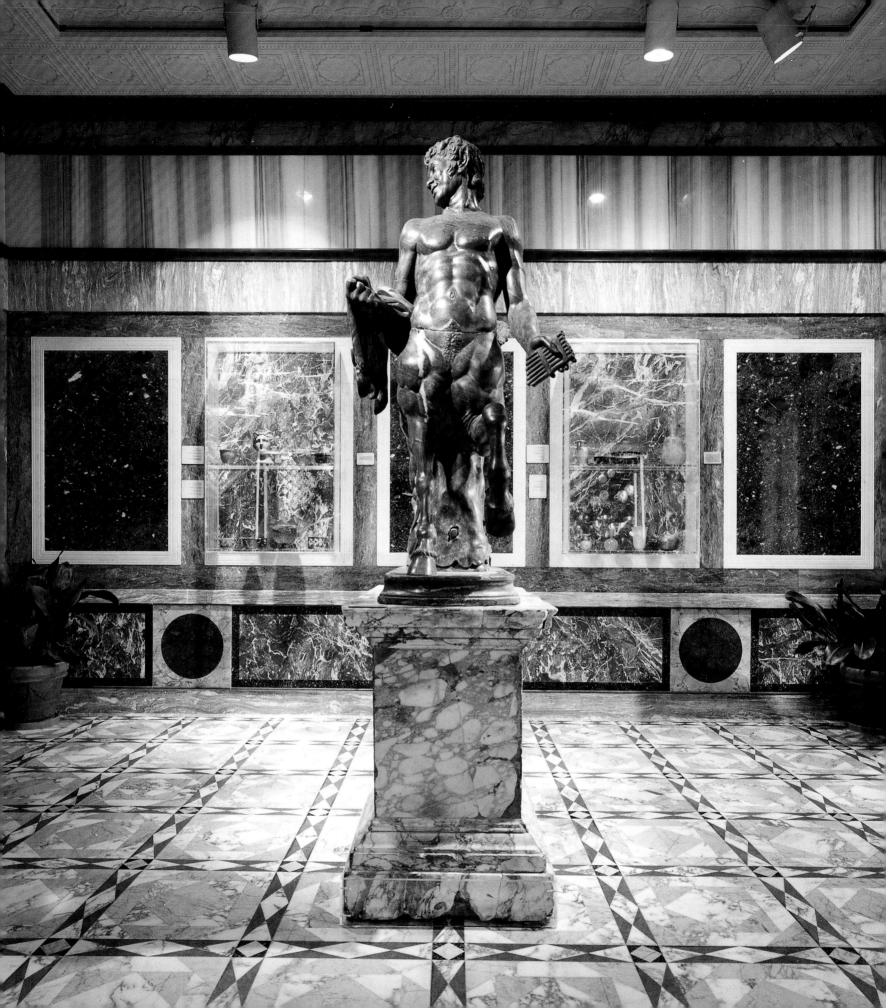

cornices, and elaborate lintels. In two galleries, ancient mosaics were set into the floors—one was actually cut to fit among four small columns. Also, two columns of pink Aberdeen granite purchased by Getty from Lansdowne House in London (the Robert Adam–designed drawing room, where the columns originally stood, and the dining room were dismantled in the 1930s when streets were widened) were incorporated to flank the doorway between the Room of Colored Marbles and the Basilica.

For the opening, Neuerburg had originally intended to furnish some of the spaces with replicas of ancient furniture. In preparation, he commissioned the construction of several elaborate pieces in Naples that copied carbonized objects found in Herculaneum by the excavator Amedeo Maiuri—including a wooden bed with intarsia work and a *lararium*, or small shrine for household deities (fig. 63). The first Curator of Antiquities, Jiří Frel, objected to the notion of replicating furnishings. He was concerned that the public would be hopelessly confused as to what was ancient and what was re-created. In the end, the replicas were never used in the Museum (though some, such as the *lararium* shown here, are carefully preserved in storage).

Both Getty and Frel were aware that the antiquities collection still was not extensive enough to fill the space available in the new museum. For this reason, Getty was advised by Neuerburg and Fredericksen—in consultation with Frel—to purchase the entire Greek and Roman inventory of a New York gallery of ancient art (the Royal-Athena Gallery) in 1971. Though their primary intention was to obtain the kinds of smaller objects—such as statuettes, terracotta and bronze vases, and glass—that would have furnished an ancient villa, Getty and Frel actually succeeded in adding some fairly large objects as well as some significant Greek and Etruscan pieces. Included in this purchase were the statue of a pantheistic goddess,

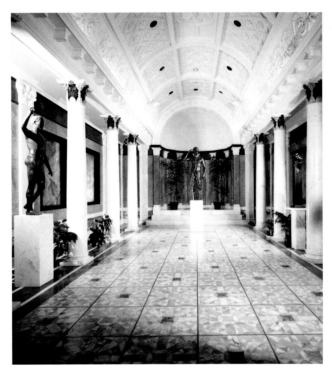

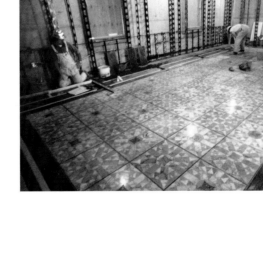

opposite

Figure 57. The completed Room of Colored Marbles as it was installed in 1983 with the nineteenth-century replica of the young centaur in *rosso antico* marble in the center

Figure 58. The Basilica completed and installed with bronze sculpture, ca. 1980

Figure 59. The floor of the Basilica in the process of installation. Its pattern was copied from an original found during the eighteenth-century exploration of the Villa dei Papiri.

Figures 60-62. The Temple of Herakles in the Getty Museum (ground plan and elevations in fig. 60) was designed specifically to showcase the Lansdowne Herakles. The room's magnificent marble mosaic floor was copied from the first floor discovered in the original Villa dei Papiri. Fig. 61 shows the floor being installed before the rest of the room was completed; fig. 62, opposite, shows the Temple finished with the statue in place.

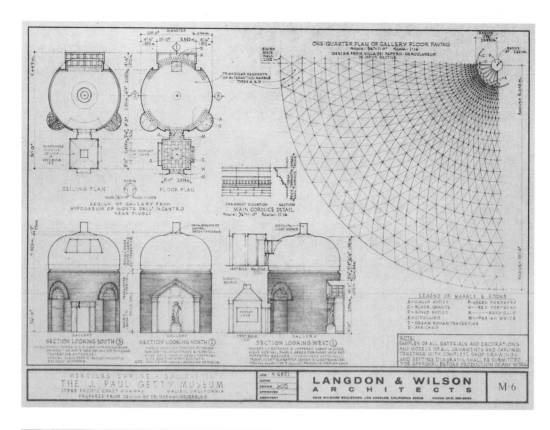

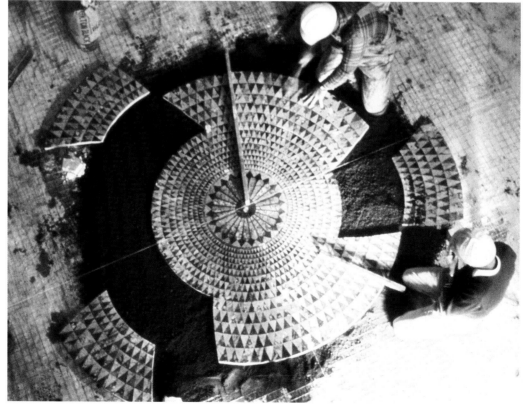

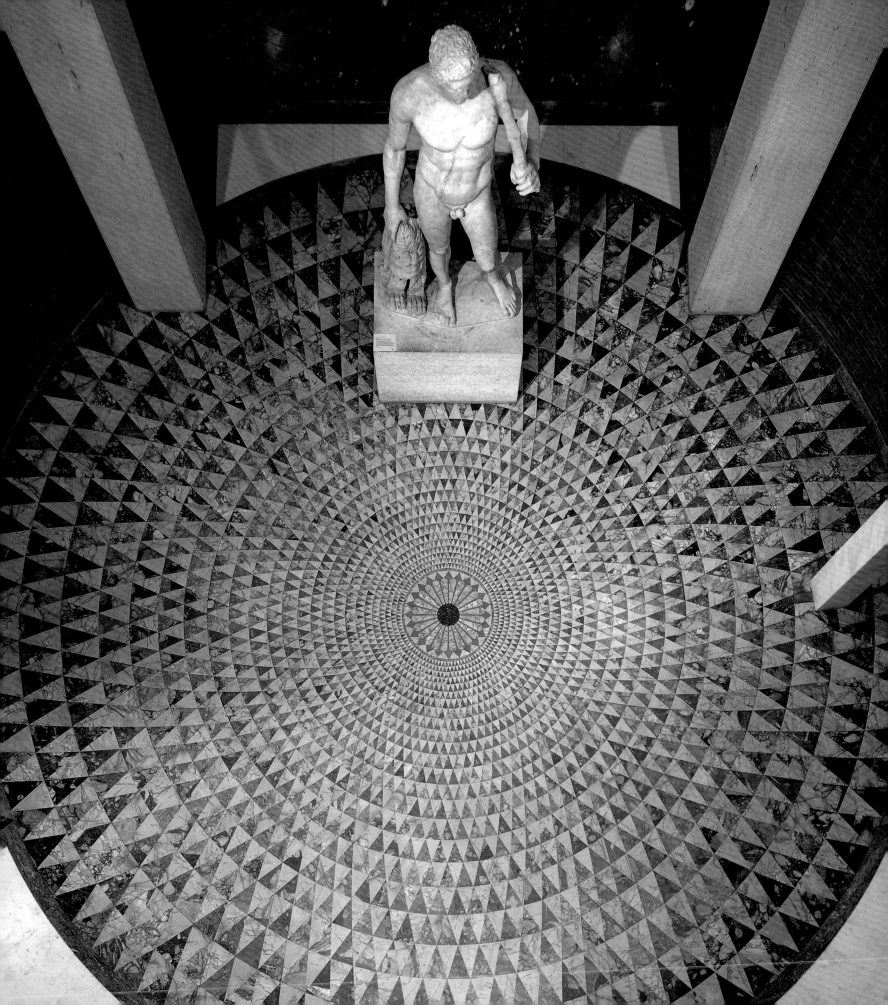

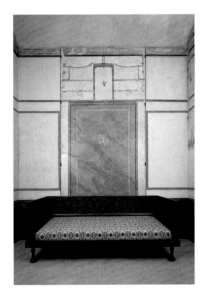

Venus-Hygieia (fig. 64); some good Greek,
Etruscan, and South Italian terracotta vases,
including a fine black-figured *pelike* (a type of
storage jar) by the Theseus Painter, a large group
of *bucchero* vessels, and South Italian animal-
head *rhyta*; several examples of Etruscan tufa
sculpture; and a Cypriot limestone kore.
The purchase also brought the Museum its first
Cycladic objects and a number of important
Greek and Roman funerary monuments (including a grave marker of Posideos and Herophanta
and one of Popillius and Calpurnia. The acquisition showed the same kind of indiscriminate
buying for which Getty had once criticized
William Randolph Hearst, but the addition of
more than 350 pieces filled out the collection
very nicely with examples of the minor arts.

In the design of the building, the obviously
Roman architectural elements were limited
to the first level, which was used exclusively
to display antiquities. The design of the upper
level—which first housed the collections
of paintings, French furniture, and decorative
arts, and later also included the collections
of European sculpture, old master drawings,
illuminated manuscripts, and photographs—
was more generic in character, with mostly
carpeted or wooden floors, painted or fabric-
covered walls, and simple suspended ceilings
typical of Beaux Arts museums around the world
(fig. 65). Only the galleries for French furniture
and decorative arts were given more distinctive
treatment; there, antique paneling enhanced
the setting where these fine collections were
displayed. Neuerburg designed only one elaborate colored marble floor for the upper level—
a baroque design well suited to the later collections of paintings and French furniture—and
it was placed in the elevator vestibule. There
were few windows, as natural light was not
considered advantageous to the display of these
collections, and over time the small number of

windows that did exist were covered to reduce
the light levels and provide more wall space.

One late addition to the project was the
small Garden Tea Room just to the west of the
Museum building (figs. 66, 67). Though initially
opposed by Getty, who saw no need for such
services, it was added for the convenience of
visitors, as there was little opportunity for
refreshment in the area. Its pseudo-Roman style
matched the Villa, although the structure had
nothing to do with the original plan for the Villa
dei Papiri. Set against the hillside just in front

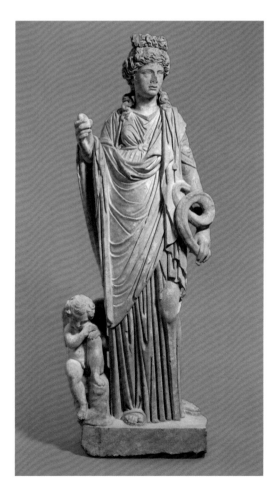

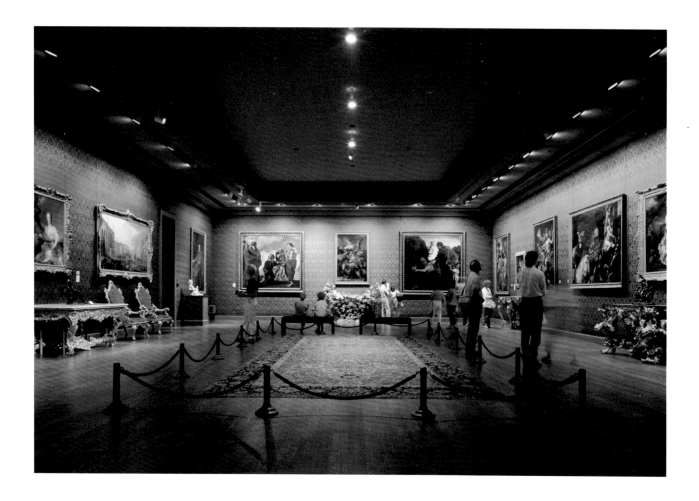

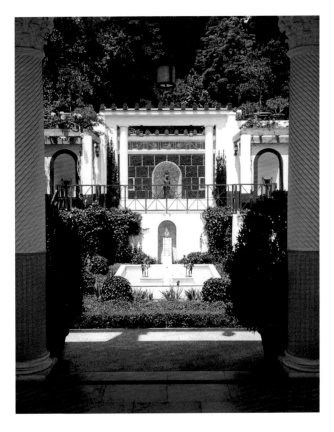 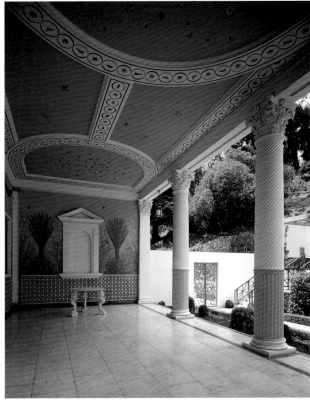

Figure 66. View from the West Porch of the Museum to the Garden Tea Room, with the square fountain based on an original in the House of Loreius Tiburtinus in Pompeii before the podium and the small *nymphaeum* at the back of the terrace just above it

Figure 67. View down the West Porch of the Museum building, with the Garden Tea Room just opposite. Garden murals by Garth Benton were inspired by originals such as the wall shown in fig. 68 from the House of Livia in Rome.

of the grand West Porch, this modest building was composed of two symmetrical pavilions joined together by a landscaped terrace with tables. One pavilion functioned as the servery, and the other as protected indoor seating. Between the two pavilions, a small wall fountain (*nymphaeum*) flowed out into a square basin with a bronze statuette of a maiden in its center. Like the bronzes in the Museum's two peristyles, this little figure was a cast made by the Chiurazzi foundry from the mold of an ancient model found in the outer peristyle of the Villa dei Papiri. The wall behind the fountain was covered with rusticated faux-stone masonry in red and blue up to the level of a blue glass-mosaic frieze of sea nymphs that filled the space just beneath the roofline. Inspired by a similar structure in the House of the Skeleton at Herculaneum, the design of this wall enlivened the otherwise fairly simple restaurant, which was set on a high podium and accessible only by four sets of narrow stairs.

Another niche in the front of this podium, set just beneath the *nymphaeum* between the two central flights of stairs, held a second fountain with a statuette of Silenus sitting atop a bloated animal skin from which water flowed down a series of small marble steps into a square basin. In the center of the basin, a stepped pyramid also spouted water, which ran down its four sides toward four bronze figures of Cupid at the corners of the pool. The fountain was based on an elaborate model in the House of Loreius Tiburtinus in Pompeii, but the bronzes were all Chiurazzi copies of figures found in the Villa dei Papiri.

The broad West Porch of the Museum itself, with its twisted fluted columns copied from those of the Villa San Marco at Stabiae, was later adapted to become part of the Tea Room seating area. The walls and ceilings, decorated with Garth Benton's paintings inspired by garden frescoes from the House of Livia in Rome (fig. 68), the House of the Fruit Orchard in Pompeii, and other Roman and Pompeian villas, provided the perfect setting for casual outdoor dining.

The gardens of the Museum were likewise carefully planned to be historically accurate, using only species of plants identified in the excavations of the gardens of Pompeii and Herculaneum. The landscape architects Emmet Wemple and Associates, and especially project director Denis Kurutz, carefully studied the excavation reports of Wilhelmina Jashemski and other Pompeian archaeologists before creating their designs. Many of the seeds and bulbs were imported from Italy and propagated in nearby nurseries to be acclimatized to the Malibu environment. The more formal Outer and Inner Peristyles were organized with paved walkways and geometrically trimmed box hedges that surrounded the plant beds and reflecting pools. Rows of laurel trees, pomegranate trees, ivy topiaries, and oleander bushes were symmetrically introduced along the length of the *viridarium*. Their evergreen foliage, harmoniously framed by the boxwood, provided year-round lushness in the garden (fig. 69). Heirloom roses of the type used in antiquity to make perfume filled the small beds in front of the laurels and pomegranate trees, together with irises and acanthus plants (fig. 70).

The peaceful, shaded East Garden, originally intended to be an aviary, included an accurate replica of an elaborately decorated wall fountain from the House of the Great Fountain in Pompeii, as well as a central circular fountain built to accommodate water lilies and other aquatic plants (figs. 71–73). The larger Herb Garden (fig. 74), on the west side of the Outer Peristyle, was modeled on an ancient kitchen garden, with various fruit trees (including pear, apple, fig, and peach) and terraces of olives as well as expansive beds of herbs used by the ancient Romans for medicine and cooking.

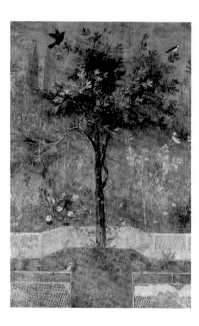

Figure 68. Garden frescoes in the House of Livia, Rome

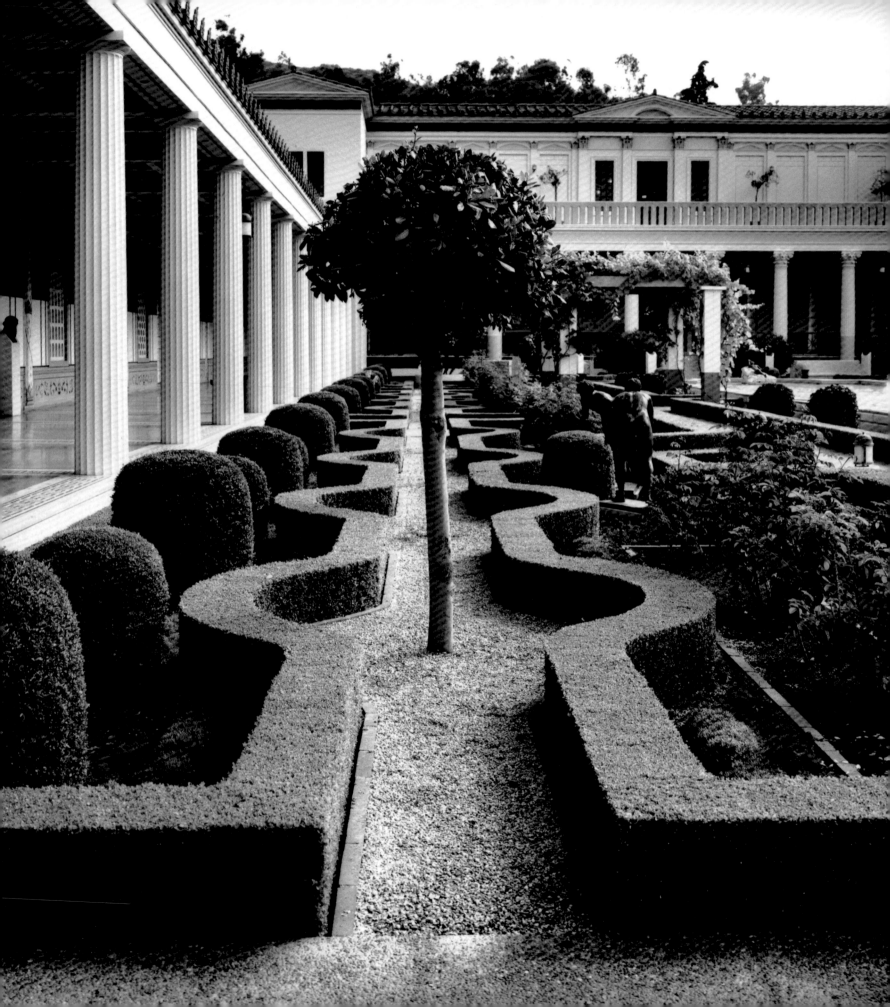

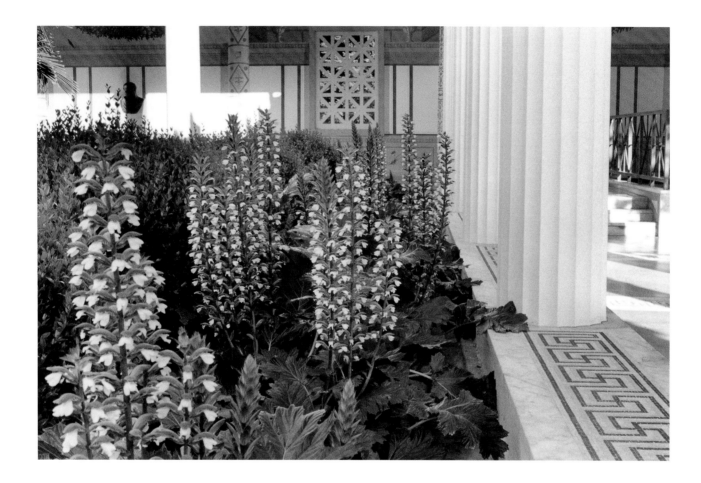

opposite
Figure 69. View of the Outer Peristyle garden looking toward the Museum's south facade. Symmetrically trimmed box hedges bordered the rows of laurel trees that ran parallel to the Doric porticoes.

Figure 70. In summer, luxuriant acanthus plants filled the southeast corner of the Outer Peristyle garden.

Figures 71–73. Though both fountains in the East Garden (fig. 71) were based on ancient sources, only one was a faithful copy. The colorful arched fountain against the back wall replicates a well-preserved original in the House of the Great Fountain in Pompeii (fig. 72), imitating its central stepped cascade for the falling water as well as its intricate mosaic decoration and the large stone theater masks that decorate its supporting pilasters (fig. 73).

opposite
Figure 74. The Museum's Herb Garden, to the west of the Outer Peristyle, was planted with fruits and fragrant plants known to have been used in the preparation of foods and medicines in ancient Rome.

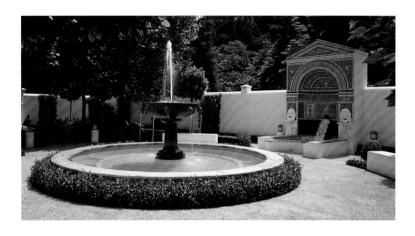

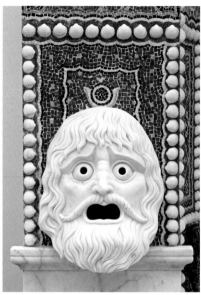

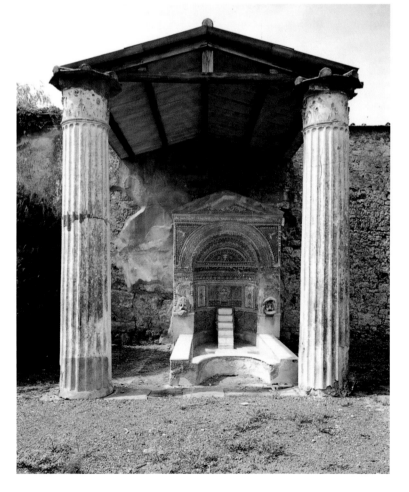

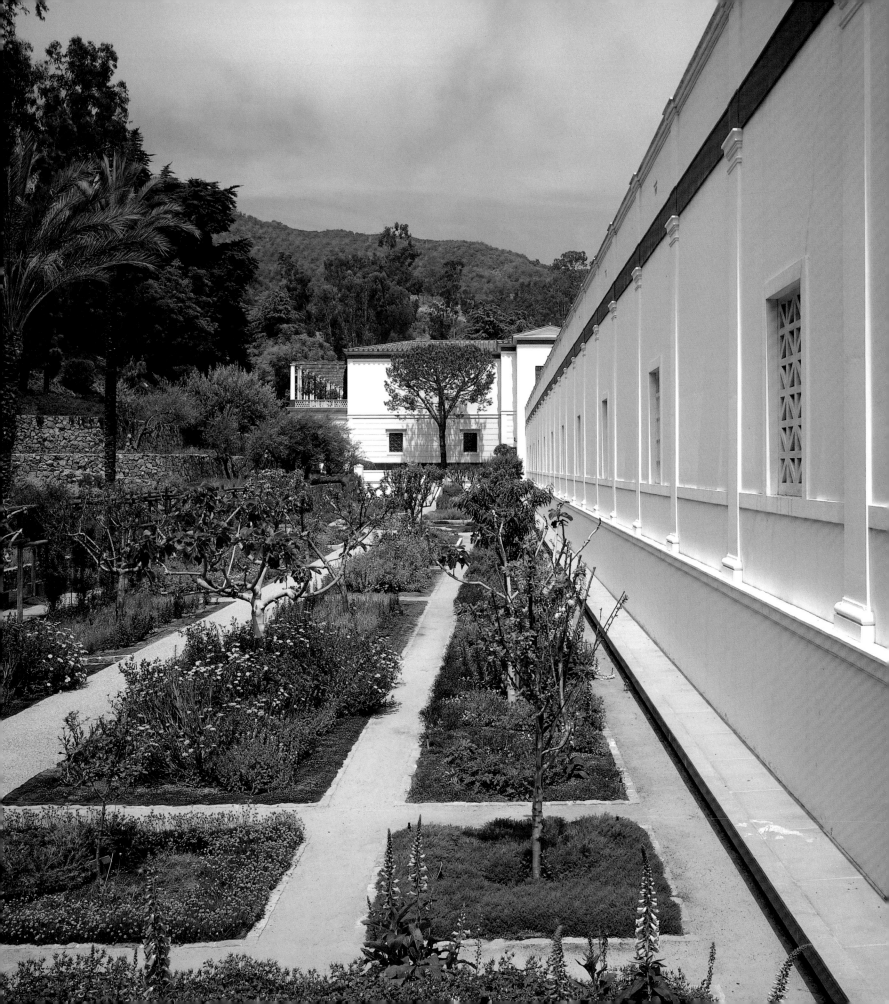

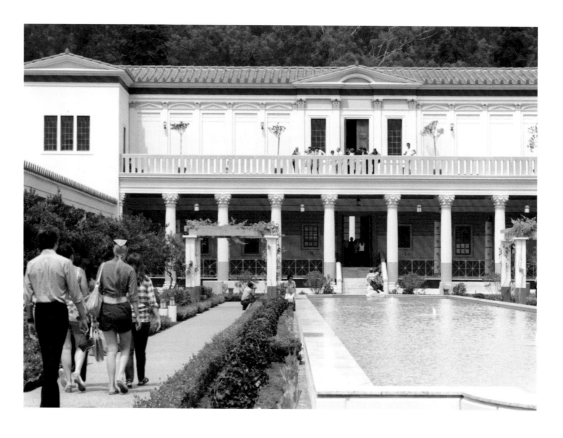

Figure 75. Some of the first visitors arriving at the newly opened Getty Museum, January 1974

It provided a casual space for visitors to take a rest from the galleries and to enjoy the sun and the views over the Pacific.

On January 16, 1974, the Museum opened to the public for the first time. It was greeted by vicious reviews from critics, who detested the derivative pastiche and considered the notion of re-creating an ancient building more appropriate to a movie set than an art museum. But as much as the critics reviled it, the public loved it, arriving in droves. Over the years, the Museum became one of the most beloved sites in Los Angeles (fig. 75). Indeed, the public appreciated it as much, if not more, for its lush gardens, photogenic porticoes, and colorful, opulent materials as for the collections it housed. Meanwhile, the Museum's original home, the

Ranch House, was gradually converted into office spaces, though quarters were kept ready in case J. Paul Getty should return.

THE CREATION OF THE GETTY CENTER

In June of 1976, J. Paul Getty died at his home in London at the age of eighty-three. Although he had always said that the Museum would be provided for after his death and had actually endowed the Museum with $32 million by the mid-1970s, the magnitude of his largesse was unexpected. He left his entire personal fortune, then estimated at $700 million, to endow the Museum. The will was first challenged by his family, who did not dispute the Museum's right to the money (since it had inherited the $1.3 billion trust established by Getty's mother) but took issue with the assets of the Museum being controlled by a board of trustees instead of by the family. Next, the Internal Revenue Service sought to collect the majority of the estate ($628.6 million) in taxes, claiming that the Museum did not qualify as a charity. The litigation was finally settled in 1982, and the Museum received the funds—which by that time had grown to $1.2 billion—unencumbered by any restrictions.

At the time, the Museum was the only program supported by the J. Paul Getty Trust, and the international art world reacted immediately with fear and resentment. Such an endowment, larger than that of any other museum in the world, would make it possible for the Getty to control the art market, and this dominance would drive up the costs of works of art for every other institution. It could also lead to the plundering of European collections that had already been depleted by American collectors and institutions earlier in the century.

Recognizing the immense possibilities and responsibilities that such resources presented, however, the Board of Trustees appointed a new president and chief executive officer, Harold Williams (fig. 76), to develop a broad range of programs that could contribute to the "diffusion of artistic and general knowledge," the mission formulated by Getty in the original Trust.

In 1983, after a period of travel and exploration to determine the needs and identify the areas where support could do the greatest good, Williams recommended that the Board establish six programs in addition to the Museum: the Getty Conservation Institute, the Getty Center for the History of Art and the Humanities (later to become the Getty Research Institute), the Art History Information Program (later to become the Getty Information Institute), the

Getty Center for Education in the Arts (later to become the Getty Education Institute), the Museum Management Program (later to become the Getty Leadership Institute), and the Getty Grant Program (later to become the Getty Foundation). His intention in expanding the activities of the Trust was to support research not only in the arts and humanities but also in areas closely linked to the visual arts—such as conservation, education, and management, which were integral to the kinds of work already being done in the Museum. These new programs would allow for broad input from specialists around the world and, he hoped, have greater international impact. The application of new technologies, especially computers and video, showed great promise for both the collection and the diffusion of knowledge; the Art History Information Program would explore these technologies and their usefulness, until it was disbanded in 1999. Because the resources allowed the Trust to extend support to scholars and projects not under the auspices of its own institutions, the Getty Grant Program was initiated.

At the same time, Williams and the Board made another momentous decision—to select a site where they would construct new buildings to accommodate all of these programs, including the Museum. The only exception was the Department of Antiquities; the Board decided it should remain at the Villa in Malibu, which was built to house that collection so appropriately.

For the Villa, this decision was both positive and inevitable. From the start, a particularly uncomfortable tension had existed between the later, nonancient collections and the replica building that housed them. While Getty clearly had thought about the appropriateness of a pseudo-Roman *villa marittima* for the display of his antiquities, apparently he had not considered the contradiction inherent in housing old master paintings and French furniture and

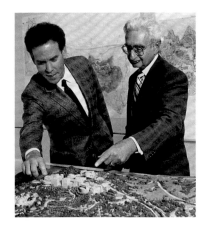

Figure 76. Getty Trust President Harold Williams (right) and Vice President Stephen Rountree discuss details of the model of the Getty Center. Rountree would oversee the construction of this massive project before starting on the renovations of the Villa site.

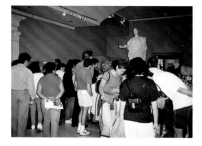

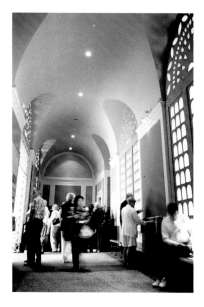

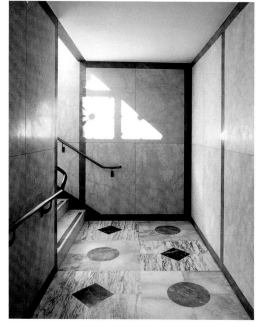

Figure 77. One of the galleries of ancient sculpture filled with visitors in 1997, just before the Museum closed for renovations, illustrates the crowded conditions in which the growing collections were displayed.

Figure 78. The vaulted space off the southeast end of the parking garage that led visitors to the elevator and stairs did not provide an appropriate entrance into the Museum.

Figure 79. One of the two staircases at the north end of the garage that led to the Outer Peristyle

decorative arts in a replica of a building that would have predated them. As funds for acquisitions had increased, the collections of paintings and French decorative arts had grown in size and significance. With this growth, the building's inappropriateness for their display, as well as its space limitations, had become ever more apparent.

To be fair, in Neuerburg's plan, the most Roman elements of the building—including spaces specifically adapted from the Roman house plan, such as the Atrium and the *cubicula* (bedrooms)—were restricted to the first level, which housed antiquities. The upstairs spaces did not include classical architectural elements. And because the levels of light and humidity had to be carefully controlled in both the paintings and the French furniture and decorative arts galleries, the plans for these spaces included few openings for natural light—in sharp contrast to the galleries on the lower level, which

had both windows and doors opening onto the gardens on every side.

In fact, except for the nearly hidden staircases and single elevator, the upper level had little connection to the lower one, or indeed to the building that housed it. Originally, only twelve windows looked out on the Inner Peristyle from the upper level (three on each side of the enclosed square), and six opened onto the Atrium (three on the west end and three on the east). Two large windows in the upper elevator vestibule looked out to the ocean over the Outer Peristyle, and two more looked out from the upper West Porch onto the Garden Tea Room. Aside from those—and a strangely futuristic curved window cut into the dome of the Temple of Herakles, allowing a view down to the elaborate marble mosaic floor— the public spaces on the second level did not communicate with the gardens or galleries of the ground floor. Two small rooms on either end of the South Balcony on the second level did have windows looking out on two sides, but they were used as offices until the years just before the Villa closed for renovations, when they became galleries.

Although there had been little enough to start with, natural light was gradually excluded from the upper-level galleries almost entirely. In addition, one of the large rooms for paintings was remodeled to include interior walls that would provide more display space. Cases were added to the corridor surrounding the Inner Peristyle to accommodate the expanding collections of silver and ceramics. Finally, with the addition of the new collections of illuminated manuscripts, photographs, drawings, and European sculpture, it became clear that either a new wing or a new building was needed to properly house the Museum's nonancient collections.

It was also obvious that, once these collections were removed, the Museum would need to be significantly refurbished to make the

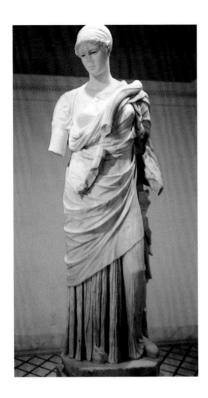

upper-level galleries suitable for the display of antiquities, as that collection had also grown dramatically. The addition of large pieces of sculpture as well as several private collections had strained the confines of the first level. When the antiquities collection was small and had few large sculptures, the Los Angeles County Museum of Art (LACMA) had generously lent the Getty Museum several large pieces from its Hope and Lansdowne collections. Early images of the Villa show LACMA's statues of Athena and Hygieia (fig. 80) standing in the alcoves that had been created for such large-scale pieces on either side of the Atrium, while a great krater (two-handed bowl), a throne, and a colossal bust of Athena filled the area of the Atrium near the West Porch. The Hope Herakles and Lansdowne Athlete had occupied the niches in the Museum's Temple of Herakles. Because the Getty now needed the space to display its own collections, these pieces were returned in 1987. Fortunately, LACMA had prepared a new gallery to house these great sculptures, and they were welcomed back to a display space perfectly suited to their imposing scale.

The first private collection to be added to the Getty's Antiquities Department, consisting of 215 engraved gems and cameos, did not take up too much space (fig. 81), but the second, which included more than four hundred Greek vases (fig. 82) and vase fragments of exceptional quality, did. Walter and Molly Bareiss (figs. 83, 84) had begun assembling their collection in the 1950s and had focused on red-figured vases made in Athens between 510 B.C. and 480 B.C., generally acknowledged by scholars as the greatest period of Greek vase production. The collection—which included masterpieces by such artists as Psiax, Onesimos, Douris, the Brygos Painter, and the Berlin Painter, as well as more than one hundred complete black-figured amphorae (storage jars), kraters, and drinking cups (fig. 85)—originally came on loan to the Museum for an exhibition mounted in 1983. Since Getty himself had had little or no interest in Greek vases and the Museum's first curator had collected mostly South Italian pottery and fragments, the acquisition (which was part purchase, part gift) significantly upgraded the Museum's holdings in this area.

Figure 80. The Hope Hygieia lent by the Los Angeles County Museum of Art on display in the Atrium of the Museum, ca. 1987

Figure 81. Engraved Etruscan scarab from the late 5th century B.C., showing a kneeling archer

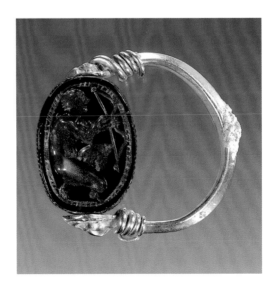

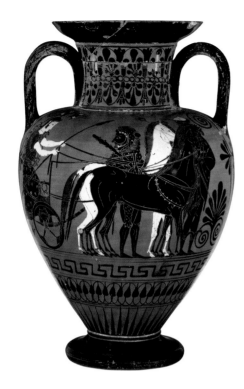

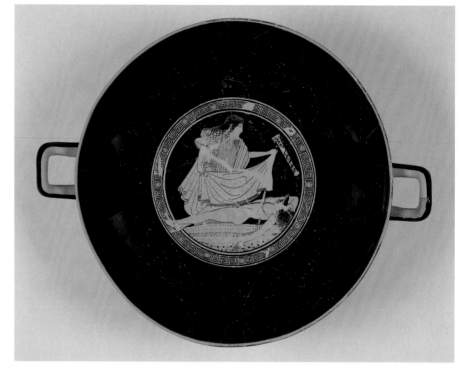

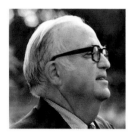
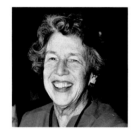

Figures 82-85. The amphora by the Bareiss Painter (fig. 82) was named for the collectors Walter and Molly Bareiss (figs. 83, 84), who assembled a remarkable collection of ancient vases acquired by the Museum in 1985-86. The collection also included the famous cup by the Brygos Painter showing the suicide of Ajax (fig. 85).

A third collection, purchased in 1985 through an agent for a private collector in New York, brought the Museum ten masterpieces of marble and bronze sculpture. The objects ranged in date from the Cycladic period of about 2500 B.C., represented by a magnificent statuette of a harpist (fig. 86), through a fourth-century-B.C. marble table support in the shape of griffins attacking a doe (fig. 87) to the Roman *Portrait Head of a Balding Man* from the third century A.D. The objects' extraordinary quality and state of preservation immediately made them highlights of the collection. In 1988, a dealer in New York offered the Museum the

opportunity to buy a smaller group of Cycladic objects from the European collectors Paul and Marianne Steiner, including three large female figures of the folded-arm type (fig. 88).

But the Museum's greatest opportunity came in 1996—just before the Villa was closed to the public for renovations—when Lawrence and Barbara Fleischman (fig. 89) of New York presented the Museum with the possibility of acquiring their collection of more than three hundred bronzes, terracottas, marbles, and vases. Like the Bareisses, the Fleischmans had been collecting ancient art since the 1950s; unlike the Bareisses, however, they had bought

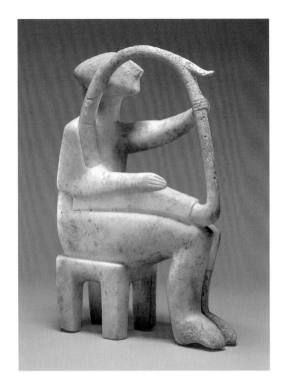

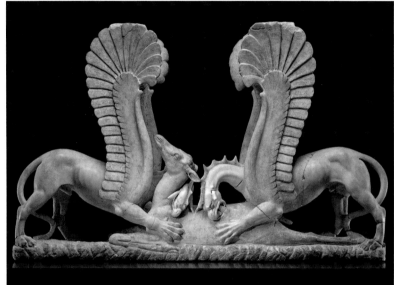

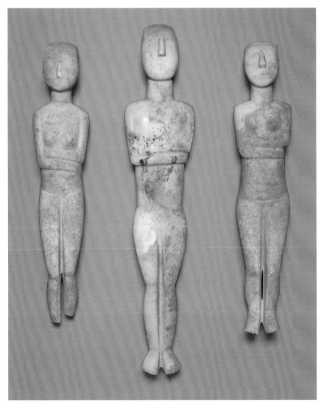

Figures 86–88. Important
examples of ancient sculpture
acquired by the Museum
in 1985 and 1988 from
private collectors included
the Cycladic seated harpist
(fig. 86), the magnificent
painted table support
with two griffins attacking a
fallen stag (fig. 87), and
three large Cycladic female
idols of the folded-arm variety
(fig. 88).

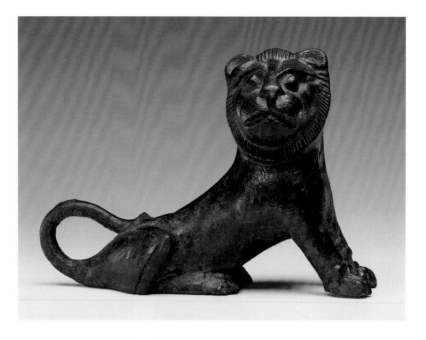

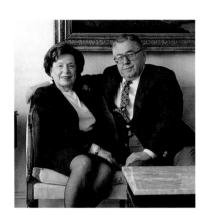

Figures 89-92. New York
collectors Barbara and
Lawrence Fleischman (fig. 89)
acquired ancient art of
all periods and in all media.
Among the many master-
pieces now in the Getty collection are the Archaic
bronze statuette of a lion
made in ancient Sparta
(fig. 90), the unique Hellenistic
bronze *lebes* decorated with
the relief protome of a satyr
and inlaid with silver (fig. 91),
and a Roman two-handled
silver cup showing Odysseus
in the Underworld (fig. 92).

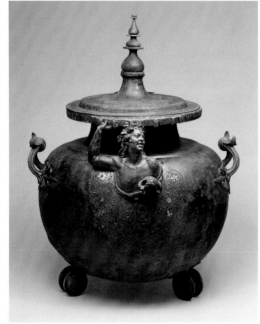

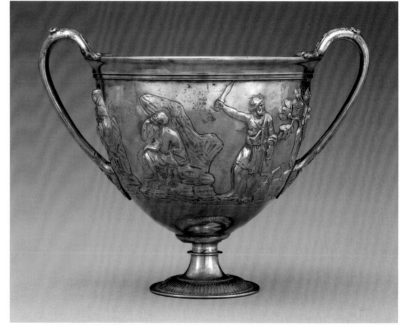

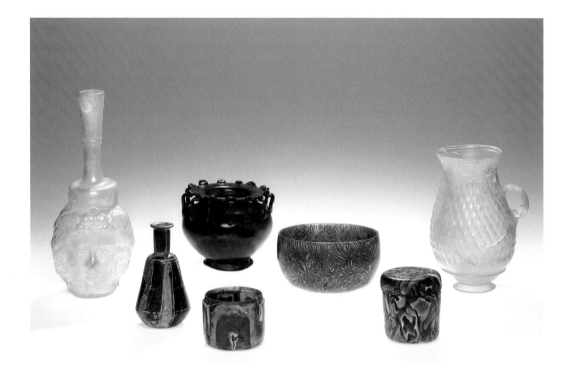

objects in all media and of all periods. Key pieces in the collection included two Greek bronze lions from the Archaic period (fig. 90); an Etruscan Late Archaic painted terracotta plaque; a unique Late Hellenistic bronze *lebes* (mixing bowl) decorated with a satyr's protome in high relief and floral patterns with silver inlays (fig. 91); a Greek Late Hellenistic marble statue of Tyche, goddess of good fortune; a magnificent Roman bronze head of the young Bacchus; a Second Style wall painting of a landscape seen through glass; and a Roman silver *kantharos* (wine cup) with scenes of Odysseus in the Underworld (fig. 92). As with the Bareiss collection, the acquisition was part gift and part purchase.

It should be noted that collecting did not stop while the Villa was closed for renovations. In 2003, the Museum had the opportunity to purchase 380 of the major pieces from the distinguished glass collection formed in Germany by Erwin Oppenländer (fig. 93). He had begun collecting in the 1930s, and the collection included pieces ranging in date from an Egyptian *krateriskos* (small mixing bowl) of 1500 B.C. to Islamic objects of the eleventh century A.D. The collection also included examples of most glassmaking techniques, both blown and molded. Among the most stunning pieces are three examples of gold band glass, several important vessels of mosaic glass, over thirty pieces of core-formed glass, a mold-blown beaker with mythological figures, a large lotus-bud beaker, and several snake-thread bottles.

As the Museum's collection grew, so did the staff that was needed to care for it. The Ranch House had slowly been transformed from a private residence with some large public gallery

Figure 93. The Antiquities Department's most recent acquisition is 380 pieces of ancient glass from the collection of Erwin Oppenländer. The vessels shown here represent some of the most important glassmaking techniques, including (counterclockwise from left) a mold-blown beaker, a gold-band flask, a gold-band *pyxis*, an agate glass *pyxis* with lid, a faceted one-handled jug, a mosiac bowl, and a vessel with thirteen handles.

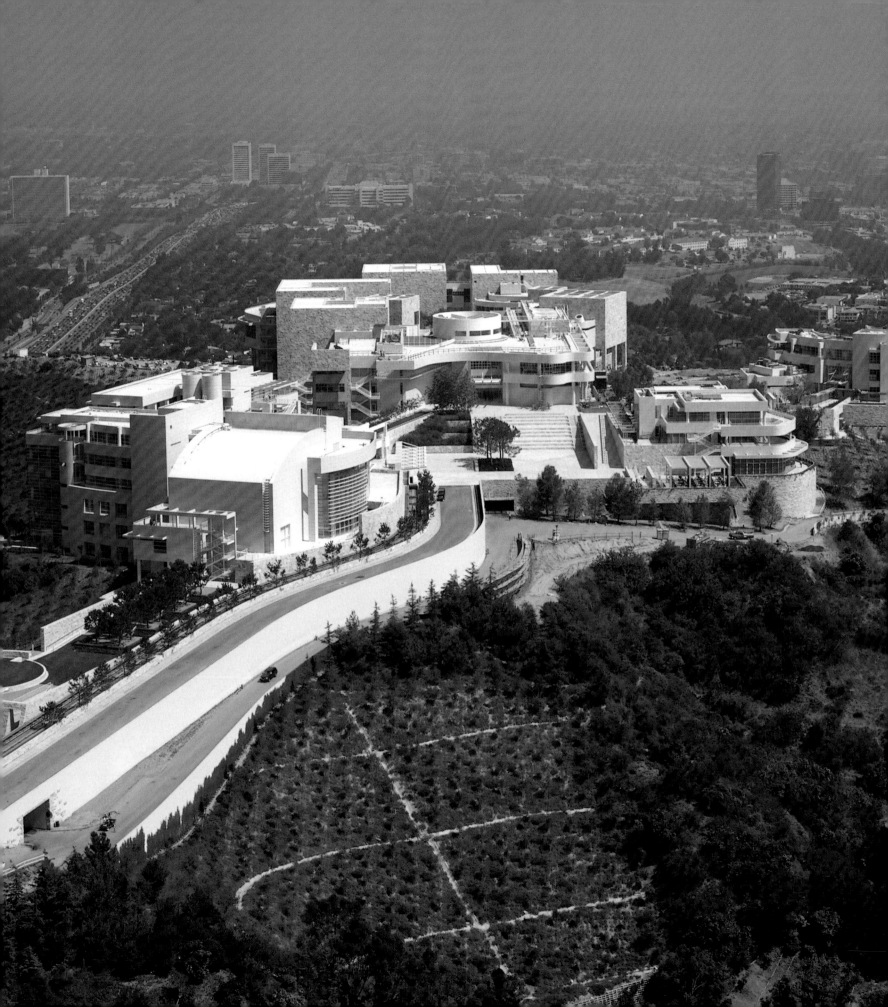

spaces into an office building that housed part of the administrative staff as well as Publications, Education, Accounting, Personnel, Academic Affairs, offices for guest scholars, and the mail room. The conservation laboratories, which had originally been accommodated in the basement of the Museum near the collections in storage, had moved up to the former entrance courtyard on the east side of the Ranch House in 1984. Antiquities Conservation occupied the large gallery on the ground level of the Ranch House that had once been used to display the ancient sculpture collection. This space was used for the treatment of large, heavy sculpture, while the light-filled room above that had once held French furniture and decorative arts was now designated for the treatment of vases and small objects. Additional laboratory buildings were constructed on two sides of the tiled courtyard that still held the fountain decorated with monkeys. The laboratory for the conservation of paintings was adjacent to the so-called Blackburn residence on the north, and the laboratory for the conservation of decorative arts was located on the south.

The Blackburn residence was actually a wing of the Ranch House, connected to it by a large arch that spanned the driveway. Once home to J. Paul Getty's ranch foreman, Ralph Blackburn, and his wife, Earleen, the Museum's first receptionist and switchboard operator, this space was renovated in 1984, to house first the curatorial offices of the Antiquities Department and later the Paintings Conservation offices, Education, Photographic Services, and the Slide Library. The three guest cottages that originally provided housing for staff members who lived on the property were gradually converted to office space for Public Affairs, Exhibition Design, and Education.

In 1983, after purchasing a large undeveloped tract of land adjacent to the San Diego Freeway in West Los Angeles and conducting an international search for an architect, the Getty Trust engaged Richard Meier & Partners Architects, of New York, to design the six buildings that would comprise the new Getty Center and house the Trust's expanded programs. Beset by political, aesthetic, and physical challenges, this large, complex project would take thirteen years to complete (fig. 94). It opened to the public in December 1997.

The Museum in Malibu remained open until just a year before the Getty Center opened, even as the nonancient collections were slowly being moved to their new home for installation. But on July 6, 1997, when the paintings collection was about to move to the Center, the Villa's doors closed to the public. Over the next year, the entire antiquities collection was also moved to the new site so that the much-needed renovation of the Villa could begin. Antiquities formed the basis of the new museum's opening exhibition, *Beyond Beauty*. Following that, a small portion of the collection was on view in temporary galleries on the lower level of the Center's West Pavilion until May 2004, while the rest of the collection was housed in the Center's storerooms.

opposite
Figure 94. Aerial view of the Getty Center designed by Richard Meier in west Los Angeles

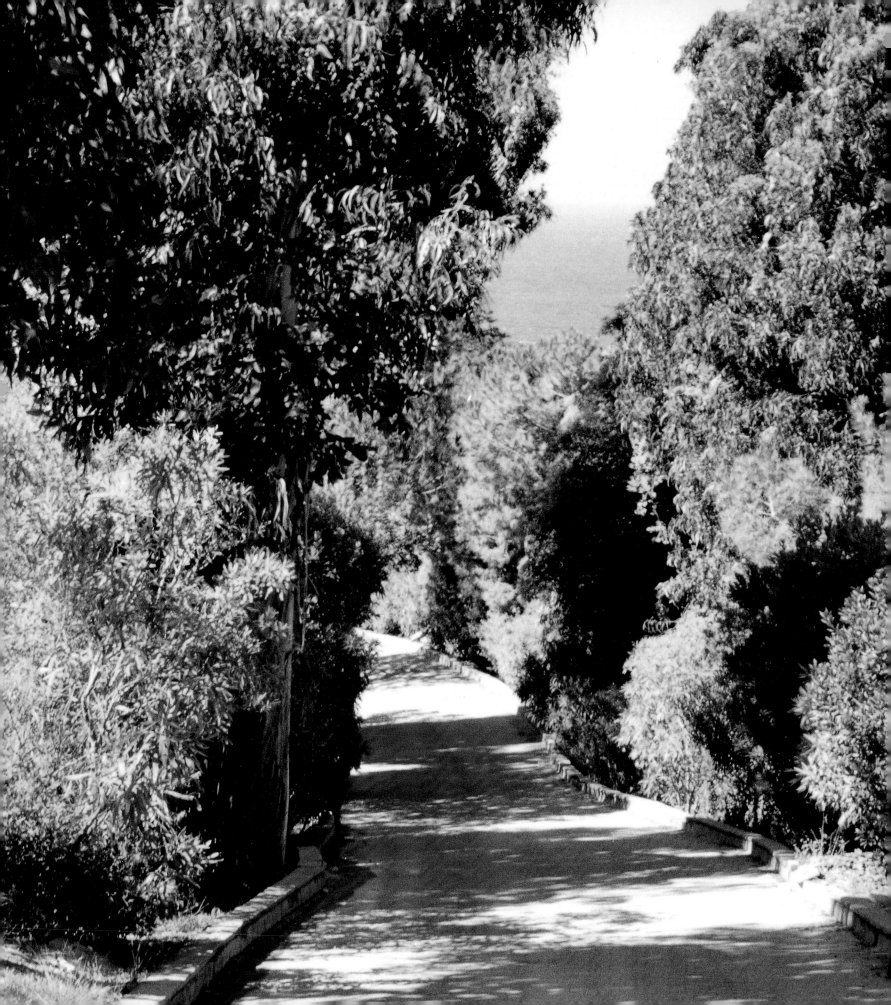

3 The Villa Renovation Project

The planning for the renovation of the Villa had begun as early as 1987. During the years of active growth of both the collection and the staff in the 1980s, it had become clear that there were a number of things that needed to be done to both the building and the site to bring them up to current codes for safety and accessibility. The fire roads were too narrow for the latest models of large fire trucks (fig. 95); the servery of the Tea Room, accessible only by stairs, was unavailable to the disabled; the slope of the Auditorium floor was too steep for a wheelchair, and safe exiting in case of fire required a new stairway that would lead directly to the outside. The Ranch House had no climate control and provided no access for the disabled. Over time, its original spaces, both living quarters and galleries, had been subdivided to accommodate offices and laboratories without any coherent overall plan. Correction of these and other problems had been deferred, with the permission of the City of Los Angeles, until the Getty Center was completed, but those issues would have to be addressed in the new plans.

At the same time, there were several objectives for the renovation that, while not essential to the project, came to be considered as highly desirable improvements. During the building's many years of service to the public, its problems as well as its strengths had become obvious.

The first objective, and perhaps the most important one, was to create a proper entry sequence for the Museum that was suited to its

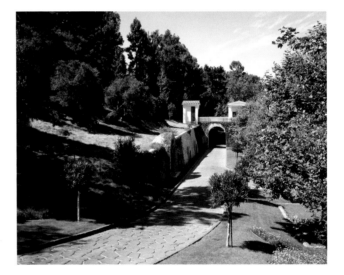

function as a public space. In the first century B.C., the Roman architectural historian Vitruvius wrote that a *villa suburbana* (country home) was entered through its peristyle, and Neuerburg had followed this idea in Malibu by having visitors enter through the Outer Peristyle. Unfortunately, this entry did not necessarily serve either the public or the collection very well (fig. 96).

The main parking area was beneath the Outer Peristyle, with a smaller, open parking lot (the so-called camper lot) located a hundred yards away up the hill. Arriving at either place, visitors had to ascend, by means of stairs or a small elevator near the southeast corner of the garage, to the Museum and its gardens. With

opposite

Figure 95. View looking south on the fire road that ran around the back of the Malibu property

Figure 96. The East Road running alongside the Museum with its original pseudo-Roman paving. This paving had to be replaced with smooth asphalt in the late 1980s to facilitate art deliveries.

just two small restrooms, no place to check a coat or bag, and no access to wheelchairs or strollers, this entry sequence afforded few of the services now expected in most public facilities. Later, an information desk was added in the basement to provide visitors with maps and guides to the collection (see fig. 78), and eventually visitors could obtain wheelchairs and strollers at a security desk just inside the Museum basement doors (in an area not intended for public access). Neither the small elevator nor the four staircases (see fig. 79) from the underground garage, uninviting and hard to find, prepared the visitor for what was waiting above. The entry experience simply did not do justice to the magnificence of the architecture.

The entry sequence did nothing to promote the Villa as a museum. After arriving in the Outer Peristyle, visitors usually walked the length of the garden and passed through the entrance vestibule to a second garden, the Inner Peristyle. Both of these spaces were filled with twentieth-century copies of works of art found in the original Villa dei Papiri rather than with genuine antiquities. Only after turning around one quarter of the Inner Peristyle did the visitor finally enter a gallery and encounter a real work of art. Not surprisingly, visitors often found themselves confused about which works were ancient and which were modern.

Because the first galleries of antiquities were two large rooms adjacent to the Atrium, the visitor usually passed through these spaces before entering, from the side, the Atrium—the true center of a Roman house. This awkward off-center arrival obscured the axial symmetry of the building and left many visitors perplexed about exactly where they had come in. Though a small building, it was a particularly disorienting one—indeed, as a scholar of antiquities who was a frequent visitor commented, "I have no trouble in the Louvre and the Met; this is the only museum building in which I get lost."

Vitruvius's statement that the entrance would have been through the peristyle made sense for the Villa dei Papiri when it was first built, before its large outer peristyle was added in the second half of the first century B.C. Its basic plan was that of a Roman house in which the private living quarters were arranged rather symmetrically around the atrium's gracious public space. The entrance to the original villa was not likely to have been through its *tablinum*, which opened directly onto a portico overlooking the sea. An entrance from the north through the smaller inner peristyle, however, would have taken a visitor fairly directly to the atrium. Recent excavations of the building still have not uncovered its entrance, so any claim about a historically accurate entrance remains speculative at best. Nevertheless, the original entrance to the house clearly could not have been through the large and later outer peristyle.

From the Museum's perspective, it seemed preferable to create an entry sequence that would provide more parking for both visitors and staff, and would also welcome them with more public services. The ideal arrival path would also allow visitors to see the building and its largest gardens from the exterior; that way, the public would have an opportunity to understand and appreciate the re-created building before entering it. Finally, upon entering the Museum, visitors would come into contact with works of art from the collection before enjoying the pleasures of the gardens. The best way to accomplish this goal seemed to be to have visitors enter the building through the West Porch and directly into the Atrium.

Another important goal of the renovation project was to bring more natural light into the gallery spaces, especially on the upper level, and to allow more visual communication between the two floors. This could be achieved to some extent simply by unblocking existing windows that had been closed over time (fig. 97).

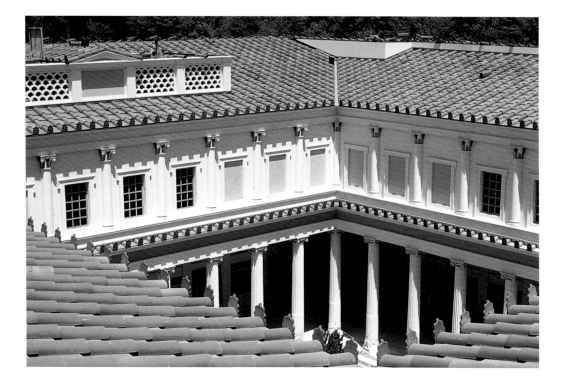

In addition, creating new windows in spaces where blind frames suggested they would have been originally (in Neuerburg's imagined second-century B.C. phase of the original villa) could transform the gallery surrounding the Inner Peristyle on the second level, and incorporating skylights in the two largest galleries on the upper level would provide the best possible environment for exhibiting antiquities, especially marble sculptures, which are shown to their greatest advantage in natural light. (Earlier technical studies of the building had concluded that these two ceilings were the only ones in the Museum that could be safely cut to accommodate skylights.)

Finally, the large Atrium (fig. 98) needed the benefit of the natural light that had been such an important aspect of original Roman interiors (see fig. 28). In an ancient villa, this light would have come from the *compluvium* in the roof, which was open to the sky. At the Museum, another source of light could be provided by increasing the number of openings in the plaster screen around the upper level of the Atrium; this would also create better communication with the galleries on the second level, which would now have additional windows and skylights. In the House of the Samnites at Herculaneum, which inspired the decoration on the Atrium's upper level, one entire end of the wall is open to the sky between the engaged columns on the supporting wall (fig. 99).

Though several special exhibitions had been mounted at the Villa (the last one, *A Passion for Antiquities: Ancient Art from the Collection of Barbara and Lawrence Fleischman*, was presented in the fall of 1994), the installation of such shows always required parts of

Figure 97. View into the Inner Peristyle from the southwest corner of the roof. The three original windows visible in the center of each side of the upper level had to be covered inside to protect the light-sensitive collections on display in those spaces.

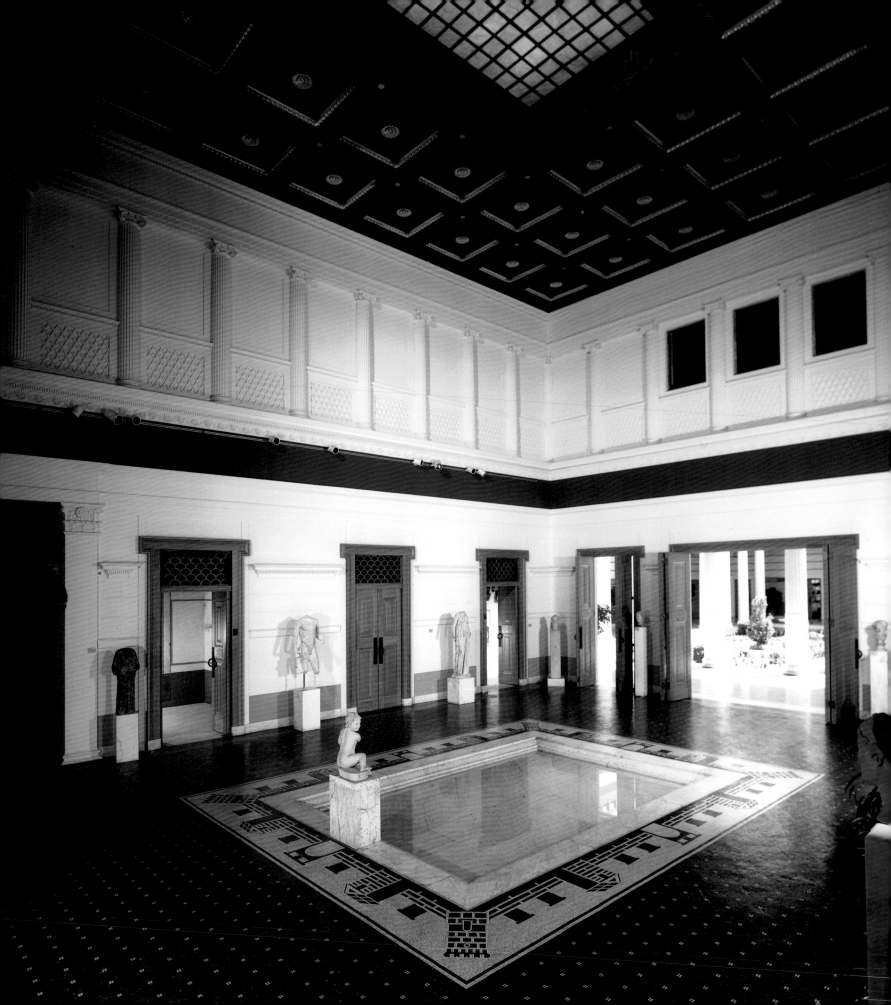

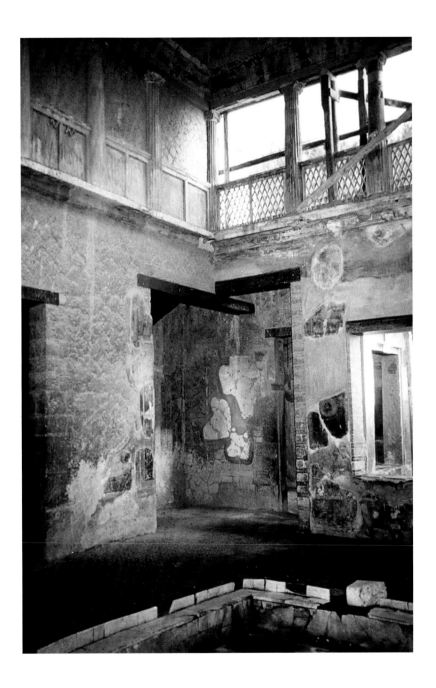

opposite
Figure 98. The Atrium
of the Museum in its original
state installed with ancient
sculpture and wall paintings
in the *cubicula*. The only links
between this grand central
space and the upper level
were the three windows at the
east and west ends of the
plaster screen. These opened
into galleries of paintings and
European sculpture that
otherwise had no connection
to the Roman architecture.
The grille and faux alabaster
of the *compluvium* in the
ceiling were lit from behind to
simulate daylight.

Figure 99. The atrium of
the House of the Samnites
at Herculaneum. The plaster
screen on three sides
of the upper level served as
Neuerburg's model for the
Museum's Atrium. The fourth
side had real latticework
at the bottom between the
columns and was open to
the sky.

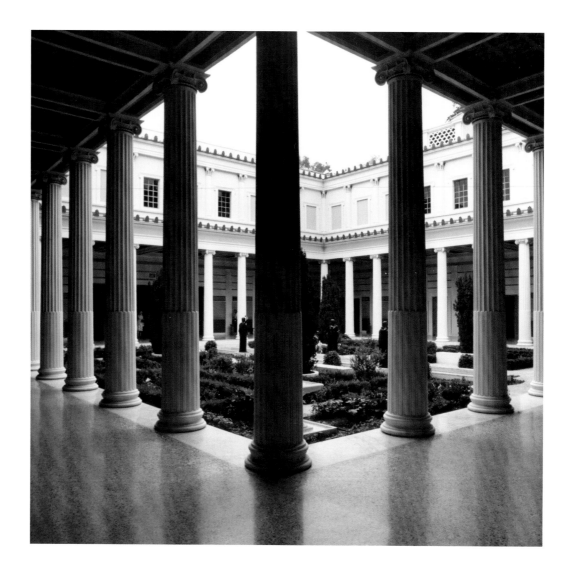

Figure 100. The Inner Peristyle in its original state. Chiurazzi foundry replicas of the bronze maidens from the Villa dei Papiri stand along the sides of the long central fountain. All of the galleries around this space had at least one and sometimes two doors that were open to the interior garden.

the permanent collection to be removed from display. With the entire Museum now devoted to a single collection—antiquities—the staff generally agreed that special exhibitions would be an important way of encouraging visitors to return often to the Villa and of keeping the site active. Exhibitions would also provide the staff with opportunities to pursue interesting research on the collection and the latest discoveries in the field, and would allow the Getty to promote the arts of other cultures, both ancient and modern, not represented in its own collection. To present such shows properly, it would be necessary to create a suite of galleries that could be devoted exclusively to special exhibitions. The spaces would need to be arranged in a clear sequence so that an exhibition concept would unfold for visitors in an intelligible manner.

From the start, it seemed best to put this sequence on the second level. Nearly all of the galleries on the first level had at least one door to the Inner Peristyle that was always open during visiting hours. Because one of the great pleasures of walking through these spaces had always been the constant alternation of indoor and outdoor experiences, it would have been unfortunate to close these doors in order to control a visitor's movement (fig. 100). In contrast, a block of gallery spaces on the second level could easily be connected internally without sacrificing the enjoyment of the adjacent interiors. Additionally, the second level could be climate controlled; to do so on the first level would require closing all of the doors and entirely changing the nature of that space.

The suggestion to locate the sequence of special exhibition spaces on the second level of the Museum focused attention on yet another awkward aspect of the building. For visitors, accessing the second level had always been something of a puzzle. Though one staircase was centrally located beside the passenger elevator in the entrance vestibule, and two others, though less visible, were clearly marked (one in the northeast corner of the Inner Peristyle and the other in the southwest corner of the Atrium), no one could ever find them. Discreetly tucked behind heavy oak doors, they were generally overlooked and underutilized. If visitors were to find and enjoy the proposed new special exhibition galleries, better access would have to be provided. The building needed a prominent staircase that would lead directly from the Inner Peristyle to the upper level. And if the Atrium were to serve as the new public entrance hall, the stairway would have to be clearly visible from this central space.

Because of the Museum's location in an earthquake zone, protecting the collection has always been a high priority. While the shell of the building, fortunately, had been well constructed, the interior walls did not have the strength to support heavy works of art. At the same time, attaching pedestals and cases to the floors frequently required drilling and patching the marble tiles, which proved unsightly over time. It was decided, therefore, to include in the gallery plans an art-support system within the walls and an anchoring system within the floors, both of which would allow for the safe attachment of heavy objects such as marble reliefs, cases, and pedestals.

Beyond improving the public's entrance in and movement througout the building, and upgrading the conditions for displaying the collection within the galleries, there was much work to do on the site. Perhaps most critical was the need to expand the available parking, which had been inadequate from the beginning. When the Museum opened in 1974, it had parking for approximately 260 cars. The construction of some paved spaces for staff in the back of the property increased that number to 291. But this was still grossly inadequate. During the last year of operation before it closed for renovation, the Museum welcomed some four hundred thousand visitors; although many of them did indeed come by public transport, additional parking would be required if the Museum were to accommodate both passenger cars and tour buses on the property.

Both curators and conservators hoped that in the renovation process, the conservation laboratories could once again be directly connected to the Museum. When space in the Villa became tight, the conservation studios had been moved out of the Museum basement and into parts of the Ranch House and two purpose-built structures on the courtyard beside it to the east. While this solution provided more room for large projects, such as the reassembly of large sculptures or mosaics, it meant that any object requiring treatment had to leave the secure environment of the Museum to be transported

Figures 101. Scene from a performance in the Inner Peristyle of *The Wanderings of Odysseus*, an adaptation of Homer's *Odyssey* created by Oliver Taplin, directed by Rush Rehm, and produced in 1992. Small stages were constructed over the central fountain and in the four corners of the garden, and the audience sat on all four sides of the colonnade.

Figure 102. Scene from a performance in the Inner Peristyle of Plautus's *Cassina*, produced in 1994 and directed by Michael Hackett. A large stage was constructed on the north side of the garden for this presentation, done in conjunction with the exhibition *A Passion for Antiquities*.

opposite
Figure 103. View of the Museum taken from the original fire road northwest of the Ranch House looking south to the ocean

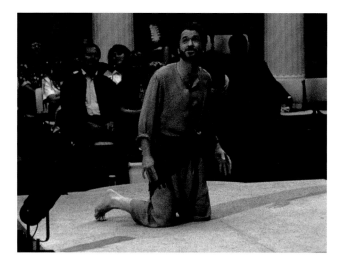

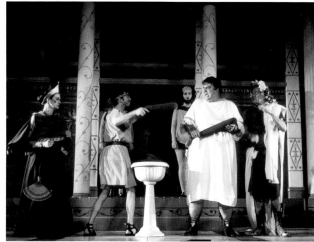

by truck up the hill to the laboratories. This process was not only time consuming but also exposed pieces to risks, which could be reduced by creating a tunnel to connect the laboratories directly with the Museum storage areas.

The Museum never had either a loading dock or a designated freight elevator—one elevator served both passengers and art—so plans would need to be developed for facilities necessary to ensure that works of art could be both safely delivered to the Museum and safely moved around the site. Up-to-date service equipment and controlled spaces would be needed to support the ambitious program of regularly scheduled special exhibitions planned for the renovated Museum.

Live concerts of classical music and theatrical productions related to works of art in the collection had become a popular part of the Museum's programs over the years, but—for lack of any other suitable space—they had been mounted in the Atrium or the Inner Peristyle under less-than-ideal viewing and acoustic conditions (figs. 101, 102). Planning the improvements to the site outside the Museum afforded the perfect opportunity to add a small outdoor theater designed for these activities, which were now considered basic to the Museum's public mission.

The final intention was to make more of the site accessible to the public. In his will, J. Paul Getty had made it clear that he wanted the public to enjoy the beautiful Cañon de Sentimiento that encloses the Villa and provides magnificent views out over the Pacific (fig. 103). These instructions had to be balanced with the neighboring homeowners' need for privacy, but the slopes of the canyon walls above the Villa could certainly provide space for more pathways and gardens.

All of these improvements were specifically related to the Museum and its activities for the public. But since the permanent collection on display was now to be limited to antiquities, the directors of the various Getty programs began to discuss possibilities for expanding the activities on the site to include functions of the Getty Research Institute and the Getty Conservation Institute. The concept of a center that would promote research and conservation as well as exhibitions related to classical art and culture emerged.

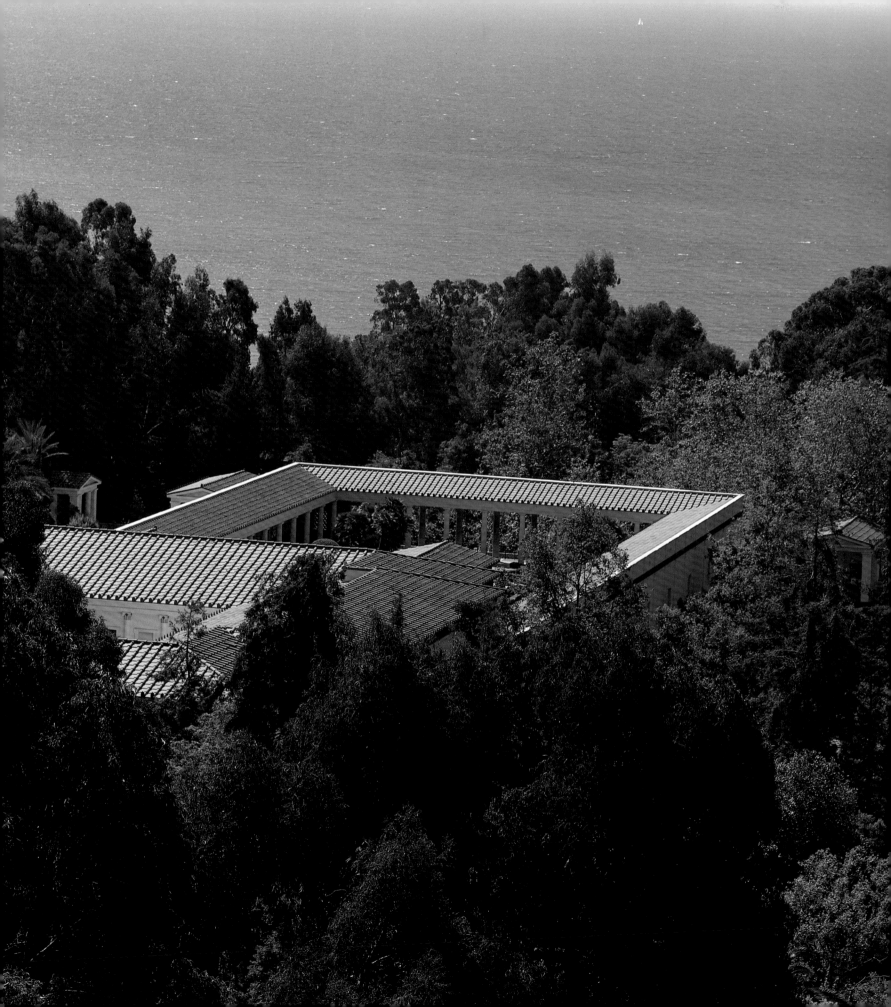

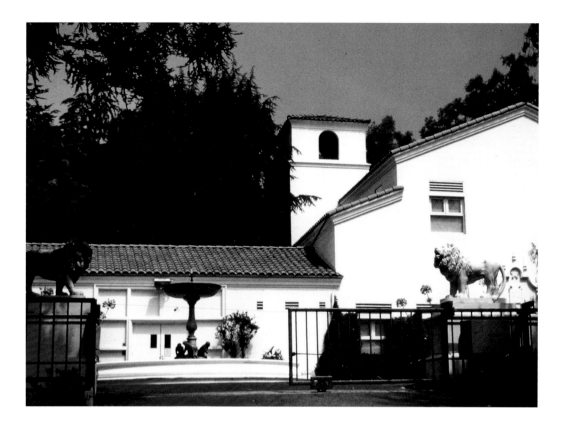

Figure 104. View of the Monkey Fountain and the east side of the Ranch House, including the extension built originally to display ancient sculpture. The extention was converted in 1985 to serve as the Antiquities Conservation laboratory and workshop space.

To represent the research aspect, a Villa Scholars program was conceived, smaller in scale than the Getty Center Scholars program and more narrowly focused. To make it practicable, new offices for the guest scholars and the administrators of the program would have to be factored into the planning. And because the scholars, as well as the curatorial and conservation staff, would need a small library to pursue their work at such a distance from the Getty Center, a branch of the Research Institute's main library that would include a good selection of the Institute's twenty-five thousand standard texts on antiquity and related subjects would also have to be accommodated on the site.

Staff at the Getty Conservation Institute had for many years hoped to create a program to train students in the conservation of archaeological and ethnographic materials. No such strictly defined program existed in the United States—in fact, the only two programs of this nature that were operating at the time the program was conceived were in England and

Australia—and the Villa seemed to offer the ideal setting for creating teaching laboratories side-by-side with the working laboratories of the Museum. By joining forces with the University of California, Los Angeles (UCLA), which took responsibility for hiring the staff and defining the curriculum, the Conservation Institute ensured that graduates of the program would finish their studies with a degree from a respected and accredited university. The Getty was to contribute the laboratory facilities, a training classroom, and offices for the program director and supporting staff on the Villa site, so these elements also had to be added to the expanding renovation plans.

As these discussions developed, it became clear that the Museum building alone would not be adequate to house all the activities now envisioned for the site. The Ranch House, existing laboratory buildings, cottages, and even the old barn that was used to store groundskeeping equipment presented possible spaces for expansion, but all would need to be thoroughly renovated if they were to be adapted to new uses, and they were not necessarily the right size or in the right location for those uses (fig. 104). Everyone involved in the discussions quickly recognized that before any renovations or expansions could be considered, the project needed a master plan for the whole site, and it would be best to hire professionals to assist the group in that planning exercise.

SITE PLANNING: THE SELECTION PROCESS

At this point, in the spring of 1993, the president of the Getty Trust and the program directors decided to organize a competition to select a site-planning architect or architectural firm appropriate for the Villa project. Bill Lacy, at that time president of the Cooper Union in New York and secretary of the Pritzker Architecture Prize, had led the successful search for the architect of the Getty Center, and everyone was confident that he was the right person to define the parameters and process of the new competition. A selection committee was designated that included Museum Director John Walsh and Associate Directors Deborah Gribbon and Barbara Whitney; Conservation Institute Director Miguel Angel Corzo; Research Institute Director Salvatore Settis and Deputy Director Thomas Reese; Getty Trust President Harold Williams and Vice President Stephen Rountree; and myself. The distinguished New York–based architectural critic Ada Louise Huxtable and the respected historian of Roman architecture William MacDonald were also included in the selection committee as outside experts.

Because no written program existed for the site—in fact, the Getty team wanted the architects selected to assist in drafting such a program—it was impossible to invite architects to submit models or plans of what might be done.

Also, because the project involved the renovation of a very popular public landmark, it required the participation of an architect who would be respectful of the Villa, who would understand and appreciate the classical model on which it was based, and whose personal style would not conflict with the building. For these unusual circumstances, Lacy devised a selection process that was unique at that time. In the first step, the selection committee researched potential candidates and, during two days of meetings, on May 12 and 13, 1993, ultimately identified a group of twenty-four architects and firms whose built or planned works seemed appropriate in style and spirit for the Villa project. These architects and firms were then invited to submit written statements of interest and slides of projects that would support their candidacy. Of the twenty-four, twenty submitted statements and slides. The committee then met in Los Angeles on July 20 and 21, 1993, to review the slides and statements. At the conclusion of these discussions, they had narrowed the group of candidates under consideration to six. Purely by chance, two were based on the East Coast (Machado and Silvetti Associates and Kallmann McKinnell & Wood Architects, both of Boston), two were on the West Coast (Frank Israel of Israel, Callas, Chu, Shortridge Design Associates; and Hodgetts + Fung Design Associates, both of Los Angeles), and two were in Europe (Alvaro Siza of Oporto, Portugal, and Juan Navarro Baldeweg of Madrid, Spain).

All six finalists were then invited to come together to Los Angeles for two days, September 14 and 15, 1993, to hear a description of the program firsthand from the president of the Getty Trust and from the program directors and their staffs. The intention of this bold step was not to produce discomfort among the candidates but to make certain that the process was

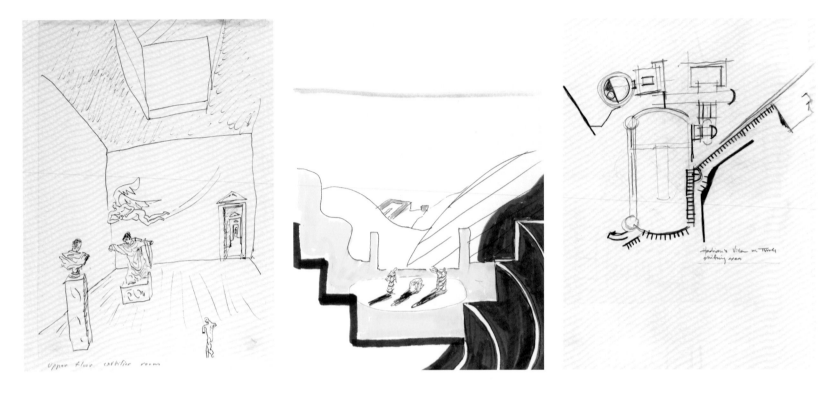

Figures 105-7. Left to right, drawings from the sketchbooks of Alvaro Siza (a skylit gallery), Juan Navarro Baldeweg (the outdoor theater), and Frank Israel (Hadrian's Villa at Tivoli)

completely fair to all. No written document existed that could be distributed, and Lacy was worried that a series of presentations on the same subject over a period of weeks or even months would be uneven and could unfairly disadvantage some of the candidates.

For two intensive days the group had the opportunity to discuss the history of the original Villa dei Papiri, find out about the various programs envisioned for the Villa site, and learn about both the positive and negative aspects of the site, as gathered from the experience of the staff members who had worked in the existing buildings. After these sessions and a tour of the site, each candidate was given a generic eleven-by-fourteen-inch sketchbook along with instructions to return the book in two weeks with ideas and proposals for the reorganization of the site. Again, the simplicity

of this requirement was intentional. The pool of candidates included very large firms as well as architects working on their own, and it was obvious that some competitors could commit more staff and resources than others to present lavish proposals if these had been requested. Like the group briefing, the sketchbook was intended to equalize the competition and put the emphasis on ideas rather than elaborate models or designs. Finally, the candidates were at liberty to explore the canyon and all the existing facilities on their own.

The sketchbooks submitted by all the candidates were extraordinary, each offering a wealth of original ideas that never repeated the suggestions of the others (figs. 105–7). Following the receipt of these documents, the selection committee visited the studios or offices of each candidate to discuss the ideas submitted and the manner in which the project would be developed and managed internally. The committee also made a point of seeing some examples of the built work of each candidate, and it interviewed some of each firm's clients to get a sense of the architects' working relationships. The West Coast candidates were the first to be interviewed (on October 28 and 29, 1993), because both could be easily visited in Los Angeles. The two European firms were the next to receive the committee (on December 6–10, 1993). The East Coast visits were unfortunately delayed by the Northridge earthquake of January 17, 1994, which disrupted the selection committee's scheduled flights from Los Angeles. Those visits were finally completed on February 22 and 23, 1994. At the conclusion of the last interviews in Boston, the committee repaired to the headquarters of the American Academy of Arts & Sciences in Cambridge, Massachusetts, to review what it had seen and learned. Following intense discussion, the field was reduced to two top contenders, and in May 1994 Harold Williams selected the team of Machado and Silvetti, of Boston, to undertake the renovation and expansion of the Villa site.

CREATING A MASTER PLAN

Starting in the fall of 1994, the team from Machado and Silvetti began monthly visits to Los Angeles—a grueling schedule that would continue for the next eight years, first for research and preparation of the Master Plan and later for design development. In part the purpose of these trips was to get to know the site and its problems, and in part it was to become more familiar with the evolving program for the Villa. Since no written program existed, it was important for the architects to get a clear notion of what the Getty wanted to do with the site before a plan could be drafted. Rodolfo

Machado and Jorge Silvetti brought to the project great strength and experience as site planners. Their work on the master plans for Princeton University and the city center of Providence, Rhode Island, prepared them well for the challenges presented by the steep-sided canyon. Also, because both architects had traveled and worked extensively in Italy, they were intimately familiar with the great monuments of Roman architecture.

Machado and Silvetti's monthly meetings in Los Angeles alternated between sessions that focused on the Villa's renovation and discussions that concentrated on the organization of the site. Langdon Wilson Architecture, a local firm familiar with California building codes and regulations, was selected to work with Machado and Silvetti in the planning process as executive architects. Langdon Wilson had prepared the original working drawings and had overseen the construction of the Museum from 1971 to 1974. Led by Richard Sholl, Douglas Gardner, and Niall Kelly, Langdon Wilson's representatives were key players during the first phase of the project's development.

Recognizing the significant scale of the project, the Getty Trust had assembled a formidable team to manage it, under the direction of Stephen Rountree. The team included Curt Williams, who had overseen the building project team for the Getty Center; Hy Tiano; and later, Corbin Smith. Working under John Walsh, on the Museum side, this writer and Karol Wight, Associate Curator of Antiquities, attended all site-planning and design meetings.

One key decision that had to be made during the first months of discussion concerned the fate of the Ranch House. The building's central location would influence the plans for anything that could be done on the site. Though it might have been easier and ultimately less expensive to demolish the Ranch House and replace it with a more flexible, modern structure,

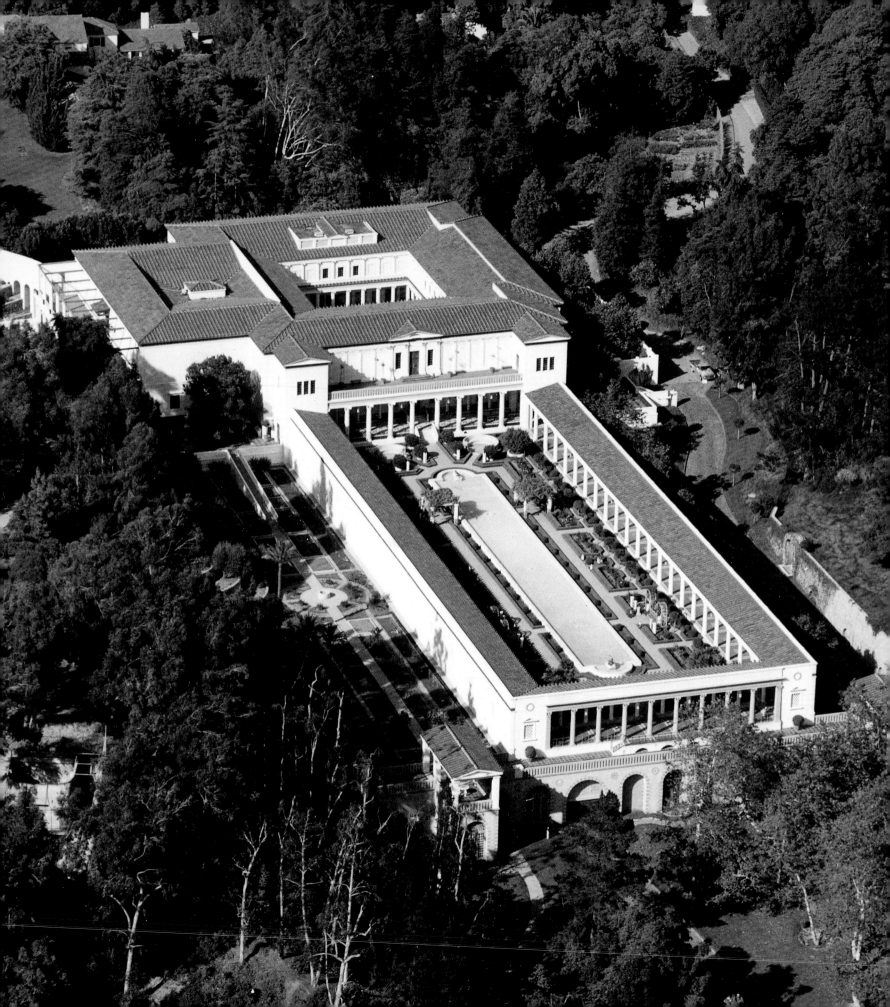

John Walsh persuaded the Villa project group and the Board of Trustees that the building ought to be saved and reused. While Walsh recognized that it was architecturally undistinguished, he felt it had played a significant part in the institution's history—first as J. Paul Getty's residence on the property and later as home to the original Getty Museum—and thus it deserved to be preserved and refurbished for use as office or library space.

Another important directive for the project came from Harold Williams. Since the Villa site (fig. 108) was to house the activities of at least three of the Getty Trust's operating programs, Williams felt it was important that the site plan both reflect this collaboration and make each component visible to the visitors. This directive's most obvious impact was on the public entrance to the site—in order to represent all of the programs equally, entry should no longer be through the Museum but should be external to the building itself. In the earliest and most simplistic attempts to implement this, the site was subdivided into program-specific buildings: for example, the Ranch House came to represent the Research Institute's presence, and the former Paintings Conservation laboratory represented the Conservation Institute. These structures were in the back of the property, however, which was not open to the public. In order to make them more visible, the entrance would need a high vantage point, and the landscaping at the back of the Museum building, heretofore carefully planned to protect the privacy of the Ranch House and conservation laboratories, would need to be opened up. Assigning existing buildings to individual programs also came with an important corollary— any new architecture on the site would have to serve and be shared by all of the programs.

In the spring of 1995, Jorge Silvetti and Rodolfo Machado were ready to present their first concepts for the reorganization of the site to the Getty staff. In their judgment, the most important issue was the location of parking. The second was the problem of directing the visitors to the West Porch of the Museum, which would now serve as the entrance to the building. And the third was the need to provide visitors with a prospect from which they could see all parts of the site displayed before them, including the Ranch House and the conservation laboratories, where programs of the Research Institute and Conservation Institute would be housed.

At this point, the architects conceived of a public entrance to the site that would be more centrally located. They suggested having visitors drive up the east road beyond the original Museum building and then park in a new subterranean garage located approximately where the old groundskeeper's barn stood. Exiting this structure, visitors would follow a broad pathway, a kind of Appian Way, along the north side of the Villa, with the Museum exterior on the left and new, glass-fronted conservation laboratories visible on the right, offering a behind-the-scenes glimpse at ongoing work. This pathway would finally lead to the Entrance Porch— and would provide an entry sequence much like the one that Machado and Silvetti had proposed in its original competition sketchbook. In this plan, the theater would be distant from the rest of the buildings on the site, located on a hillside high above the Ranch House where a natural hollow offered views out to the sea. Unfortunately, a quick estimate of the cost of this scheme made it clear that it would be impossible—one element alone, the proposed funicular for transporting theater patrons up to the dramatic new structure, was estimated at $16 million.

About this time, the project teams from both the Getty and the architectural firms were feeling a new pressure that was related to the cost of the Getty Center. Damage to the partially

opposite
Figure 108. Aerial view of the Museum prior to renovations

completed buildings suffered during the 1994 earthquake had required expensive repair work, and the price tag for the project was now far beyond its original anticipated cost. Concerned about adding the cost of extensive renovation in Malibu to the already inflated cost of the Meier-designed Center, Williams and Rountree cautioned against proposing any major interventions at the Villa in the near future. They made it clear that they wanted to develop a master plan that would incorporate all of the changes and expansions anticipated to take place on the site during the next twenty years. At the same time, they proposed that the project move forward in two phases. Phase I, to be implemented immediately, would provide for necessary upgrades to the site (mainly widening the fire roads, making all areas accessible and safe for exiting, and, if possible, adding an outdoor theater and a loading dock); for the modification of the Paintings Conservation laboratories and offices so they could be used by the projected UCLA/Getty master's program on the conservation of ethnographic and archaeological materials; and for the creation of the programmatically symbolic new entrance, which would be exterior to the Museum building itself. Against the advice of the architects, this phase would not include new or expanded parking. In Phase II, additional parking would be added to the site, together with office space for future growth and additional facilities not incorporated in the first phase.

The twenty-year Master Plan was presented to the Board of Trustees in September 1995 and approved. At the same time, it was decided that only the plans for Phase I would be developed fully for implementation. Neither the Getty team nor the architects received this news happily. Creating a distinctive new entrance exterior to the Museum *without* relocating the parking, which currently existed only beneath

the Museum building and at the south end of the site, presented the greatest challenge. Once this new entrance to the site had been located, the second major problem would be how to get the visitors from the parking area to the Entrance Porch of the Museum, the only building on the site that would be open to the public. This would have to be accomplished without emphasizing the apparent lack of logic for those familiar with the site: visitors who were used to parking beneath or near the Museum's Outer Peristyle would now have to follow an extended pathway along the exterior of the building in order to enter the site "properly"—that is, from outside the Museum building. Finally, the lack of space for all the needed or wanted programmatic improvements (such as an enlarged bookstore, a more functional auditorium, an enclosed loading dock) made everyone question the wisdom of this approach.

After considering several options, the architects proposed a new scheme. If a large subterranean garage could not be constructed in Phase I, at least the traffic patterns could be simplified. Their plan separated public visitors from staff members, deliveries, and business visitors by suggesting two different entrances—the public would still enter, as in the original site plan, from the Pacific Coast Highway (fig. 109), while the staff and all other business visitors would enter from Los Liones Drive at the northern end of the site and would park at the back of the property.

This solution, which was to have a major impact on later architectural developments, was quickly accepted as the most workable means of resolving the problems of circulation and public parking. It did not address the lack of adequate parking for staff and business visitors, however, nor did it resolve the issue of the new entrance or the difficulty of getting the public from the existing parking area to the

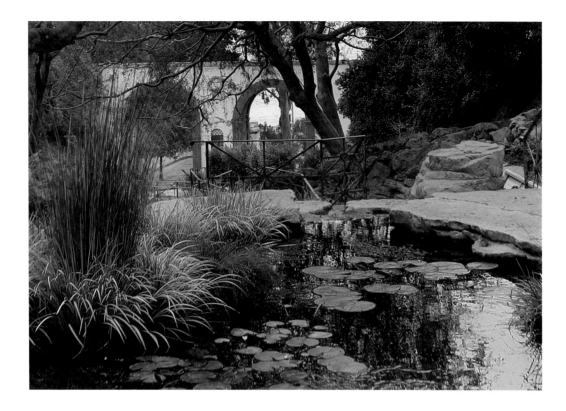

Entrance Porch of the building, at least for the first phase of construction. Interestingly, the answer to this puzzle would also be the key to providing the visibility desired by all the programs on the site. It would offer the solution for integrating the new architecture on the site with the old in an intelligent and appropriate way.

Among the chief criticisms of the original Museum building offered by the staff to the architects had been the lack of a proper entrance and the absence of expected public amenities —there was no place to check a coat or bag, no space for wheelchairs or strollers, and no real provision for orientation materials or information. Now that the site would be home to several programs, the kinds of information available would have to expand. Moreover, everyone hoped that the facility for providing these services, like the entrance to the site, would not be located inside the Museum building. With this in mind, the architects proposed in the first phase to construct a separate Entry Pavilion— a kind of enclosed outdoor space, buried in the hillside but open to the sky—adjacent to

the two existing parking areas on the southwest side of the Museum's Herb Garden. Within this inviting space, visitors could get their first introduction to the Villa site and its various activities with wall maps, banners, and brochures. They would also find restrooms, a checkroom, and wheelchairs and strollers.

Of necessity, the level of the Entry Pavilion, like the parking, was somewhat lower than the level of the Entrance Porch. Thus visitors would have to ascend, either by stairs or by elevator, to a walkway that would lead them to the Entrance Porch. Considering how to resolve this transition, the architects asked themselves, "What would happen if the walkway were raised above the Museum building, allowing the visitor to look down on the Villa as if it were an artifact in the landscape, similar to the ruined villas one looks down on when entering the excavated site of Herculaneum?" (figs. 110, 111). From such a vantage point, the visitor would also clearly see the Ranch House and conservation buildings in the distance.

Figure 109. Public entrance to the Villa site directly off Pacific Coast Highway. In order to lessen the impact on traffic on this already heavily traveled road, the Master Plan for the site proposed having staff and business visitors enter and exit through an alternate gate at the back of the property.

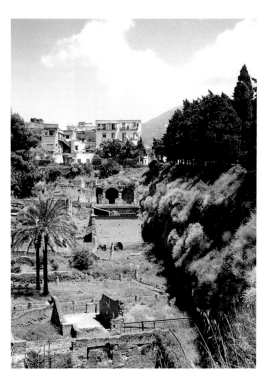

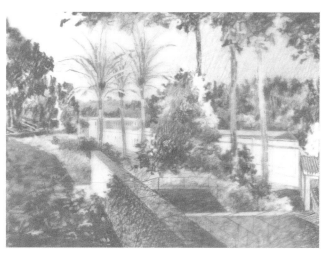

Suddenly the concept was clear—the Villa would be the equivalent of an ancient structure revealed at an archaeological site, set within the steep walls of the canyon as if originally buried deep in the earth. The new structures to be added to the site, such as the Entry Pavilion and the Outdoor Theater, would define the building's limits, not competing with it but enhancing its originality and uniqueness. This reinterpretation of the original building as an artifact would become the guiding principle that helped define the project overall.

Machado and Silvetti had already decided that their new buildings, including the Outdoor Theater, would not attempt to imitate the Museum's existing architecture or real ancient villas in any way. Rather, the buildings would be clean, simple, modern structures that would surround the Museum building, treating it like a work of art in a frame. The discreet palette of materials they originally proposed were intended to complement the materials used in the Museum itself—concrete, bronze, and glass. To make the poured surfaces interesting, however, and to expand on the concept of the Museum as an excavated artifact, the walls of

the surrounding new structures were to be textured at different levels and incorporate narrow bands of colored stone, evoking the various strata, or layers, of earth that would have buried the building.

At this time, the Getty Center was nearing completion, and the rich cleft travertine used to sheathe many of its surfaces had attracted great attention from all who visited the site. The rough, golden stone, which had also been widely used in ancient Rome, was becoming synonymous with the impressive new Getty Museum. To create a subtle visual link between the two locations, the architects added it to the list of materials to be used as strata in the new architecture at the Villa site.

The concept of the elevated entrance and the perspective of the Museum as an artifact surrounded by strata walls won immediate approval from the Getty team. Machado and Silvetti's intuitive appreciation of the appropriateness of an archaeological conceit for the Master Plan confirmed the wisdom of the selection committee's choice, and the principal elements of the plan now fell easily into place.

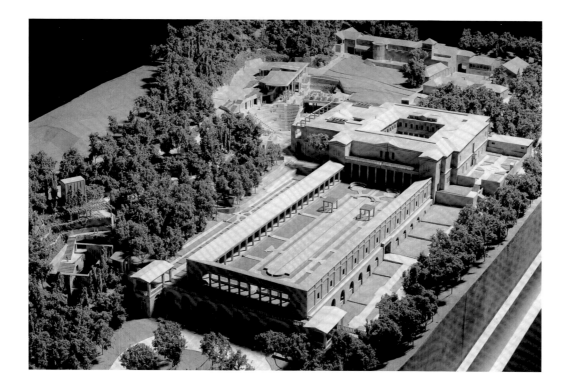

FROM TWO PHASES TO ONE: CONSOLIDATING THE PROJECT

The turning point of the project came some three years later, however, after the opening of the Getty Center in 1997. In January 1998, immediately after the opening, Harold Williams retired as president of the Getty Trust. His successor, Barry Munitz, at first continued to support the phased construction of the Villa project but then quickly expanded Phase I at the urging of the Trustees, in particular Ramon C. Cortines, to include a new parking structure for the public on the site of the old camper lot.

At about the same time, the Conservation Institute and UCLA finally reached an agreement to develop a master's program on the conservation of archaeological and ethnographic materials. Though many of the classes related to the program would be held at UCLA, the laboratories and offices for the director and teaching staff would have to be accommodated at the Getty Villa, and the old Paintings Conservation laboratory was simply not adequate for this purpose. Considering all the problems that arose from the phased construction—the continued

inadequacy of parking, the lack of needed facilities and growth space during the last phase, and, not least of all, the specter of an extended legal battle to secure permits whenever the second phase was initiated—Munitz ultimately realized that the Getty was adopting a self-defeating approach to this important project. In November 1998, he persuaded the Board of Trustees to increase the budget and to approve the construction of the entire Master Plan in a single phase.

While this decision put great pressure on the architects and Getty staff to plan and design everything that the Master Plan provided for—including new conservation laboratories, a second parking structure for staff and business visitors at the back of the site, and a twenty-thousand-square-foot office building for future expansion—it was greeted with great rejoicing by all involved with the project. Finally, the coherent logic of the Master Plan itself had triumphed—the carefully conceived adjacencies of related functions and interlocking spaces would be preserved intact, and construction would respect the unity of the design (fig. 112).

Figure 112. Large model for Phase I of the Villa Master Plan built in 1996, showing the new turnaround, drop-off area, and loggia in front of the Outer Peristyle, the Entry Pavilion, the raised Museum Path, the Outdoor Theater, and the enlarged Cafe (with Museum Store beneath) and its terrace for outdoor seating. The Auditorium, under the Ranch House lawn, is not visible, and the new construction planned for the North Campus in Phase II was not yet included.

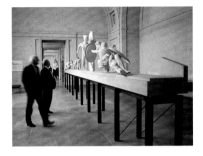

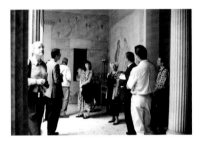

Figures 113, 114. Principal architects from Machado and Silvetti joined Getty Museum staff on two study trips to Europe to see related buildings and installations. The first, to Denmark, Germany, and Switzerland, included a visit to the Glyptothek in Munich to see the display of ancient sculpture, among them the marbles from the temple of Athena Alea on Aegina (fig. 113). On the second trip, through south Italy and France, the group visited the Villa Kerylos at Cap-Ferrat outside Nice (fig. 114).

CREATING A COMMON VOCABULARY FOR DISPLAY

The firm of Machado and Silvetti was recognized for its expertise in site planning; however, the architects were less knowledgeable about the requirements of a museum interior appropriate for the display of antiquities—how to provide effective and flexible lighting to enhance the objects; what kinds of colors and patterns could be used in the floors and on the walls to complement the Villa and not compete with the collection; and what kinds of technical infrastructures had to be placed within the walls and floors to allow flexibility in the installation while providing maximum protection in case of an earthquake.

It was clear that the key Machado and Silvetti team (Jorge Silvetti, Rodolfo Machado, and Tim Love) and the Getty Museum principals (Merritt Price, Head of Exhibition Design, and myself) should agree on possible approaches to renovation and installation and establish a shared vocabulary of references for the Museum in particular. To accomplish this, the group traveled together to see museums of ancient art, ancient buildings, and replicas of classical buildings that might serve as instructive models or sources of inspiration for the Getty Villa's renovation.

The first trip (November 17–26, 1995) took the group through northern Europe and included visits to the Ny Carlsberg Glyptotek and the Thorvaldsens Museum in Copenhagen, the Pergamon Museum and Altes Museum in Berlin, the Glyptothek and Antikensammlung in Munich (fig. 113), the recently restored Pompejanum (Ludwig I's re-creation of the Pompeian House of the Dioskouroi) in Aschaffenburg, the Staatliche Kunsthalle in Karlsruhe, and the Antikenmuseum und Sammlung Ludwig in Basel. Foremost among

the design elements explored at these important institutions were natural light, wall and floor colors, and case and pedestal designs.

A second trip through southern Europe (May 19–30, 1996) included gardens as well as museums, ancient sites, and collections. The list of participants had expanded to include Machado and Silvetti associates Mimi Love, Conrad Ello, and Peter Lofgren; Getty Museum Director John Walsh, Associate Director Barbara Whitney, and Associate Curator of Antiquities Karol Wight; garden specialists Richard Naranjo and Michael DeHart; and landscape architect Denis Kurutz. The trip started in Naples, where the primary objectives of the visit were, naturally, the ancient sites of Pompeii and Herculaneum as well as the Imperial Villa at Oplontis. At these sites, the group focused on the boldness of ancient pigments, the various types of mosaic patterns, and the different sources of natural lighting within domestic spaces. The small theater of Pompeii made a particularly strong impression on the group, since they were looking for models that could be adapted to the Getty Villa site. In addition, the group toured the National Archaeological Museum of Naples, which houses the major finds from Pompeii and Herculaneum, as well as the Villa Floridiana, the Villa Pignatelli, the newly restored Museo di Capodimonte, and the Royal Palace at Caserta, with its extensive eighteenth-century gardens.

In Rome, the group visited the Palazzo Ruspoli and the Palazzo Altemps—both Baroque buildings now at least partially reused as museum spaces — and the ancient monuments in the Fori Imperiali and at Hadrian's Villa in Tivoli. From Rome, the group traveled to Cap-Ferrat in the south of France to see the Villa Kerylos (figs. 114, 115) (an early-twentieth-century re-creation, designed by the French classicist Théodore Reinach, of a Greek house

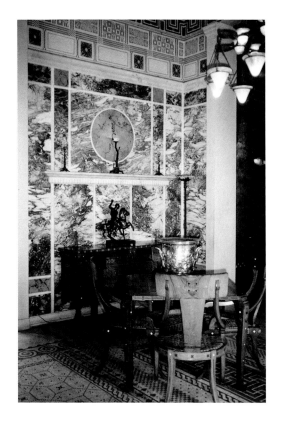

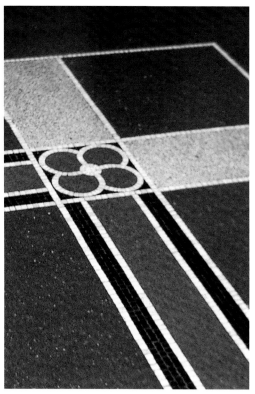

from Delos) as well as the nearby Villa Rothschild and the Villa Les Cèdres botanical gardens. The tour ended in Paris with visits to the Louvre, the Musée de l'Institut du Monde Arabe, and the Musée Picasso.

At the completion of these two trips, the small group most closely involved with the Villa project had a shared sense of great excitement about the work ahead as well as an intimate familiarity with a number of key references that would be important for the planning process. Several of the buildings and sites visited would ultimately provide sources of inspiration for important details in the Villa. The floors of the Ny Carlsberg Glyptotek (fig. 116) influenced the colors, patterns, and use of mosaic and terrazzo

throughout the Getty Villa; the second level of the Thorvaldsens Museum (fig. 117) was the prototype for the new vaulted corridor on the Museum's second level; the houses of Pompeii and Herculaneum served as the primary sources for wall colors and decorative floor patterns that could be adapted to the terrazzo medium; the former Hôtel Salé—the beautifully restored seventeenth-century building that houses the Musée Picasso—included the model for the handrail cut into the marble that clads the wall of the East Stair; the dome of the Pantheon in Rome provided the model for the dome of the Temple of Herakles; and the small theater of Pompeii (fig. 118) was the ideal size and shape for the Villa's new Outdoor Theater.

Figures 115, 116. Examples of two interiors that influenced the designs for the Museum's gallery spaces. The Villa Kerylos at Cap-Ferrat (fig. 115), an early-twentieth-century replica of a Greek house on Delos, contained lighting fixtures and furniture that could be adapted for the Museum building. In the Ny Carlsberg Glyptotek in Copenhagen (fig. 116), the colorful terrazzo and mosaic floors incorporated elaborate designs that helped to organize the installation of the collections.

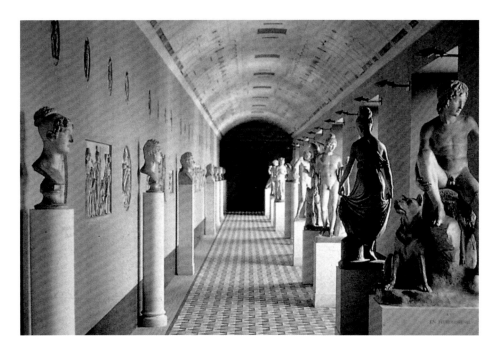

Figures 117, 118. The sculpture gallery on the upper level of the Thorvaldsens Museum in Copenhagen (fig. 117)—with its arched ceiling and windows in the wall surrounding the building's interior court—served as the inspiration for the vaulted corridor that runs around the Inner Peristyle on the upper level of the Museum. And while the architects did not intend to replicate an ancient theater at the Villa, the small theater at Pompeii (fig. 118) had the same intimate, comfortable proportions they wanted for the new performance space.

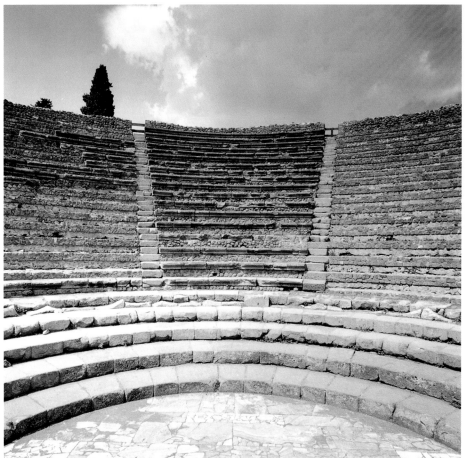

LEGAL BATTLES

Following the development of the Master Plan, attorneys for the Getty Trust began the process of applying for permits from the City of Los Angeles. Around the same time, the staff of the Museum held an evening event at the Villa to present the project to the neighbors who lived on either side of the Malibu property for discussion and comment. Though they provided little feedback at the meeting, the neighbors were clearly concerned about the Getty's intentions.

The first public hearing before the zoning administration, on December 7, 1998, lasted some seven and a half hours without a break—the longest public hearing on record in Los Angeles at that time. And as the plans moved through the city's approval process, the hearings held about the project became increasingly rancorous. Following the ultimate approval by the zoning administration, the neighbors appealed the decision to the city council. The hearing before the full city council (on December 15, 1999), though more limited in time, proved to be equally acrimonious. But in the end, the plans won the unanimous approval of the council.

Unsatisfied with these results, a group of the neighbors appealed for another hearing with the California Coastal Commission, which has wide-ranging authority over land use on or near the California coast and meets alternately in northern and southern California every other month. The commission recognized both the magnitude of the project and the importance of the dispute and managed to accommodate the hearing fairly quickly in its agenda. Again, in spite of heated debate, the majority of the commission approved the Villa plans, and the project seemed to be on its way.

On January 18, 2000, the Getty's attorneys were informed that a coalition of neighbors had filed suit in the California Superior Court against both the Getty Trust for proposing the Villa plans and the City of Los Angeles for approving them. Though the first decision on this suit, rendered on October 25, 2000, went against the Trust and the city, this ruling was overturned on appeal. On October 21, 2002, the California Supreme Court finally determined that the project was appropriate to the site and could be built as planned. The long legal battle, which had cost the project four years of construction time, was finally over.

PLANNING FOR THE INSTALLATION OF THE COLLECTION

Once the Master Plan was complete and architects and clients alike were satisfied that all of the various components of the program had been accommodated successfully, a smaller team of designers and executive architects began to work together with the Getty's antiquities curatorial staff and Exhibition Design staff to plan the installation of the collections in the Museum galleries. Certain basic facts about the building and the collection were critically important to this process. First, it was difficult, if not impossible, to control the way the visitor moved through the existing gallery spaces. The ground plan of the Museum did not suggest an obvious sequence, and most galleries had two or more doors through which the public could enter and exit. On the ground floor, nearly every gallery had at least one door (and several had two) that opened onto the Inner Peristyle. One of the pleasures of California—and, indeed, a feature that made the reconstruction of a Roman villa so appropriate in this location—is the year-round sunny, dry climate that is so similar to that of the Bay of Naples. Part of the charm of visiting the Museum during its first

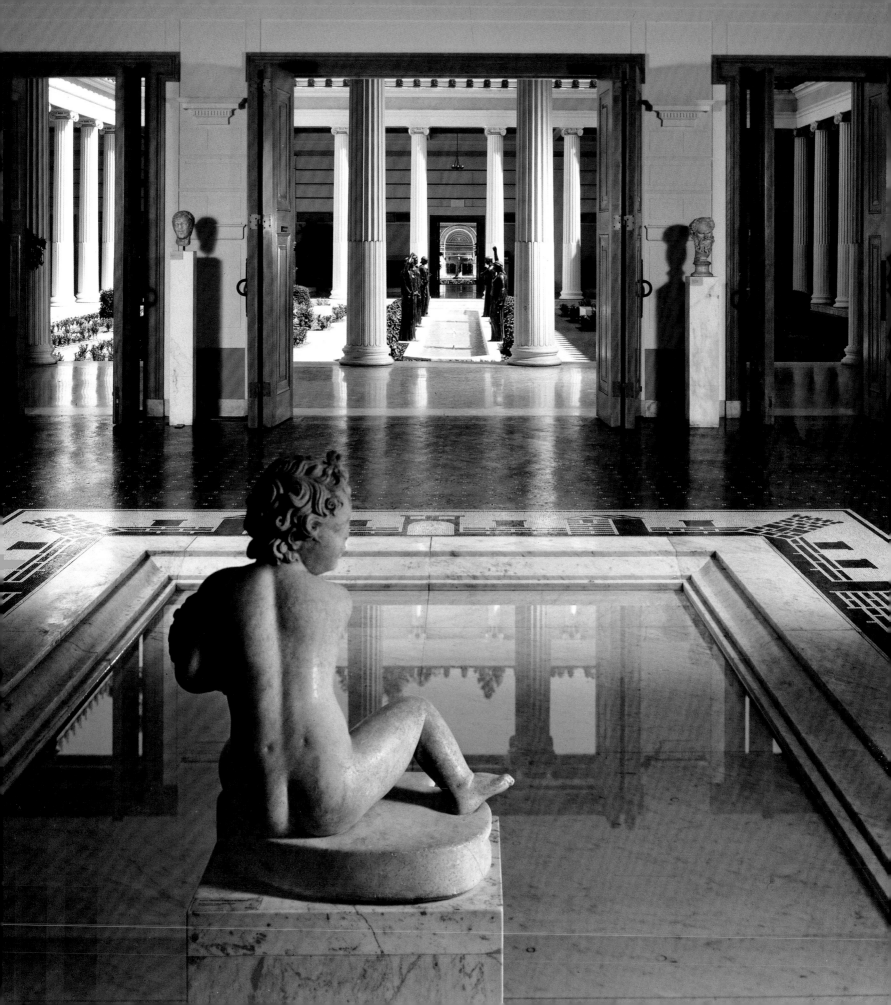

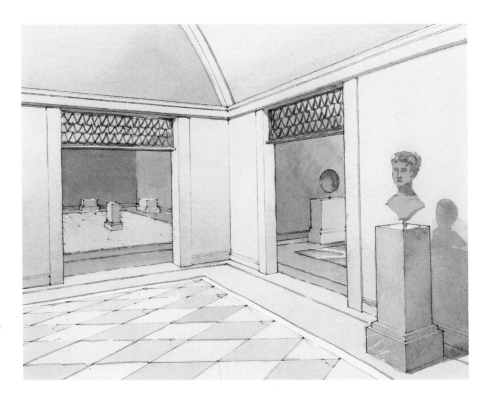

twenty-three years of operation had been the experience of moving between interiors filled with art and the lush, sunlit exterior court-yard. Everyone believed that this openness had to be maintained.

To provide ease of movement between inside and outside, the solid-oak gallery doors on the first level had always been open to the gardens during public hours. Indeed, the Atrium was completely open on both ends, so visitors could pass without impediment between the Inner Peristyle and the West Porch, which formed part of the Garden Tea Room, with its re-created *nymphaeum*. The gallery off the Inner Peristyle directly opposite the Atrium was also open on both sides, allowing a vista straight through the building from the west door of the Atrium to the shady East Garden (fig. 119). There, the colorful mosaic fountain (copied from the House of the Great Fountain in Pompeii) provided a focal point in the center of the garden wall. Architects, designers, and curators all agreed that this axial view had to be preserved, as it is essential to visitors' apprecia-tion of the original building plan.

Early in the planning process, conservators had noted that the first level's openness would make it difficult to maintain environmental control of its exhibition spaces, even with a posi-tive pressure system. Clearly, the ground level would not be appropriate for special exhibitions, especially of loan objects, which would require both well-defined, directed pathways of move-ment and stringent climate control. Instead, a sequence of gallery spaces on the north side of the upper level was identified that could be linked internally to provide an ideal space for temporary displays. With their multiple openings, many of the other galleries on the upper level (fig. 120) presented some of the same challenges as those on the first level. Most of these galleries opened onto a central enclosed corridor that

would also function as exhibition space, so there was no problem in allowing for easy movement between interior and exterior space.

Ultimately, the many routes available to a visitor walking through the galleries helped determine the approach to the installation of the collection. Since there was no predictable pathway, any effort to establish a sequence based on chronology or medium, for example, would be futile. Because each gallery had to function as a self-contained unit, a thematic or iconographic installation seemed to offer the best solution.

In fact, an installation based on imagery was extremely well suited to the nature of the collection. Formed principally over the second half of the twentieth century, when the market for antiquities was becoming ever more restricted, the Museum's collections of Greek, Roman, and Etruscan art were strong but incomplete in many key areas. Opportunities to acquire the kinds of large-scale Greek sculpture, Geometric ceramics, Minoan bronzes, or Roman wall paintings that distinguish the

Figures 119, 120. The Museum's important axial view (fig. 119, opposite), photo-graphed here from the west end of the Atrium's *impluvium* through to the large fountain in the East Garden, had to be preserved in the reno-vation of the building. The multiple openings of many of the galleries on the upper level were maintained in the renovated Museum (fig. 120).

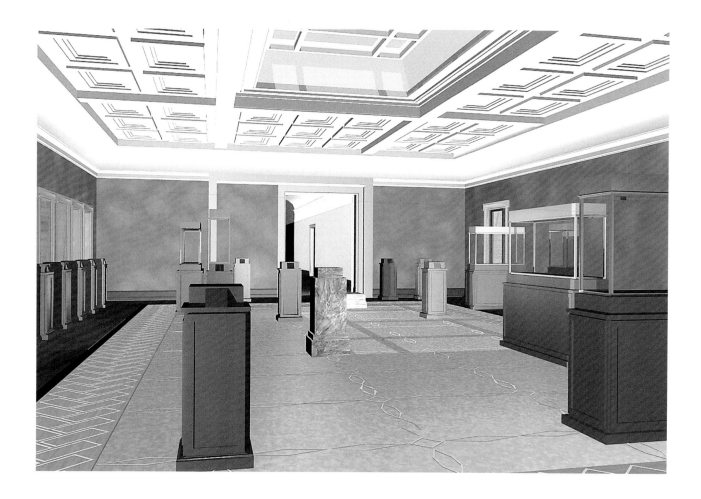

Figure 121. The process of planning the gallery interiors and the installation of the collections took three years. Simulated spaces modeled on the computer allowed for experimentation with various color combinations on floors, walls, and ceilings.

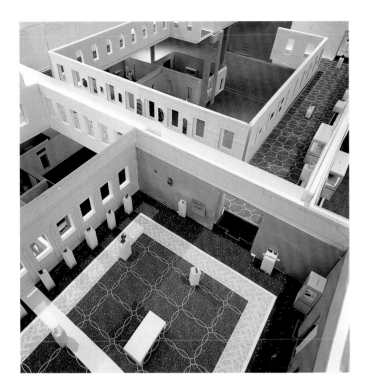

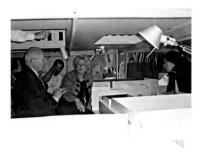

Figures 122, 123. Once preliminary decisions about gallery colors and floor patterns were made, the large foam-core model of the entire building (fig. 122) was decorated accordingly and mounted on two levels to allow the architects, curators, and designers (fig. 123) to check the perspectives from one space to another and to consider the relationships between adjacent rooms.

antiquities collections of older institutions were rare, and those that presented themselves often raised difficult questions about provenance and exportability. A subject-based installation allowing objects of various types and periods to be displayed together to support each gallery's overarching theme—such as Gods and Goddesses, Theater and Dionysos, or Stories of the Trojan War—would make the best use of the objects in the collection.

The decision to place a self-sufficient display in each gallery was also helpful in planning the color schemes for the gallery walls and floor designs (figs. 121–25). To support one of the project's main objectives—to connect visually the two levels of gallery spaces—each of the permanent collection galleries (and even the special exhibition spaces to a certain extent) needed to relate to one another in their use of basic materials such as terrazzo, crown moldings, and plaster walls. But these rooms did not have to look the same. On the contrary, there was a strong rationale for making them so different from one another that each theme would have its own identifiable space.

The team concluded that each gallery should vary in color from all spaces that were adjacent to it or were visible from its doors and windows. At the same time, the view through any portal should present a harmonious unity, with no visual clashes. With this in mind, the installation team prepared a palette of colors drawn from ancient Roman wall paintings. The architects had already done valuable preliminary work on this aspect of the interiors. After the trip to Pompeii and Herculaneum, they had prepared an elaborate series of color schemes based on their close observations of the ancient originals; these templates became an indispensable resource (see pp. 184, 185).

In the early stages of planning, it was decided that all of the gallery walls would be coated with color-imbued plaster to give depth and a more authentic texture to the surfaces. However, though such surfaces are durable, they cannot be easily touched up or repaired. Given that installations would change fairly regularly and that the building's constant daily use would inevitably lead to deterioration over time, the design team decided to select only three galleries for this special wall treatment. Located on the first level, these spaces included the two large galleries on either side of the Atrium (Galleries 104 and 114) and the Temple of Herakles (Gallery 109), which were all intended for the display of the permanent collection.

Whether covered with painted or color-imbued plaster, every wall would have to be able to display objects. The thematic installations planned for all of the galleries included some massive marble reliefs, mosaics, and ancient wall paintings that might be either mounted on the wall with supporting brackets or enclosed in heavy vitrines. In addition, pedestals and the tops of large display cases would need to be bolted to the walls so they would be less likely to topple over in the event of an earthquake.

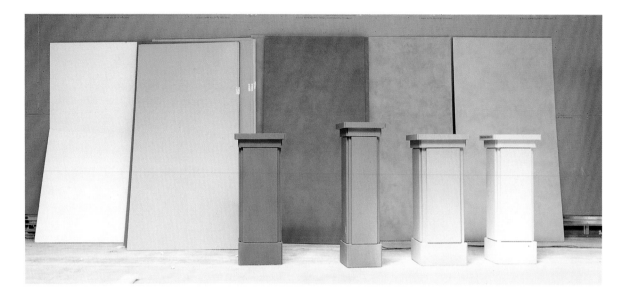

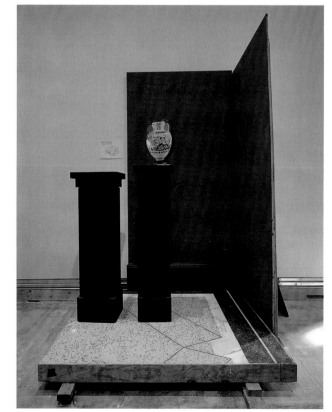

Figures 124, 125. Refining the colors selected for the walls, floors, and gallery furniture required several stages of decision making. Possible wall and pedestal colors were first set up in gallery daylight conditions (fig. 124), and then accurate corner conditions for each gallery were created with selected wall, floor, and pedestal colors (fig. 125).

To provide the infrastructure necessary to carry heavy loads (and to avoid having to cut the walls to access the structural concrete), the architects worked with Museum conservators and preparators to devise an art-support system that could be built into the fabric of the walls (fig. 126). In each gallery space designated to house the permanent collection or special exhibitions, horizontal bars of inch-thick steel were mounted on frames of hollow steel uprights at four different heights. Drilled with threaded holes at regular intervals, these beams are capable of supporting thousands of pounds without stress, and their carefully measured placement allows maximum flexibility in the installation process.

The gallery floors—all in combinations of terrazzo, marble, and mosaic patterns of varying complexity—were given an important role in organizing the display space within each room. Every floor was designed to have a black terrazzo border, framed on the inner and outer edges with strips of white marble tesserae (the inner strips are double in the larger galleries and single in the smaller ones). The area defined by this border, which varies in width according to the size of the room, was intended to accommodate all the pedestals and cases set against the gallery walls. The central terrazzo field of each floor, sometimes set off from the black zone by a band of marble or an elaborate mosaic pattern, was planned to have a different color keyed to both the hue of the wall and the kinds of objects to be exhibited in the space (figs. 127, 128). (The only exceptions to this rule were the galleries for special exhibitions and the space designated for family activities, in which the floor surfaces would be uniform black terrazzo to provide a more neutral surface for the changing displays of different materials.) A variety of repetitive motifs from ancient mosaics were adapted to provide the patterns formed by the bronze divider strips in the large expanses of terrazzo

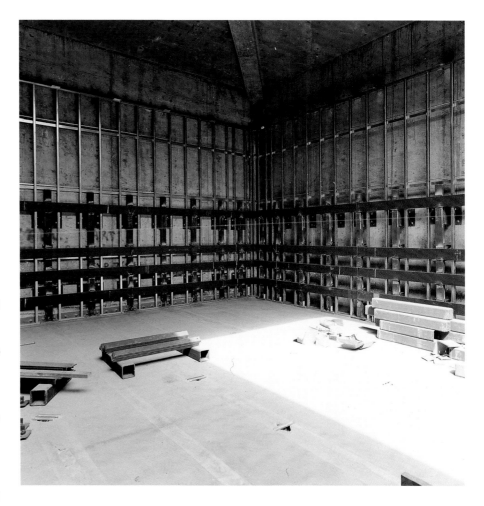

Figure 126. The art-support system, hidden behind every gallery wall, allows very heavy objects and cases to be attached simply and safely.

Figures 127, 128. Machado and Silvetti architect Mimi Love created a remarkable variety of patterns for the terrazzo and mosaic floors of the Museum based on ancient Roman mosaic designs (fig. 127). The different color used to set off central floor space is framed in every gallery by a border of black terrazzo intended to define the space for the exhibition furniture, such as cases or pedestals, that needs to be attached to or be in close proximity to the wall (fig. 128).

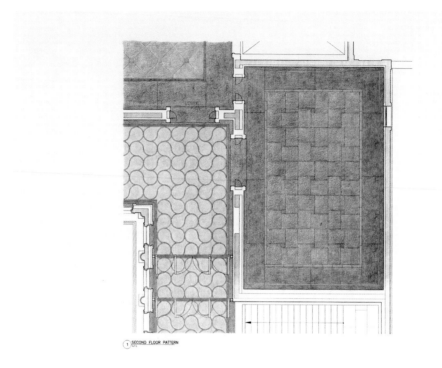

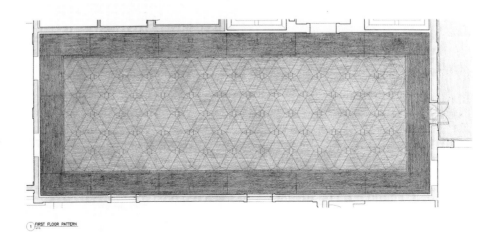

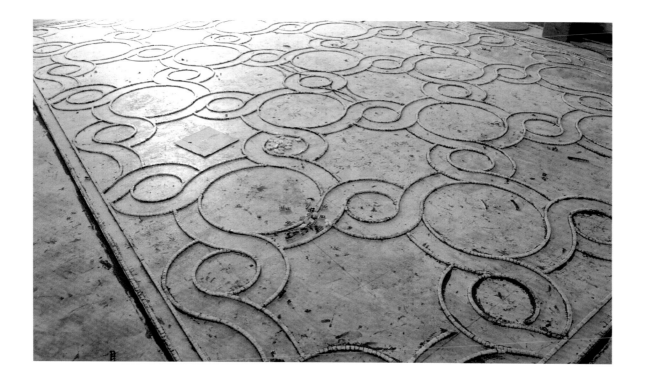

filling the centers of most of the floors (figs. 127–31).

Mindful of another project goal—to provide for the safe attachment of cases and pedestals to the floor in order to prevent movement in an earthquake—the designers, under the guidance of Mimi Love, artfully marked the points of intersection in the bronze work of the floors with square, round, and diamond shapes that could be removed from the surrounding surface. In the fabric of the floor beneath each of these shapes, they planned to embed a metal box in the fabric of the floor (an "attachment point") that, when connected with proper conduits, could provide electrical power and access to computer data as well as secure fastening for the exhibition furniture (figs. 132, 133). Only two floors on the upper level, the elevator vestibule and the floor of the vaulted corridor that surrounds the Inner Peristyle, could not accommodate the power point system. Located directly above some of the most elaborate ceilings on the first level of the Museum, they could not be drilled to provide access to the necessary electrical conduits. They also received no bronze dividers

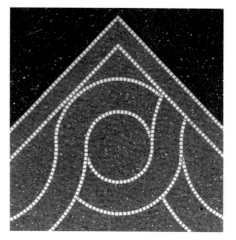 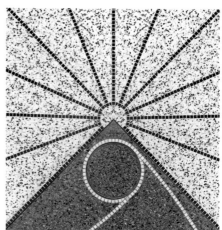

Figures 129–31. Patterns in the most elaborate floors were created with small marble tesserae laid by hand before the colored terrazzo was poured (fig. 129). Details of the finished floors (figs. 130, 131) show how carefully these mosaic patterns, executed in both black and white stones, had to be resolved in the corners.

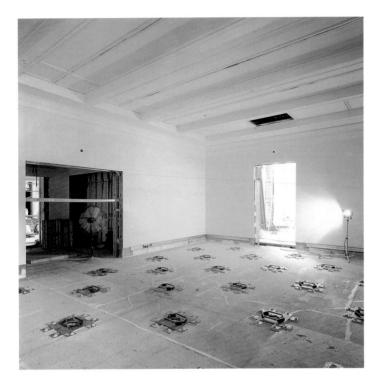

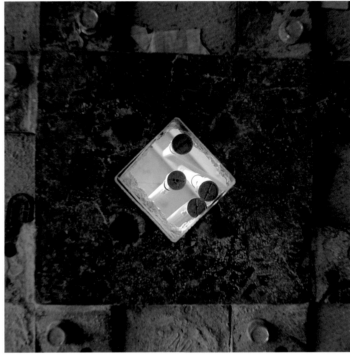

Figures 132, 133. A regular grid of attachment points built into each gallery floor allows pedestals, cases, and even information terminals to be safely located in the space with great flexibility (fig. 132). Conduits for power and data are visible within the open box of an attachment point (fig. 133), which also provides hardware for the secure attachment of pedestals and cases.

in the terrazzo, but their elaborate patterns, formed with white marble tesserae, were also drawn from ancient mosaic models.

Of necessity, the decisions made about both the installation program and the designs for the galleries (including color selections and floor patterns) influenced the development of the ceiling patterns, lighting, and even exhibition furniture. Lighting had always been a problem in the Museum galleries, where both the tracks for spotlights and the general ambient lighting were inadequate and inflexible. Early in the discussions with the architects, the decision was made to adopt two basic approaches to the articulation of the ceilings. One would reflect a kind of simple beamed ceiling that seems to have been prevalent in Roman domestic architecture. The other would echo the more elaborate

coffered ceilings often used in grander public spaces, such as atria or peristyles. Both would allow for the lighting fixtures to be hidden in between and alongside the relief elements, whether coffers or horizontal suspended beams.

For the second-level gallery surrounding the Inner Peristyle, a unique solution was proposed—a vaulted ceiling. Because it had to accommodate ductwork and pipes, the vault could not be a true semicircle above the cornice, but the arched ceiling provided a graceful unity to this space, which was reinforced by the uniform wall color and curving floor pattern. Suspended light fixtures would have introduced an unfortunate visual interruption in the sweep of the ceiling, so a system using slot lighting was incorporated into the repetitive latticelike pattern of the vault.

Finally, the black borders of all of the terrazzo floors, planned originally as a kind of organizing device for the placement of wall-related cases and pedestals, powerfully influenced the design and color of the exhibition furniture (figs. 134, 135). Experience with the display of ancient works of art, especially marbles, had long persuaded the curators that dark pedestals would show the objects to the greatest advantage. Since the gallery baseboards (which also hid raceways for electrical power and data connections) were to be painted nearly black to complement the floor border, the design team proposed using the same dark tone for the bases of the cases and pedestals, at least for those located in that zone of terrazzo. In this way, the bases would blend in with the floor and baseboards and become a discreet background for the display. (For displays with objects of various media—which could include bronzes, vases, terracottas, jewelry, or glass—the cases would have neutral, light interiors with colors selected to work with, but not match, the wall color of each gallery.) An experiment gauging the visual impact of pedestals of different colors on the interiors of the terrazzo floors quickly convinced the curators that choosing a uniform dark tone throughout for the exhibition furniture was aesthetically preferable to using a hodgepodge of gallery-specific colors; it was also more practical. Thus the decision was reached that all the bases of the display furniture (except the built-in cases, which would be finished in white oak and bronze to match the doors and windows) would be painted in the near-black finish, providing the last important detail in the complex design for the gallery interiors.

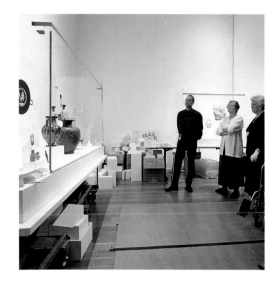

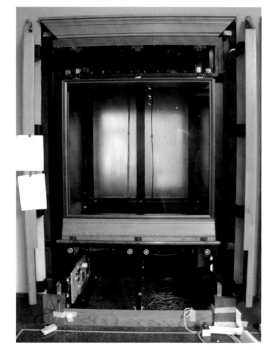

Figure 134. Curators and exhibition designers spent months creating case layouts with both mock-ups and real objects. This process allowed them to give the case manufacturer (Glasbau Hahn in Frankfurt, Germany) accurate dimensions for each piece of gallery furniture.

Figure 135. One of the built-in showcases prior to assembly offers a glimpse of the complex inner workings, including fiber-optic lighting, power-operated glass front, and the provision for creating a stable environment (microclimate) inside the vitrine.

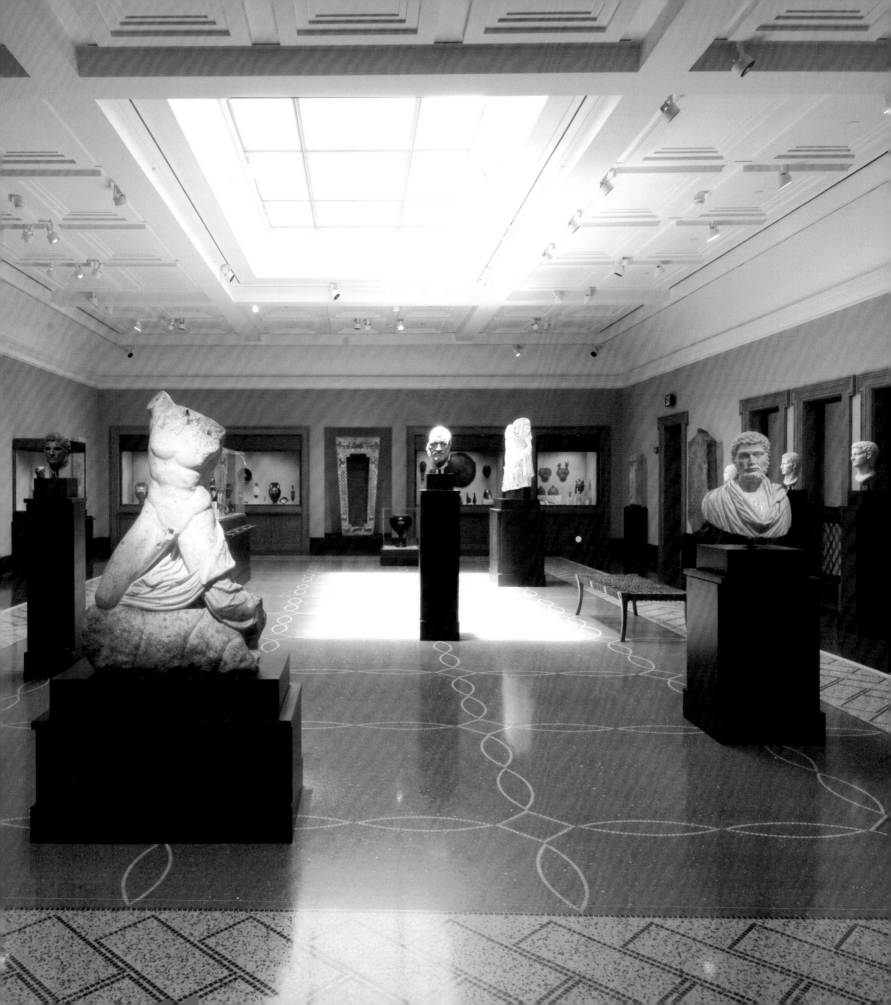

4 A New Beginning

Since it opened to the public thirty-one years ago, the Getty Villa has been a unique monument in American architecture. Beloved by some, reviled by others, it powerfully expresses its founder's vision of what a good public space should be, especially one dedicated, in part at least, to exhibiting works of classical art.

It is remarkable to have the opportunity to redo such a building from top to bottom—to make not only the changes impelled by practical and legal reasons but also those improvements meant to enhance the physical structure and the various purposes it serves. It is rarer still to be able to rethink an entire site—to change the patterns of circulation on the property and relocate some functions into new architecture. The architects, curators, administrators, and designers of the Getty Villa project have been privileged to share this unusual experience. We began the process of defining the renovation and expansion program with a list of objectives. For the last twelve years, we have pooled our knowledge and ideas to create a dynamic environment intended to promote the appreciation and preservation of the arts and cultures of classical antiquity.

The Museum building is now presented from the outside as a magnificent artifact within the excavated landscape. On the inside, it can finally be appreciated in a unified way—the galleries of the upper and lower levels are physically and visually related, and natural light fills most of the display spaces (fig. 136). Works of art and furniture can now be installed safely and changed easily, thanks to the art-support system in the walls and the attachment points in the floors. In addition to improving and expanding the areas for the permanent collections and special exhibitions, we have added new facilities for research, conservation and conservation training, and performance. Works of art will now be delivered to the Museum and transported between the collections in storage and the conservation laboratories through secure interior environments where objects are protected. Public amenities such as the Cafe and Museum Store have been augmented and made accessible to all.

To achieve these goals required resilience, innovative thinking, patience, and great commitment from the team of design architects working under the inspired leadership of Jorge Silvetti. It is most appropriate now to turn the story over to him, as he offers his own perspective on the project's careful planning and execution.

opposite
Figure 136. The incorporation of new sources of natural light, such as the skylight in this upper-level gallery, has fulfilled one of the primary objectives of the renovation project, providing a more suitable environment for the display of ancient artifacts.

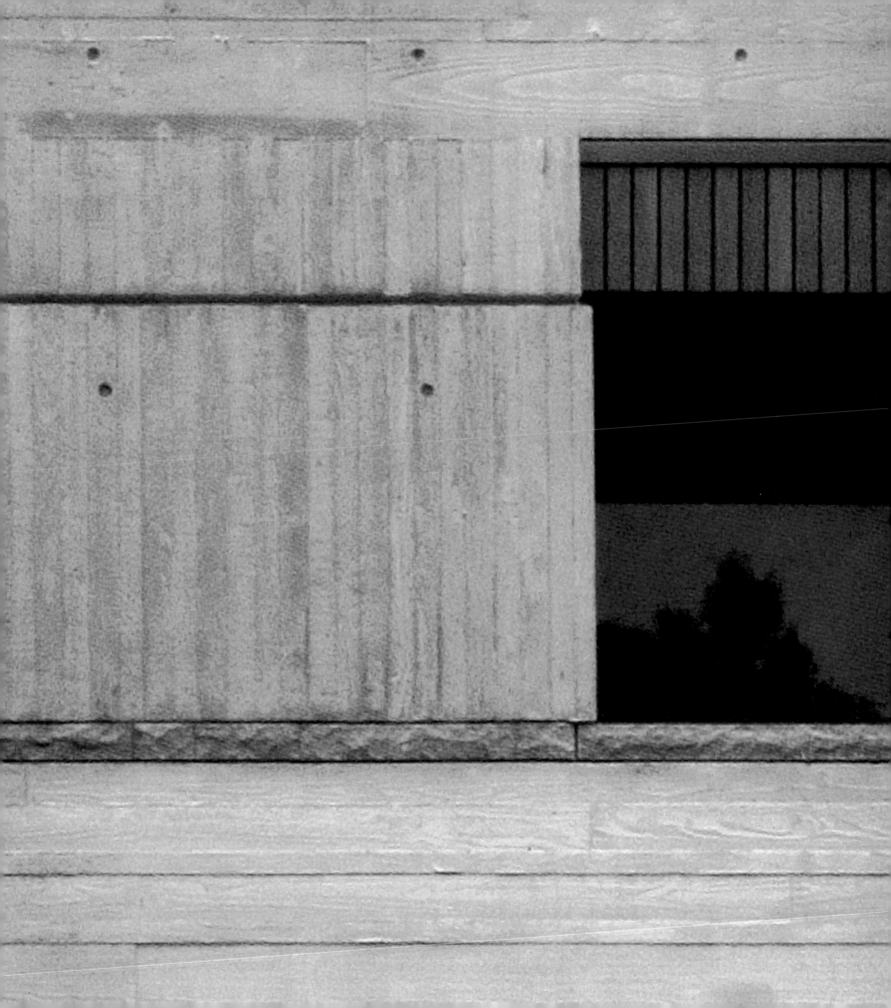

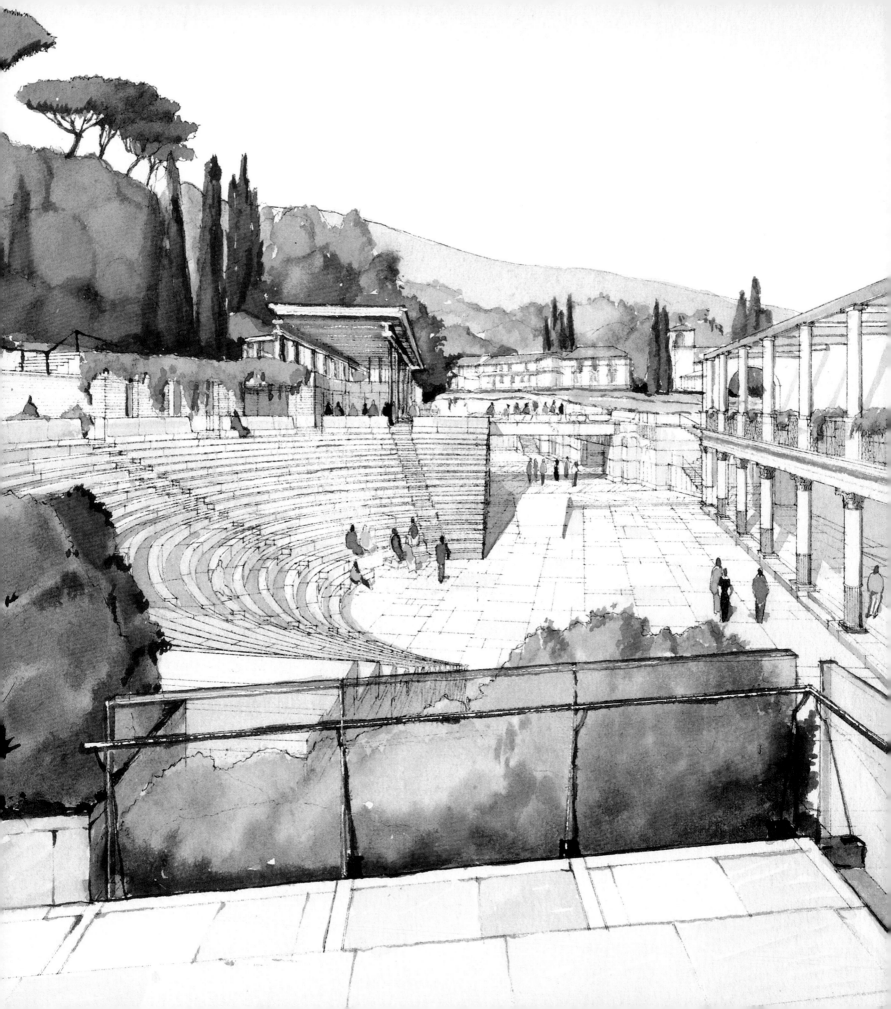

PART II

The Getty Villa Reimagined

JORGE SILVETTI

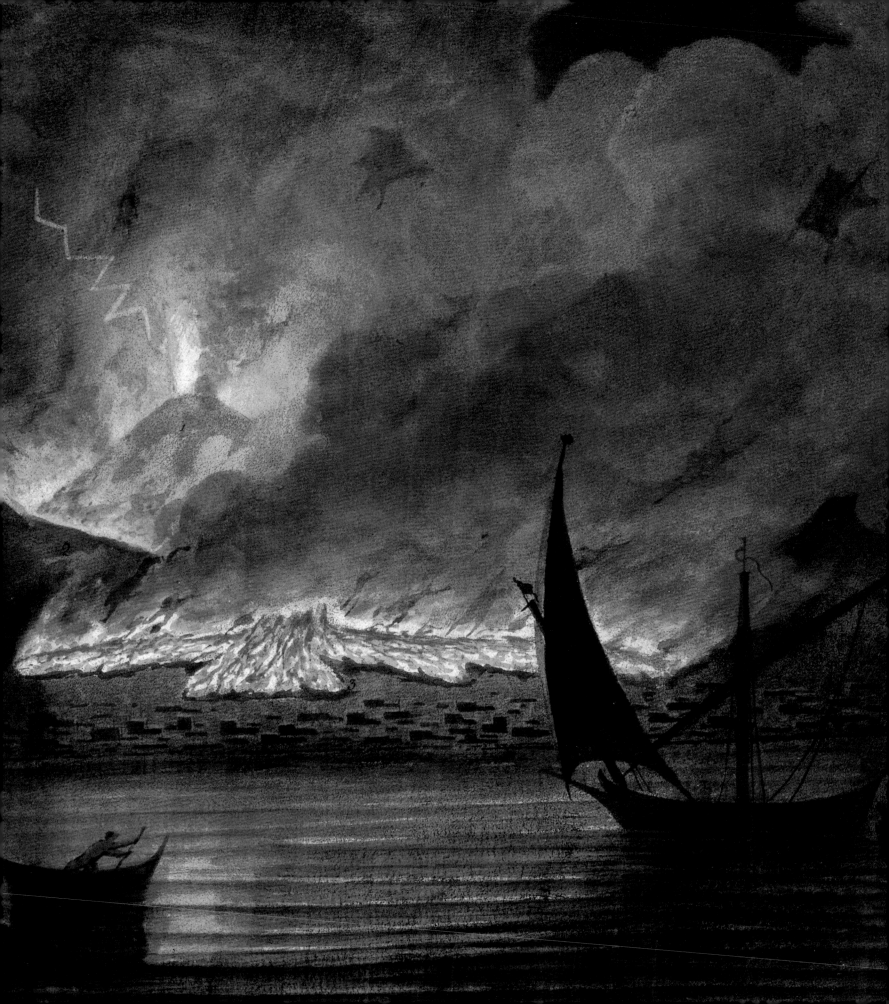

Prologue

I

BURIED UNDER THE ASHES

The beginning of the Master Plan and Architecture for the Getty Villa has a precise date—Friday, October 29, 1993—and like most important moments in this complex story, it was marked by an unusual occurrence that seemed to underscore the project's singular nature. On that date, all six finalists for the competition to select the project's architect gathered at the Villa for a two-day briefing about the site and program and to hear the thoughts and aspirations of representatives of the many entities that composed the Getty Trust at the time. Our small architectural and urban design firm based in Boston was represented by its two partners, Rodolfo Machado and myself, who by then had been working together for more than twenty years and as the firm's partners for almost a decade. The Getty Trust was represented by its president, the directors of its component entities, and the professional staff members who would be involved in discussions and decisions pertaining to the Master Plan. The non-Getty members of the jury that would select the architect, all prominent in the field of architecture, also attended. It was an impressive group, and we could not have wished for people with better credentials or finer sensibilities.

We gathered in the Villa's Founders Room, a cramped, somewhat disconcerting space done in a 1960s corporate/clubby décor and dominated by an oil portrait of J. Paul Getty. It felt heavy, dark, and crowded, and—lacking what the Romans called "decorum"—it would continue to feel out of place with the colorful Roman villa during the coming years. However, it was the only room suitable for our monthly meetings until construction began in 2000, and it was there that we heard presentations from many of the principal players. Most memorable to me, because of the topic and the speaker's credentials and fame, was Professor William L. MacDonald's account of the Villa dei Papiri in Herculaneum—the Getty Villa's direct inspiration—and the circumstances surrounding Mt. Vesuvius's eruption in A.D. 79 (fig. 137). Professor MacDonald's vivid presentation was full of emotion and pathos; in the dark Founders Room he brought to life the scenes of terror, anguish, and despair, and conveyed the centuries-long calm that followed after the ashes settled and the existence of some of these places was forgotten. It was what we needed—emotion together with a sense of historical reality—for the suspension of disbelief necessary for architects of my generation to engage seriously with the Getty Villa. I would say that, almost without exception, every architect in the room had a problematic relationship with the building that one of us would be asked to redesign: namely, that even in 1993 our understanding of the creative process was still firmly and unquestionably rooted in modernism. Thus, we believed that it was immoral to copy previous forms, and we shared modernism's relative

opposite
Figure 137. *View of the great eruption of Vesuvius . . . night of the 20th of Oct.r 1767.* Sir William Hamilton, Campi Phlegraei . . . (1776), Plate vi, vol. 2

Figures 138-41. Examples of decorative elements preserved from the original Museum building in their present, restored condition. The color palette shown was reconceived and changed as part of the process of reimagining the whole Villa.

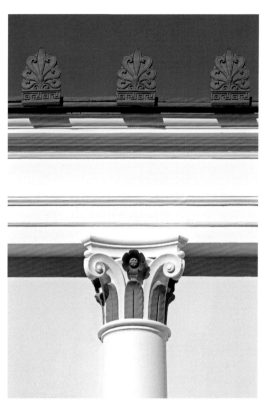
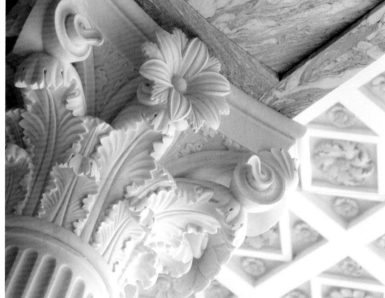
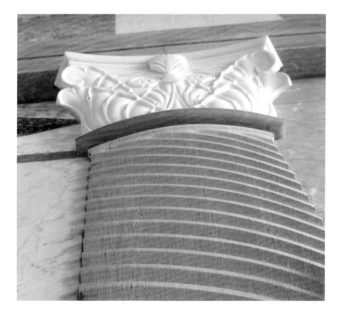
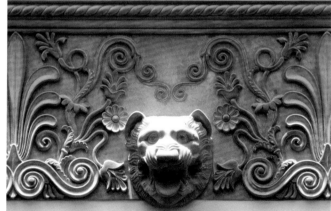

uneasiness with the use of historical precedents and with replicas.

After the briefing, we visited the grounds. As we emerged from the dark room into the Inner Peristyle and what had been a benign California morning, we were not only blinded by the daylight but were soon covered by a dusting of white ash falling from the sky. There was a moment of silence and disbelief. Were these ashes real? Was a volcano erupting in Southern California? Would we all soon disappear? Or was this just a mise-en-scène constructed by the Getty to reinforce the verisimilitude that this building had always sought? Laughing but nervous, we soon learned that the ashes were being carried by the Santa Ana winds from wildfires that had been burning in Southern California for the past few days, indeed right behind the hills that shelter the Villa.

What a provocation to our imagination those few moments had been. We were transported back almost two millennia to that tragic day in Campania. We felt the consequences of a natural and human catastrophe and could, for a moment, visualize the Villa in Malibu—even if for a moment—as the setting of that experience and the embodiment of a historical event. Those stubborn white ashes also gave us a powerful taste of the intellectual and artistic struggles that were to come in the months and years ahead as we tackled the architectural dilemma of dealing with a replica of a Roman building that no one had seen since A.D. 79!

THE COMPETITION

At the end of the two-day meeting, one thing became clear: our most serious architectural problem resided well beyond the obvious difficulties of solving the major planning issues —providing parking, accessibility and an entry sequence; accommodating more visitors and increased museum services; remodeling the existing structures and designing new buildings, and so on. How, while addressing all those technical, functional, and programmatic issues, were we to infuse new life into a replica of a classical building and its surroundings? As architects, we found ourselves then—and still do now, more than a decade later—in a culture in which historical replicas have lost most of the educational and artistic value they might have had in previous times. Today, historical, literary, or mythological images are brought back to life in order to be consumed as commodities; they are presented as "themes" to enjoy rather than as sources of knowledge or as genuine aesthetic experiences.

In the last two decades, this phenomenon has transformed some cultural institutions— chiefly, art and natural history museums—for the worse as they became mostly distributors of products and images. Yet the Getty Villa still retained the innocence of a replica that had been conceived more as one individual's folly than as a conscious consumerist undertaking. J. Paul Getty deliberately chose the Villa dei Papiri for his model and scholar Norman Neuerburg as his archaeological consultant. He also chose to reproduce the Villa's decorative elements painstakingly and faithfully and, finally, to offer only limited access and amenities to visitors— all attesting to the modesty and honesty of his intentions (figs. 138–41). Yet, by 1993, in a strident society propelled by a booming economy, Disney had become the universal paradigm of all commercial successes based on the idea of a replica as human experience, and the use and acceptance of "thematization" in major real estate and cultural development had also taken hold (fig. 142). This created a dangerous atmosphere for redeploying the Getty Villa, by then a paradoxically "humble" replica with no aspirations other than J. Paul Getty's personal desire to house his collection in a building that would, as

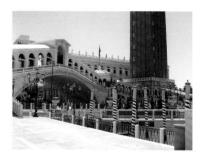

Figure 142. The Venetian hotel and casino in Las Vegas provides an exemplary case of "thematization" as a tool of real-estate, entertainment, and commercial development in late-twentieth-century America.

PROGRAMMATICALLY: we can contextualize
the villa by developing along it the new
Museum component of THE CASTS ROOM.
Unlike the Beaux Arts type, which was
a mere repository of exemplary pieces,
in its new version will consist of an
exhibition of architecture & urbanism
i.e models of buildings, fragments
of them and models of entire cities

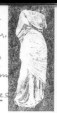

AS A MUSEUM OF ARCHITECTURE & URBANISM, ITS VEHICLE
WILL BE ARCHITECTURE ITSELF, IN OUR
OWN INTERPRETATION OF ROMAN SPACE & MATERIALS

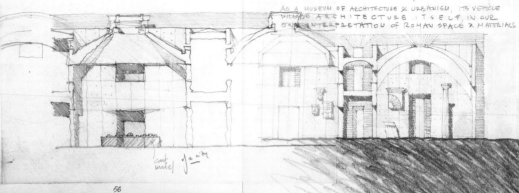

cast
model of a city

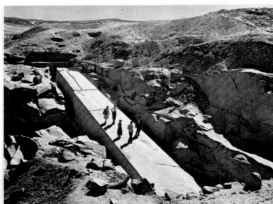

One of the most memorable sites we have
ever seen..... and a very didactic one, too:
about materials (and their passage
from nature to culture), about technology
about landscape art, and about power.

food for thought, as they say...

he said, "be what...a good museum should be," one that would be the most appropriate for his collection of Greek and Roman art.

The dangers and traps were many, and they were real and scary! A variety of conceptual challenges faced the Getty Villa and its would-be architects at the time, but none would compare with the difficulties posed by the tempting trap of "thematization." We knew then that if we were to be chosen, our struggle would be to preserve the dignity of the building's original idea while erecting new facilities that reflected contemporary ideas and trends in museum management, expanded accessibility, and increased public attendance. To this challenge we later added the coherent coordination of the Museum's programs with those of other Getty entities, such as the Research and Conservation Institutes.

We returned to Boston for two weeks of intense work on our submission for the competition. Those days required hard work and hard thinking, but they were also delightful days of toil and chat. The method of selection—by submitting a sketchbook rather than a finished project—relieved us of the typical pressures of competitions, which require rapid and forced synthesis. None of that would be reflected in our sketchbook. We let our ideas flow, almost as a stream of consciousness of interconnected, but not necessarily linear, thoughts that surged, bounced, mixed, and transformed themselves, some ending up in ideas that are still alive in the new Getty Villa, others that went nowhere but did serve to open doors to further investigations. It was an intense dialogue among architects— between Rodolfo Machado and me, to be sure, but also between the two of us and the team we had put together for these two weeks. As such, the dialogue was not so much about words but about drawings, sketches, books, photocopies, slides, postcards, and memories. We displayed this heterogeneous treasure of artifacts in the sketchbook, using the fragments and loose pieces to convey ideas, images, and hypotheses (figs. 143, 144).

To the untrained eye, our sketchbook may look like a chaotic display of non sequiturs, a series of disconnected ideas about classical architecture, parking arrangements, tree specimens, theater design, wall construction, botany, and the like. But to the focused and knowing eye, the scribbles, comments, paste-ons, and drawings are the loose components of a corpus of elements in search of a narrative that would give them final form and meaning. The selection committee seems to have deciphered the enigmatic structure of the book, discovered its buried story, and constructed a positive hypothesis as to how we would develop our ideas. We got the job on May 10, 1994, after the committee had visited both our office in Boston and our built work, which was not extensive at the time but was demonstrative enough of our sensibility and our mode of working.

This happy outcome was preceded by other unusual occurrences: the Getty team's first attempt to visit our office, in January 1994, was canceled when the Northridge earthquake struck on the day before the scheduled visit; by the time the committee finally arrived, the local work that they were going to visit—a large and recently finished private house outside Concord, Massachusetts (fig. 145)—had been severely damaged by fire. As we attempted to show what remained, the small bus transporting the selection committee became stuck in the ice on a remote rural side road for two gelid hours. Ashes, earthquakes, fires, and ice storms—were the gods of Olympus trying to tell us something in this prologue to the task we would soon be called on to perform? In Concord on that icy afternoon, neither Rodolfo nor I thought for a minute that we would ever get the job of redesigning the Getty Villa.

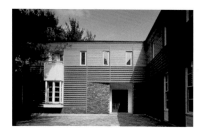

opposite
Figures 143, 144. Sample pages from the Machado and Silvetti competition sketchbook

Figure 145. Private residence, Concord, Massachusetts, designed by Machado and Silvetti Associates, 1992–94. It was completely reconstructed in 1994–95 after a fire.

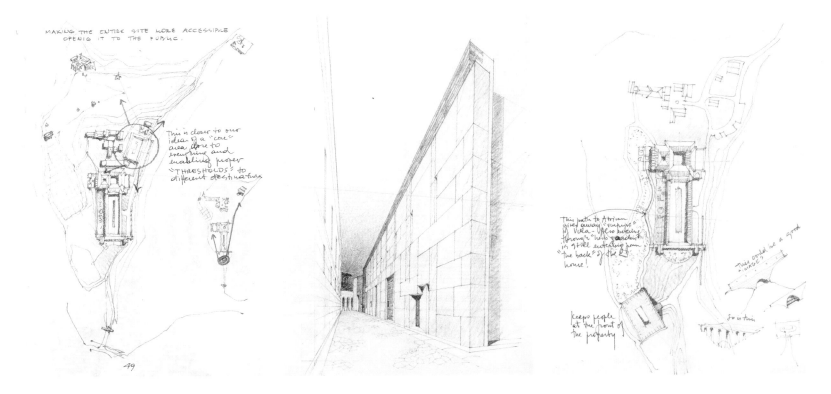

Figure 146. Site plan with the public entry sequence from the parking area at the northeast corner of the Museum building

Figure 147. Perspective of a narrow street along a new building as part of the public entry sequence seen from the north

Figure 148. Site plan showing an alternative public entry sequence from the south

opposite
Figure 149. Proposed concrete wall for the north facade of a new building

Figure 150. Proposed Italian stone pines on the crest of the site's western slope

In practical terms, among the many interrelated ideas it recorded, our sketchbook contained a preliminary plan that addressed mainly the pressing issues of parking, accessibility, and the relocation of the entrance to the Museum; it would serve as the beginning scheme for the project (fig. 146). It called for the garage to be located in the area immediately northeast of the Museum building. Visitors would enter the Villa at its gate on the Pacific Coast Highway and pass by the Museum building on its east side on the way to the parking lot. From there, visitors would have a short walk to the new entrance—during which they would encounter buildings offering an expanded program of visitor services along a relatively narrow street between the existing Museum building and the new structures (fig. 147). The new buildings would be "assembled" as a string of classically

but abstractly inspired spaces built in concrete (fig. 149). The dimensions of the gardens would be expanded and their Mediterranean flora increased by the inclusion of Italian stone pines (fig. 150). It is worth mentioning here that the sketchbook also contained an alternative parking solution in which the garage was located in the existing parking area (called the "camper lot") southwest of the Museum, with pedestrian access following a path on the west slope above the Herb Garden (fig. 148). While long forgotten during the early years of design, this plan was later "recovered" and a version of it eventually became the built solution—validating the fertile and productive characteristics of the sketchbook competition method.

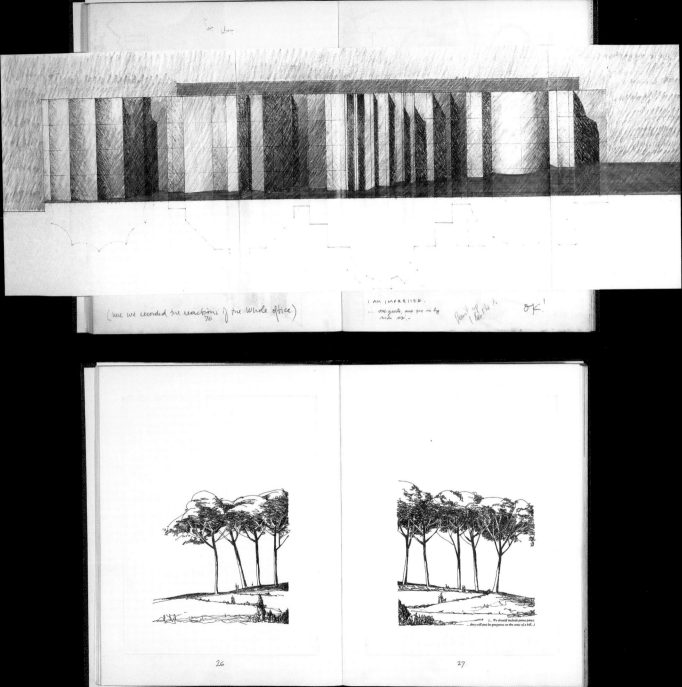

(here we recorded the reactions of the whole office)
70

I AM IMPRESSED.
... one gents, one give one by
books etc.-

Pour up light
idea

OK!

(... We should include pinus pinea.
...they will just be gorgeous on the crest of a hill...)

26

27

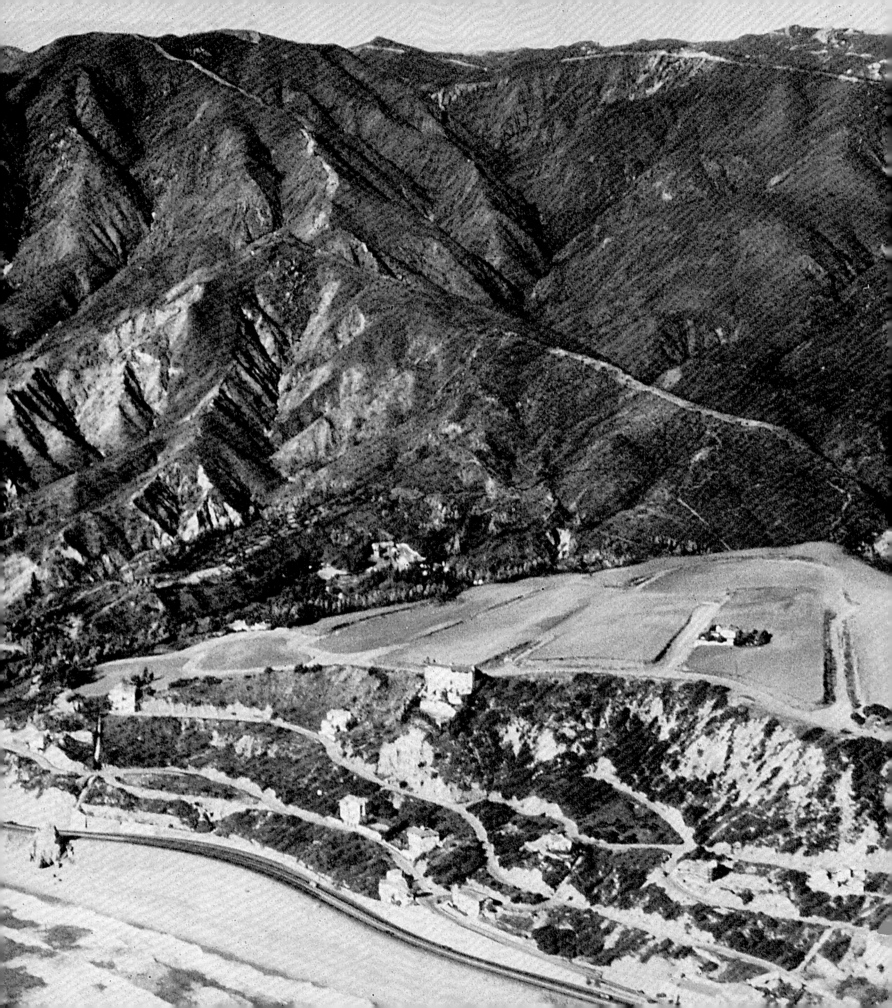

2 Staking Out the Field

MACHADO AND SILVETTI

When we entered the competition, our office had never employed more than twelve people; within a year we had tripled in size, and in two years we had a staff of almost fifty people. In the life of every successful practice, there is a job that produces momentous change; for us, the Getty Villa was that job. While such changes necessarily transform firms into new entities, growth poses inherent dangers that always relate to the change of atmosphere in the workplace and its effect on creativity and final results. We tried, successfully I believe, to preserve the same "small" studio environment by maintaining a structure that fostered dialogue, exchange, and critique. We expanded the Getty team one member at a time, and we kept the principal project staff throughout the process, guaranteeing consistency and efficiency over a period that proved to be much longer than anyone had expected.

As the office quickly grew and took on other commissions, we realized that each project should have just one partner in charge of it, which was a new mode of working for Rodolfo and me (fig. 152). But we made sure that the partner *not* in charge of a particular project served as its in-house critic and, in the case of the Getty, regularly visited the site and attended important client meetings. The main responsibility for the Getty, however, was mine. Rodolfo was the partner who had engaged more directly with the clients of two other important projects at the time: Robert F. Wagner, Jr., Park in Manhattan and Scully Hall, a dormitory at Princeton University. Additionally, my academic involvement with classical architecture and my familiarity with ancient sites made this division of responsibilities the most logical. From then on, Rodolfo and I, who had always worked together on each design—in the same space and sometimes at the same desk—would develop new modes of communication that would ensure the continuity of the fruitful and exciting dialogue we had started in architecture school in Buenos Aires in the 1960s.

GETTING STARTED, PROGRAMMING

We were often in Los Angeles during those first few months, and we were constantly surprised to discover how many more people worked at the Getty than we had ever imagined. It seemed that those first trips mostly involved meeting people—and then meeting more people. Everyone was cordial, open, supportive, enthusiastic, and ready to help—and all of them definitely had ideas of their own about the Villa! We also learned that there were many "entities" of the Getty spread all over town.

At this point, too, we helped select the local associate architects that the Getty, after its experience constructing the Getty Center in Los Angeles, thought would facilitate our work

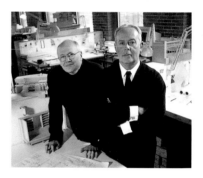

opposite
Figure 151. Photograph taken in the 1930s of the Cañon de Sentimiento—future site of the Getty Villa—showing the dramatic topographical conditions of Southern California's coastal mountain range

Figure 152. Jorge Silvetti (left) and Rodolfo Machado in their Boston office, April 1997

in Malibu. Together we interviewed five local firms, each of which had long-standing associations with design firms like our own, and we agreed upon Langdon Wilson as the most appropriate. Langdon Wilson had collaborated with Norman Neuerburg on the original Getty Villa, and it would offer us invaluable assistance, acting as our technical partner during the project's design phases.

These early ventures into the institution were encouraging and warm, but they did not offer a clear picture about how we were supposed to proceed. While searching for clues, we attended the very first working meeting with the Villa design committee sometime in the summer of 1994. There, we were the ones to advise our clients on how to "get started." As architects, we knew already that this project presented at least two concrete and daunting physical conditions to contend with: on the one hand, a very rich, complex, and topographically difficult site and, on the other, a whole set of functioning buildings, gardens, and infrastructure that the Getty was committed to preserving, restoring, and reusing (fig. 153). It was obvious to us that these two realities would seriously affect whatever project and program the Getty might eventually formulate, were it ever actually to settle on anything at all! Thus, our first fundamental recommendation contradicted what the committee thought the initial steps of the work would be. Unlike the process that had been followed for the design of the Getty Center—in which an extensive initial phase of programming had taken place before any physical, three-dimensional idea had taken shape on paper—for the Villa, we proposed what we thought was the only choice in a situation with many fixed elements: to program and design concurrently.

The ease with which the Getty accepted this methodology surprised us, as we are accustomed to encountering more resistance from

clients whenever we propose something different from what they originally had in mind. Yet it is to the Getty's credit that its committee members immediately and clearly understood the sort of creative process that would be required in this project and, from day one, followed our recommended path. In so doing, they guaranteed not only that we would experiment with where to locate, for example, a new loading dock (which had to serve large trucks in a difficult-to-access canyon site already occupied by various structures) but also that, as we explored real design solutions to this difficult problem, we would discover site potentials that suggested new programmatic ideas, ones that could not have been conceived in the abstract. (In this example, the process led to the idea of establishing a service tunnel to the loading dock.)

Architecture's eternal struggle to find forms that serve functions is never linear, nor is it one in which one endeavor dominates the other. In the case of the Getty Villa site, in which we found extremely difficult physical constraints (such as a main building situated at the bottom of a deep canyon, the ever-present danger of landslides, the difficulties of access, etc.), we established a process that allowed the site itself to exist not as a passive and silent entity but as an active participant that could "speak," as it were, and tell us about its hidden potentials. For us, that has always been the most fruitful approach. Our strategy was simply to "listen" to the site's voices while ignoring, if only for a moment, the needs of the program, so that we could see how those needs could be redefined for the better after we had "heard" what the site had to say about it. A similar model of "listening" to contextual issues other than topography will become evident as this story unfolds, relating in particular to the way our thinking process incorporated the fundamental "content" of the Villa program—namely, archaeology, antiquities, and conservation.

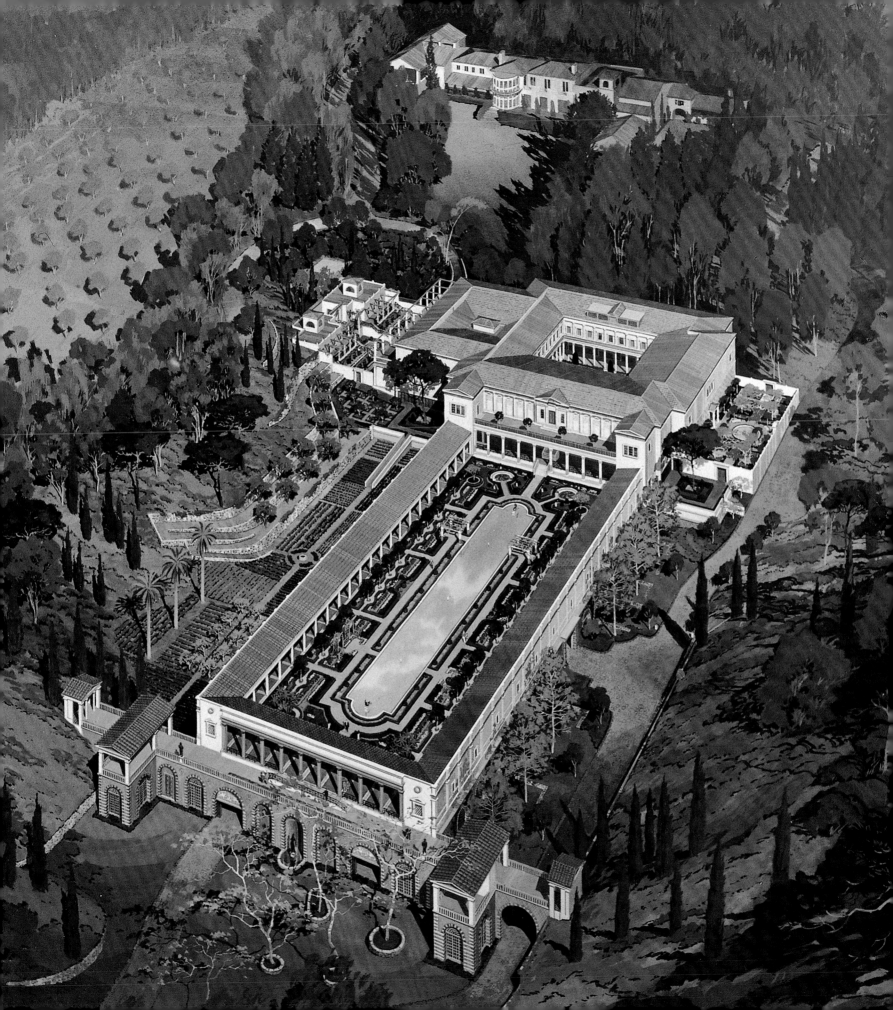

THE FIRST FORMALIZATION OF THE PROGRAM

By January 1995, the first formalization took shape and was presented to the Villa design committee (figs. 154, 155). I use the word "formalization" rather than any of the other terms commonly applied in the initial architectural design process — such as *concept*, *pre-schematic design*, or *parti* — because what we presented was none of these. Rather, it was an almost direct translation of programmatic desires, understood within the broad aims of the Getty Trust's mission statement, an attempt to allocate those desires to concrete places and to establish spatial relationships among the places and the site that made sense and were allowable by site conditions. But nothing more. No narratives of a higher order other than common sense, function, and size applied. We made no attempt to align the project with a particular architectural trend or to reaffirm traditional values. A quick look at our formalization gives a clear idea that

First Master Plan
JANUARY 1995

Figures 154, 155. This is the architects' first formalization of the programmatic needs responding to site conditions and the Getty's stated mission for the Villa site.

Key:
M Museum (existing)
H Ranch House (existing)
T Outdoor Theater
P Parking structure
C Cafe
L Art conservation laboratories and research facilities
F Funicular

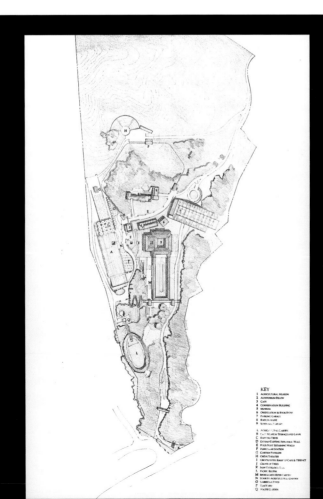

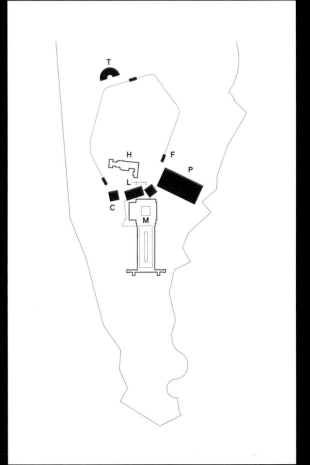

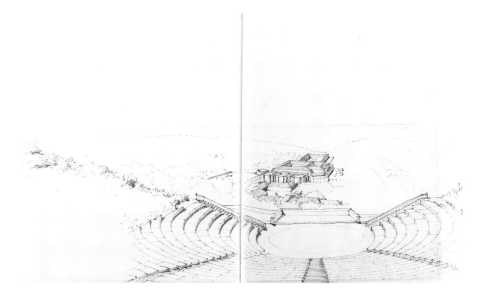

it was more a display of needs and aspirations than a project. Unattractive as it may look, it was a key moment in the process because it represented concretely what so far had been merely abstract ideas in the protagonists' minds. It provided a first (and perhaps shocking) impression that brought a sense of reality and a wealth of knowledge to all those involved, allowing them to grasp how big things were, how they could be placed and fitted on the site, how structures related and affected one another, and so on.

In addition, tentative and unresolved as it was, the cost of the project was first estimated at this stage. It is hard to remember now whether that estimate was even in the ballpark, so to speak, but programmatic requirements and site expectations would prove to be too costly even for the famously rich Getty. Thus, for example, the positioning of the outdoor classical theater —one of the most strongly desired new programmatic elements, which we had placed high up on the property on a privileged natural bowl that would provide the audience with the spectacular background of the Pacific Ocean— would prove to be prohibitively expensive if it were to be made accessible to six hundred spectators, who would have to be transported by funicular or similar means (fig. 156). Similarly, many other aspects of the site and the program were tested in this scheme, and we were left with fresh knowledge about them. From this step (which at the time appeared uninspired), a series of fundamental conclusions followed that allowed us to move on to the very first version of the Master Plan, in which most of the seeds of the new Getty Villa were planted—and that now, in retrospect, proves the value of our seemingly perfunctory formalization.

CONCLUSIONS OF THE FIRST MASTER PLAN

At this point, the committee came to the following conclusions:

- The outdoor theater could not be up the hill and would have to be placed nearer the other public areas, thus ensuring easy access to performances and other uses for large groups.

- Each entity at the Getty that would have a substantial physical presence at the new Villa—principally, the Museum, the Research Institute, and the Conservation Institute—wanted its own architectural identity. Yet, as all the space in the Museum building itself clearly was going to be assigned to the Museum, the question to be resolved was how the Research and Conservation Institutes could appear distinct in a context where the allure and singularity of the Museum building's size, location, and material richness seemed unbeatable.

- The limitations of suitable space for a parking garage required that this crucial component be an underground facility.

- While no conclusive decision was made at this point regarding the important component of the auditorium, the scheme made it

Figure 156. The Outdoor Theater, as described in the competition sketchbook and reproposed in the initial Master Plan, was located in a natural bowl high above the property with the Pacific Ocean as the stage backdrop

clear that the original auditorium in the basement of the Museum building would be not only very expensive to remodel but also extremely difficult to adapt to current accessibility standards.

Overall, one of the most valuable insights gained at this stage was the extent of the site's limitations: theoretically, we had sixty-four acres to play with, but in reality various key elements—

the topography of the canyon, the locations of major existing buildings that were to be preserved and reused (a position that the Getty clearly established at our first meeting, when we proposed, perhaps in typical architects' fashion, that all existing structures except the Museum be razed), and the need to open, relate, and coordinate all of this with accessible circulation —reduced drastically the areas where the programs could be deployed. In a surprising reversal of the promise this large site originally held,

A New Center of Gravity

Figure 157. Due to functional and topographic demands, the notion of a "center of gravity" emerged. This completely changed the initial concept of the new Getty Villa from an Arcadian collection of bucolic garden structures into an inevitable concentration of functions around the new entrance to the Museum. The existing natural slope, occupied by an inadequate cafeteria (the Garden Tea Room), became the felicitous choice for the location of the Outdoor Theater, which in turn generated and organized all the other moves that followed in successive versions of the Master Plan.

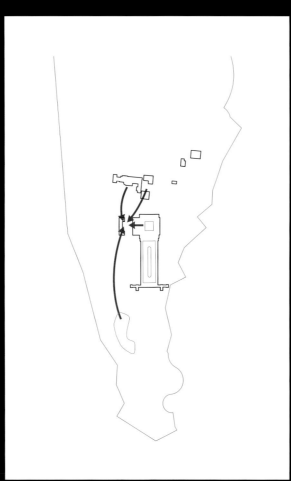

there suddenly seemed to be no space left for what we needed!

However, as we watched the site appear to contract rather than expand, we began to see this "negative" tendency as a source of new inspiration. The need for a real *center of gravity* for the Villa began to take shape in our minds: it would be a hub of activities, encounters, and exchanges, rather than (as in our original idea) an Arcadian dispersal of the programmatic components in an ever-expanding series of gardens and retreats in the larger site (fig. 157).

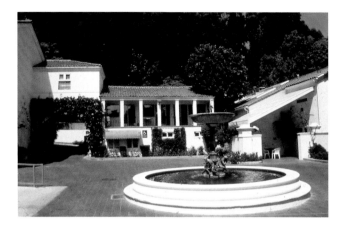

RELOCATING THE OUTDOOR THEATER

The next phase started with a few promising and fundamental developments. First, Harold Williams, President of the Getty Trust, decided that each of the Getty programs participating at the Villa would be assigned an existing building that would be remodeled according to its specific needs: to the Museum, the Roman Villa; to the Research Institute, the Ranch House; and to the Conservation Institute, the laboratories around the area known as the Monkey Court (fig. 158). All of the new buildings would be for shared public-use functions—for example, outdoor theater, food services, parking, auditorium, and visitor services. It was a wise and Solomonic decision that dissipated the growing tension and left everyone satisfied, or at least silent. Even more important, the decision made sense architecturally and practically: the logic of maintaining the Museum in the old Villa was unassailable; in addition, the domestic scale of the Ranch House, as well as its relatively remote location and commanding views, made it ideal as a haven for scholars, and the old laboratories would require only an upgrade and some modification to continue to perform their conservation functions. It also made sense politically to devote time and energy to thinking about

new buildings for new public functions without privileging any particular entity.

The next development, and from our point of view the one with the most important consequences for the project, involved relocating the Outdoor Theater. While there was no particular reason to worry about this more than any of the other important issues, in my mind it loomed larger than the rest. Although the program and the site already were rich in opportunities for public amenities, the idea of an outdoor theater in such a setting fascinated me, and I had probably imbued this piece with as yet unwarranted potential. But I came into the project with strong views and biases about this unique building type, views I had developed over many years of travel and from my passion for antique sites, where I had encountered some of its most exquisite examples (fig. 159). For me, outdoor classical theaters are marvelous structures that propose multifaceted meanings. They are undoubtedly spaces for spectacle, but they are also architectural gestalts that can be made to belong to the landscape or to the fabric of the city. Equally important, they are open forms that can be used in so many ways other than the one for which they were originally created. In addition, an outdoor classical theater easily

Figure 158. The Monkey Court, shown here in around 1994, functioned as the hub of art conservation activities until the Museum in Malibu closed in 1997. Although reconceived and redesigned as part of this project, the original character of the court and its placement at the heart of the conservation operations has been retained.

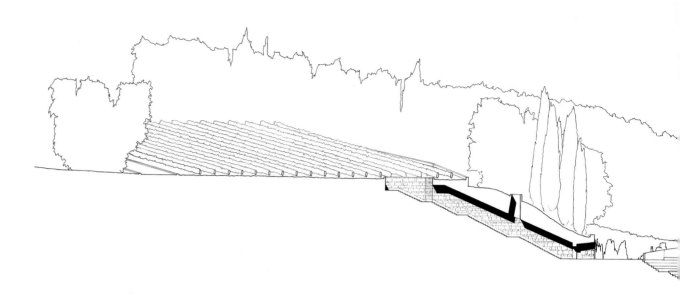

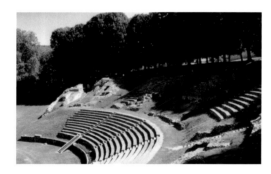

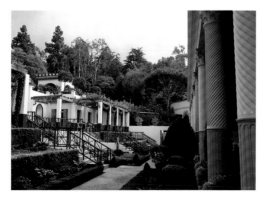

Figure 159. A Roman theater, Autun, France

Figure 160. The Tea Room, shortly before the Museum closed in 1997

and directly communicates its function—yet it brings with it a dense sense of history and timelessness that encourages personal interpretation and inventive uses. It is a quintessentially engaging architectural form.

For all these reasons, I had invested both the design and location of an outdoor theater with great importance. I shared with many on the team the sadness of losing the truly spectacular location that we had proposed, high above the Ranch House with the Pacific Ocean and Channel Islands as the backdrop. Undoubtedly, this would be hard to top! Yet, in retrospect, losing our first choice for the location challenged us to think harder and became a real opportunity for creativity. In the end, such undeniable loss generated a move that was to be pivotal for the project.

I obsessed after that meeting about the Outdoor Theater's location. Shortly afterward, I had an insight that—like many other good ideas in this project—crystallized during

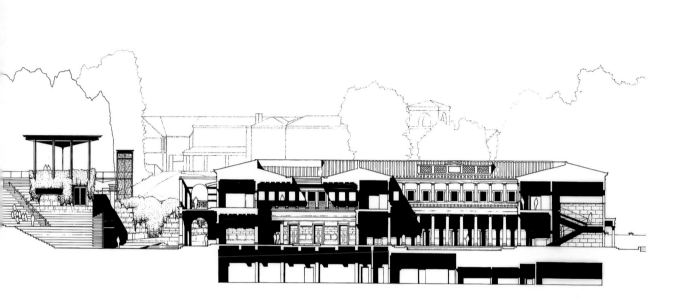

a flight home from Los Angeles. I made a little sketch on an American Airlines napkin—now mislaid—that few people, including my flight companions Peter Lofgren and Tim Love (our firm's associates in charge of the Getty master planning design team), believed was viable. However, it proved to be a defining move that brought us directly into the next and highly productive stage of the project. Specifically, I proposed to locate the Outdoor Theater down the hill, and I placed it where it stands today: on an axis with the new main entrance to the Villa, resting on the natural slope against which the Villa's unfortunate, dysfunctional Tea Room, which had been added shortly after the Villa's construction, still stood (fig. 160).

Back in Boston, Rodolfo, who is always happy when things fall on some axis, supported the move and allayed my growing doubts. It was clear to me that such a move was histori-cally incorrect, because no ancient theater abuts a Roman house; theaters were located close to

the forum, in other public areas, or outside the city. But the tensions generated by working with a historical replica were already beginning to bother me. How were we to achieve historical correctness in a California canyon with respect to a replica of a Roman villa that nobody had ever seen, adjacent to a remodeled 1920s ranch house that loomed vigilant from the hill above? I also felt that the theater's new location would create a stunning and memorable juxtaposition of buildings and become a potent magnet for the visitor. Just as importantly, the Outdoor Theater, when seen as a stairway, could be conceived as a springboard for a gentle climb to the gardens above, which we were also supposed to be developing at that time (fig. 161).

Figure 161. The location of the Outdoor Theater, nestled against a natural slope just west of the Museum, was originally part of a larger concept of linking the Museum's entrance to future gardens on an existing upper plateau via a tunneled stairway.

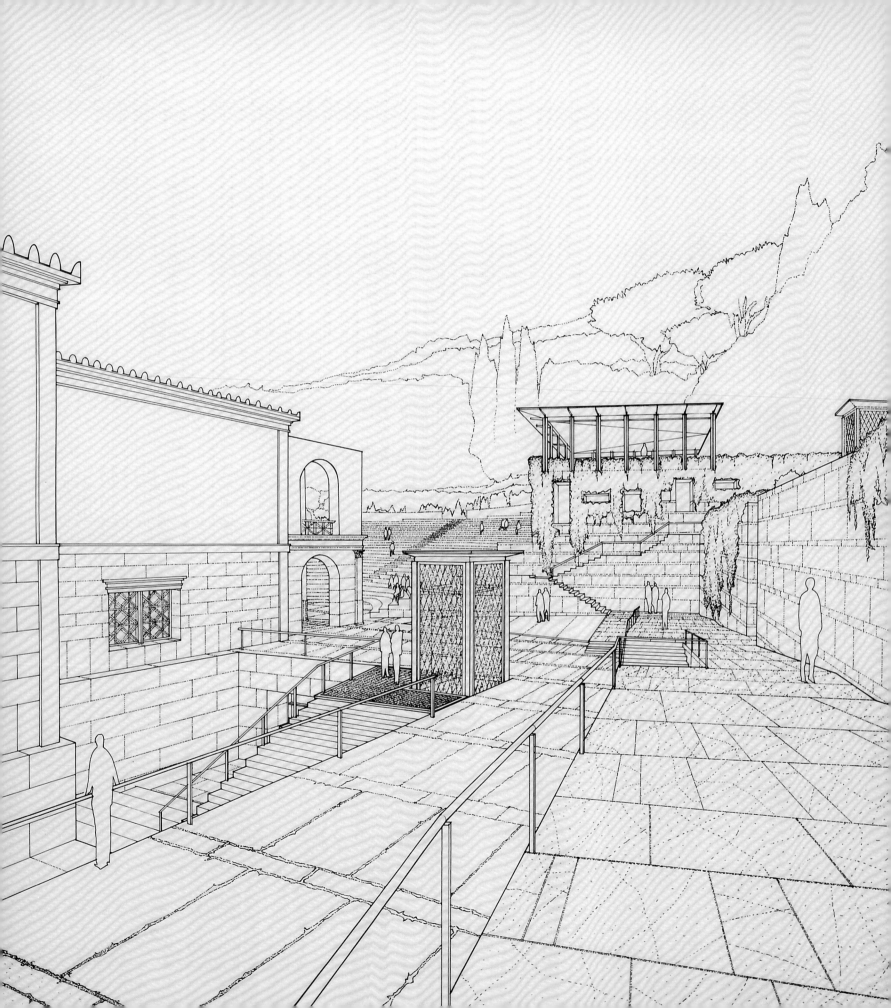

3 Deciphering the Language— Interpreting the Site

IMPACT OF THE OUTDOOR THEATER'S NEW LOCATION ON THE MASTER PLAN

The Getty enthusiastically accepted our proposal regarding the new location of the Outdoor Theater, and I was able to overrule my skeptical team. The effect of this move on the project was profound. At this stage, we were still relying on the access solution laid out in our competition sketchbook, which had visitors arriving from the underground parking structure in the area northeast of the Museum. With the relocation of the Outdoor Theater, we could strengthen the focus of attraction at the main public destination, which now would be not only the entrance to the Museum but also a gate to the still-unexplored areas of the site further up the hill and beyond. Moreover, everyone agreed that a feature with multiple uses would be a tremendous asset in the vicinity of the Museum. The Outdoor Theater would offer not only a venue for performances but also new and logical ways of handling the arrival of large groups of people—who could gather on the theater's steps for orientation—without having to steal much-needed square footage from the main building.

Finally, with the Outdoor Theater's relocation, a new area hitherto unimagined began to develop naturally at its foot: a public plaza that would remain in all future stages as the heart of the Getty Villa and that was soon to embody

the attributes we were seeking for the configuration of a new center of gravity in the site. Slowly but inexorably, all public services and facilities began to gravitate toward this node, led by the small Cafe that we placed on the perch above and to the north of the Theater (fig. 162).

THE MASTER PLAN IN TWO PHASES

New ideas, plans, and alternatives were offered, and meetings and more meetings were held during the project's first year. In April 1995, after a few iterations of the new directives and the relocation of the Theater (figs. 163, 164), the Getty made another momentous decision, which, though reversed years later, had an indelible impact on the project's direction and on the choices we were to make in the general organization of the site. The Getty announced that the Master Plan would be conceived and developed in two phases (see figs. 174–77). The initial phase would be of limited scope, involving the basic required upgrades in accessibility throughout the site and the minimal changes necessary to get visitors to the proper Museum entrance by way of its West Porch and Atrium. The first phase would have no provisions for major new buildings, not even the much-needed parking garage. With the Outdoor Theater and the small Cafe as the only exceptions, all new buildings (and their programmatic content and

opposite
Figure 162. Perspective from summer 1995 showing the visitor arrival path, connecting a public parking structure north of the Museum (not shown) with the new center of gravity of the Getty Villa. Organized around a large plaza, this "hub" of public programs and activities is bracketed by the Museum entrance to the east and the Outdoor Theater to the west (left) and a small cafe pavilion to the north (center).

consequences) would be deferred to the second phase, which would focus on new services and buildings, such as the garage, a restaurant, and an auditorium.

No explanation for this decision was offered, but we came up with one of our own: the construction of the Getty Center was continuing concurrently with the Villa project, and at that particular moment press accounts of the total costs and presumed overruns were embarrassing for the officers of the Trust.

Thus, the decision to reduce the scope and expenditure of the Villa project could be interpreted as a demonstration of the Trustees' fiscal discipline. For us, however, it made no sense, as either a planning or a financial decision, for an organization such as the Getty to postpone construction of elements essential to fulfilling its stated mission. Nevertheless, for the next year we simply had to contend with this planning twist, which had tremendous consequences for the design.

Master Plan
MARCH 1995

Figures 163, 164. This early version of the Master Plan still follows the basic ideas of public access and circulation studied in the original sketchbook. From an underground garage northeast of the Museum, visitors make their way to the central plaza in front of the Museum's new entrance via a path along the north side of the building. With the Outdoor Theater in its new hillside location west of the Museum and the Cafe to its north, the visitor arrives at the Villa's new center of gravity, from where the Museum itself and expanded gardens high above the Theater beg to be explored.

Key:

M   Museum (existing)
H   Ranch House (existing)
T   Outdoor Theater
P   Parking structure
C   Cafe
VS Visitor Services building
L   Conservation laboratories
        and research facilities

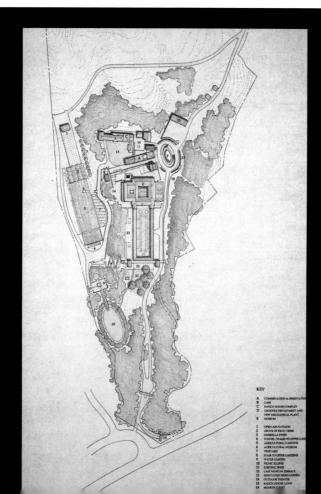

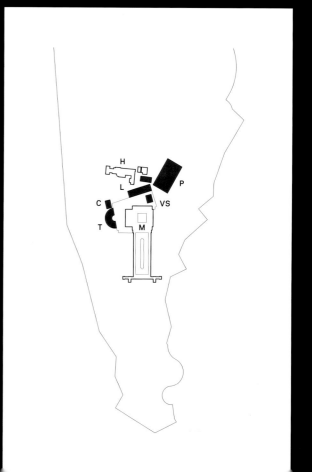

THE ENTRY PAVILION—
THE OTHER KEY COMPONENT

The immediate result of this change in plans was twofold. On the one hand, we felt personal sadness. The rich promise of the new Villa that had unfolded during the first year of work was suddenly postponed to an elusive "second phase," replaced by an impoverished and perfunctory upgrade that would, at most, bring the site up to current standards of accessibility and might very well be all we were ever going to get. On the other hand, the omission in the first phase of the garage, together with the directive to implement in that phase the new entrance to the Museum on its west side, forced us to look for a solution to a problem that at first had seemed intractable: how to bring the public from the existing parking areas (the camper lot and the garage under the Outer Peristyle) to the new entrance, bypassing the entire length of the Museum as the visitor's first experience (fig. 165).

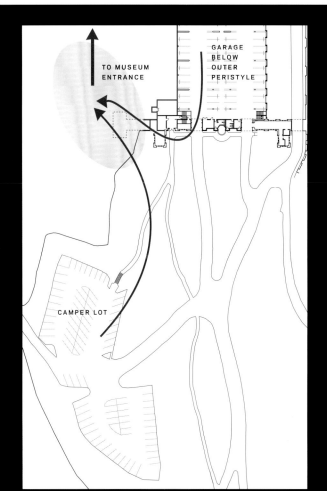

Figure 165. The strategic location of the Entry Pavilion addresses the challenge of bringing visitors to a single point of orientation from two separate parking areas to the east and south, from the garage below the Outer Peristyle, and from the camper lot to the south. From this new arrival point, patrons are transported via stairs and elevators to a hillside pathway leading northward to a terrace above the Theater Plaza and entry to the Museum.

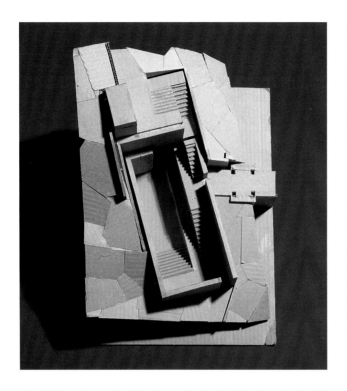
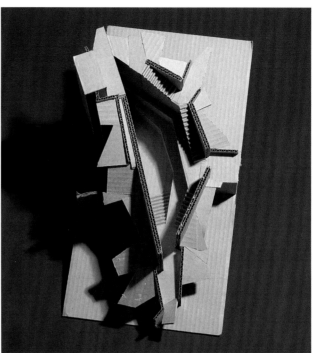
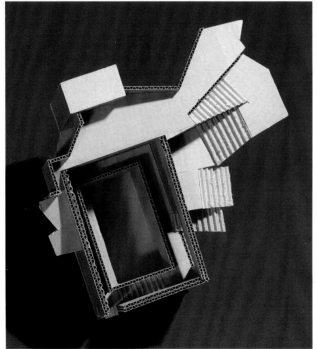
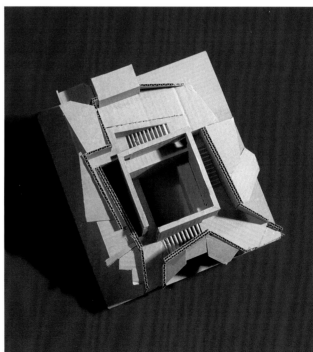

Again, this new difficulty proved to be the source of what is probably the most imaginative architectural piece in the ensemble: the Entry Pavilion—an entirely new and, for a while, highly contested element that would be key from then on in the development of the final scheme (figs. 166–69).

In attempting to achieve the required first-phase entrance sequence—that is, to bridge the gap between the existing parking area and the new door—we soon realized there was no apparent route for the visitor to follow that would avoid the Museum building. For a while, this seemed to be an unsolvable dilemma, as our only two options were both unacceptable. The current route, through the building itself, was an impossible proposition, as it would contradict the whole effort to have people enter the Museum from the outside through its "proper" door on the West Porch (fig. 170). An alternate route, through the Herb Garden, would negotiate the distance without entering the building,

opposite
Figures 166-69. Cardboard study models of alternative designs for the Entry Pavilion (1995–96)

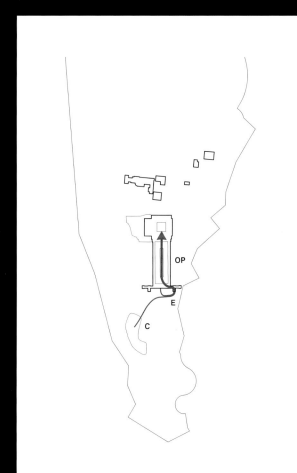

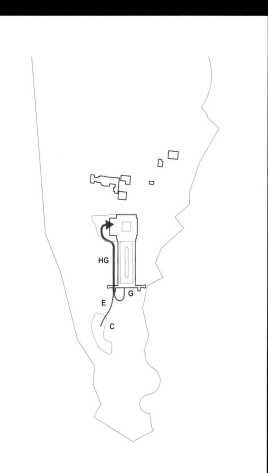

Figures 170, 171. Original pedestrian entry sequence (fig. 170), from the camper lot (C) parking area to the Museum via an elevator (E) in the southeast corner of the Outer Peristyle (OP). Alternative pedestrian entry sequence (fig. 171), studied during the master planning process, which leads visitors to the Museum's new entrance along the west wall of the Outer Peristyle via the Herb Garden (HG).

Key:
C   Camper lot
E   Elevator
HG Herb Garden
OP Outer Peristyle
G   Garage

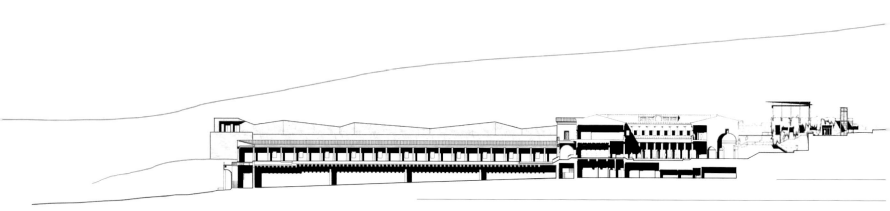

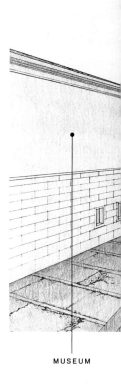

MUSEUM

Figure 172. Site section
through Museum and Ranch
House, showing the roughly
75-foot vertical climb
from the camper lot in the
south to the Ranch House
terrace in the north. Considerable differences in levels
in the public areas of the new
Getty Villa presented
both design challenges and
opportunities.

opposite

Figure 173. Phase II panoramic perspective showing
visitor arrival area north of
the Museum's new entrance.
A new visitor services
building (foreground, at right),
providing an auditorium, bookstore, and general entrance
control from parking areas
further north, would have
acted as the threshold to the
Museum, Outdoor Theater,
and Cafe beyond, all of which
would have already been built
as part of the Phase I plan.

but it would continue to rely on the Museum's mass as its only physical support along its path; the Museum structure would dominate the visitor's entry and thus overshadow the role of other Getty entities that were also part of the new Getty Villa—precisely the experience we were trying to avoid (fig. 171). After exploring this latter possibility in many variations, we reaffirmed our conviction that the new entry sequence should be conceptualized as an entrance to the Getty Villa as a whole and not exclusively to the Museum. To achieve that, we had to find a spatial buffer between that imposing building and whatever path the visitor would be asked to follow. This squared well with the desires of many on the committee and with our own aspirations to prolong the entrance experience of the visitor. Equally important, it offered an opportunity to articulate Mr. Getty's stated desire to open the Villa site to the public as much as possible. However, this conceptual clarity was not as easy to find in the reality of the site topography. So, we revisited an alternative in our competition sketchbook, one that, when we originally proposed it, had appeared far-fetched in comparison with the then-preferred northern approach to the new entrance (see fig. 148). Suddenly, the sketchbook's high pedestrian route on the west slope above the Herb Garden was the more

realistic option—if only we could negotiate the visitor's ascent elegantly, imaginatively, and efficiently. This is when the beginnings of the Entry Pavilion concept began to take shape.

While this was taking place, we were also working on what continued to be for everyone the "real" project: the architectural resolution of the full program that would be implemented in the second phase. In attempting to find a way to move from the first through the second phase, the idea of how to resolve the "dilemma" of the entry sequence in the first phase appeared. As in the most favored alternative in our competition entry, the full project assigned the bulk of the major development of the new programs to the areas immediately north of the Museum build-ing, with multileveled structures that negotiated the considerable differences in level between the Museum and the Ranch House and conser-vation laboratories. Somewhere between the footprint of these structures and in the 75 feet that existed between the camper lot and the ground level of the Ranch House, we needed to accommodate in the final phase all the new pro-grammatic components. Not surprisingly, with such drastically different levels occurring over a short distance, our project evolved with an entry sequence in an intermediate level (+194' [indicates 194 feet above sea level]) between the Museum's entrance level (+176') and the

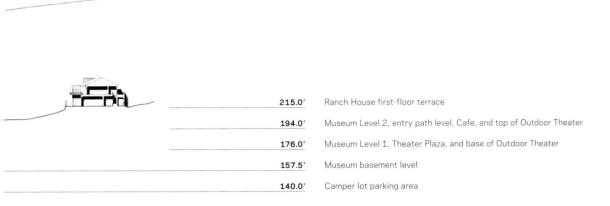

215.0'	Ranch House first-floor terrace
194.0'	Museum Level 2, entry path level, Cafe, and top of Outdoor Theater
176.0'	Museum Level 1, Theater Plaza, and base of Outdoor Theater
157.5'	Museum basement level
140.0'	Camper lot parking area

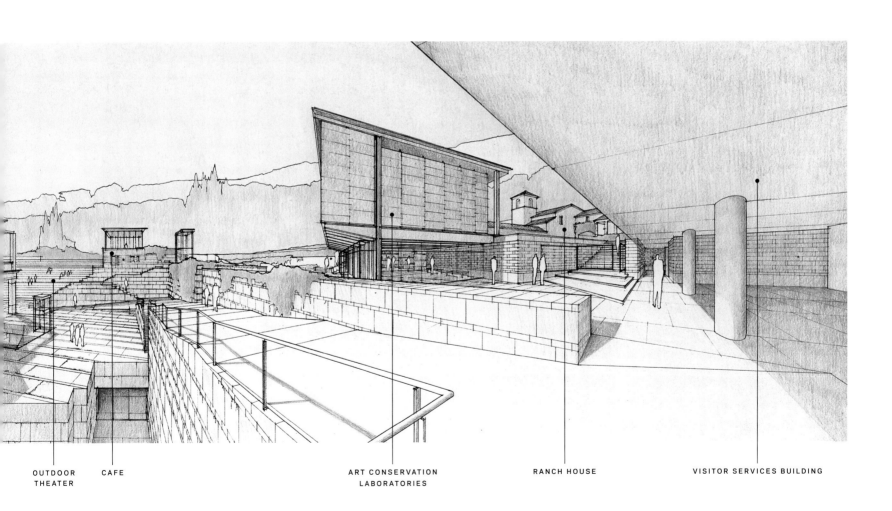

OUTDOOR
THEATER

CAFE

ART CONSERVATION
LABORATORIES

RANCH HOUSE

VISITOR SERVICES BUILDING

upper building's ground floor (+215') (figs. 172, 173). This odd condition would remain until the end, and in spite of our doubts about its validity, we became accustomed to it, accepted it, and finally discovered its unique potential. But that will become clear later, for the Entry Pavilion concept was the instrument that would allow us not only to resolve complexities of vertical circulation but also to give conceptual validity to the experience of entering the Museum and its grounds.

TRUSTEES' MEETING OF SEPTEMBER 1995— THE SECOND MASTER PLAN

For the September 1995 Trustees' meeting, we proposed a two-phased project whose functional success relied heavily on a "reversible" entry-sequence solution that could change its role as it changed directions from Phase I to Phase II. This meant that in Phase I the path performed as an entry sequence, in a northerly flow, from the existing parking facilities in the south

Master Plan, Phase I
SEPTEMBER 1995

Figures 174, 175. Visitors would enter from the Entry Pavilion in the south via a garden pathway along the west slope above the Museum building leading to a central plaza.

Key:

M Museum (existing)
H Ranch House (existing)
T Outdoor Theater
C Cafe
EP Entry Pavilion

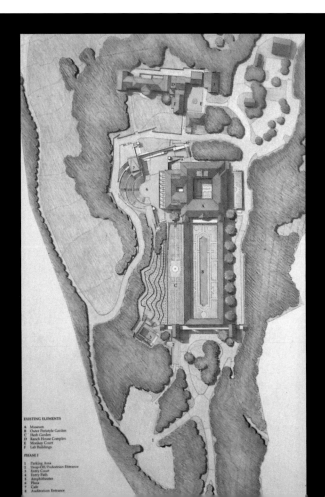

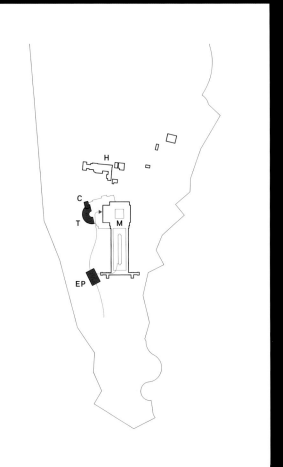

to the entry plaza in front of the Outdoor Theater via the Entry Pavilion, which would serve both to orient visitors and to transport them, either by elevators or garden stairs, to the middle level of the path (figs. 174, 175). Later, whenever Phase II was implemented, visitors would arrive at the plaza from the north (figs. 176, 177). The former entry path would revert to a southerly flow and take on its definitive character as a tranquil "back road" open to visitors exploring the site beyond the plaza and into the gardens. Visitors could either step down into the Herb Garden or climb up to a garden path that would take them through the west-slope gardens and then into the former Entry Pavilion. Consequently, the Pavilion would itself become a garden folly providing the major vertical circulation that would eventually bring visitors to the proposed upper gardens, which would be developed in the large plateau, formerly a lemon grove, above the main buildings of the Villa (+230'). Still, both phases would share the center

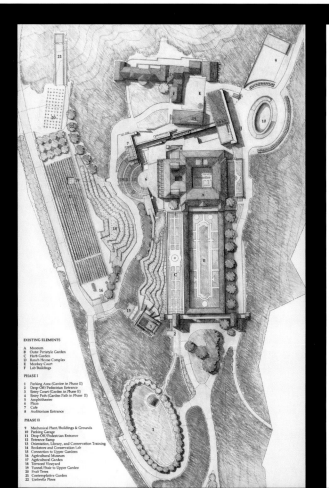

EXISTING ELEMENTS

A   Museum
B   Outer Peristyle Garden
C   Herb Garden
D   Ranch House Complex
E   Monkey Court
F   Lab Buildings

PHASE I

1   Parking Area (Garden in Phase II)
2   Drop-Off/Pedestrian Entrance
3   Entry Court (Garden in Phase II)
4   Entry Path (Garden Path in Phase II)
5   Amphitheater
6   Plaza
7   Cafe
8   Auditorium Entrance

PHASE II

9   Mechanical Plant/Buildings & Grounds
10   Parking Garage
11   Drop-Off/Pedestrian Entrance
12   Entrance Ramp
13   Orientation, Library, and Conservation Training
14   Bookstore and Conservation Lab
15   Connection to Upper Gardens
16   Agricultural Museum
17   Agricultural Garden
18   Terraced Vineyard
19   Tunnel/Stair to Upper Garden
20   Fruit Trees
21   Contemplative Garden
22   Umbrella Pines

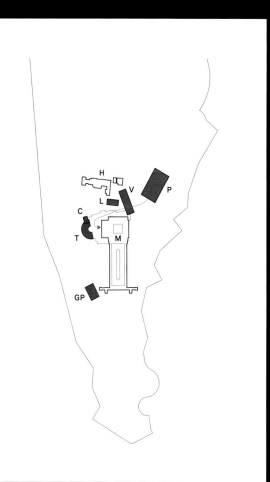

Master Plan, Phase II
SEPTEMBER 1995

Figures 176, 177. The direction of the Phase I entrance sequence is reversed in Phase II. From a new parking facility to the north, patrons would arrive via a new visitor services building and descend by way of a long ramp into a central plaza. Consequently, the former Entry Pavilion would become a garden destination beyond.

Key:

M   Museum (existing)
H   Ranch House (existing)
T   Outdoor Theater
P   Parking structure
C   Cafe
V   Visitor Services building
L   Conservation laboratories and research facilities
GP Garden Pavilion

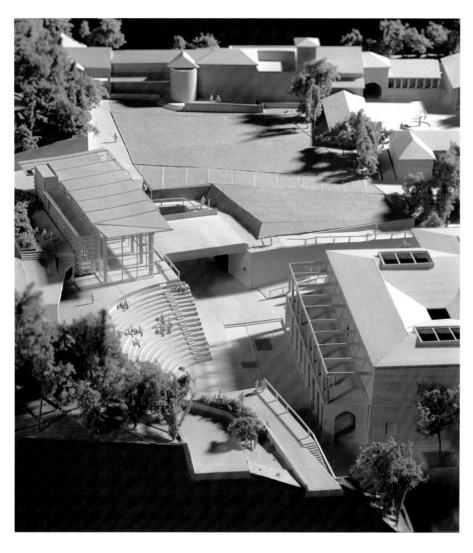

Figure 178. Site model showing new buildings surrounding the Theater Plaza and the entrance to the Museum. Clockwise starting with the Museum at right, the Museum Path, the Outdoor Theater, the Cafe, the Ranch House, and the new lawn over a 250-seat, partly subterranean auditorium

of gravity, namely the plaza in front of the Theater, which by now had been firmly established as the hub of the Getty Villa, and which would henceforth be called the Theater Plaza.

Thus, with the path in its two incarnations connecting the Entry Pavilion/garden folly with the Theater Plaza at an intermediate level, it was possible to succeed in connecting all the components of the Villa at a more neutral middle level, as well as to create the buffer between the Museum and an independent entry sequence. In terms of character, the reversal of the path's role was also consistent in each phase. It would be very active and "inevitable" in the first phase. In Phase II it would become just the opposite, a route for visitors to discover at the end of a Museum visit, a path followed by those who were curious or who sought out the more guarded and secluded areas beyond the busy plaza. In this final configuration, we would find sandwiched, as it were, between preexisting buildings and at different levels—a plaza, an outdoor theater, an auditorium, a bookstore, outdoor eating facilities, a fountain, stairs, and elevators (fig. 178).

While we were not yet openly addressing issues of architectural vocabulary, materials, and expression, the project already had a distinct character insofar as it established a clear strategy of intervention. Looking at the project's final plan, we first notice that all new interventions are articulated according to an orthogonal grid different from the one defined by the existing buildings. This is a contemporary architectural and urbanistic technique used to clarify and highlight "newness" in relationship to existing conditions. It is a truly widespread technique that is sometimes abused: it can impart graphic clarity without offering many spatial rewards.

I want to state clearly here that this solution was not imposed on the Getty as part of our standard vocabulary. Rather, the "rotated grid,"

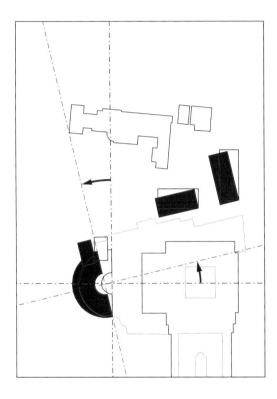

Theater in this strategic location (fig. 179). Thus, by opening views up the hill and giving breathing space to the plaza, we established a perceptible and distinct orientation that would be associated, by extension, with all new buildings. In this way, the distinction between old and new in our project would not be dependent entirely on the architectural look and the style of the new buildings—a welcome condition that released us from the pressures of having to compete with the Museum building for architectural presence.

The Master Plan received an enthusiastic approval by the Trustees, and the recommendations that followed supported all the main points proposed by the design, specifically confirming that:

- Each institution of the Getty Villa needed to be represented on the site.

- The main door to the Museum should be through its West Porch and Atrium.

- The new plans (Phase I and Phase II) should open up the site to visitors and staff.

Figure 179. Diagram showing the geometric rotation of the Outdoor Theater, from its idealized north-south orientation parallel to the Museum's West Porch, to its more advantageous location conforming to the slope of the west hillside. This move widens the area of the Theater Plaza and opens up views of the Ranch House and coastal mountains to the north.

a very rare feature of our projects, resulted from a reasoned, step-by-step process that we followed in order to establish the precise location for the Outdoor Theater. In earlier versions, our first instinct was to orient this key component in an obvious direction: parallel to the facade of the Museum. But soon it became clear that the open space created in between would be insufficient as the main public open area of the project and that it would be difficult for the upper buildings to be part of the scene generated by such a plaza. In addition, given the topography, it was not possible to move the Outdoor Theater further to the west, so as to widen the plaza and gain views to the upper hill. Rotating the Outdoor Theater to follow the natural direction of the west slope became the only logical move if we were to keep the

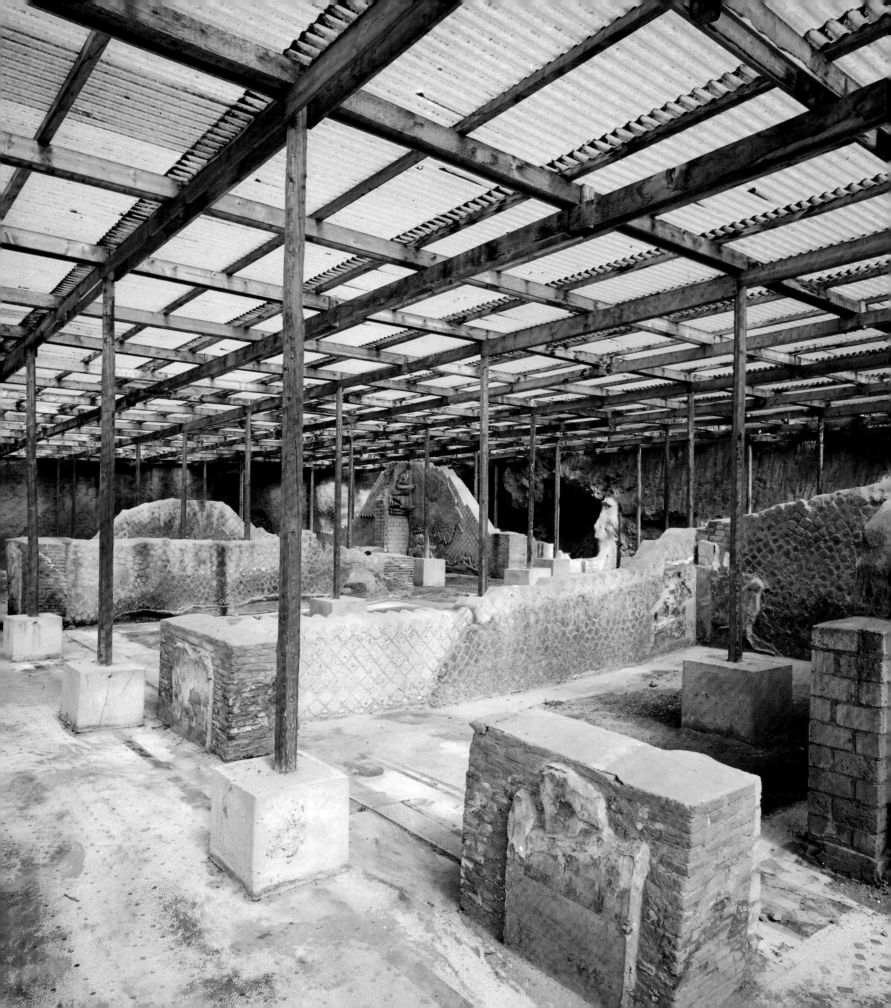

4 # Tectonic Shifts and the Unearthing of the Villa

WORK AND PAIN

The terrain having been "staked out," as it were, we began to work intensively to develop the principles, ideas, and design strategies expressed in the Master Plan. We began a process of acquiring knowledge systematically in each area of the program, site, and buildings. It involved knowledge that might be found in libraries, in other sites around the world, and from talking to experts in various fields. This period, roughly from September 1995 to September 1996, was a fertile time, when the creative process flourished—knowledge was acquired, discoveries were made, and interpretations were realized. Just as important, we developed strong personal ties with the Getty staff involved in the project.

During this period, we at Machado and Silvetti chose to organize ourselves into two teams: the "new buildings team," led by Conrad Ello, and the "existing buildings team" (with two subteams, one for the Museum and another for the Ranch House complex), led by Mimi Love. Coordination of the overall project—overseeing the harmonious synthesis of the many components of this complex job and its successful construction—was in the hands of Tim Love until 2002; after that it fell under Conrad Ello's growing responsibilities.

Ironically, during this time a freak accident rendered my right shoulder and arm useless other than for basic movements, and I temporarily lost the ability to draw—a situation that sporadically recurred for three years and through four surgical interventions. Naturally, this meant that, with the exception of very small rough sketches, I could not conceive and draw up my design ideas more or less at the same time; instead, other members of the team had to draw what I imagined. This proved to be both humbling and rewarding, confirming what we all say about the design process—namely, that it is first and foremost a true team effort, though rarely do we see that idea so vividly expressed! This also forced my "immersion" into the digital world that was slowly transforming our office. To this day, I use computers without really knowing how it all works, by sitting next to colleagues who "draw" on the screen for me.

TRAVEL

If we were to choose one aspect of that eventful year, from fall of 1995 through fall of 1996, that had the greatest impact on the project's development, it would be the two trips we made to Europe to visit archaeological sites, antiquities museums, and other relevant locations. Each journey focused on two important goals: first, to acquaint ourselves with the state-of-the-art approaches to exhibiting classical antiquities in European museums, and second, to experience as thoroughly as possible the Roman architectural sources of the Getty Villa (figs. 180–84). Broadly speaking, while each trip corresponded to one of those objectives, and our forays were separated in time by half a year, it is impossible for me to measure separately the impact each had on the project.

It was a year of learning whose impact we could fully appreciate only later, as each of us reflected on what we had discovered and how those discoveries changed not only our work on the Villa project but also our other work and interests. For me, certainly, it affected the curricula I developed for courses I taught at Harvard. I found that the study of the Roman house—one of my chief research topics since beginning the Getty Villa project—could give my graduate students and me a paradigm of great value in understanding and synthesizing many aspects of architecture even today. More dangerously, it turned me on to the beauty (and great cost!) of Greek vases. Certainly, we all came away changed in how we thought about museums and their attendant design issues (display, color, lighting, character). We acquired substantial historical knowledge about how space, color, building type, and plants were formally articulated and physically used in antiquity. And we were intrigued and puzzled by the intellectual and experiential dilemmas and the delights that originals, "replicas," and precedents still pose in the history of architecture.

But the most valuable acquisition by far was the bond established between the Getty team and our own during these journeys. The experiences, images, and knowledge that we internalized and brought back became common and constant reference points we all would draw upon in the years that followed, as we discussed, assessed, or simply speculated about the design of the Villa, the new buildings, the public spaces, the furniture, or the gardens.

We had, simply, developed a *common vocabulary* that allowed us to talk about the project and its ideas—a priceless tool whose frequent absence from many design processes might help explain their failures. Furthermore, we developed a shared "taste"—however odd this may seem—based more on an understanding of and respect for what the others liked or disliked than on a shared aesthetic.

Not surprisingly, the topic that interested me the most throughout this experience was the manner in which the "antique" was and is presented and re-presented to our eyes by different artists, architects, collectors, amateurs, and scholars throughout the centuries-long Western obsession with the art and artifacts of classical antiquity. It also proved that there is no single, correct approach in dealing with the "antique." Indeed, there are many approaches, and only the most intelligently creative ones endure. We saw archaeological sites where the stratification of eras is vivid and palpable as one literally descends through space and time into the past; we saw others where the contemporary topography merges seamlessly with the remnants of past landscapes. We saw spaces that were almost intact and others where the fragmentary antique remains exert severe demands on the beholder's imagination. We saw some originals that had been restored with great accuracy through a painstaking devotion to sources, and others where interpretation had prevailed over authenticity, with the designer's sensibility superseding knowledge and connoisseurship.

We also saw practical aspects, such as museum galleries where the effects of direct natural light on antiquities were tested and galleries where not even the slightest ray of sunlight was permitted to fall upon the figures. We visited spaces where bronze, ceramic, and marble can be seen only against a neutral, abstract, off-white color that blurs all architectural clarity,

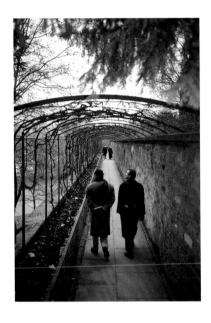

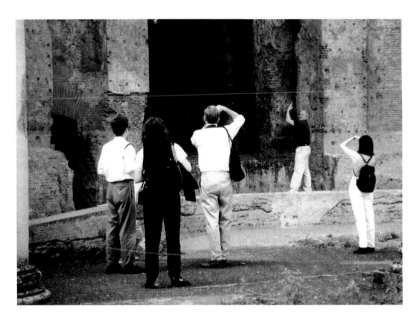

Figures 181-84.
clockwise from top left
The Pompejanum, in Aschaffenburg, Germany, November 1995 (fig. 181); Hadrian's Villa, May 1996 (fig. 182); Pompeii, May 1996 (fig. 183); Herculaneum, May 1996 (fig. 184)

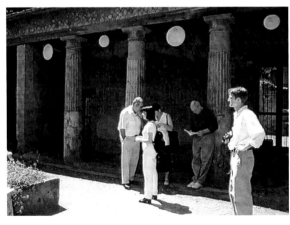

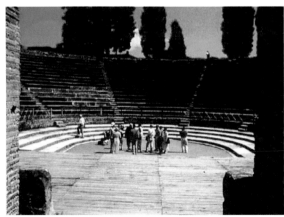

and spaces where the same handful of classical materials can be seen against a rich and even exuberant palette of classical colors that express hierarchies of space and architectural elements, transforming every wall into a stage set against which the classical artifact can "perform." Indeed, we came back well armed for a frontal attack on our most difficult problems, which the complex Master Plan maneuvers had so far postponed: how to remodel our replica of a Roman villa and how to introduce new buildings around it—all this on a site that, during three decades, had acquired the flavor of the southern Italian Mediterranean settings where ancient Roman maritime villas were built and that displayed unabashedly its trophy, the reincarnation of the Villa dei Papiri.

We made certain decisions without much discussion, some even before returning to the States. For example, we agreed that natural light would be brought into the galleries as much as possible and that the Roman color palette of southern Italian classic domestic environments would be used, not only to expand the original and more modest color scheme at the Villa but also to replace some colors that had already been employed.

Other design decisions were less evident. Not surprisingly, it would take us months of concentration, imagination, and much rumination to "discover" the design decisions that pertained to the architecture of new buildings, structures, and spaces that would inevitably bear the signature of Machado and Silvetti. Given our approach to architecture, those decisions would require from us not just the deployment of a particular vocabulary but, fundamentally, a supporting concept, an overall idea. And on this account, the knowledge we brought from our site visits, together with the personal experience that most of us had accumulated over the years, constituted the "treasury" from which we would extract our inspiration.

THE NEW ARCHITECTURE

For the new architecture that we would create to encompass all of the shared functions, public services, and amenities, we paused and looked at what we had already proposed in the Master Plan. On close inspection, it turned out that the plan contained a strong hint of a direction to follow, one that would guide the process toward the development of a convincing and exciting architectural language. This guiding image was that of "archaeology" itself, which, upon our return from our travels, struck us as being embedded in what we were already doing. The Getty Villa presented a variety of aspects that had long given us headaches: the lack of a clear "ground floor"; the difficulties associated with moving people up and down slopes, ramps, and stairs; the inherent contrivance of our proposed new entry sequence, in which we would take visitors up in order later to bring them down.

These "inconvenient" features, which we were fighting against or had been attempting to ameliorate since day one, slowly but surely turned out to be the source of the project's conceptual strength: the site became something not unlike what we had just experienced in Herculaneum—today, half-excavated, but real and visible right below the present-day town, where one moves from one level to another, from the present to the past, from one era to another, and in doing so makes "archaeology" a tangible and lived experience (figs. 185, 186).

Moving around the Getty Villa site, which we were so carefully crafting in order to resolve a complicated topography, was in fact analogous to the experience of visiting the Villa dei Papiri itself (fig. 187). Navigating the site demanded that we move vertically through the earth's striations in order to "discover" the Villa. Our multilevel project, with interconnected buildings at different heights, alluded to the multilayered and simultaneous existence of different conditions, which were all attributes that could, with care, knowledge, and taste, be articulated using an appropriate architectural language to establish the character of the new Getty Villa.

Throughout this text, just as in our work, I often make use of the terms *language*, *vocabulary*, and *syntax* to describe our design's qualities. This analogy has a long tradition in architectural theory and history, and its use is thus intentional in our thoughts and work, particularly at the Villa. Indeed, what we produced, after identifying archaeology as the characteristic image to pursue in the design of the Villa, was not simply a vocabulary defined by a palette of materials and details. More precisely, it was an operational system that, like a grammatical framework, would allow us to make decisions and to assign materials, details, and a finite set of formal motives to locations and functions in a particular way and with specific roles, so as to articulate or relate each design element with every other in consistent ways.

Thus, thinking in terms of a system or a grammar rather than of a style, our vocabulary at the Getty Villa is not historicist, because it does not rely on nor does it use any classical elements or icons such as those derived from the classical orders and ornaments. Our vocabulary is, in fact, quite contemporary insofar as materials, forms, and elements are concerned. As a system, however, both the historical and thematic references emerge from the way this contemporary vocabulary is deployed: historically, it relates to the original buildings and to the landscape (through formal and conceptual symmetries, hierarchies of components, alignments, and proportions); thematically, it reinforces at each instance the "image" of the site as *a place of discovery and exploration*, one in which history is represented by the layers accumulated over time and not by a style or specific iconographic program.

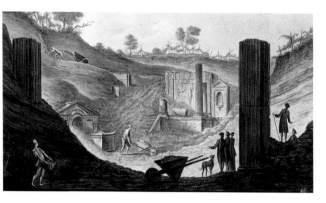

Figure 185. Print depicting eighteenth-century archaeological excavations in Italy

Figure 186. A photograph from the 1930s of the excavations at Herculaneum shows the stratification between the Roman town below and present-day city above.

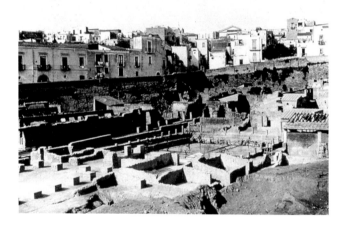

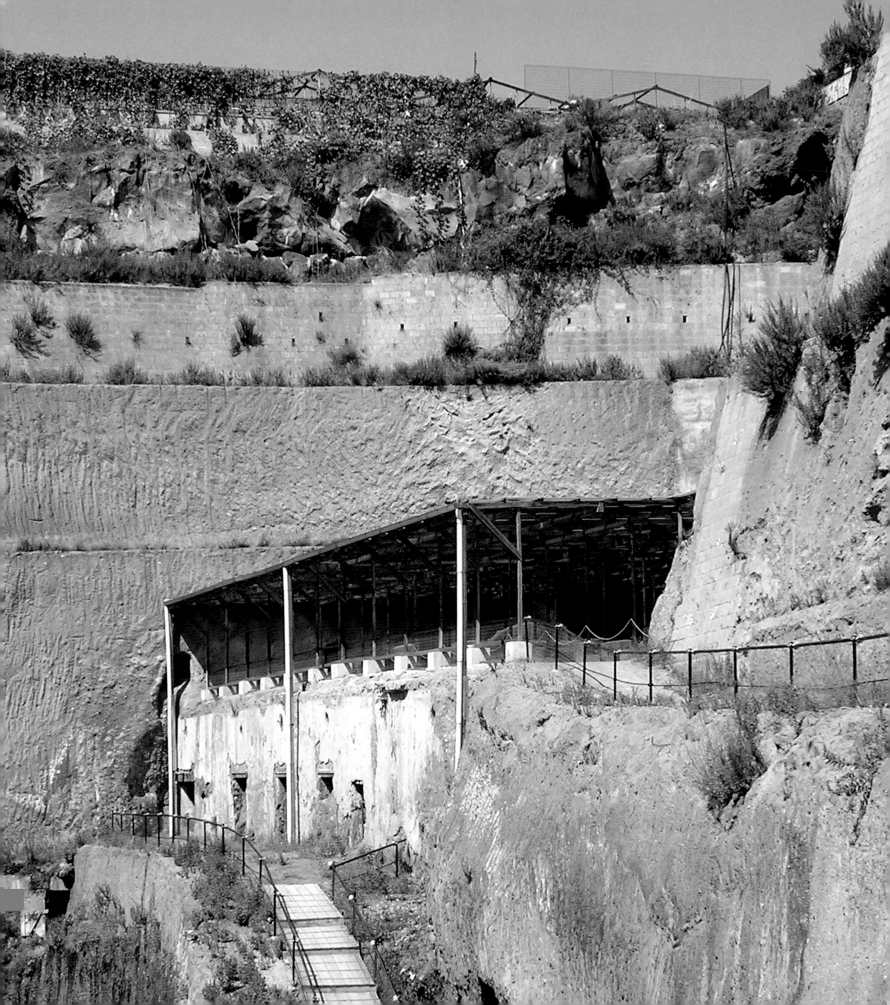

Perhaps the best example of what we attempted in terms of creating a language that would "speak" for the new Getty Villa is what we called the *strata wall*, a term that describes the layered surfaces of all walls facing the public areas. In this, the most pervasive yet diverse component of the system, each "stratum" is defined by a distinct material, such as concrete, stone, or wood. The strata wall gives identity and unity to all the new buildings and creates continuity throughout the site in what could otherwise have been a rather fragmented ensemble of unrelated structures. Its appearance, materials, and function are the subject of the next two chapters.

To further extend the language analogy to architecture, we can consider its materials, details, colors, and forms as the elements and "protagonists" that can be used to tell a story—an architectural story, to be sure, but one that would be coherent, interesting, and, at the same time, consistent with the institutional goals and content. In hindsight, this process of systematization, with its implications of rules and operations, perhaps appears overly structured, formal, and dour to the reader, but that perception can be attributed to the difficulty of trying to convey with words what in practice is a stimulating, flexible, and ever-changing proposition of articulating ideas, materials, and a site by means of an architectural narrative.

As we were attempting to reflect this guiding image in our project, Getty design committee members came to one of our meetings with an idea that had emerged from a recent discussion about the kind of institution the new Getty Villa would be. The Getty had realized as soon as the project started that it was not just addressing the reuse of existing buildings and grounds, but that it had the opportunity to create a new entity on the site. The Villa was not going to be a smaller version of the grand project taking shape in Brentwood, nor simply a museum of antiquities: the new Villa would become a "center for comparative archaeology," where all its components—Museum, Conservation Institute, Research Institute, Education Institute —would promote the study and understanding of archaeology. Was the Getty influenced by what our design suggested, or were we induced to adopt the image of "archaeology" as our guide because the Getty itself was moving in that direction in defining how the Malibu site would function? There is no clear answer, of course. All I can say is that the chronological convergence of ideas represents the best example of what a good design process should be: a productive dialogue between an educated, curious client and architects who are ready to listen and learn—a client whose ideas will change along with the design ideas presented, who has sophisticated institutional ambitions, and who trusts the architects to realize those ambitions in inspiring physical settings.

Furthermore, I found even more instructive the fact that the convergence of institutional goal and architectural concept served more as a tactic than as an enduring policy. By the end of the project, the institutional makeup of the Getty had changed. The "entities" no longer had the same roles and complex hierarchical relationships, and the idea of a center for comparative archaeology was abandoned in favor of a more fluid and open institution. Yet the communion of institutional, expressive, and aesthetic purposes served, at a crucial moment, to give the project an exhilarating impulse.

With the articulation of this programmatic goal, the client's vision clicked with that of the architects. The theme played right into the architectural and landscape forms that were taking shape on the ground. In a nutshell, a unique institution—supported by its collections, exhibits, research, and conservation activities—

opposite
Figure 187. Ongoing excavations reveal the archaeological and geological strata at the Villa dei Papiri

was promoting archaeology as a scholarly, professional, and intellectual endeavor, all for the benefit of the public, academics, and connoisseurs. This would take place on a site that seemed to illustrate, as it were, the very act of archaeology, not through a literal representation of such activity but through the experience of the site and its contents, which were beginning to suggest more and more a place for exploration and discovery.

Ultimately, it was not just the image but also the logic of "the archaeological site" that served to establish a manner of thinking and a rationality of images, a vocabulary of elements and a syntax of relationships—all of which proved defining even at this early stage of the project. It established a basic conceptual theme that from then on would allow us to resolve in a consistent way the myriad landscape and site problems and the architectural vocabulary of the new buildings that we were to design. In "archaeology," we found the theme of the narrative and the source of the architectural vocabulary.

THE STRATA WALL

Thus, at this consequential moment, both the design of the new Villa's institutional programs and the design of the architecture of its new buildings and its site converged on a clear, concise conceptual image. The convergence occurred not by thinking abstractly about how this or that should look, but simply by squarely facing the problem at hand and interpreting plans we had already developed using the architectural grammar that had emerged in the process.

By this time, it had become clear to the architects, engineers, builders, and managers that, because we would have to build so many structures, roads, and public spaces against

the slopes of the canyon, one of the project's most imposing structures would be not dramatic spans or heroic forms (expressive opportunities that architects hope for) but rather massive retaining walls. This unavoidable reality gave us the basic building and landscape organization of horizontal terraces. At first sight, the canyon would appear to restrict the architectural possibilities, because many structures would have to integrate themselves with the topography and it would no longer be possible to design buildings as free objects in space (as proposed in the first phase, in 1995). Instead, structures would now lean against the hills, thus losing their sculptural potential to play three-dimensionally against the landscape. Seen from a different perspective, however, it was clear that the basic structure of the landscape we were getting with the retaining walls would suit the original site's Mediterranean inspiration.

The architectural interpretation of this broad organizational principle began by following the logic of such structures (heavy and solid, with few openings) and of the site's horizontal stratification into many terraced levels (figs. 188, 189). It began to yield the results that we see today. The design of the retaining walls (and, by extension, of all walls) would follow the notion of thick, rich horizontal layers made out of earthy materials. We were still far from the final design of these walls, but the simple and systematic organization of vertical planes that today we see realized in diverse incarnations of different complexity and material expression is the direct result of a formal synthesis achieved in the summer of 1996. It embodied ideas and aspirations in a material system that made it possible to methodically interpret and design all the ingredients of the project concurrently; that formal synthesis encompassed the major components of the

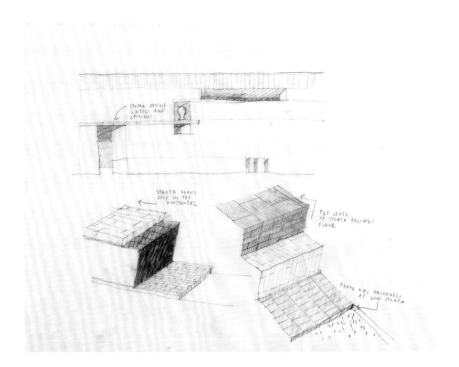

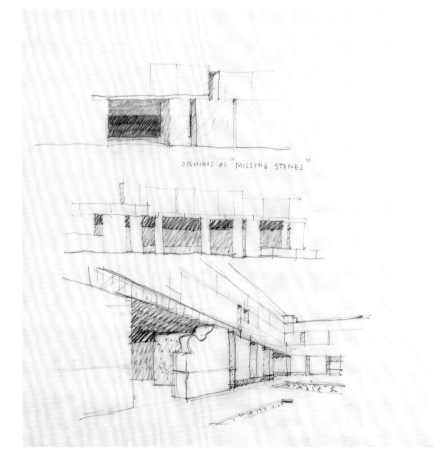

Figures 188, 189. Early sketches of the strata wall concept. The stratification of different masonry materials allows for the interpretation and resolution of different architectural demands and conditions on the site's many levels, for example, walls, vertical openings, floors, stairs, landings, etc.

Figure 190. Early study of the 250-seat Auditorium as a freestanding structure adjacent to the Cafe and Museum

Figure 191. Model of the Auditorium in its present location under the Ranch House lawn, which has been removed in the model

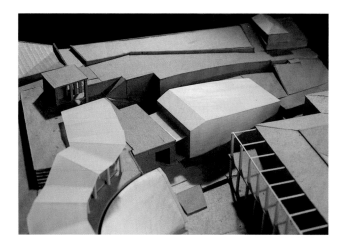

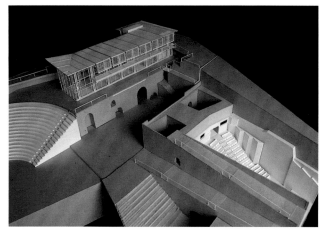

Master Plan, the guiding image of archaeology, and the architectural language's many voices.

THE MASTER PLAN OF 1996

Finding an overreaching architectural idea that would allow us to investigate the site and the program further gave us confidence. It encouraged us at every step to look for fresh opportunities and to discover new potential locations for an ever-growing program in an ever-shrinking usable terrain. For example, as pressures were mounting owing to the difficulty of accommodating all the programmatic requirements of the Museum in its existing building, the original basement auditorium, which we were initially charged with simply upgrading and remodeling, was jettisoned altogether, and we were forced to search for a new and better location. The Auditorium would be a prime amenity of the new Getty Villa and a place destined for large numbers of people, so this was a good move in its own right. Remodeling and refitting the existing auditorium in that inconvenient location would have been very costly and never would have achieved the high standards for multiple uses expected today in a museum facility of this caliber.

As the Auditorium emerged from the depths of the basement, though, there was no doubt that it would have to find a home in the areas near the site's new center of gravity, the Theater Plaza. Yet, as noted before, while such a center was now one of the most firmly established conditions of the Master Plan, it was nonetheless a restricted and relatively small area that was getting more crowded by the day. Many attempts were made to locate a 250-seat auditorium in a building somewhere around this focal point; however, it became evident that the actual area available was not only small but

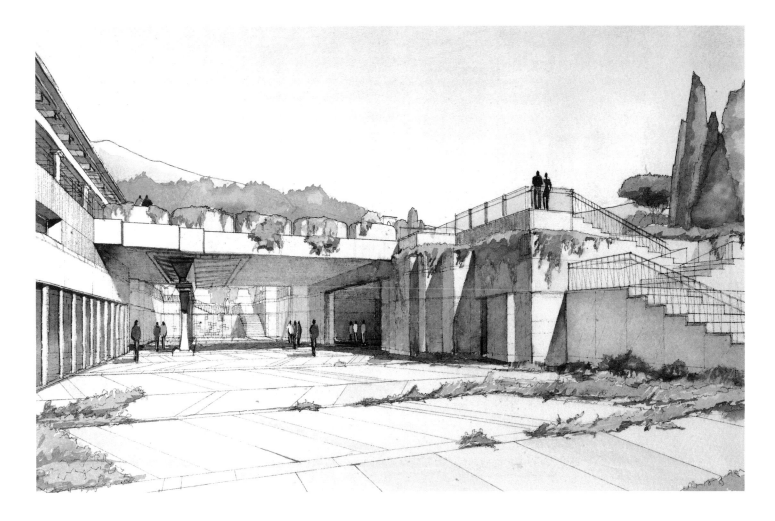

already dominated by the massive Museum building (figs. 190, 191). Erecting another substantial structure in its proximity would dangerously diminish the quality of the public areas, would confuse the logical hierarchy of spaces that the new entry sequence was trying to promote, and, worse yet, would generate a competition among buildings—both for attention and for space—that could never be settled.

The Auditorium found its place in an intermediate condition, effectively buried under the Ranch House lawn, but with its southwest corner exposed to the Theater Plaza. In our final plan, this semiburied condition would become the strategy we followed in locating most of our buildings (fig. 192). The Cafe (which evolved into a larger facility), the Museum Store, various educational facilities, and the Entry Pavilion would soon follow this pattern, with most of their volume hidden against the slopes of the canyon or under other buildings and only one or two sides exposed to the public areas.

Figure 192. Perspective study of an early version of the Auditorium in its definitive, partly subterranean location north of the Museum (Auditorium entrance shown at center). The Ranch House lawn conceals it from above, while its western and southern sides are exposed to the Theater Plaza.

Figure 193. The Outdoor Theater, conceived as a distinctive architectural piece disengaged from the strata wall

opposite
Figure 194. The Entry Pavilion, the other distinctive architectural event, was conceived as an unprecedented, open-air room partially buried in the landscape.

Thus, in the northern area of the Theater Plaza, a substantial collection of buildings and programs, structured in a complex and intricate juxtaposition of volumes, levels, and topographies, provides a vibrant and articulated formal backdrop to the public space without ever overwhelming it with its intrinsic massive size. Buildings "disappear" under the hills, revealing only their public fronts. As a result, this compact organization of programs and buildings creates a public space that is highly animated by architectural forms and materials. It supports a variety of choices for the visitor, all taking place at an intimate scale that promotes human contact, spontaneous interaction, and a direct architectural experience. Moreover, what we have

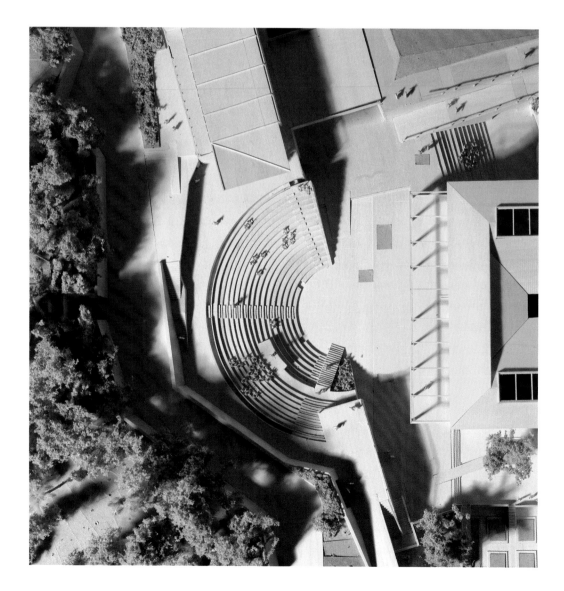

created in that area is a veritable collection of
buildings and activities—including a "bridge,"
an outdoor foyer for the Auditorium, a shop
front for the Store, a sunken courtyard, a public
fountain, various public stairs, covered and
open-air outdoor eating areas—that evoke an
ideal of urbanity.

In this charged, intense corner of the project, the strata wall rapidly evolved from design
concept to design tool, giving us the confidence
to imagine and design the public face of all these
programmatic components. As an expressive
design tool, it confirmed its appropriateness
because it could be adapted and reinterpreted
in each one of these conditions without violating
its nature. In this way, it helped contribute to
establishing a relaxed sense of unity throughout
the site.

EXCEPTIONS TO THE RULE

As with any rule, we made exceptions: first for
the Outdoor Theater (fig. 193) and then for the
Entry Pavilion. Against the continuous, fluid
architecture of the strata wall, which aimed
more at framing the Museum than at con-
fronting it, the Outdoor Theater was designed
to stand out, disengaging itself from the strata
wall (which in this one instance appears to pass
behind a building). By misbehaving, so to speak,
while in the company of quieter and more
obedient fellow buildings—by emphasizing its
historical incorrectness (no ancient theater
would have been located so close to a villa) and
its undaunted objecthood—it shines as the
unique artifact that it is. I believed strongly that
the Theater's uniqueness among the elements
of the ensemble deserved special architectural
treatment. Moreover, its physical nature is
ambiguous. On the one hand, it is modest in
bulk, occupying very little real space as it
spreads over the natural slope of the terrain.

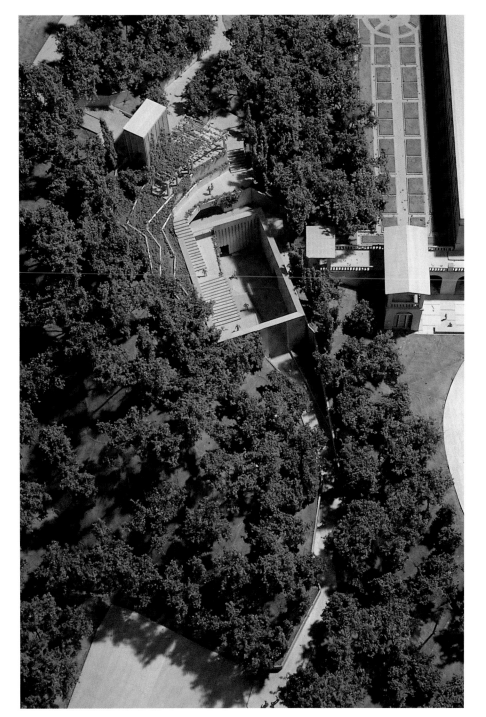

Figure 195. Unveiling of
the large Phase I model
on the porch of the Museum
at a meeting of the Trustees
in September 1996

On the other hand, its overt and sweeping gesture of welcome and embrace is imposing, allowing it to assert itself next to the Museum without overloading the site with volume and weight. It is, in many ways, the easiest piece to comprehend in the new ensemble. Yet it is also the strangest piece in the way it presents itself to the visitor: approaching from the south and at the end of the entry path, one sees it as an outgrowth of the landscape; at its northernmost tip, it is distinctively an object in space.

The Entry Pavilion is the other element that violates the "rules" of the strata wall (fig. 194). Its exceptionality is more intrinsic and rooted in its conception as a unique, unprecedented piece. Indeed, it results not from a design decision to treat it differently (the case with the Outdoor Theater, a piece that in itself is conventional) but from its spatial and programmatic nature. As the first architectural experience for a visitor to the Villa, this roofless concrete "room," semiburied in the west slope, offers neither historical nor conventional architectural referents that would guide the beholder in interpreting its meaning; as such, this surreal piece could only be consistent with itself. To counter the perils of the Entry Pavilion's potential autonomy from the rest of the project without compromising its uniqueness, we used its only shared attribute—its very exceptionality—to pair it with the Outdoor Theater. We treated both structures with identical surface material: sandblasted concrete with a distinctively colored aggregate. Thus, each of these two pieces of the entry sequence maintains its unique identity, yet both share a "functional" marking as the beginning or the end of the entry experience.

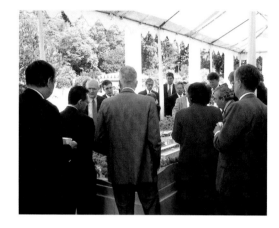

THE TRUSTEES' MEETING OF SEPTEMBER 1996

With all this progress, we prepared our presentation for the important Trustees' meeting of September 1996 (fig. 195). The project had evolved along the lines approved a year earlier, but certain realities had now sunk in. Indeed, while the project would be implemented in two phases, it was clear that an ever-increasing number of programmatic elements would need to be included in the first phase, such as a fully developed restaurant, a new auditorium, and a new bookstore (figs. 196, 197). The second phase was taking shape, to be sure, but it was more a hypothesis for the future than a commitment to a plan—or, at least, that was our designers' perception. In fact, for this important meeting we were asked to prepare an elaborate wooden model that detailed only the first phase of the project. To this day, that model has served to describe the Getty's plans for its new Villa. The continuing reliance on our old model, which reflects only Phase I of the superseded Master Plan of 1996, proves that even though major and drastic changes have altered the plan since then (such as adding the North Campus facilities in

1998), the fundamental elements that define the new Villa already existed in that early plan.

In short, this plan contained:

- The new entry sequence, including the Entry Pavilion, Museum Path, and drop-off improvements at the southern end of the Villa.

- The new Theater Plaza, bounded by the Museum, the Outdoor Theater, a 300-seat cafe with indoor and outdoor seating, a 250-seat auditorium, a bookstore, and miscellaneous educational and support facilities.

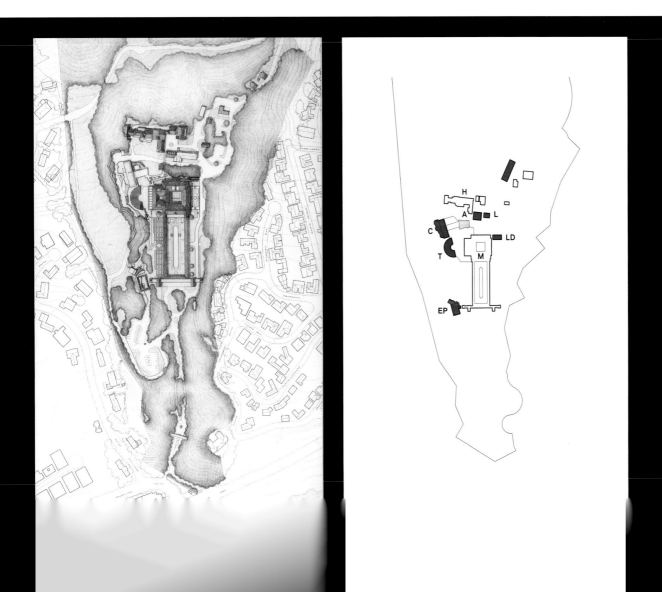

Master Plan, Phase I
SEPTEMBER 1996

Figures 196, 197. This iteration of the Master Plan retains many of the elements and characteristics of the September 1995 Phase I plan. The key differences include a larger cafe (by now a full-service restaurant), a new loading dock at the east end of the Museum, and the new subterranean location for the Auditorium.

Key:
- **A**   Auditorium
- **C**   Cafe
- **EP** Entry Pavilion
- **H**   Ranch House (existing)
- **L**   Conservation laboratories and research facilities
- **LD** Loading Dock
- **M**   Museum (existing)
- **T**   Outdoor Theater

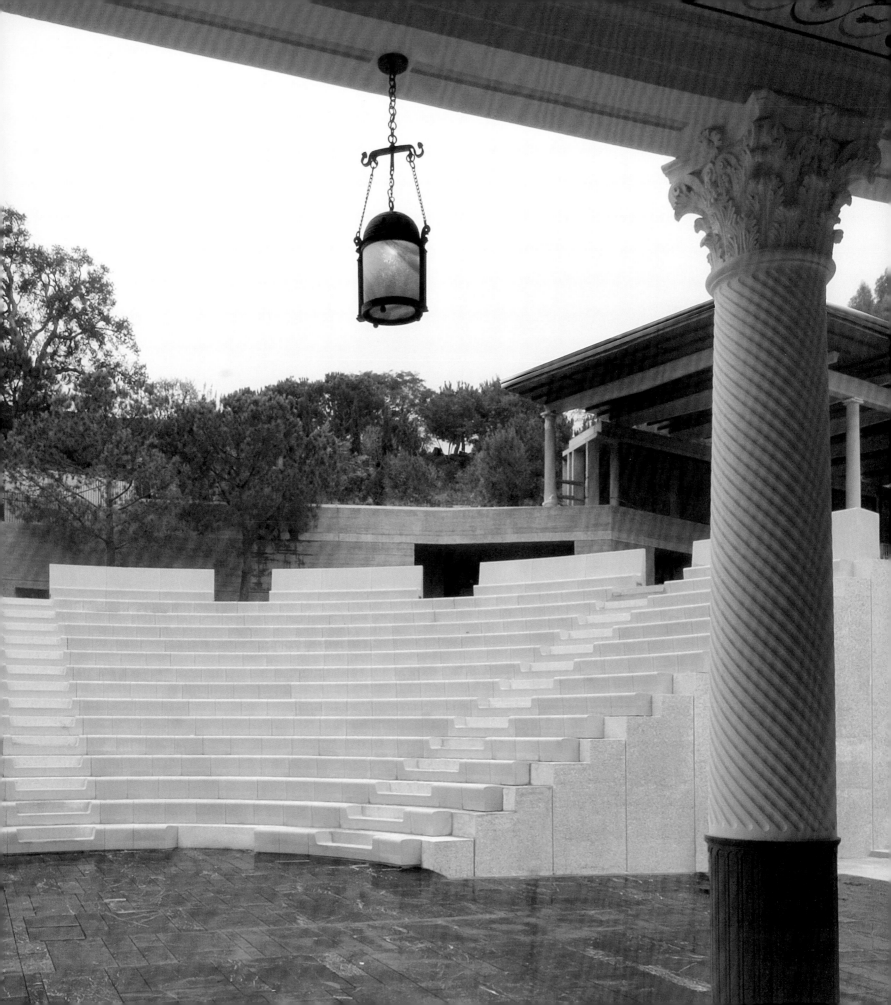

5 Systematic Exploration and Extraordinary New Findings

THE GETTY CENTER OPENS

The two years that followed (1997–98) saw intense development of the project's many elements. The more tedious aspects of this period—myriad consultations, meetings, and more meetings, trials and errors, bureaucratic frustrations, and the like, which characterize any design and construction project—have no place in this narrative. But a handful directly affected the project's evolution and are essential to record so that the reader can grasp the complexities and vicissitudes of the undertaking.

The opening of the Getty Center in Brentwood in December 1997 exerted a powerful impact on our project, and it could not have been otherwise. While its effect was largely indirect, there was no way that a concurrent Getty construction project such as the Villa, still in its creative stages, would not be influenced by all the news coming from Brentwood.

Simple quantitative questions arose. Parking again became a hot issue: Were we planning enough of it at the Villa? Visitors' services and amenities followed suit: Did we have enough bathrooms at the Villa? Did we need an orientation theater? Was the picnic area well sited and large enough to handle school groups? Did we have adequate storage for coats, umbrellas, and strollers? These questions would lead to broader concerns regarding a perceived shortage of space at the Center, and later to thinking

of the Villa as a "space resource" for the Trust at large, rather than a place dedicated exclusively to the archaeology and classical programs for which it was originally conceived. Such concerns coincided with a change of administration at the Getty, followed by inevitable adjustments to the institution's mission. Hence we saw both new programs and new strategies emerge. Specifically, we initially received a charge to include twenty thousand square feet of generic office space in the Master Plan. Soon after, we saw a momentous shift in the overall planning and implementation strategy: the new Villa was to be achieved in one single phase—whatever was going to be built would be built all at once.

While this came as a surprise, it was easily understood by those of us who had followed the process closely. Since the beginning of the project, in meetings and exchanges, the Getty had kept its neighbors and their neighborhood associations informed of the plans to remodel and expand the Villa. As the plans became firm and the time to move forward was approaching, there was a sense that apprehensiveness and perhaps hostility were developing among local residents, especially concerning the disruptions that a large construction site would impose on the area for years. The Getty saw it as a gesture of goodwill to eliminate its two-phase strategy, thus compressing the building activity into a "one construction site/only once" policy. In June 1998, we were instructed to reformulate the

opposite
Figure 198. The Outdoor Theater and Cafe seen from the West Porch

Master Plan as a building and institutional operation to be achieved in a single intervention.

This clean and simple gesture had serious
policy implications, for the Getty realized that
its promise to the neighbors to build only once
carried with it the burden of making now all
the necessary decisions about its total and future
needs. Hence, the initial request that we build
generic office space was soon superseded by
a more elaborate program incorporating more
than thirty thousand square feet of office and
conference space, new loading and grounds
maintenance facilities, and a chain of interrelated
program expansions.

THE EMERGENCE
OF THE NORTH CAMPUS

In rapid succession, many other decisions were
made on matters that had been left in limbo
for the hypothetical second phase. For instance,
when it was decided to build new state-of-the-
art conservation laboratories to replace the old
ones adjacent to the Ranch House, the Getty's
commitment to preserve the character of the
original residential areas on the site meant that
they would be built pretty much on the same
footprints that shaped the Monkey Court. It
followed that, consistent with the earlier decision to separate public entrances and parking
facilities from nonpublic ones (with a southern
public entrance and parking, and nonpublic
northern access and parking), and given that the
additional generic office building would cater
to staff and scholars—in short, not to Museum
visitors—these programs found their natural
place in the area east of the Monkey Court,
next to the nonpublic parking. Of course, the
additional programs created increased parking
needs. This led to the decision to build two
large garages: a 200-stall facility dedicated to

staff and business visitors arriving from the
northern entrance via Los Liones Drive, and a
250-stall facility used mostly by Museum visitors
coming by way of the Pacific Coast Highway
and positioned on the existing camper lot site, a
lower plateau southwest of the Museum proper,
which originally served as overflow to the
original garage under the Villa (figs. 199, 200).

These planning issues were quickly decided,
and an entirely new condition emerged that
provided still more opportunities for rethinking
and conceptualizing many other elements. The
size of the garage at the northern edge of the
site forced us to focus on the entire area north
of the Museum and east of the Ranch House,
where certain features of the terrain exacerbate
the clash between buildings and topography.
Indeed, immediately above the Museum, the
canyon turns sharply to the east, and the slope
of the west hill becomes more accentuated. This
allowed us to bury most of the garage, leaving
only its southeast corner showing above ground.
Nevertheless, what emerged was substantial
and imposing, because the bulk of the garage's
volume created a podium on the level of the
existing Monkey Court, which offered a more
ample space for expansion. The new buildings
could all be deployed on this plateau in a
way that would maintain a positive relationship
with the scale of the Ranch House.

In any case, with new "real estate" to work
with, the footprint area of the Ranch House
complex doubled in size. In order to implement
the shared desire to recapture the proportions
and character of the original Monkey Court as
a hard-scape plaza with a fountain in the center,
this new area of the Getty Villa was conceived
and developed around two very distinct courtyards. On the one hand, there was the "new"
Monkey Court (officially renamed the Conservation Court), surrounded by laboratories on its
four sides so that not only were the proportions

and character of the original evoked but its function was replicated too. On the other hand, the office and conference spaces and other facilities were developed around a new courtyard of similar dimensions. However, that courtyard was organized more as a green cloister, with its northern side overtaken by the slopes of the hills and natural landscape that cascade down and into it, bringing a dramatic confluence of nature and architecture to this remote corner of the site (fig. 201).

At the "hinge" between these two courtyards, a staff cafe was added, because it was becoming clear that the food services in the public areas could not accommodate a larger staff as well, and because it would make sense to provide a quieter and simpler restaurant for the staff, scholars, and non-Museum visitors. This active yet simple new programmatic component complemented the aforementioned cloister's role, which acts as a transition from the natural landscape that receives the visitor from the

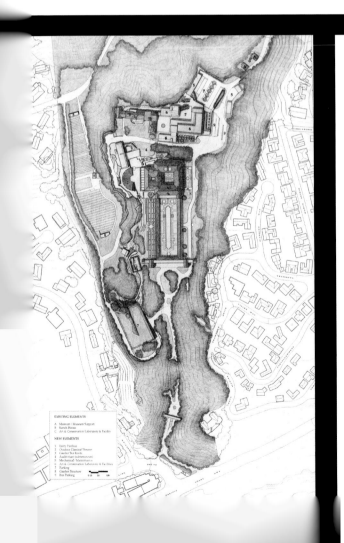

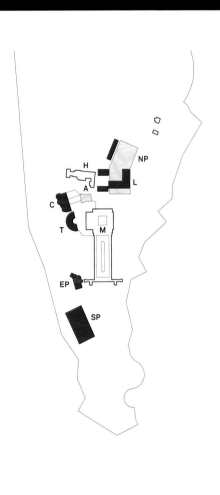

Final Master Plan
SEPTEMBER 1999

Figures 199, 200. This final version of the Master Plan incorporates new programs in the North Campus, as well as two new parking structures. This single-phase plan was fully and faithfully implemented in the Villa's construction and renovations between 2000 and 2005, largely as shown in these drawings.

Key:

A	Auditorium
C	Cafe
EP	Entry Pavilion
H	Ranch House (existing)
L	Conservation laboratories and research facilities
M	Museum (existing)
NP	North Parking (staff)
SP	South Parking (public)
T	Outdoor Theater

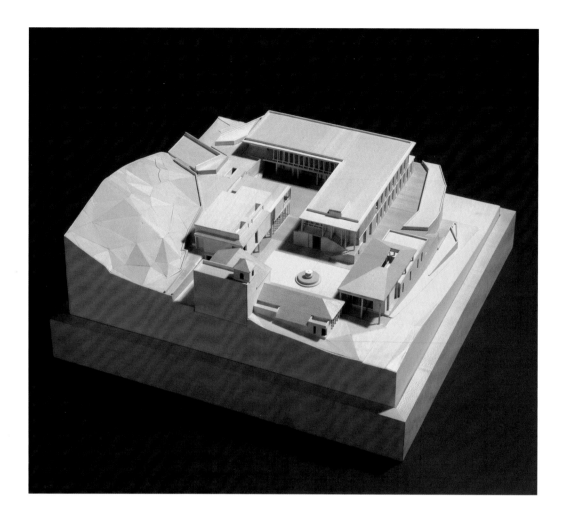

Figure 201. Site model showing the new buildings and the two courtyards of the North Campus

business and service entrance to the north, and also provides the access and threshold from the parking area into the upper complex and the Villa beyond (figs. 202, 203). In short, the staff, as well as those coming to a conference, to the laboratories, to the library and research facilities, or to the classrooms, would enter the site at this point, and could quickly and easily find their destinations in the entirely new complex north of the Museum without interfering with the public activities of facilities to the south. What had started as a simple upgrade to J. Paul Getty's old residence, the Ranch House, became a full-fledged academic and administrative complex, which from then on was referred to as the North Campus.

The North Campus plateau allowed us to sort out and organize the nonpublic working areas with an ease and simplicity that brought a definitive clarity to another major programmatic component of the Master Plan: the service areas. Again, the area's actual physical shape produced a logical interpretation of its attributes and suggested new possible uses. We had now acquired a large "podium." This is a very ancient and clever architectural device, one that the Romans had deftly used to differentiate in a building between what needs to be revealed and what needs to be concealed; what is figure and what is ground; what is accessible and what is restricted. Our podium fulfilled this role well by indicating a way to resolve the whole service area for the Villa, which until then had been too close to the entrance or other public amenities.

Given the prominence of the southeasterly exposed corner of the podium, together with the

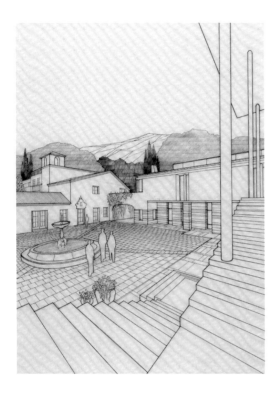

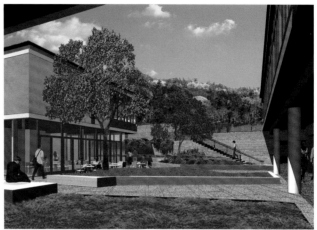

Figure 202. The new Conservation Court preserves the original fountain and the general configuration, scale, and function of its surrounding buildings.

Figure 203. This computer rendering of the new Office Court—a cloisterlike space—shows the staff entrance from the garage (right), and the relationship of the courtyard to the hillside and native landscape, as well as the new staff cafe (left) as a hinge between the Office Court and the Conservation Court (the Monkey Court).

removal of the second-phase entry sequence from this area, the space left between the garage and the northeast side of the Museum almost naturally became a service court. This change from what had been, until recently, the most public area of the now-defunct Phase II was not unwelcome. Three years into the project, and with most planning decisions already made, we were still trying to find a location for the Museum's loading dock and freight elevators (fig. 204). We had attempted—without success—to place these facilities on every possible point along the Museum's east and northeast sides away from the public areas. Due to the lack of space in and around the Museum proper, we could never find a location that would accommodate the maneuvers of delivery trucks necessary for the safe unloading of art. Because

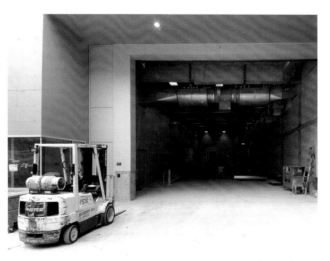

Figure 204. The loading dock located below the Office and Antiquities Conservation buildings

Key:
1 South Portico   **6** Stairway
2 Restrooms   **7** Herb Garden
3 Information Desk   **8** Arrival Balcony
4 Coat Check   **9** Museum Path
5 Elevators

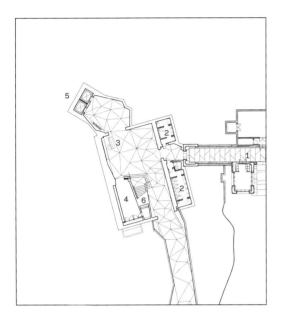 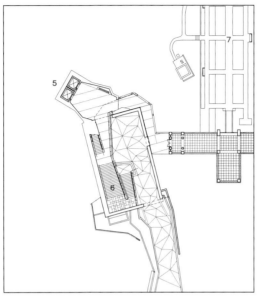 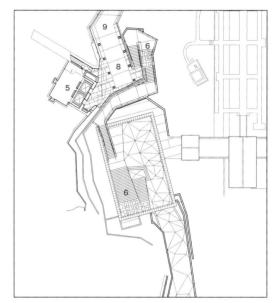

Figure 205. The experience of the reimagined Getty Villa begins here at the ground level of the Entry Pavilion, which houses key visitor services (e.g., orientation/information desk, public restrooms, coat/parcel check, etc.) and which has direct connections to parking and drop-off areas.

Figure 206. The intermediate level of the Entry Pavilion, where visitors can choose to end their Museum visit by way of the gardens

Figure 207. On the upper level of the Entry Pavilion is the terminus of stairs and elevators from levels below, initiating the garden promenade northward toward the Theater Plaza and the entrance to the Museum.

the new structures in the North Campus would require larger foundations and excavations, we were now manipulating the ground in that area, making it easier to resolve the service area's geometric and spatial demands. The most satisfactory resolution was to locate all loading-related facilities in the garage/podium building; thus, the need for a tunnel arose naturally—fulfilling an old (and virtually forgotten) desire to join the conservation laboratories with the Museum. That goal now could be achieved together with the full set of programmatic requirements for its service areas.

MORLEY CONSTRUCTION

About this time, another defining event occurred: the selection of the general contractor, Morley Construction Company (at that time already engaged as general contractor for Rafael

Moneo's Our Lady of the Angels Cathedral in downtown Los Angeles). After a rigorous search in early 1997, during which several candidates were interviewed and heavily scrutinized by all of us involved, Morley emerged as the unanimous choice for this complex renovation and expansion. Initially, it would be involved in developing the project's budget and schedule and would serve as our "sounding board" while we began to explore the project's myriad details and constructability. Eventually, this talented team would build the new Villa complex. The choice proved to be the correct one, as the technical experience Morley had gained from the Cathedral—whose schedule by now had overtaken ours in Malibu—would later pay significant dividends during the construction of the Getty Villa. Moreover, the personal relationships that were established years before construction was to begin would streamline communications and spawn a long-term esprit de corps. More important, Morley's early selection allowed its entire team to learn the project's common architectural language together with the rest of us, while it was developing, such that nuance and detail were eventually understood by everyone engaged in the process—from the project executives on down to the countless workers in the field.

THE DEFINITIVE ENTRY SEQUENCE

The conflation of the project into a single phase had an even more resounding consequence. The entry sequence proposed only for Phase I would become the permanent setting for the first encounter between the visitor and the new Getty Villa. The Entry Pavilion and the entry path could now exploit their potential meaning in the total ensemble. Interestingly, while no fundamental change occurred in the overall configuration of this sequence as inherited from the previous two-phase plan, the certainty of its now becoming permanent allowed us to realize fully its promises and become more assertive in developing the sequence as a protracted threshold full of surprises and discoveries. Thus, the size of the Entry Pavilion became larger because it was now seen as the logical place to install visitor services like restrooms, orientation facilities, kiosks for brochures, and lockers (figs. 205–7). At the same time, the entry path could now be conceived as a landscape narrative along which the visitor could discover, one step at a time, the component elements of the new Getty Villa through framed vignettes and surprising findings (figs. 208, 209).

 As we focused on the details of this area, another potential architectural insight soon emerged. While visitors would park at a garage south of the Entry Pavilion and then walk toward it along a direct path (figs. 210, 211),

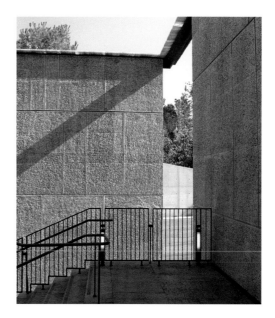

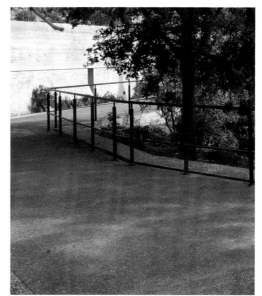

Figures 208. A landing in the Entry Pavilion

Figures 209. A section of the Museum Path

it was possible and desirable to bring cars and buses closer to the entry in order to drop off visitors before parking. A large porte cochere was then conceived by reinterpreting and redesigning the series of bricked-over arches, which previously had been a marginal aspect of the building, providing, as it did, for cars to enter and exit through its only two open arches. (Coincidentally, this was the location of the poorly conceived public entrance to the Museum via the garage.) By opening all the arches and thereby creating a real portico, we could create a properly scaled public drop-off where large numbers of visitors could find protection from the elements and proceed toward the Entry Pavilion through a dramatic tunneled gallery at its west end (figs. 212, 213).

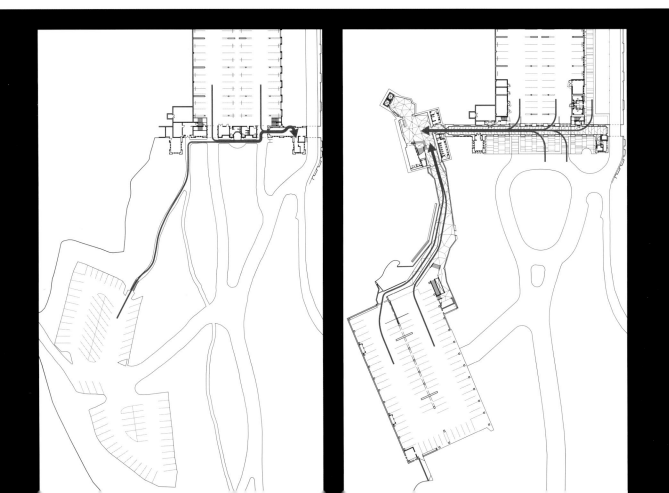

Figure 210. Diagram showing the former entrance sequence from public parking areas to the Museum's entrance via a stair and elevator at the southeast corner of the Outer Peristyle

Figure 211. Diagram showing the new arrival sequence from (a) drop-off areas; (b) an existing parking garage underneath the peristyle garden; (c) a new public garage—all leading to the Entry Pavilion

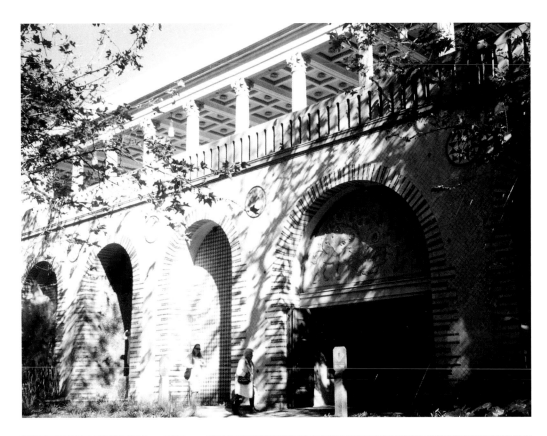

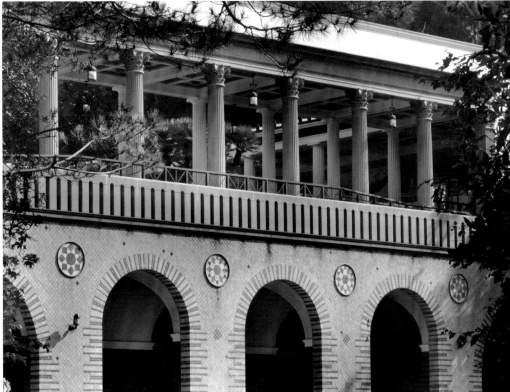

Figure 212. The Museum's south facade with the original vehicular entrance to the public garage (which also operated as the pedestrian entrance to the Museum by way of an undersized and wholly inadequate stair and elevator) under the Outer Peristyle. Note the stone and brick infill panels in the archways

Figure 213. The same view of the south facade, showing the transformation of the existing archways to create an open yet covered pedestrian connection from the existing garage and new drop-off areas to the Entry Pavilion

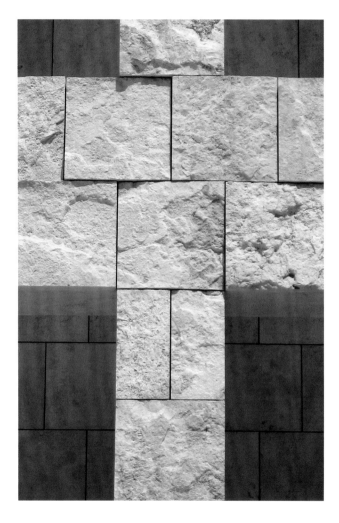

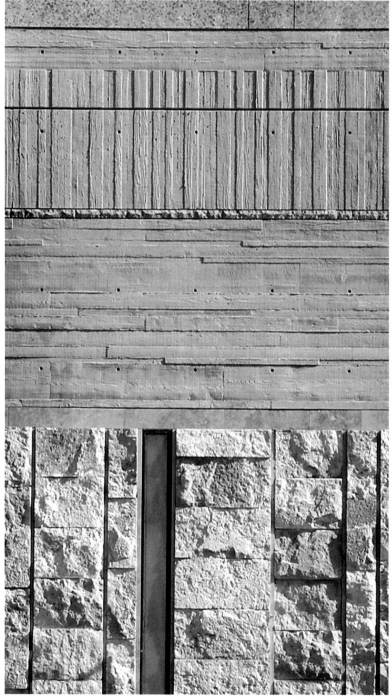

Figure 214. Partial view of Roman travertine wall cladding at the Getty Center

Figure 215. Partial view of the strata wall, showing the Noce travertine wall cladding at the Getty Villa

THE MATERIALS OF THE STRATA WALL

The opening of the Getty Center not only encouraged us to make propitious adjustments and additions to our initial architectural program but also positively affected our design by leading us into a dialogue with another architect's distinctive materials and vocabulary of forms. These were giving the Center such a strong character that we were intrigued by them. Clearly, the Villa and the Center represented two very different conceptions of architecture. In terms of planning principles, however, they were not very different.

Richard Meier's Master Plan relied on classical precedent in ways probably even more conscious and determined than our own moves at the Villa (see also J. Walsh and D. Gribbon, *The J. Paul Getty Museum and Its Collections* [Los Angeles, 1997], pp. 85–90). Other than a bare hill, Meier had received very little as "context," and he could trace the pedigree of his moves all the way to Hadrianic Roman planning; we, on the other hand, were guided and influenced as much by the limited possibilities of a crowded steep canyon and its existing structures as by planning principles.

Meier's architectural expression at the Center follows a very different direction from ours. At the Center, Meier continued his research into a modernist vocabulary of abstraction rooted in early-twentieth-century aesthetic models—a course for which he is so admired. Yet, there is a notable departure at the Center from his most characteristic earlier palette of materials. The Center is characterized by the pervasive use of rough stone in the vertical planes. The choice of Roman travertine, presented in cleft rectangular blocks some three inches thick, was an inspired and felicitous choice. These rugged, expressive components are deployed on the walls of the Center in abstract orthogonal grids, where they appear

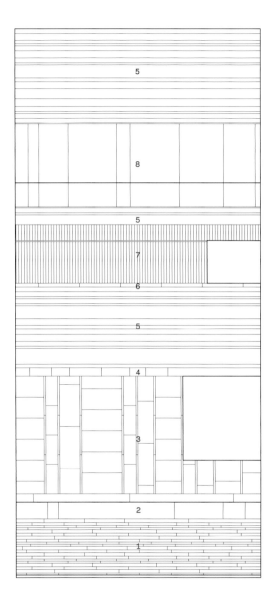

Figure 216. Elevation drawing of the various materials used in the strata wall

Key:

1 Honed China Black marble
2 Ground and acid-etched concrete with Black Raven decorative aggregate
3 Cleft Noce travertine, with honed Noce travertine "fillets"
4 Honed Noce and bronze channel
5 Horizontal board-formed, cast-in-place concrete
6 Cleft porphyry stone
7 Vertical board-formed, cast-in-place concrete and two-inch-wide solid-stock, Afrormosia wood laid vertically
8 Ground and acid-etched concrete with wine-red decorative aggregate

weightless and in suspension because of the effect produced by the quarter-inch reveal joint that sharply separates one block from the other with a crisp line of shadow (fig. 214).

We were also impressed by the iconic status the material acquired with the public. It became an instant symbol of the Getty, eventually and inevitably being sold in small cubes as souvenirs at the Center's bookstore. We realized that even though the strategies and approaches to architecture of the two Getty campuses were dramatically different from one another, the incorporation of such a lovely stone in our project

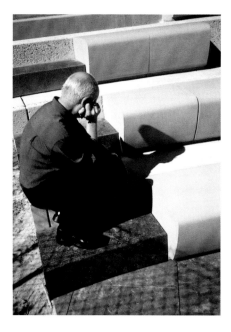
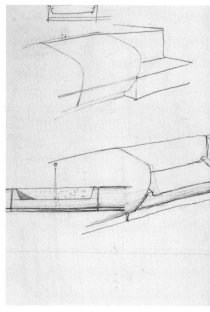
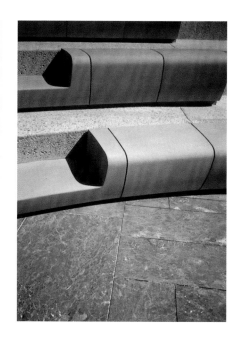

Figure 217. Early version (ca. 1999) of a full-scale stair and seat mock-up for the Outdoor Theater showing alternating steps of precast concrete and porphyry stone

Figure 218. Author's sketches of the Outdoor Theater's redesigned steps

Figure 219. Full scale mock-up showing final design integration of steps and seats

would not only give us the expressive material we were looking for but also allow us to articulate the kindred spirit of the two campuses. We achieved this bond by using travertine in a notably different way: while the stone plaques at the Center appear weightless and repetitive, the ones in the Villa's strata wall are of different sizes and are used in a hierarchical fashion (figs. 215, 216). They are the most important stratum of the wall and the heaviest of all its materials, and as such they occupy its lowest layer—at the plaza level—in an unusual bonding pattern that emphasizes the stone's weight and the reliance of each block, one on another, to "build" the structural strength of the wall.

At both the Center and the Villa, travertine's deployment clearly illustrates one of architecture's fundamental classical expressive devices —namely, that of "representing" construction. At the Center, where the buildings rely on a column grid rather than on walls for principal support, the heavy stone—a quintessential

weight-bearing material—appears as the veneer it is, with no structural function. As such, it must be deployed as weightless. At the Villa, on the other hand, the same stone, also a veneer, is used to represent the structural nature of a supporting wall. As such, it is deployed with the particular bonding pattern expressive of its weight-bearing role.

With the choice of Noce travertine—a darker, chocolate-color hue used in the Museum lobby at the Getty Center—we set in motion the final stage in defining the strata wall and making all the other decisions about materials affecting the look and character of the new buildings. The travertine stratum would be followed upward by successive layers: horizontal board-formed concrete, bronze channels and soffits, thin red porphyry stone, Afrormosia wood, vertical board-formed concrete, ground and polished concrete with integral decorative aggregate, and more horizontal board-formed concrete.

At this stage, with materials defined and every building firmly positioned, we embarked with Morley Construction upon the task of creating full-size mock-ups: first, we built our fundamental version of the strata wall; next, the theater seats (figs. 217–19), composite floor patterns, concrete, and so on; and finally, the office building in the North Campus. The experience and knowledge gained through this testing method cannot be overemphasized. Mock-up construction coincided with the addition of Bradley Johnson to our team. He arrived in 1996 to lead the technical and material development of the project in Boston and then, in 2001, in Malibu, where he was "in situ" at the Machado and Silvetti outpost at the Villa every day until the end of construction. His impressive technical expertise, coupled with his meticulous understanding of the complex and nuanced conceptual fabric of this project, had a far-reaching and positive influence on the resolution of the myriad details and systems of the project.

A NOTE OF DISSENT

Throughout the design of the new buildings, I wanted to mark all the distinctive attributes of the new architecture described in the preceding chapters. I also wanted to accentuate the unique conditions under which they emerged in relation to the preexisting aesthetic references that the Villa established so strongly and literally with the ancient world, antiquities, and classical architecture. To accomplish those goals, I introduced a somewhat mysterious sculptural form obtained by subtracting a substantial mass of concrete in the exposed northern corner of the Outdoor Theater, which I felt could easily accommodate special treatment, as it was overly massive and inexpressive (fig. 220). The sculptural form's sensuous, curvaceous configuration found no match at the Villa, and

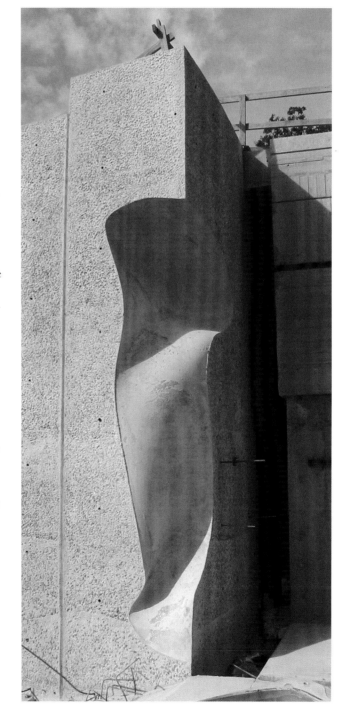

Figure 220. The controversial sculptural form, cast into the northeastern corner of the Outdoor Theater, as built in summer 2004

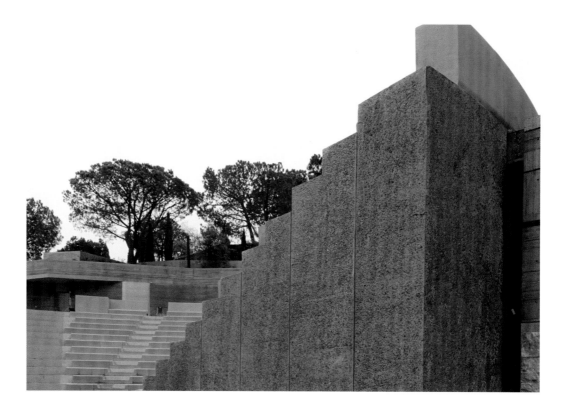

Figure 221. The Outdoor
Theater after the sculptural
form was removed in fall 2004
by filling in the void

it stood alone as an extraordinary occurrence, an "apparition" that pointed to the ineluctable contemporaneous aspect of all this architecture that at the same time was trying to be deferential to history. In this element only, there was a very conscious effort to stop the visitor with an open visual question in an otherwise smooth journey of discoveries.

Not entirely surprisingly, this "inexplicable" form was controversial as soon as it was built in the summer of 2004. In a job that was as complex and that lasted as long as the Villa project, it is remarkable that this was the only design feature on which we and the Getty agreed to disagree and that, once built, the Getty eventually chose to remove. This event illustrates well the intellectual and aesthetic dilemmas and paradoxes that the project posed to all its

protagonists. While nobody objected to the sculptural void's intrinsic formal and material interest, craftsmanship, or even beauty, its drastic departure from the overall vocabulary developed for the new buildings put the Getty and us on opposite sides. The Getty objected to its "strangeness," its lack of "belonging"— but it was precisely our intention to produce an element with such transgressive attributes. While the logic and intelligence of the arguments presented for or against such attributes made for a lively discussion, in the end the element's nonessentiality condemned it (fig. 221).

In the meantime, a host of aesthetic issues (purity vs. aberration, coherence vs. heterogeneity, orthodoxy vs. heresy, defamiliarization, transgression, and deviation) were brought to the fore, confirming once more the apparently inexhaustible capacity of "the Villa problem" to generate artistic polemics.

On our end, though, there was a strongly felt urge to address the project's self-consciousness about history, precedent, and antique models—in short, its overt referential nature, which so strongly dominated important formal decisions in the design process. For us, the project's irresistible, seductive, and treacherous play with the past required an intervention that would cause a momentary disconnect from the Villa's comfortable allusions; a finger pointing at the new buildings that would provide another key to unlock the new ensemble. While it was argued that our new buildings at the Getty Villa, with their looseness of forms, material complexity, and crafty assemblage, were the best expression of the Villa's insertion in a contemporary world, we would have preferred to add an incisive, concise sign, something to shake up the visitor with a pointed, discordant, irreducible gesture.

Such a move would have found its place in a tradition of poetic estrangement that we feel is close to our aesthetics. Such a tactic has a long life in the history of art, as exemplified by the anamorphic skull of Holbein's painting *The Ambassadors*, the Pucciniesque aria of the Italian tenor in the midst of Richard Strauss's opera *Der Rosenkavalier*, or the black-and-white silent movie clip inserted in Pedro Almodóvar's film *Talk to Her*—all flashes of dissonance in a broader coherent piece that suddenly and directly confronts the beholder with other aesthetic propositions that the artists felt were necessary to complete the message, to establish a distance, or to mark a difference.

In a project like the Getty Villa—one with such broad public ambition and loaded with all the burdens that architecture must bear as a "functional" art—such structural form was perhaps too personal and rarified for the Getty to include. After the form's removal, the Villa's

new architecture was restored to an unimpeachable aesthetic orthodoxy that could never be faulted for incoherence (and, of course, the form would never be missed by those unaware of its short-lived existence). Yet we will always feel the absence of this piece; it is the missing utterance that would have completed our discourse on contemporary architecture and our intervention at the Villa.

THE MUSEUM AS AN ARTIFACT

With the strata wall fully worked out as a physical tool to articulate the architecture of all new buildings and landscape structures, with archaeological excavation as a guiding image to interpret and develop the complexities of the site, and with the entry sequence definitively established on the west slope of the canyon and along a south-to-north direction, it required only a small imaginative leap to arrive at a conceit that would satisfy our concerns about the higher entry path and ensure the autonomy of the entry sequence that we all sought.

At this stage, the Entry Pavilion would act as a horizontal and vertical threshold that, by virtue of being partially buried in the hill, created ideal conditions for a transitional preparatory experience. Once inside the Entry Pavilion, having negotiated all the initial transactions associated with arrival (parking, check-in, information), the visitor would find his connections to the world outside severed, with the open sky the only remaining link and with nothing perceivable ahead. The enclosure would keep visitors in a state of expectation. Rodolfo and I have dreamed of creating this kind of experience ever since 1983, when we created *Taberna Ancipitis Formae—Architectorum Machadus Silvettusque Mirabile Inventio* for a show at the Leo Castelli Gallery, *Follies: Architecture for the Late-Twentieth-Century Landscape* (fig. 222).

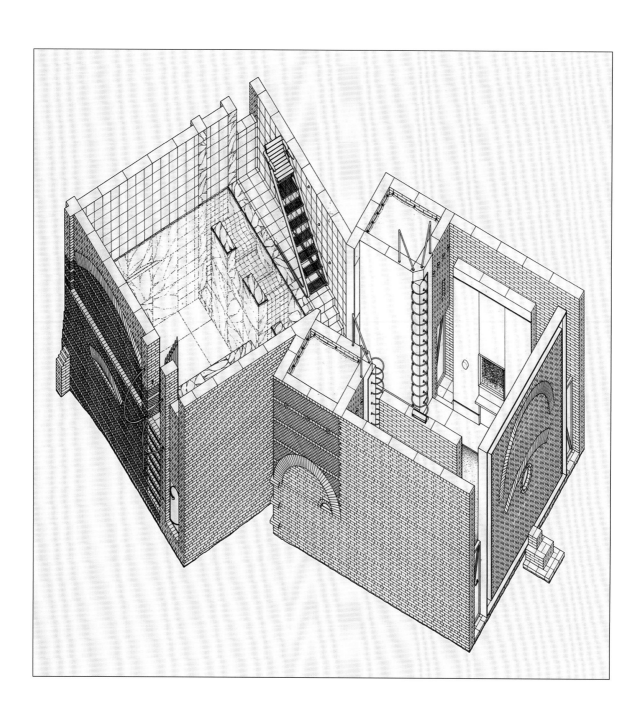

Our partially buried roofless room would be the perfect device for heightening a sense of expectation and promoting the suspension of disbelief that the Villa requires (figs. 223, 224). Ready to embark on an adventure, the visitor will naturally seek to exit this roofless chamber, and the way out is clear: the open sky and the large, conspicuous stairway—the space's dominant features—provide clear indications of what to do next in this mute and sober room. The stairs free themselves from the enclosure and meander up the slope. In reaching the end of the ascent, the visitor, who had entered the property from the Pacific Coast Highway in a straight south-to-north course, steps onto a balcony facing south and has a view that explains the topography and location without need of words. The two slopes of the canyon converging at the bottom, with the horizontal line of the Pacific Ocean horizon closing the triangle, are all that is necessary to orient visitors and to communicate the structure of the Villa's site (figs. 225, 226). A similar experience awaits those who reach the same balcony by elevator from the "grotto" located off the Entry Pavilion's northwest corner.

Visitors will have only one choice now, as the balcony is the point of departure for the path that will move them north toward the Villa's center of gravity. This trail, just above the roof of the Villa, is now the key to the story. From this modest height and along the course of its length, the Villa presents itself in a drastically different way. Instead of appearing as an imposing building at the bottom of the canyon (along, under, or inside of which one is forced to move), the Villa is seen now from above in fragments and framed by the trees—cypress, oleanders, olives, and pines—that grow on the slope. As the visitor moves along and looks down, he or she glimpses vignettes: here, a sliver of the Outer Peristyle's long walls that

offer just enough to intuit the whole; there, a portion of the parterre pattern of the Herb Garden; further along its length, a glimpse of the South Balcony of the main building (figs. 227, 228). The Villa, bracketed by quotation marks as it were, is now properly framed: it can be "observed"—or, more appropriately, it is "exposed" rather than "imposed," and this exposition allows the visitor to assume the role of spectator and to see the Villa as just one more artifact of the collection before entering it and exploring its space.

As visitors move north along this path of discoveries and insinuations, a "natural outcrop" blocks the path and the view, forcing pedestrians to travel in a sharp S around it. This short movement helps to unveil suddenly an unexpected panoramic view of the Getty Villa in its totality. Indeed, in sharp contrast with the views the visitor had been experiencing along the path—partial, and to the side—a panoramic view of the whole institution now expands in all directions (figs. 229, 230). To the left is the natural bowl that is the Outdoor Theater (which, on one's arrival, performs the role of offering a stairway leading down to the clearly visible plaza in front and at the center of the whole ensemble twenty feet below); to the right, the Museum, and, further away, the Auditorium, Museum Store, and Education Court. In front and at the same level at which he or she stands, the visitor sees the prominent canopy of the restaurant as well as its terrace bridging the open foyer of the Auditorium. Beyond and up the hill, the Ranch House is completely visible and integrated into the composition; to its right, just a hint of the North Campus is offered.

The entry sequence has not only met the functional need to organize the movement of visitors from parking lot to Museum entrance; it has also provided the opportunity to present the new Getty Villa as an institution in its totality

opposite
Figure 222. *Taberna Ancipitis Formae—Architectorum Machadus Silvettusque Mirabile Inventio.* Axonometric ink drawing of Machado and Silvetti's entry for the exhibit *Follies: Architecture for the Late-Twentieth-Century Landscape,* commissioned by the Leo Castelli Gallery, New York, in 1983

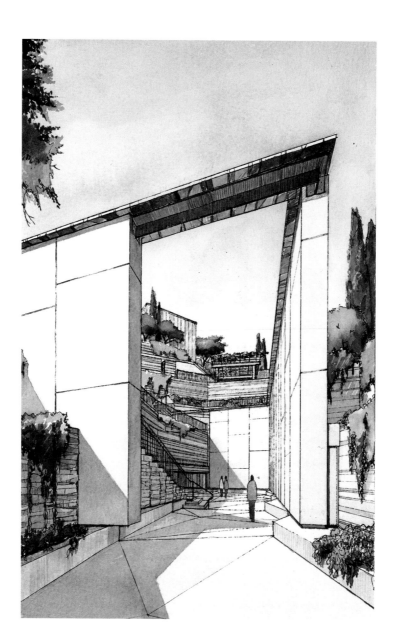

Figure 223. Entry Pavilion design rendering (ca. 1996). Arrival from visitor parking through the Pavilion's portal. From this point of entry until the landing on the Arrival Balcony, visitors experience the Pavilion as a protracted vertical threshold between the outside world and the Villa.

opposite

Figure 224. The Entry Pavilion

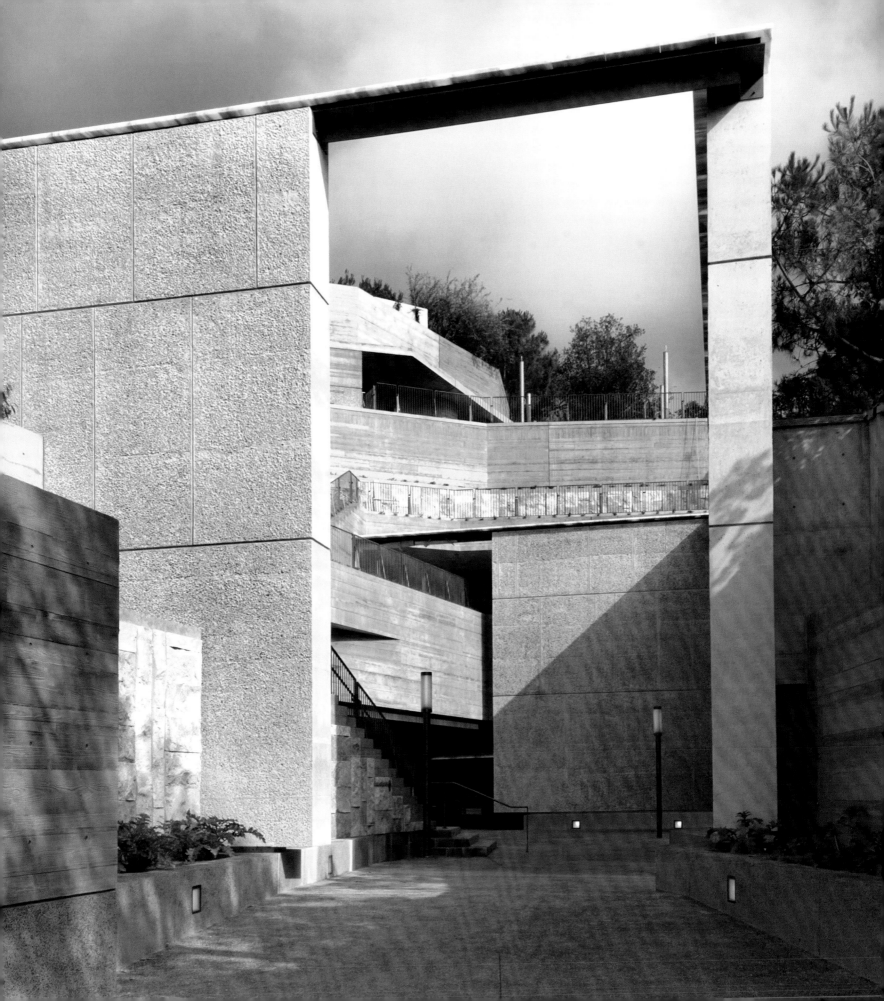

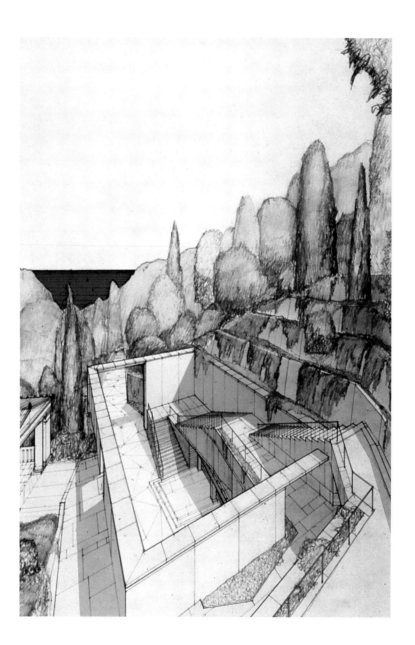

Figure 225. Design rendering of the Entry Pavilion's upper level (ca. 1996). Arriving at this dramatic overlook, visitors take in views of the Pacific before beginning their journey northward along the Museum Path.

opposite
Figure 226. The Entry Pavilion seen from its upper level

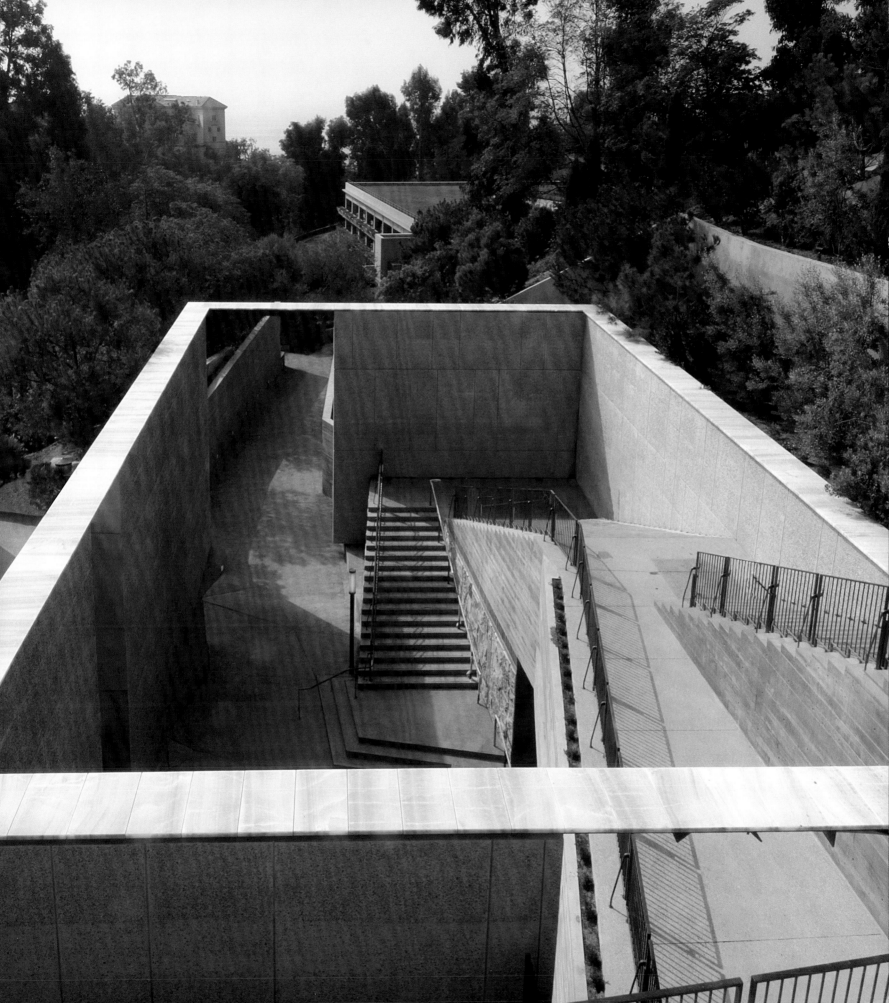

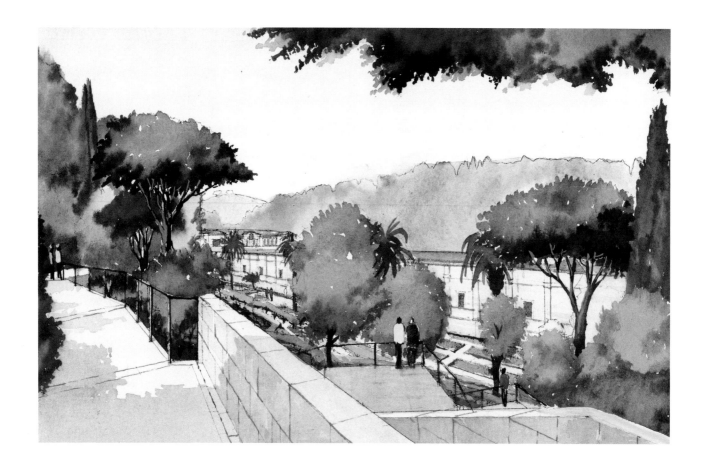

Figure 227. Design rendering (ca. 1996) of the hillside gardens, with partial views of the Museum and the path leading up to it

opposite
Figure 228. The Museum Path

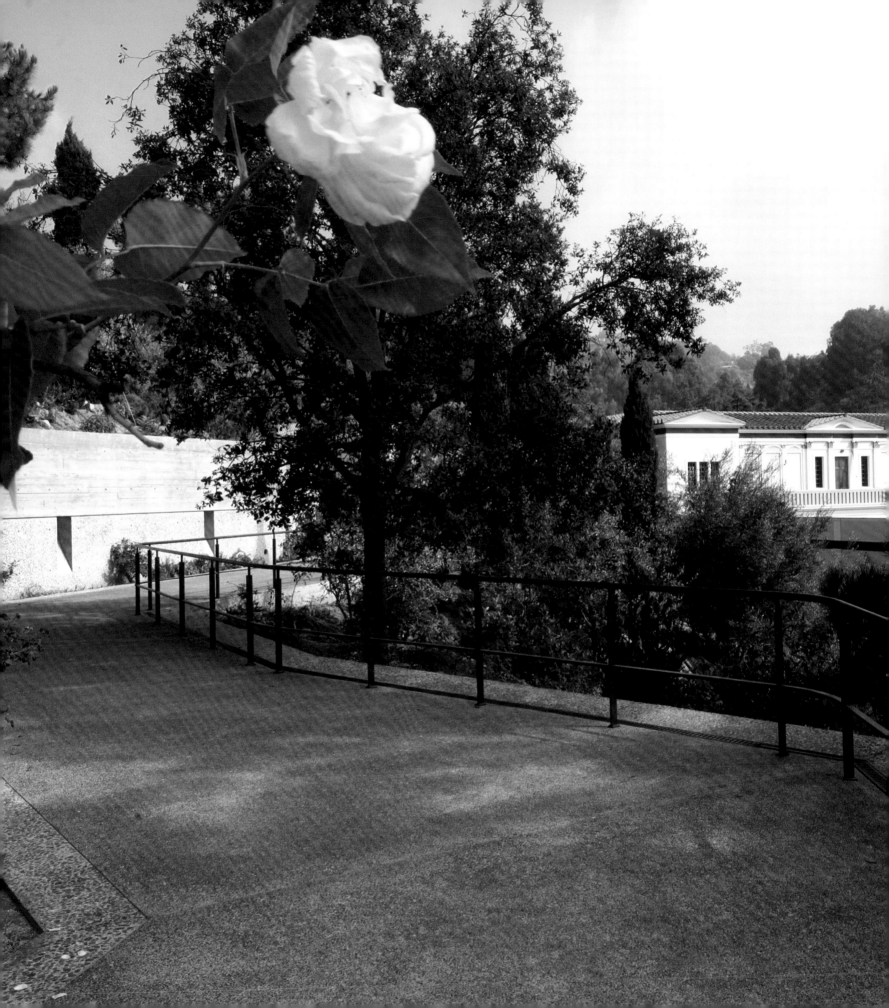

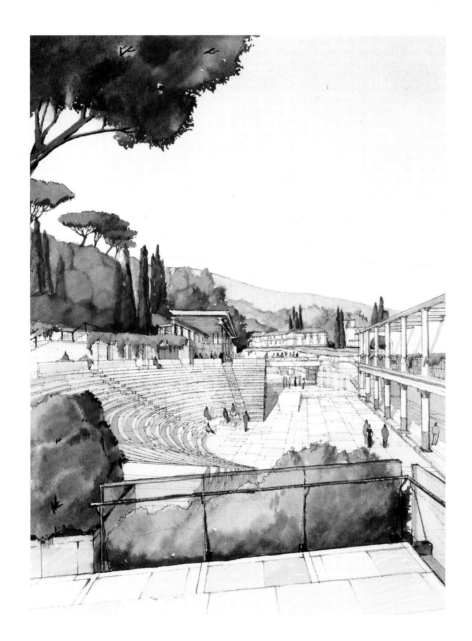

Figure 229. Design rendering (ca. 1996) of the Arrival Balcony. From this vantage point, a panoramic view of the new Getty Villa is revealed.

opposite
Figure 230. The site under construction in early 2005. Looking from the Arrival Balcony over the Outdoor Theater and Theater Plaza toward the Cafe, Museum Store, and Ranch House

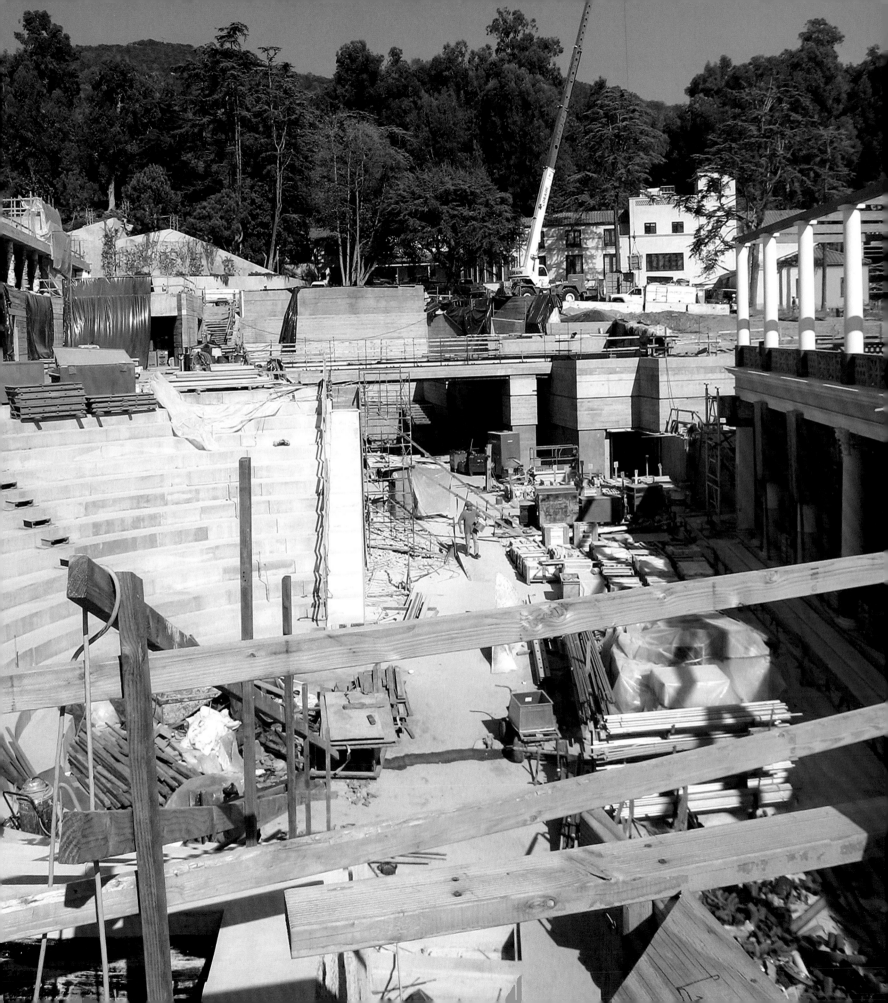

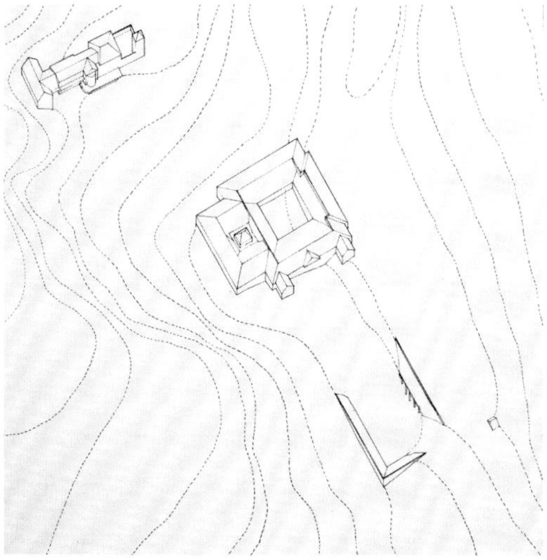

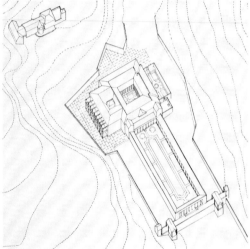

Figure 231. The Museum imagined as a buried ruin

Figure 232. The Museum "unearthed." A fictional retrospective conceit of the Villa as an archaeological site and the Museum as an artifact

ing as an artifact observed from above could just as easily have been interpreted more literally as an artifice created to stress the archaeological associations of the site. This was more an amusing association than a conscious intent, but such an interpretation now was practically inevitable (figs. 231, 232). For this reason, even as we accepted such a conceit at an intellectual level, we resisted the temptation to "thematize" the project using props, icons, and direct references to the idea of "archaeology" that is embedded in the project.

As architects, we found the idea of the Museum as an artifact exhibited in the context of an art museum doubly rewarding, because early on in the process we had to accept the loss of something dear to us: a gallery displaying a collection of casts, which we had conceived at the time of the competition. In our vision, it would have concentrated mostly on casts of classical architecture elements. Such a gallery, once found in practically all major museums and academies, now occurs hardly anywhere (figs. 233, 234)— and it would not be found at the Getty either. But with the entry sequence now focusing on the Museum as an artifact, we were recovering at least part of that experience, by observing a "sample" of classical architecture from the vantage point of the spectator, whose first experience of the Museum would be indeed that of "architecture exhibited." We were all pleased with this recovered museum experience.

and complexity, while still clearly distinguishing the major public areas from those reserved for staff, scholars, and non-Museum visitors.

Beyond both solving the functional entry problem and meeting the need to open up the site's grounds to visitors, which made the entry sequence plausible, the most notable achievement of the entry sequence involves the conceptual conceit of seeing the Museum as an artifact in the landscape prior to a Museum visit; it pleases the intellect as much as it does the senses. It took a long time, but once we "discovered" this concept, it firmly gave us the sort of insider's narrative that helped interpret, explain, and develop every single element of the project. At the same time, experiencing the Museum build-

CONJECTURES

Perhaps now is the time to pose the question, "What would have happened if…?" While historians tend to avoid this sort of speculation, I find it useful, not only to illustrate other possible outcomes but also as a way of highlighting some important, uncontrollable, and unique aspects of the design process. This is particularly

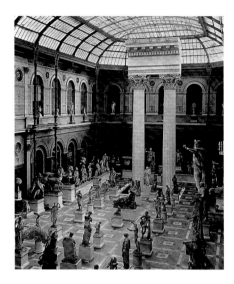 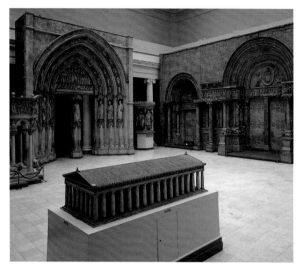

relevant in the case of the Villa project, with its many events and turning points. Because the design process is subject to the effects of unpredictable events, and because it must accommodate an abundance of coexisting yet unresolvable contradictions, it is never the linear, rational process that we hope for and that many assume it to be. In the case of the Villa, *what if* the decision in 1996 to divide the Master Plan arbitrarily into two phases had not been made? In that case, we surely would never have attempted to develop a temporary southern entrance to handle visitors. Until then, it had seemed impossible to achieve a new entry sequence from that direction; only the pressure to deal with the problems posed by Phase I of the Master Plan produced the temporary and novel idea of an Entry Pavilion.

This solution, though forced on us by the change in the Master Plan, actually turned out to be pregnant with meaning and ideas. In fact, it remained part of the project long after the ill-advised two-phase Master Plan was abandoned. By its sheer spatial, programmatic, and formal power, the "temporary" entry

sequence resisted its own demise, asserting the viability of permanent parking in the south and thus providing the key to developing a landscape narrative that resolved, with imagination and grace, a conundrum: How could we create a new entrance to the Museum through the Atrium? Moreover, without a two-phase master plan, it is very likely that the northern approach to the Museum would have established itself as the best alternative—and therefore that public parking would have been located in the north. Later, when the need to add non-Museum programs (that is, the whole North Campus) emerged in 1998, we probably would have considered placing them in the south, around the preexisting parking lot, because the northern areas would have been fully occupied with visitor services. Perhaps we have gone far enough in this course of conjecture; I hope it serves as a humbling exercise for those who think that all is explainable, that "a best solution" always exists for each design problem, and that the process evolves one step at a time.

Figure 233. Salle des Etudes Antiques, Ecole des Beaux-Arts, Paris

Figure 234. Carnegie Museum of Art, Pittsburgh, Hall of Architecture

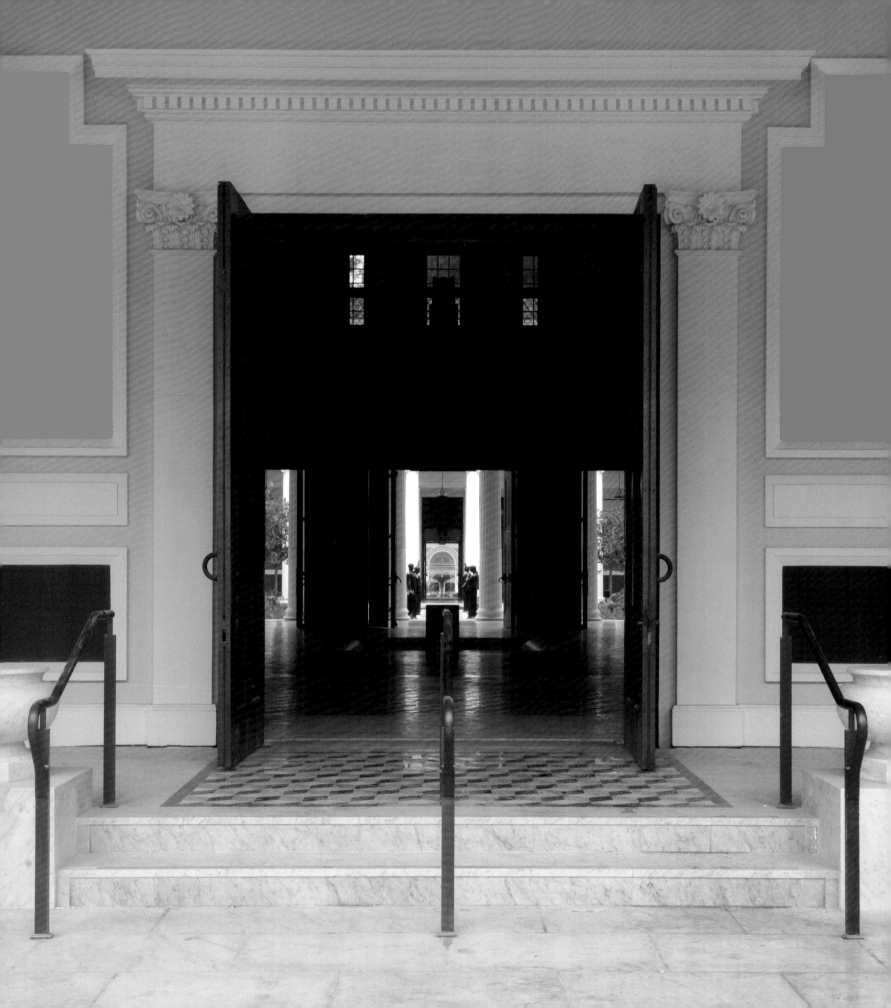

6   The Museum Restored

I have left the story of the extensive renovation work at the Museum proper, undoubtedly the main public attraction of the Malibu site, for the end of my account. The redesign of the Museum was conceived concurrently with the overall idea that guided the design of all components of the project and was never disengaged from the conceptual framework of the Master Plan. But the building's long history as a cultural icon that stood for the whole institution, its unique artistic nature as a replica of an ancient villa, and the peculiarities imposed by its function as a museum of antiquities required that this part of the job be organized and treated separately. Conversely, once the Museum's indisputable difference was established, all the other major components of the Master Plan inevitably became distinct, too, which led to the division of the architectural services into two major teams: the "new buildings team" and the "existing buildings team."

If the Master Plan's overall strategy was full of difficulties at a conceptual level, the specific approach to remodeling the Museum also posed worrisome dangers and traps. The direction that we and the Museum eventually decided to follow (that is, to continue with the design spirit of the first level throughout the building) was not as obvious at the start as it seems today. Roughly half the Museum's area needed drastic alterations in character and organization because the whole second level was not appointed to display

antiquities. Thus, because the building was so evenly split between the half (on the first level) that was already appropriate for the future exhibits and the half (on the second level) that needed structural renovation and redecoration, the project might very well have moved in directions other than the one it took. For instance, we might have redone the whole building in a third, alternative vocabulary. As we know, the Museum building was an imagined contraption, only partly faithful to an eighteenth-century plan based on an archaeological survey conducted through tunnels; the original building was—and mostly still remains—buried! Thus, no claim of absolute historical accuracy could be made for the first level, and there was no authentic building material to preserve—and so there was no indisputable obligation to maintain any of it.

Moreover, current architectural fashion at the time was promoting vocabularies and planning interventions that stressed differences through aggressive, confrontational juxtapositions, ones that produced veritable "clashes" between the new and the existing. Yet, in this intervention, there was the logical desire to establish an overall coherence between a collection of antiquities and the architecture that would house it. It would have been hard to refute the argument for developing a strategy that continued and completed the existing classical character of the building with a seamless, if

opposite
Figure 236. The East Stair seen from across the Inner Peristyle

not necessarily historically accurate, remodeling, designed to properly exhibit such a collection.

Given the importance of the project, we naturally received free advice from many architect friends and even from people in other fields. Not surprisingly, they recommended that we "smack" the Villa with a violent intervention. Hostility as a strategy of differentiation, so prevalent in contemporary architecture, is not, however, to Machado and Silvetti's taste. Such interventions may be effective, even attractive, but, in general, one-liners like that tend to exhaust themselves quickly. It was clear from our competition sketchbook that we would not follow such a course.

Still, for quite some time, while program and planning ideas were being developed and tested, we continued to ponder what our approach should be. It helped that a substantial number of entirely new buildings independent from the Museum would be required on the site; we would have plenty of opportunities to design and build our own "signature" architecture at the Getty Villa. Our broad charge—not only to restore, expand, and remodel but also to build new buildings—gave us peace of mind and a certain objectivity that helped us sort out what would be the appropriate strategy to follow for the Museum building.

While we knew early on that in our intervention on the existing Roman replica our "signature" architecture would be subtle, subdued, and not manifested through a distinctive and superimposed vocabulary, by the time we had to confront the specific design of each new building in the Master Plan, we were sure that we would not seek an architecture of confrontation. We knew that we would be gentle and "cooperative" with our own buildings, while creating something distinct, contemporary, assertive, and different. With the Museum, however, we would be guided by

the aim of improving and expanding on the referential properties of its existing architecture. Furthermore, for the Museum building alone we would adhere to an "ideal" model of a Roman house, and—rather than attempting to perfect a replica whose original still remained unknown—we would re-create its ancient character not through imitation but through evocation. Thus, the task at the Museum was one of continuing its architecture. It was also clear that whenever the original architectural fabric could not accommodate a programmatic, functional, or technical demand, such an element would not be disguised but rather dealt with honestly, openly, and amicably.

A GRAND STAIRWAY

Such was the situation with the main staircase that the Getty wanted. It had to be located in a visible and easily accessible area, be a part of the architecture of the building, and easily connect the Museum's two public levels without disorienting the visitor. Today, the solution seems obvious: we aligned the stairway with the axis on the east side of the Inner Peristyle (figs. 236–38) so that it would be visible when entering the Museum. It would be easily comprehended, yet it would be located away from the Atrium, whose otherwise generous space is claimed by the central pool of the *compluvium* and the various lines of circulation offered by its many doors. The stairway's rich materials and careful details announce its importance: it is a grand stairway. If its architectural definition differs greatly from other elements of the Museum, it is simply because there were no grand stairways in ancient Roman domestic architecture to use as a precedent.

The Roman house was primarily a ground-floor type of operation; second floors were rare

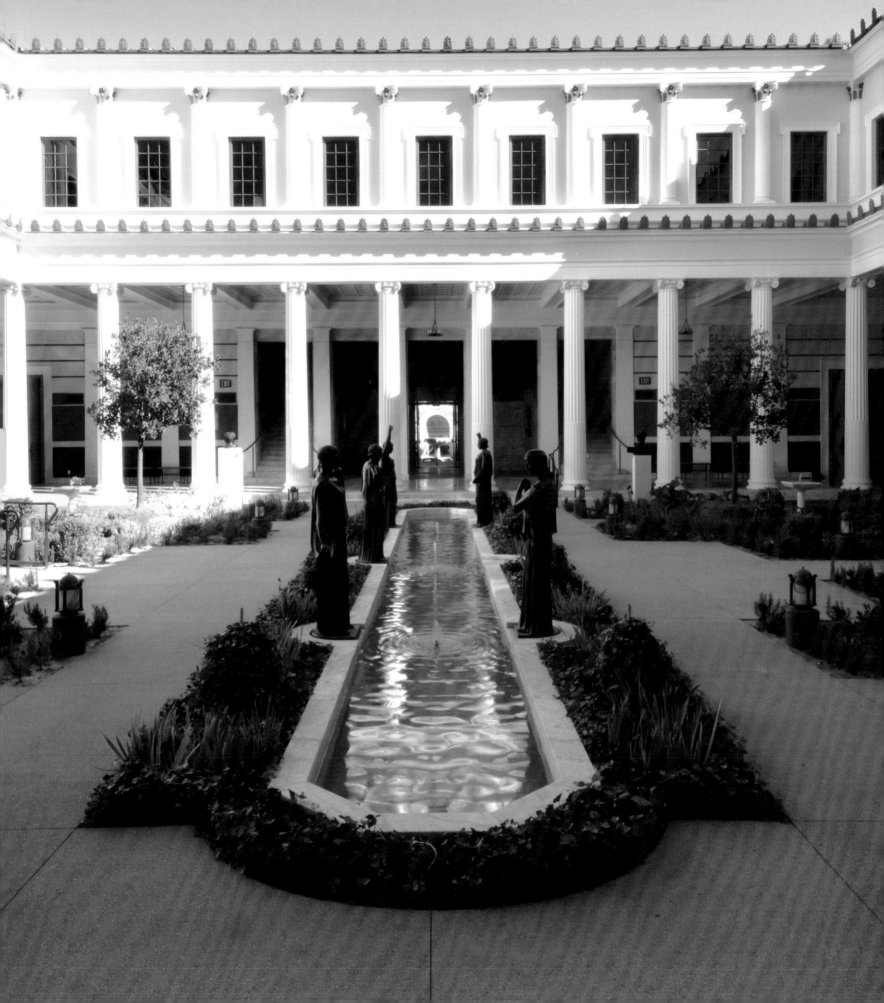

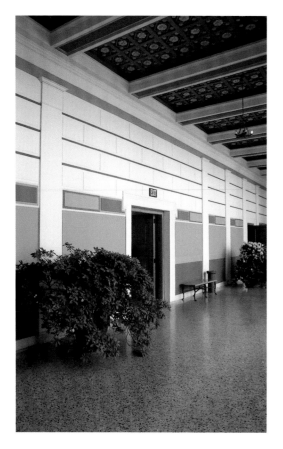

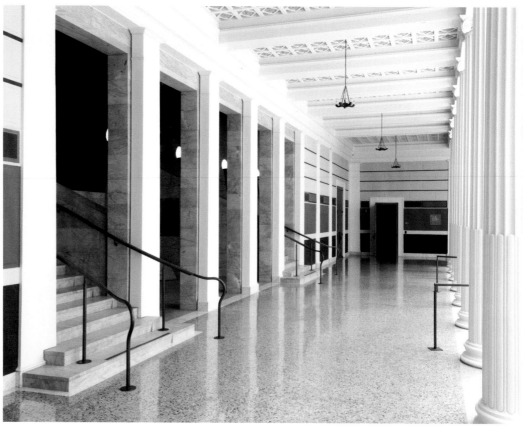

Figure 237. The east side of the Inner Peristyle before renovation

Figure 238. The east side of the Inner Peristyle after galleries were removed to accommodate the East Stair

and always less important in the hierarchy of spaces. In this sense, the entire second level of the Museum is not only a hypothetical element but also an improbable one. We had to invent a stairway for a Roman house, and we did not feel the need to fake or hypothesize anything.

The East Stair, as it became known, is organized following strict bilateral symmetry, which collects the flow of visitors coming from both sides of the Inner Peristyle in two branches. As the branches rise, they flank the ground-floor passage to the East Garden. The branches meet at mid-height at an ample landing, where circulation converges in a central trunk, which subsequently divides again, forming two diverging branches for the final ascent. The stairway confirms in every move the main west-east axis of the Museum, now completely restored to its ideal condition by the placement of the public entrance from the Theater Plaza and through the Atrium (figs. 235, 236).

To achieve the height necessary for the stairwell, space had to be appropriated from existing galleries and rooms, creating a unique, "un-Roman" space. The East Stair is one more anomaly in this "villa"—another example of the dilemmas and ambiguities we constantly found in addressing the renovation of this replica. We decided to express the double height of the staircase by constructing the whole space and the stairway itself as an independent architectural piece inserted into the fabric of the original building. To achieve this, we covered the walls and floors entirely with a single material, *amarillo triana*, a warm, butter-colored marble from southern Spain. *Amarillo triana* is not used anywhere else in the Museum; thus, it lends an unmistakable identity, continuity, and weight to the large space that joins both floors and firmly grounds its volume at the entrance level (fig. 239). Because the central part of the stair would have to "fly" from the middle level landing to the upper level, this half is treated in an entirely different manner—as a lighter "bridge" component that spans the two landings (fig. 240). Structural and functional elements of this part were made of bronze, railings were made of glass, and while those of the "stone" part were carved into the marble walls, they morphed into wood when they disengaged themselves at the bottom (figs. 240, 241). The transition from one level to the other is grand and comfortable, and the experience of moving through the space is memorable—one of many such moments the Museum offers visitors. The experience is enhanced by the radiance emanating from the unique marble and bronze trimmings as they are bathed with natural light coming from the Inner Peristyle and from an upper window, which we added for that purpose (and also to further connect the Museum visually with the least visible and least used sector of the site, its east side). The East Stair is perhaps the best example in our work of an intervention in a historic fabric in which a foreign artifact candidly exhibits its distinctiveness while at the same time makes the effort to be part of an ensemble of elements.

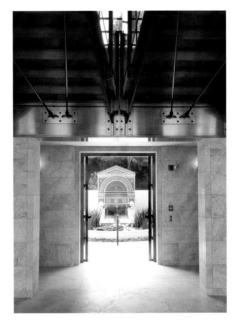

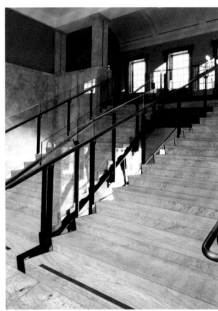

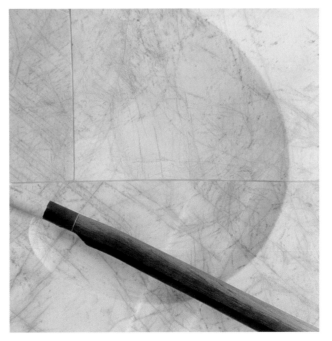

Figures 239-41. Details of the East Stair

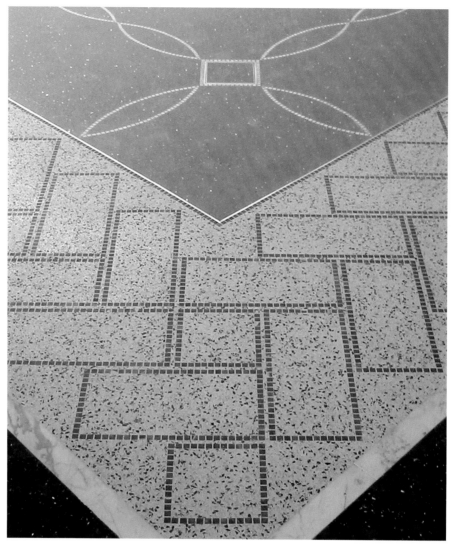

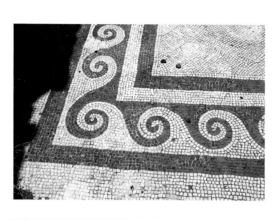

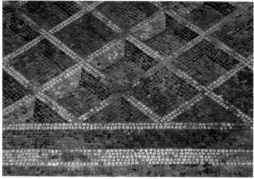

Figure 242. Detail of Roman mosaic floor pattern at Hadrian's Villa in Tivoli

Figure 243. Detail of Roman mosaic floor pattern in Herculaneum

right
Figure 244. Corner detail of floor pattern

opposite
Figure 245. General view of the Women and Children Gallery with floor pattern as designed prior to art installation

FLOOR PATTERNS

The development of floor patterns for each gallery follows the same logic. While designing and sizing the patterns in reference to required electrical and seismic support grids—7 feet 6 inches in the permanent galleries and 5 feet in special exhibition galleries—we considered many of the two-dimensional mosaic patterns that ancient Romans used to decorate the floors of their rooms (figs. 242, 243). Again, we made no attempt to achieve historical rigor—there is no replica here. Rather, our attitude of conscious reference to historical decorative patterns respects rules of either dynamic or passive composition, proportions, repetition, and framing but goes its own way in terms of materials and dimensions. Our floor-pattern designs for the Museum are constructed of terrazzo in different color combinations, with bronze, mosaic, and marble motifs and detailing (fig. 244). The pattern units here are considerably larger than those usually found in Roman floors simply because some of the rooms in the Museum are much bigger than rooms customarily found in Roman domestic spaces (fig. 245). The resulting rich variety of patterns, together with the wall colors, jolt the visitor, as each gallery proposes a surprising and distinctive visual experience (figs. 246–51).

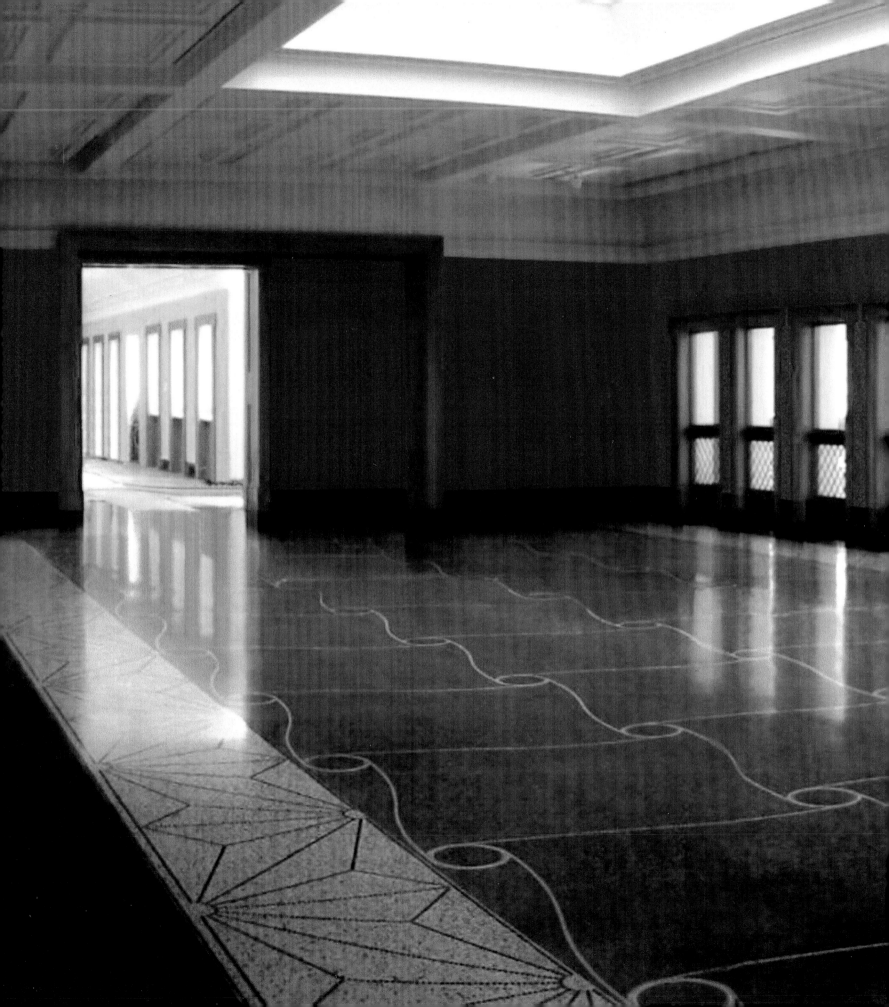

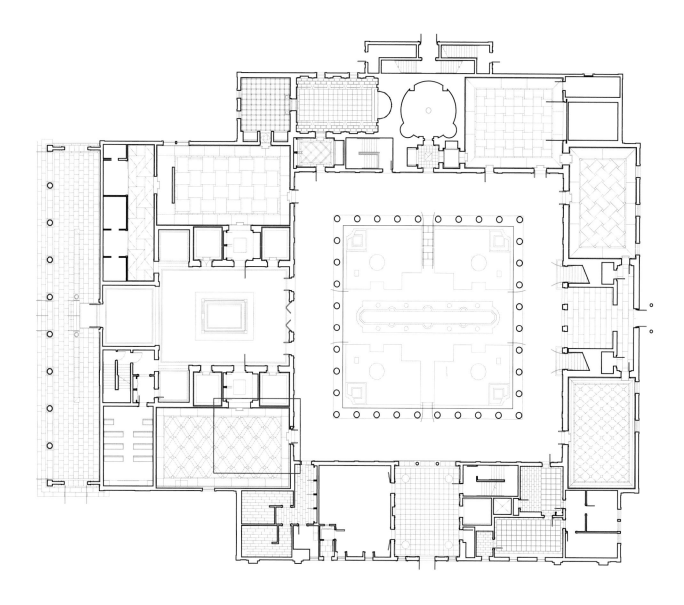

Figure 246. Museum Level 1 Plan, showing gallery floor patterns

Figures 247, 248. Plan detail of floor pattern in area indicated above and the floor as installed

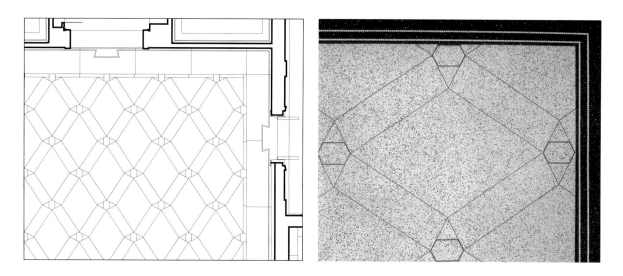

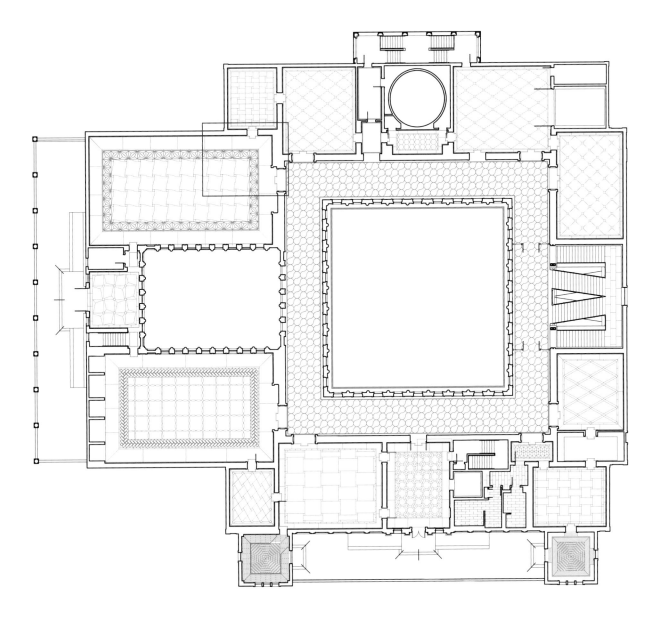

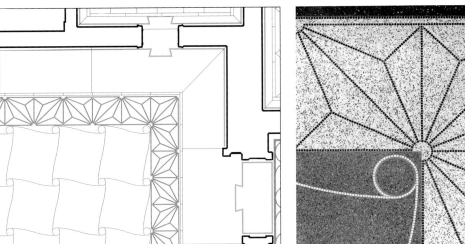

Figure 249. Museum Level 2 Plan, showing gallery floor patterns

Figures 250, 251. Plan detail of floor pattern in area indicated above and the floor as installed

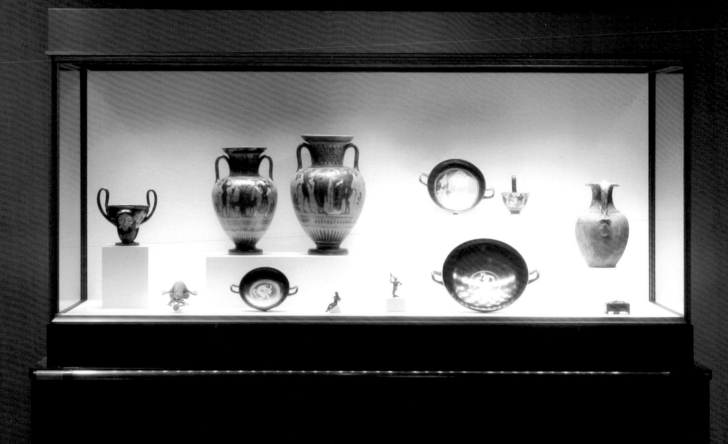
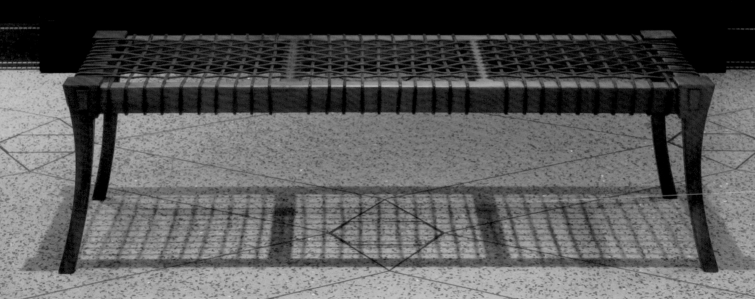

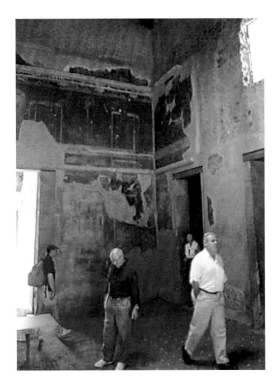

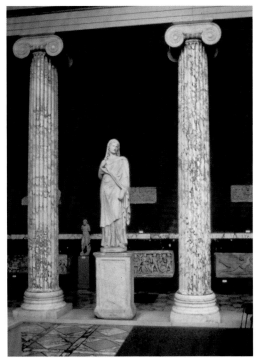

WALL COLORS

Selecting and assigning wall colors proved to be one of the most intricate, labor-intensive, and delicate undertakings of all the work done in this immense redesign (fig. 252). While we all agreed to work with the southern Italian palettes that we studied during our second European trip (figs. 253, 254)—and from early on our color sketches reflect this decision—picking the "right" color was another story!

First we developed several templates showing abstract combinations of colors in which each combination registered only the percentages of each color while ignoring the specific design, pattern, or ornamental detail that such a palette might have had in the original room (figs. 255–57). The Antiquities Department then made a preliminary selection of actual wall colors based on current ideas of the actual content of the future galleries. Then, after the floor patterns and wall colors were tested together in a reduced-scale cardboard installation model constructed in the Museum's Exhibition Design Department at the Getty Center, a full-scale mock-up of a room's corner was constructed. The mock-up, which contained all the elements that needed to be tested, was then brought to the empty Museum building, where we attempted to match, one by one, each floor pattern to each gallery wall-color scheme. These had been prepared in large sample boards.

The process took years to complete; each encounter involved curators, architects, contractors, and other Getty staff. With each session, we moved closer and closer to the current colors—and a similar story can be told about exterior wall colors as well (figs. 258–60).

opposite

Figure 252. Men and Heroes Gallery

Figure 253. Jorge Silvetti and Rodolfo Machado touring Pompeii

Figure 254. Ny Carlsberg Glyptotek in Copenhagen

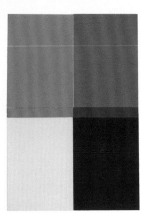

THORVALDSEN   **SCHEME C**

2108 - Chamois   1067 - Alexandrite
2097 - Amber   1699 - Inca Gold
2078 - Earth Tone
2041 - Fedora

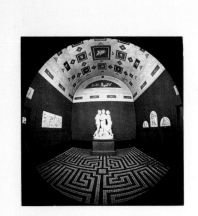

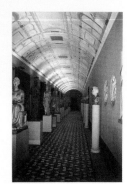

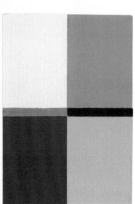

POMPEJANUM   **SCHEME B**

1150 - Milano   2306 - Anubis
1716 - Rattan   2082 - Buccaneer
1876 - Brick Dust
1601 - Chaste Fern

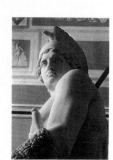

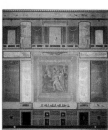

Südwand des Tablinums (13) nach der Restaurierung

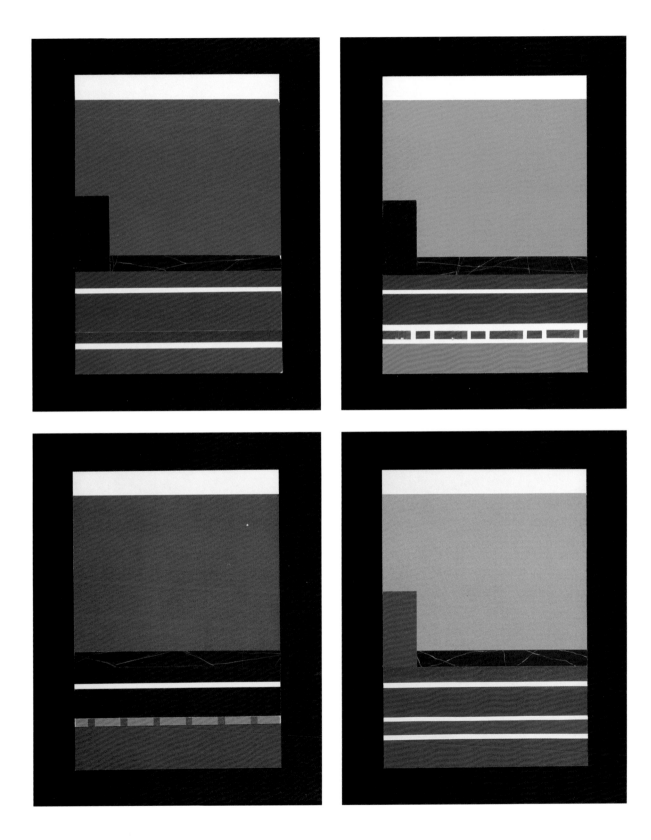

opposite, top
Figure 255. Three gallery-color studies derived from research at the Thorvaldsens Museum in Copenhagen

opposite, bottom
Figure 256. Three gallery-color studies derived from research at the Pompejanum in Aschaffenburg, Germany

Figure 257. Four of the twelve early alternative color studies for the galleries at the Getty Villa

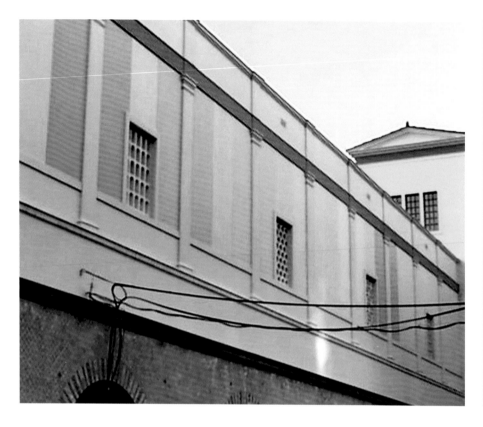

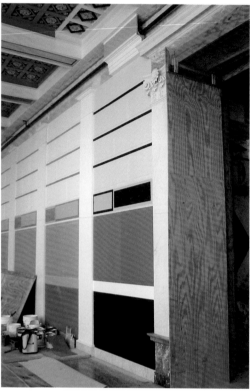

Figure 258. Color tests on the Museum's exterior wall

Figure 259. Inner Peristyle color mock-ups

opposite
Figure 260. The finished Inner Peristyle with its new color scheme

What we now have at the Museum is a building that vibrates with hues of brilliant and contrasting colors and materials based on still-visible precedents, suggesting the ambiance, if not the actual décor, of a Roman house.

The enormous effort required to produce the ineffable effect that we see today in the Museum's galleries, gardens, porticos, and walls is yet another example of the collaboration among the Getty, the construction team, and Machado and Silvetti. However, we could not have achieved that high level of sophistication, definition, and success without the indefatigable, almost superhuman, dedication and expertise that Curator of Antiquities Marion True devoted to the task. As committed as she was to all aspects of this project, in the

color selection process she was truly unsurpassed. In meeting after meeting, for color sample upon color sample, she brought her demanding eye to bear on each combination of hues, tones, and values. In her meticulous scrutiny and unflagging search for the perfect shade and juxtaposition of hues, she would often request "one more test"—a test that we probably would have not undertaken but that would, inevitably, be the combination that worked perfectly with, for example, the chosen artifacts for a gallery, its floor patterns, the light, and the general theme of the exhibit. For us as architects, it was a surprising learning process in which we found an unexpected teacher. We participated in her lessons with increasing interest and followed willingly her lead in the definition of one of

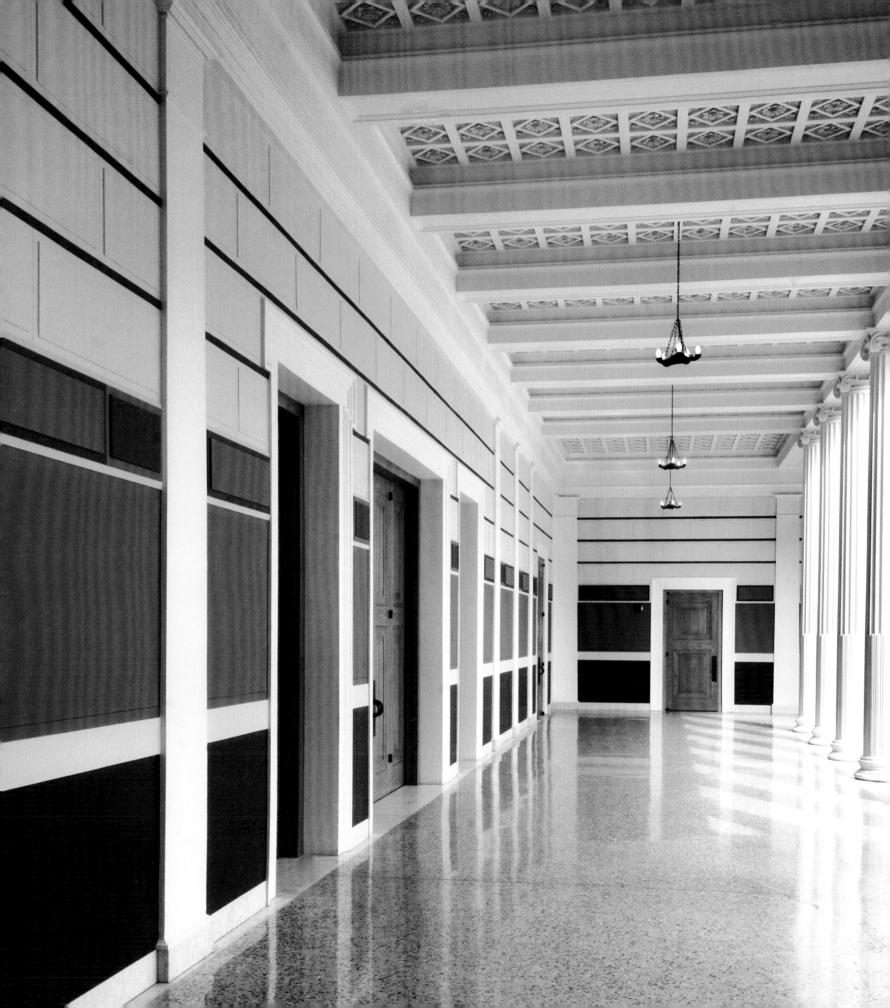

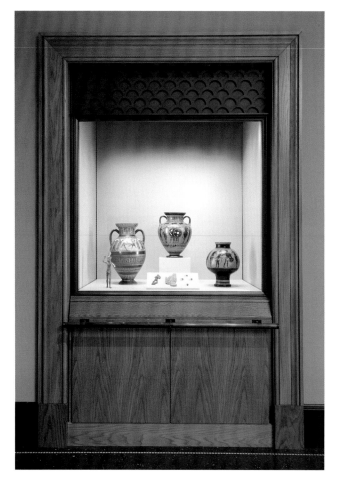

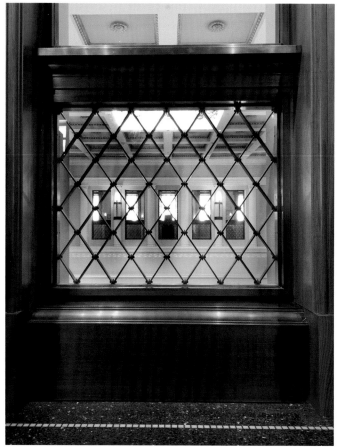

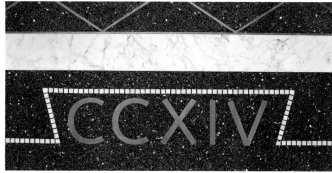

Figure 261. Display case

Figure 262. A new second-level window opening into the Atrium

Figure 263. Gallery number in Roman numerals displayed in its floor at the entrance threshold

the most distinctive features of the Museum's architecture.

To convey fully the level of detailed involvement by client and architect in the Museum's overall design, we would need to refer to too many other areas of design. Suffice it to say that the same care and commitment exercised in the design of floor patterns and the selection of

wall colors were also applied to the design of the state-of-the-art display cases, signage, lighting, ceilings, furnishings, doors, and windows (figs. 261–67). For each one of these design elements, full-size mock-ups were produced, reviewed, corrected, and re-produced—again and again, as many times as was necessary to reach a desired result.

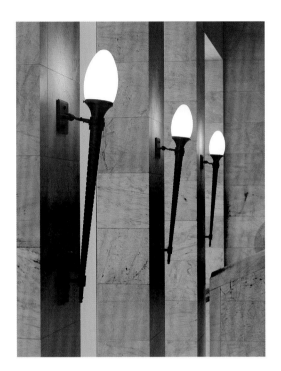

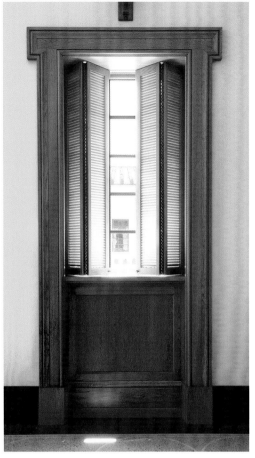

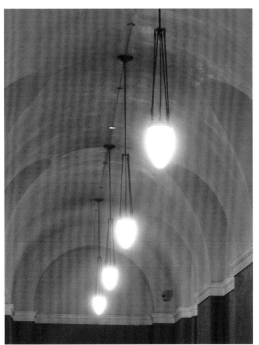

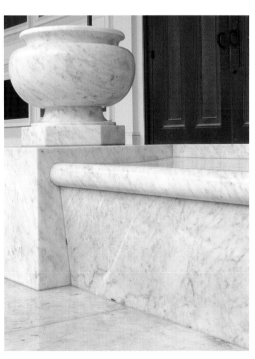

clockwise from top left
Figure 264. Bronze torchères on the East Stair

Figure 265. Shutters on the windows that now open onto the Inner Peristyle

Figure 266. Marble bench at the entrance to the Museum

Figure 267. New lighting design in the Loggia

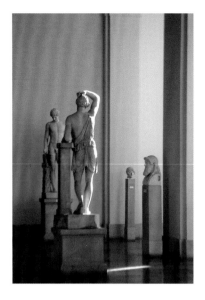

Figure 268. Sculpture Gallery in the Altes Museum, Berlin

Figure 269. The second-floor Decorative Arts Galleries around the Inner Peristyle before renovations. These galleries were organized *en enfilade* and without natural light.

NATURAL LIGHT

At the same time, no decision was easier to make than deciding to bring natural light and ventilation to as many areas of the building as was physically possible and allowable by exhibition standards. As envisioned in early drawings and renderings and corroborated by our field trips, we concluded that, whenever possible, natural light must illuminate antiquities (fig. 268). In ancient times, artifacts were created and exhibited in natural light, and the way they are shown today in the Museum's galleries reflects that (figs. 269–71). The changing opalescence of the surfaces of Pentelic marble, the differences between that Attic stone and its Parian rival, the crispness of line definition and color in red- and black-figured ceramic vases, the patina of

bronzes—these qualities all come alive when objects are bathed by the changing natural light. The important differences between such active luminescence and the stasis produced by artificial lighting were, for all of us, too clear (figs. 272–74). While not all galleries could be lit naturally (nor would we wish to abandon entirely artificial lighting), I expect the effect of the California sun moving over the Getty's collection of antiquities to be one of the redesign's major, even if unreported, benefits.

Bringing natural light to the galleries went hand in hand with opening up the Museum to views from both its interior and exterior open spaces. Visitors' orientation in relation to the galleries and to various amenities in the building, as well as to the gardens and the natural landscape, is enhanced by the many new

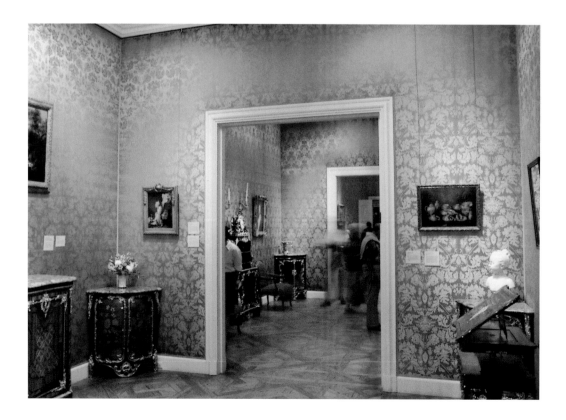

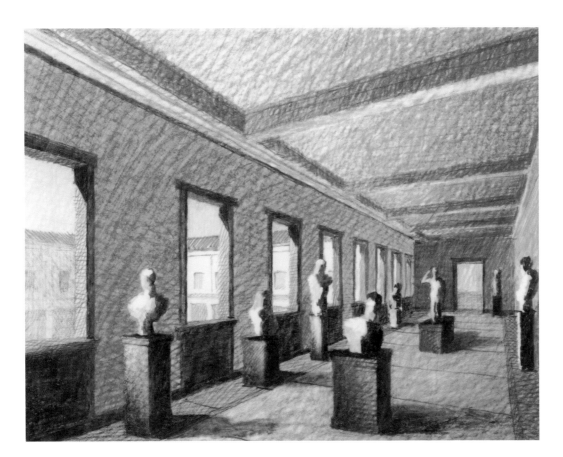

Figure 270. The gallery around the Inner Peristyle as envisioned in 1995, organized as a continuous space naturally lit by the opening up of windows

Figure 271. The gallery around the Inner Peristyle as built

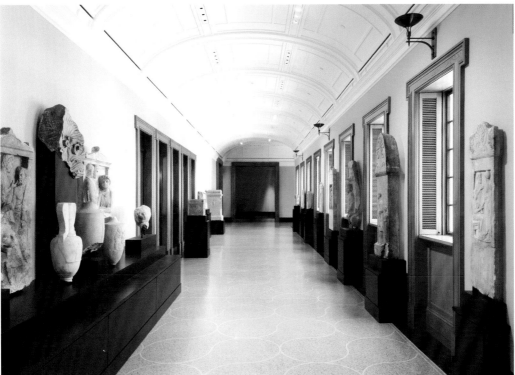

Figure 272. The Baroque Paintings Gallery before renovations (1995)

Figure 273. The same gallery space as envisioned in 1995, introducing natural light via a large central skylight and opening up windows toward the Atrium. This rendering was made from the same point of view as fig. 272.

opposite
Figure 274. The Women and Children Gallery as built. This photograph was also taken from the same point of view as fig. 272.

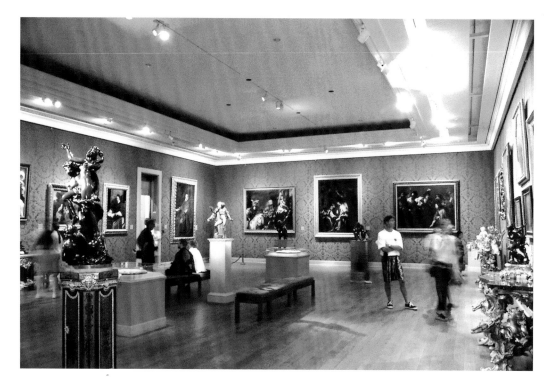

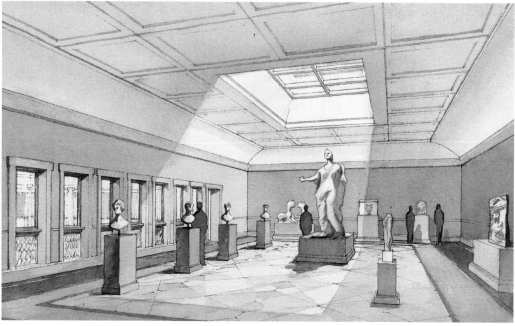

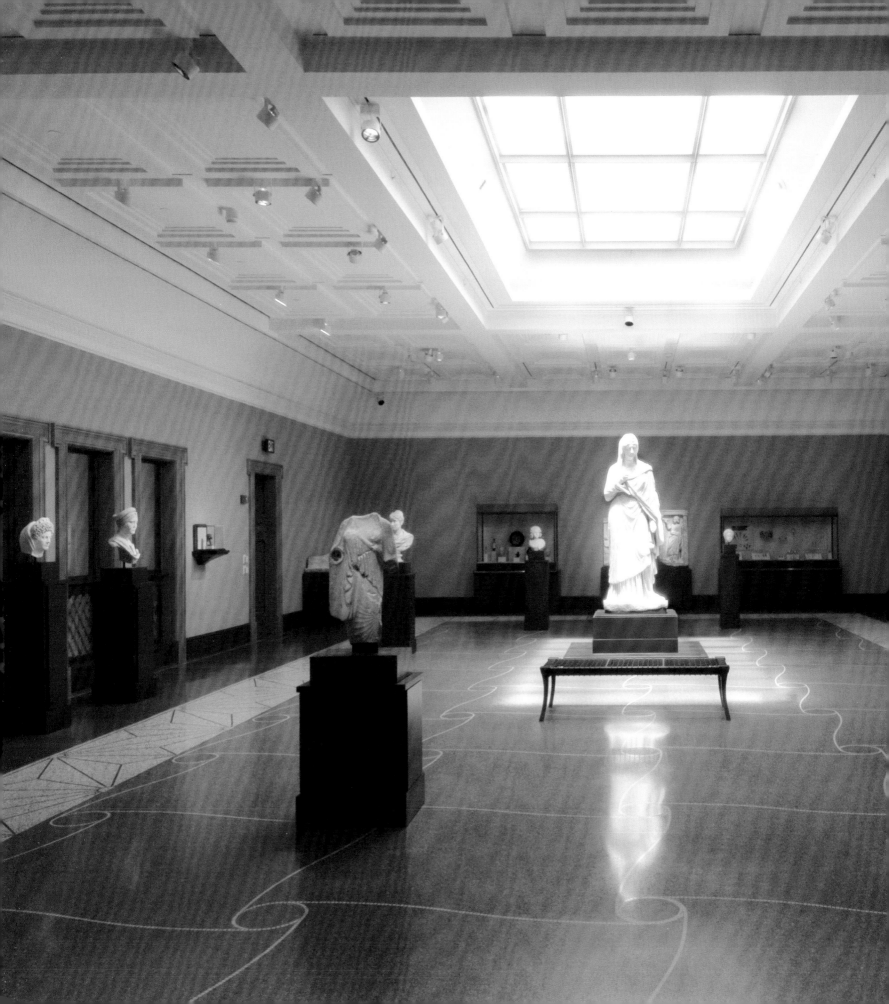

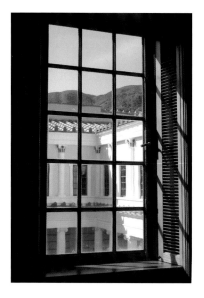

Figure 275. New window in upper level looking northwest toward the coastal mountains

Figure 276. The Atrium before renovations showing "fake" impluvium as part of the ceiling treatment

Figure 277. The Atrium, as envisioned in 1995, with all upper-level windows and the *impluvium* open. This rendering was made from the same point of view as fig. 276.

windows that were added throughout (fig. 275). This judicious and abundant piercing of the walls—sixty-three new windows were created —allows visitors to use the many reappearing reference points to track their own location in precise and easily established coordinates. Before the redesign, the visitor would lose clear contact with the exterior and, worse—given the location of stairs in an independent stairwell— would lose all sense of orientation once arriving at the second floor. Now, visitors always know where they are, can see where they have been, and can tell where they are going. While aware of their relative position, they can also observe other visitors as they move through the galleries and the outdoor spaces throughout the building. The visitor sees the art, the architecture, and other people. In our contemporary urban world,

where public space has diminished in quality and even begun to disappear entirely, the institution of the museum has evolved into a social space of prime importance. The Getty Villa has taken up that challenge, and the Museum in particular has used the remodeling and expansion as an opportunity to bring the experience of art, people, and architecture together.

A more poignant moment in this spatial transformation was achieved with the introduction of a real *impluvium/compluvium* component in the Atrium, replacing what was originally a less-authentic representation of this defining feature of the Roman house. Indeed, the previous Atrium's "window" to the sky was a purely decorative element attached to the ceiling, closed to light and air (fig. 276). In our project, it evolved into a real opening (figs. 277, 278).

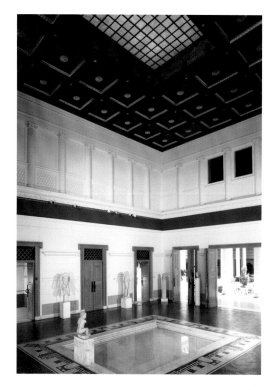

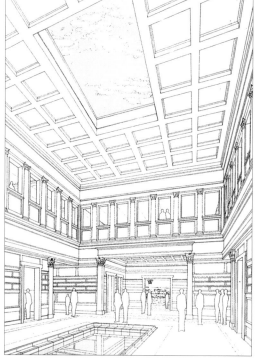

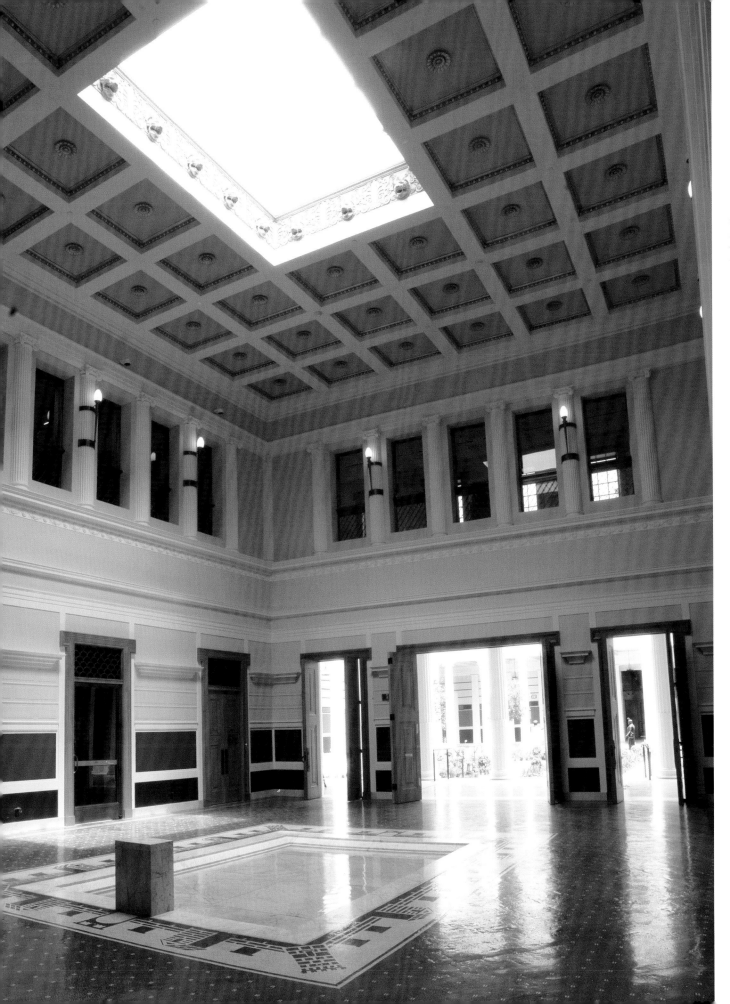

Figure 278. The Atrium as built, open to views and to the sky. This photograph was also taken from the same point of view as fig. 276.

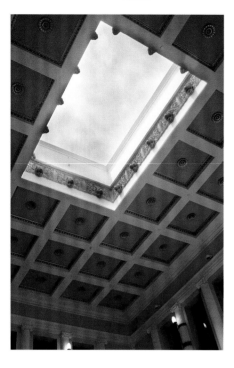

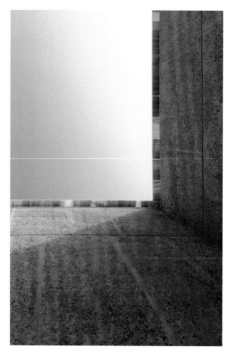

Figure 279. The *impluvium* open to the sky in the Atrium

Figure 280. The onyx cornice of the Entry Pavilion as seen against the sky

nonliteral symmetries and subtle symbols was one of our many goals. To mention just one more, hard-to-miss example: the Museum's East Stair finds its echo in the other important interior staircase, the one that brings the public from the covered area outside the Auditorium up to the cafe. The two stairs have different designs, yet they are both sculptural structures clad in the same marble—*amarillo triana*—which establishes in "another language," as it were, a correspondence with the ancient Roman house (figs. 281, 282).

This fundamental element brings a new dynamic dimension to the Atrium, arguably the busiest space of the Museum, by generating changing shadows and allowing breezes to pass through the Museum. But as importantly, it provides the opportunity to evoke the unique symbolic experience of entering a Roman house, with its unequivocal relationship to the heavens and nature.

Interestingly, the axial maneuver produced by the *impluvium/compluvium* system—which blocks the visitor's progress along the horizontal axis with a physical impediment (namely, the collecting pool of the cistern) and thus invites the eye to look up to the open sky—is prefigured exactly, but in reverse, in the experience of the Entry Pavilion (figs. 279, 280). This *other* entry threshold starts with a vertical release toward the firmament as the visitor begins to move upward, in the direction of a distant goal, only to follow a horizontal movement along the upper path through the landscape. The entry path eventually hooks up with the Museum's own axis at the project's central pivot point, where everything seems to hinge: the semicircular Outdoor Theater. Achieving these sorts of

COMPLETION

Our intense involvement with design decisions kept us all—client, architects, and builders—involved throughout every phase of the twelve-year journey. The process was a story of passion and faith in the unique public and educational mission that the Getty Villa proposes and in the possibilities of architecture to help create a "place like no other," as stated in the competition material we received in October 1993.

This account could continue, filling more pages with many other stories, examples, and illustrations—but I think that enough has been said here. All of the evolutions, developments, and changes that took place after the design decisions described in this account belong to another category of issues—one involving alterations in details, interpretation, budget, or materials. These in no way affected the fundamental forces and ideas that guided the project to completion and which are now evident at the Getty Villa for all to see, experience, and judge.

It would have been excessive to record all that here. The Getty Research Institute's archives contain a fairly complete set of drawings and models from our office that records the

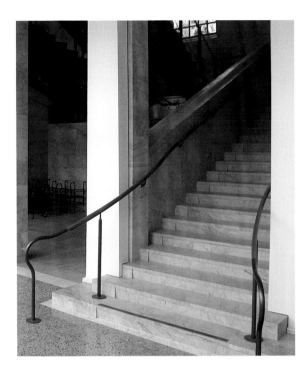
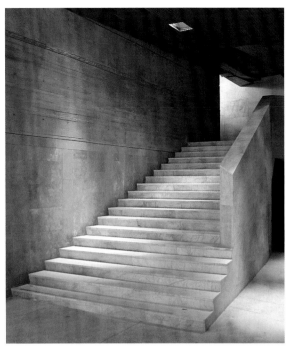

evolution of the plans for building a new Getty Villa since the time of the original competition. Additional documents that the Getty produced and now holds will complete the picture for interested readers and researchers.

PLANNING COMMISSION APPROVAL— JULY 1999

I will close with a brief account of the important external events that affected the design process. Keep in mind that over the years, while these were unfolding, the architectural design team and its Getty counterparts never ceased working on the project for an instant.

The Los Angeles Planning Commission gave the project its approval in July 1999, and, after an appeal by the Villa's neighbors, the plans were approved by the Los Angeles City Council in December of that year. The neighbors filed suit in 2000 (see p. 81). Since only the new structures were the targets of the litigation, the Museum and Ranch House renovations proceeded without incident and with little fanfare in early 2000. While we waited, the larger project

continued to be developed and refined, by then with the assistance of SPF:architects, a firm that had been brought on board as our technical partner during construction. The timing of SPF's engagement during the wait was fortuitous, as it, in partnership with Morley Construction Company, had just completed the technical drawings for the concrete work on the Our Lady of the Angels Cathedral project. SPF and Morley shared our intimate understanding of and reverence for the concrete work at the Villa, which would be so important to its overall expression.

Waiting was not easy for anybody. The Getty was concerned about the potential loss of such things as the Outdoor Theater, the Auditorium, additional parking, and education facilities—elements the neighbors contended would create more traffic, more noise, more people. And we, fearing the worst (that is, losing the Outdoor Theater and additional parking), had to prepare—painfully—alternative designs. The possibility of losing the Theater kept me awake many nights. But now, my concern was exacerbated by a fully developed project that demonstrated the Theater's real virtues. Not only

Figures **281, 282**. The *amarillo triana* stone cladding as used in both the East Stair and Cafe Stair of the new Villa

was the Outdoor Theater the element I treas-
ured most and regarded, together with the Entry
Pavilion, as the most distinctive pieces of our
firm's architecture at the Villa, it was also, at
a very basic planning level, the key to the plan's
plausibility and its laboriously achieved functionality. The Theater was also the literal and
figurative hinge on which the entire functional
and formal organization rotated.

At a more speculative level, I was convinced
—and I still am—that the Outdoor Theater
would become an icon (along with the Museum
structure itself) by which this important
Los Angeles landmark would be remembered.
Losing the Theater probably would have
deprived the reopened Getty Villa of a new
"star." When the California Supreme Court
endorsed the earlier decision of the Court of
Appeals in favor of the Getty—nine years after
we had gathered at the Villa under the falling
ashes!—we could finally celebrate, literally,
the beginning of the excavations that would
reveal the new Getty Villa in full (fig. 283).
They commenced on February 18 (Rodolfo's
birthday), 2003, and we have had quite a ride
ever since! Upon receiving news of the legal
breakthroughs, I circulated a spontaneous
e-mail to everyone on the Getty, Morley, and
Machado and Silvetti team expressing my joyful
feelings of relief and encouragement. This
short excerpt gives an insight about the working
atmosphere that permeated the job through
the years:

> As the news spread this morning on the
> ruling. . . I would like to join you all . . .
> on behalf of all at Machado and Silvetti in
> sharing the joy that the prospects of this
> action raises. Besides the sense of happi-
> ness and relief that we should feel entitled
> to express, as it is well deserved for the
> hard work, the love put on the job, and the

hardships endured, I would like to remind
[all of us] in this wonderful moment that
what is ultimately important in this ruling
is that the public good has been served.
Although you may be surprised that my
reaction as an architect at this moment
shifts to a more political arena, I must con-
fess that as the years passed and the possibility of denying Los Angeles, America
and the world a unique cultural facility
seemed more and more likely, my growing
sadness at such possibility became more
focused on the potential loss of program
than on [the danger to] my personal
professional and artistic contributions that
were embodied in our design.

And while there is no denying that we at
Machado and Silvetti can't wait to realize
our ideas and dreams as valuable contributions to architecture, I am so proud
that our efforts to serve the Getty in its
fundamental cultural and social mission to
create at the Villa "a place like no other"
. . . are now going ahead. . . . We are
now ready and reinvigorated to start this
final ride for the completion of this
extraordinary place. Congratulations!

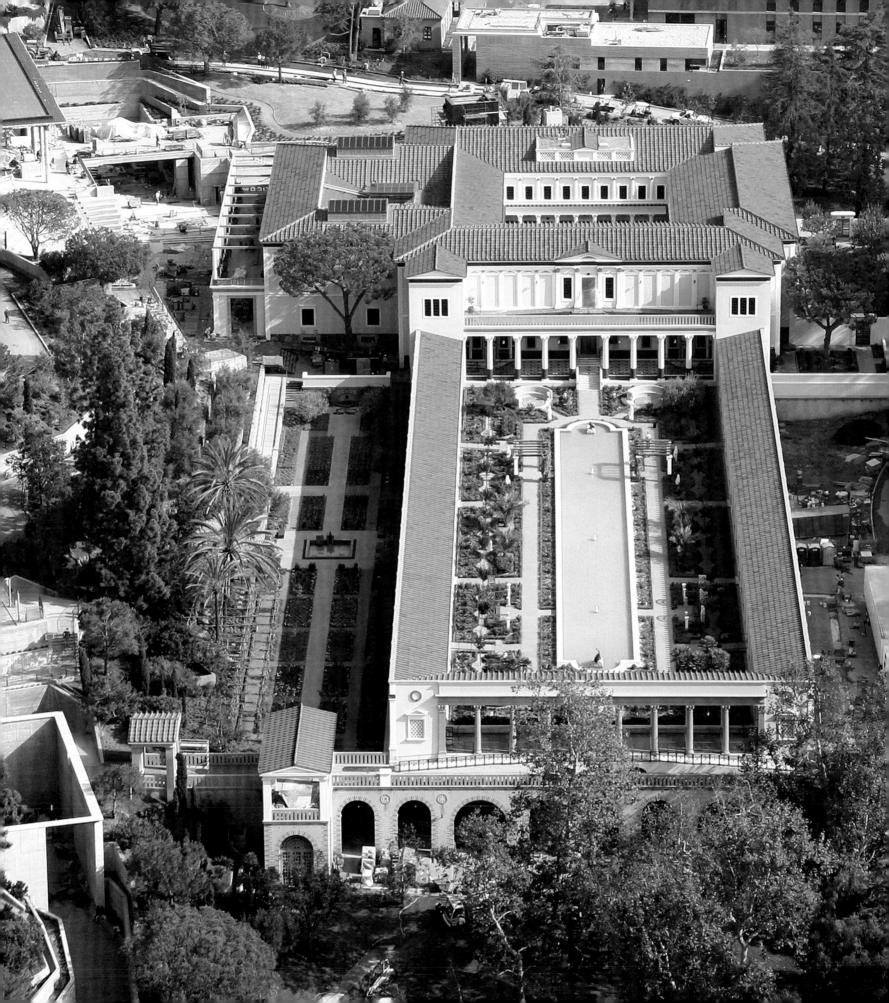

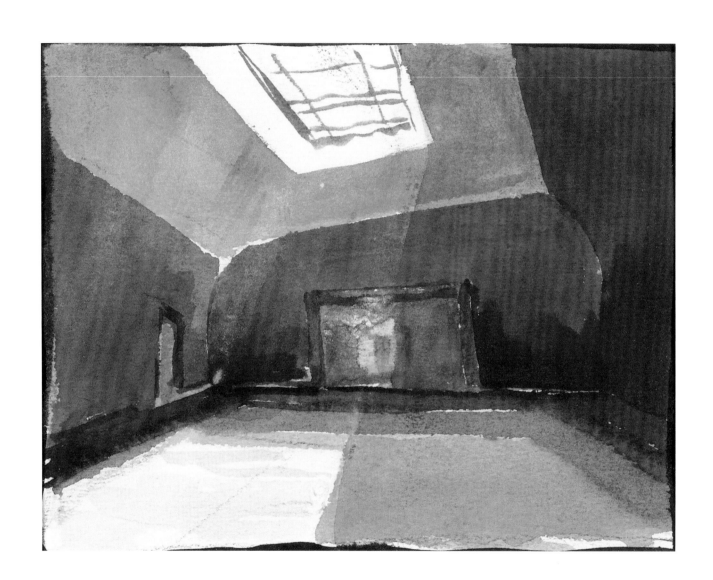

7 Epilogue

The reader holding this book will be doing so after the J. Paul Getty Museum at the Getty Villa has opened to the public and its programs are in full operation. These words, though, are being written during the last months of construction. How, then, should I close this story, when its real "ending" ought to be an account and assessment of the new Getty Villa's appearance and performance? Because this account describes the nearly twelve-year process of reimagining and building the architecture of a new Los Angeles cultural landmark, the story's conclusion should properly be *the new Getty Villa itself*. As one of the book's authors, I should not attempt to provide the visitor and reader with what are probably biased comments, nor should I do so in advance of the real tests that still await. The buildings, the gardens, the exhibits—they all should speak for themselves, in the same ways that the art and artifacts do in the galleries, ready to receive judgment. I know that the pieces forming the new Getty Villa would tell a different story than the one I just finished. It would be a story guided by effects and impressions; triggered by colors, light, spaces, artifacts, plants, and people; and interwoven with activities, memories, discoveries, sounds, and smells.

As architects, our works are the painstaking fruit of deliberations with others and with ourselves over long periods of time, the considerations of all the ingredients, visible and not, that come into play during both conception and construction. The user, however, comes with personal sets of knowledge and expectations; he or she experiences our work in moments and instants that occur at times outside our control, so the story will necessarily take another course, one induced by unforeseeable occurrences and unfathomable conditions. Throughout this text, I have used—extensively—the analogy of language to describe how buildings "speak" or "tell" a story; yet buildings are actually ambiguous in their meanings, and at times even silent if not misleading, lending themselves to a wide range of interpretations. In concluding a task such as this, it is humbling but useful to recall Rafael Moneo's reflection on this bittersweet moment of separation between an architect and his work ("The Solitude of Buildings," Kenzo Tange Lecture, Harvard University Graduate School of Design, March 9, 1985 [Cambridge, Mass., 1986], p. x):

> For a time, we regard our buildings as mirrors; in their reflection we recognize who we are, and eventually who we were. We are tempted to think that a building is a personal statement within the ongoing process of history; but today I am certain that once the construction is finished, once the building assumes its own reality and its own role, all those concerns that occupied the architects and their efforts dissolve. There comes a time when buildings do not need protection of any kind, neither from

opposite
Figure 284. Conceptual watercolor of the Museum skylight gallery, made in 1995

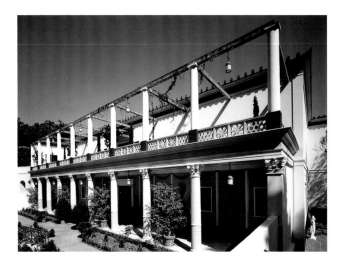

Figure 285. The West Porch of the Museum before the renovations

the architects nor from the circumstances. In the end, circumstances alone remain as hints, allowing critics and historians to gain knowledge of the buildings and to explain to others how they took their form.

Thus, I should conclude here by reflecting upon only what is possible today: the process leading to the buildings and gardens that the public is, I hope, presently enjoying. It was a remarkable process, certainly one of a kind in Machado and Silvetti's professional history, and probably unique in contemporary practice. It involved an extraordinary site; a genuine, unadulterated "architectural problem" for us to address; the rare opportunity to contribute to institution building through design explorations; the experience of coming into contact with exquisite objects of art; and the possibility of indulging in a wide range of research topics (historical, theoretical, and technical). All of this occurred while we interacted with intelligent and notable people whose enthusiasm for the project never diminished and who could, literally, open doors to resources and treasures we never could have accessed otherwise. Ultimately, it was a good

marriage of client and architect, and I publicly rejoice at its occurrence, especially at a time when these associations are often characterized by conflicts and even hostility. It has become a cliché to say that a successful piece of architecture is the product of a client's talents and efforts as much as those of the architect. The cliché could not be truer in this case, and I need to reiterate it here because it is essential in understanding the remarkable history of the process of "reimagining" the Villa.

Through a fortunate set of circumstances— including the timing of the Getty commission and its peculiar demands—the Getty selection committee was able to see, despite a long list of very accomplished candidates, that we would be particularly suited for the task, even though at the time we had only a small number of built projects. As many who know us have told us all along, this job was "made for us." We felt that way, too, throughout the process. But in many other ways, the job has "made us." None of our other projects transformed us more profoundly: professionally, intellectually, and artistically. We are different creatures than the ones who embarked on the project in 1994, feeling tense as a result of both the fascination and the apprehension provoked by the idea of working with a replica of a two-thousand-year-old Roman villa built in Malibu in 1970.

As we return the Getty Villa to its owners and to the public, we feel comfortably attached to it, with great affection for this noble and stubborn "folly." The Getty Villa convinced us that it has a positive role to play in contemporary culture. We believe that our work has equipped it to better perform that role. Certainly, the project has taught us much about architecture, about history, and about the joys of approaching architecture without aesthetic taboos and repressions, both sentiments that surprisingly still lurk in academia, journalism, and the profession itself.

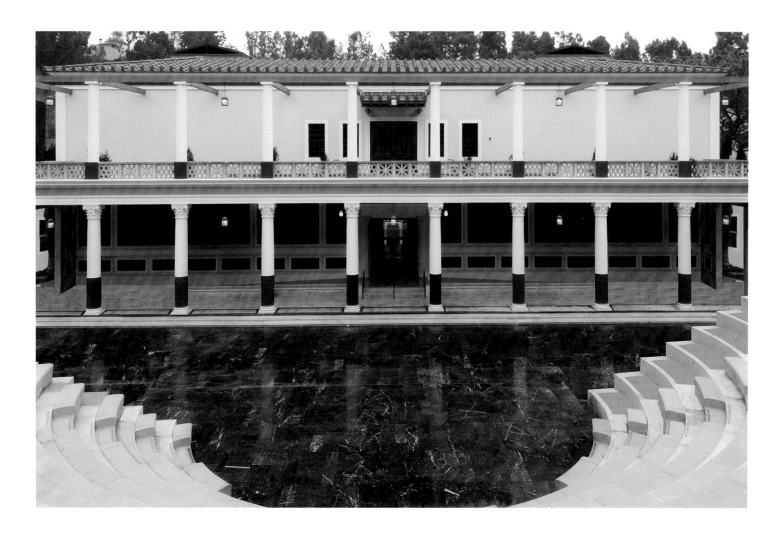

We are particularly pleased that we have been able to provide the original Museum with the company of new buildings that are unabashed in proclaiming their own identity and provenance but that did not install themselves with the intention of overwhelming the site and its original beauty. They aspire to occupy a particular niche reserved for architectural forms that represent the zeitgeist, the spirit of the time they were created. That niche has been empty for some time; it is located a good dis-tance between those that parody history and those that aim at an architecture without prece-dent. Instead, our imagination thrived among the ruins of antiquity and the achievements of contemporary architecture, drawing from both as sources for our own architecture. The peace of mind with which we straddled the clearly false dichotomy between old and new, classical and modern, conservative and progressive fueled the liberating feeling of not attaching any moralistic value to one or the other.

Figure 286. The West Porch and entrance to the Museum seen from the Outdoor Theater

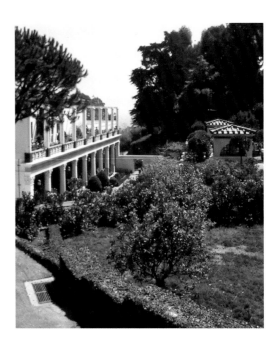

Figure 287. The Museum before renovation, looking toward the coast

opposite
Figure 288. The West Porch and Theater Plaza in the foreground and, in the background, a portion of the Outdoor Theater and Entry Pavilion

The history of human events is different from the history of artifacts, no matter how connected they may be as they unfold. The continuous presence of artifacts over time in the same space occupied by different generations allows them to be "useful" and relevant in different ways to different people during different epochs. We are giving the Getty Villa back to present and future generations, renewed in its form and mission; in doing so, we are changing its original meaning.

It is reassuring to know, though, that the Villa is not alone as an environment that intentionally attempts to evoke an idea of classical antiquity's atmosphere. It belongs to a small family of buildings that, every few decades in every century for two millennia now, have stubbornly returned—one way or another, consciously but differently—to the task of reincarnating the past. From Hadrian's Villa (ca. A.D. 120)—the personal dream of a poet-emperor to evoke his possessions in the Mediterranean—to the Getty Villa (1974), there is a string of "siblings." These begin in the Renaissance with the many responses to the "discovery" of Pliny the Younger's letters describing his villas in Tuscany and Laurentinum: the Roman baths (1834–40) by Karl Friedrich Schinkel in the Gardener's House of Charlottenhof in Potsdam; the Pompejanum (1840–48) by Friedrich von Gärtner in Aschaffenburg for Ludwig I, King of Bavaria; Prince Napoleon's Pompeian House (1856–60) by Alfred Nicolas Normand in Paris (demolished); the Villa Kerylos (1902–8) by Théodore Reinach in Cap-Ferrat; and the Roman House (1955) by Augusta Raurica near Basel, to name some well-known examples. To this company, the Getty Villa returns today —renovated, enlarged, and reimagined.

Our hope is that we have expanded the horizons of the Getty Villa as an institution by providing an inspiring setting for its ambitious

mission. We, too, held high aspirations. Recalling a phrase in the competition's brief expressing the Getty's hope that the renovated Villa would become "a place like no other," I can only say that we consciously and laboriously strove throughout this process to realize that vision. To create "a place like no other" became our own guiding motto in Boston. It led us to imagine a new environment where one could lose oneself to fantasy as well as immerse oneself in knowledge, all while enjoying artifacts of great beauty. If the new Getty Villa offers the visitor an experience that gives both intellectual as well as sensual pleasure, we have accomplished what we set out to do and what we believe the Getty sought.

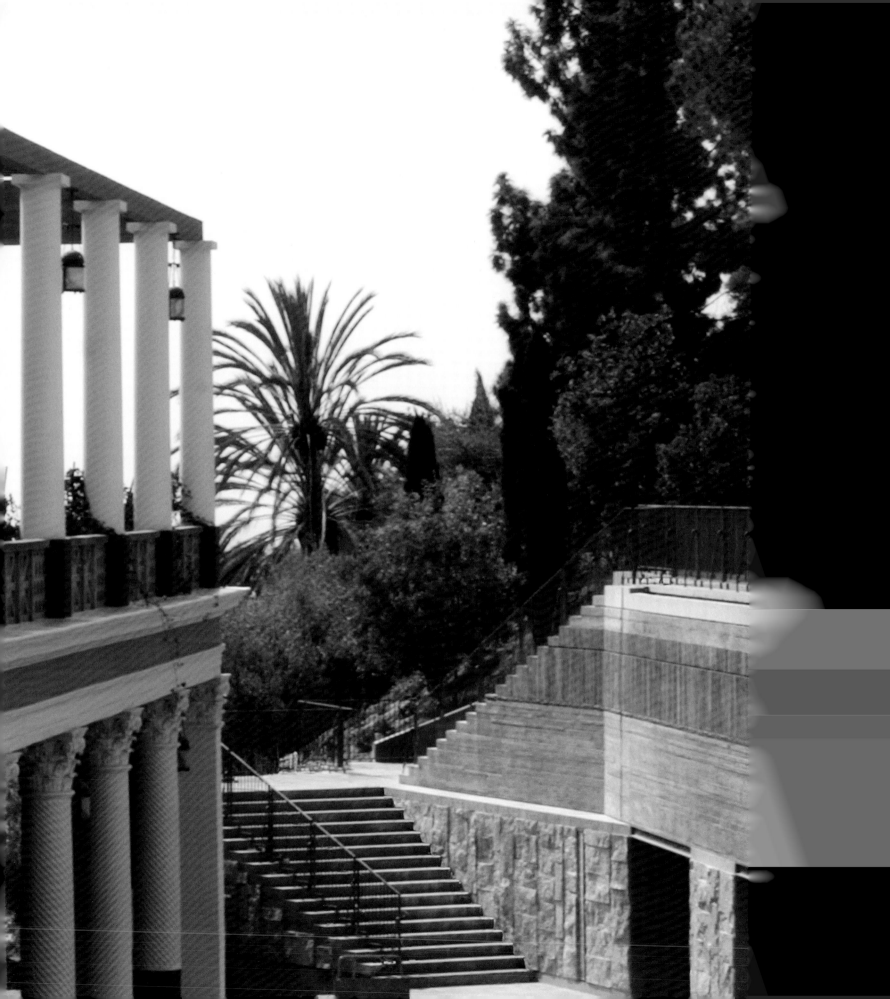

Floor Plan: Level 144'

1   Visitor Parking
2   Entry Pavilion
3   Loggia
4   Bus Drop Off
5   Peristyle Parking
6   Administration/
    Exhibition
    Preparation
7   Service Tunnel

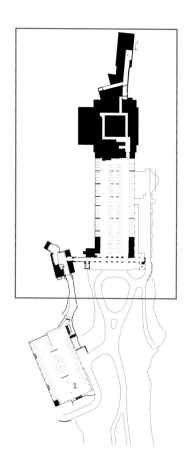

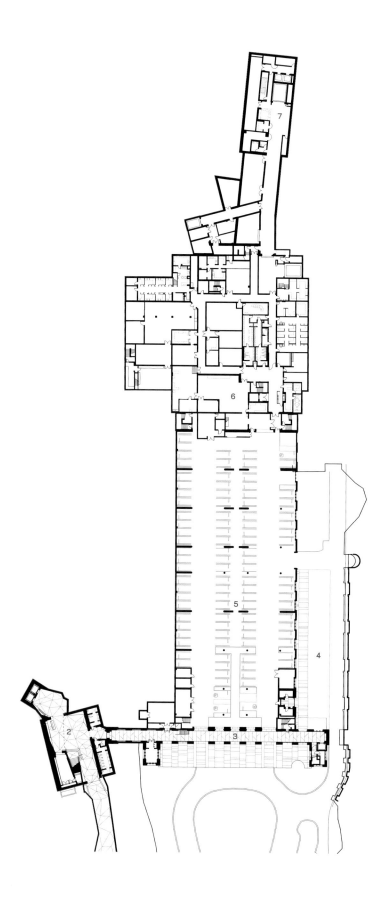

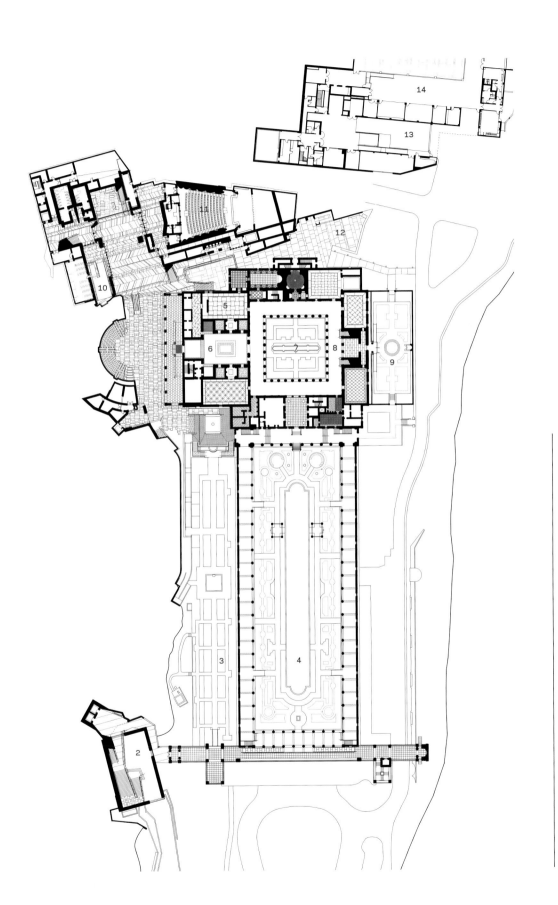

Floor Plan: Level 175'

1 Visitor Parking
2 Entry Pavilion
3 Herb Garden
4 Outer Peristyle
    Garden
5 Lower Level Galleries
6 Atrium
7 Inner Peristyle
8 East Stair

9 East Garden
10 Museum Store
11 Auditorium
12 Picnic Area
13 Loading Dock
14 Ground Maintenance
    Facility
15 Staff Parking

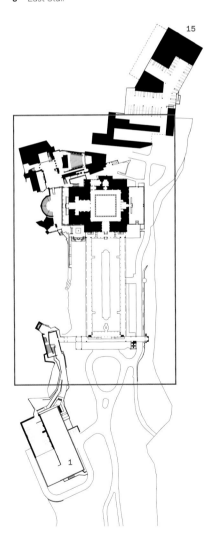

Floor Plan: Level 194'

1   Visitor Parking
2   Entry Pavilion
3   Museum Path
4   Outdoor Theater
5   Arrival Balcony
6   Upper Level Galleries
7   Cafe
8   Staff Parking

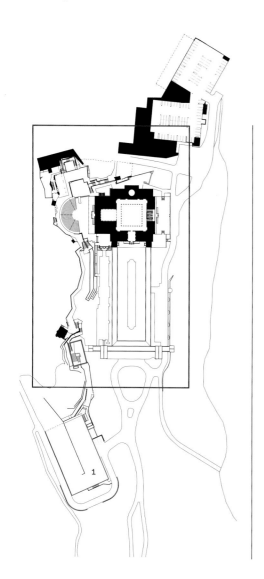

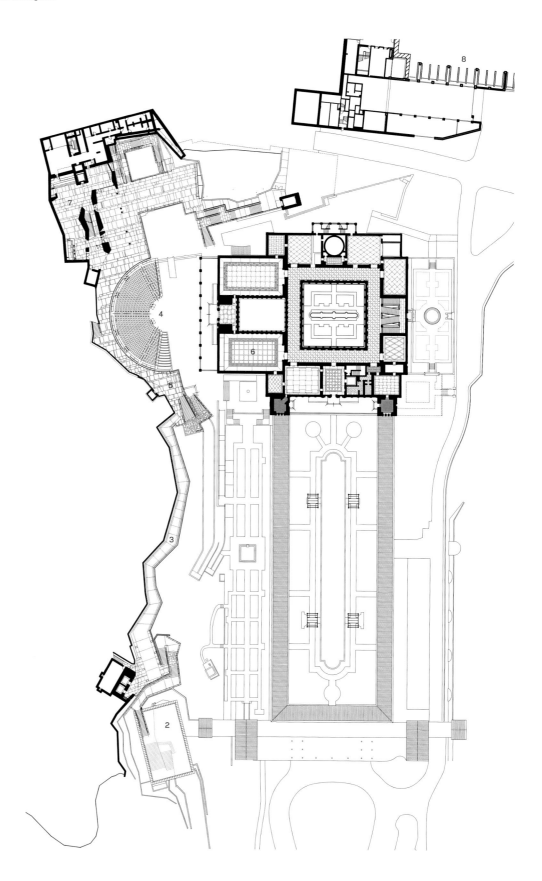

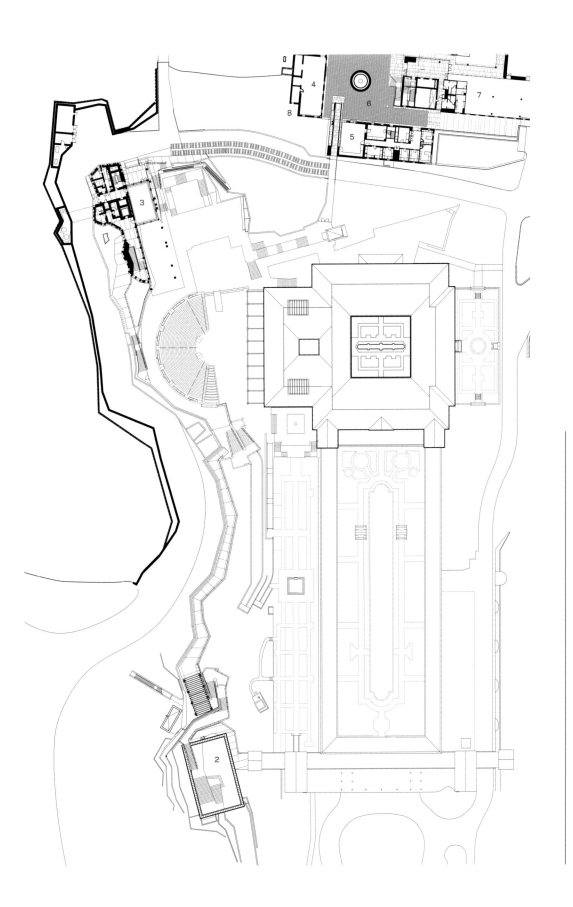

Floor Plan: Level 208'

1 Visitor Parking
2 Entry Pavilion
3 Founders Room
4 Large Objects
Laboratories
5 Organic Objects
Laboratories
6 Conservation Court /
Monkey Court
7 Office Building

8 Antiquities
Conservation
Laboratories
9 Ranch House
10 Getty Conservation
Institute Laboratories
11 Office Court
12 Physical Plant
13 Business Visitor
Parking

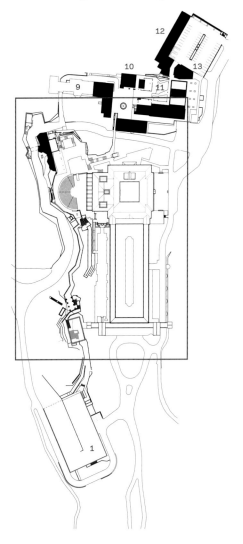

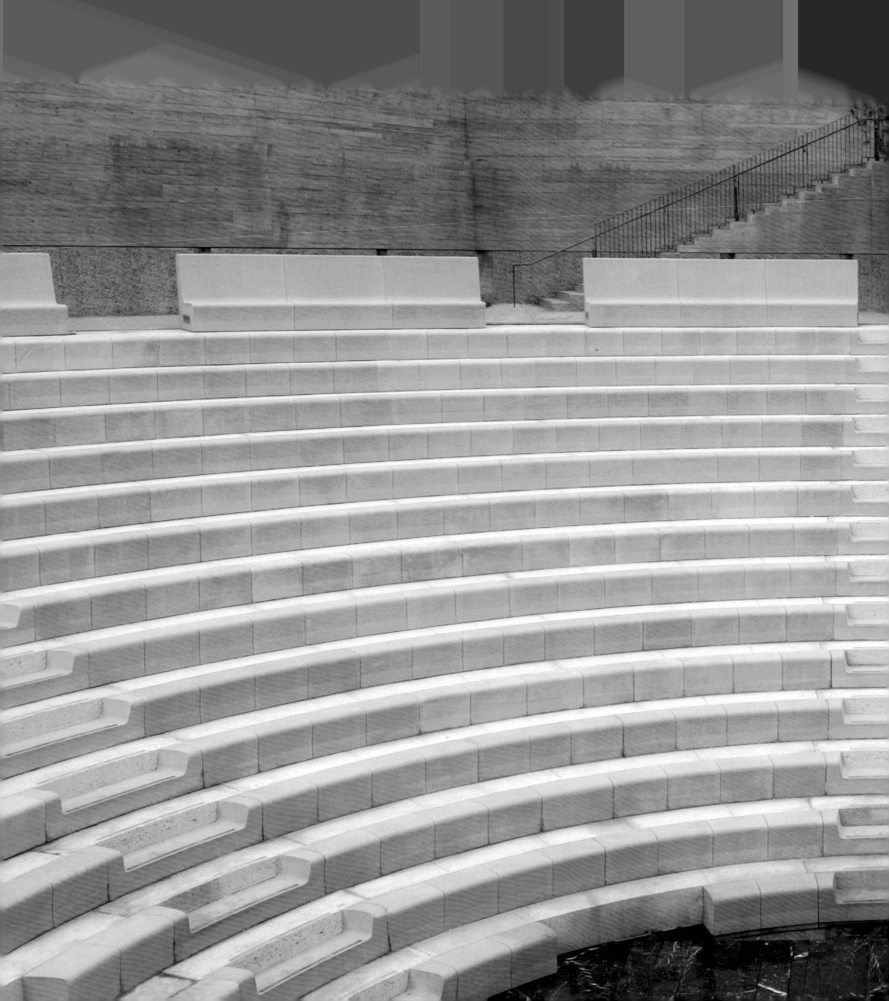

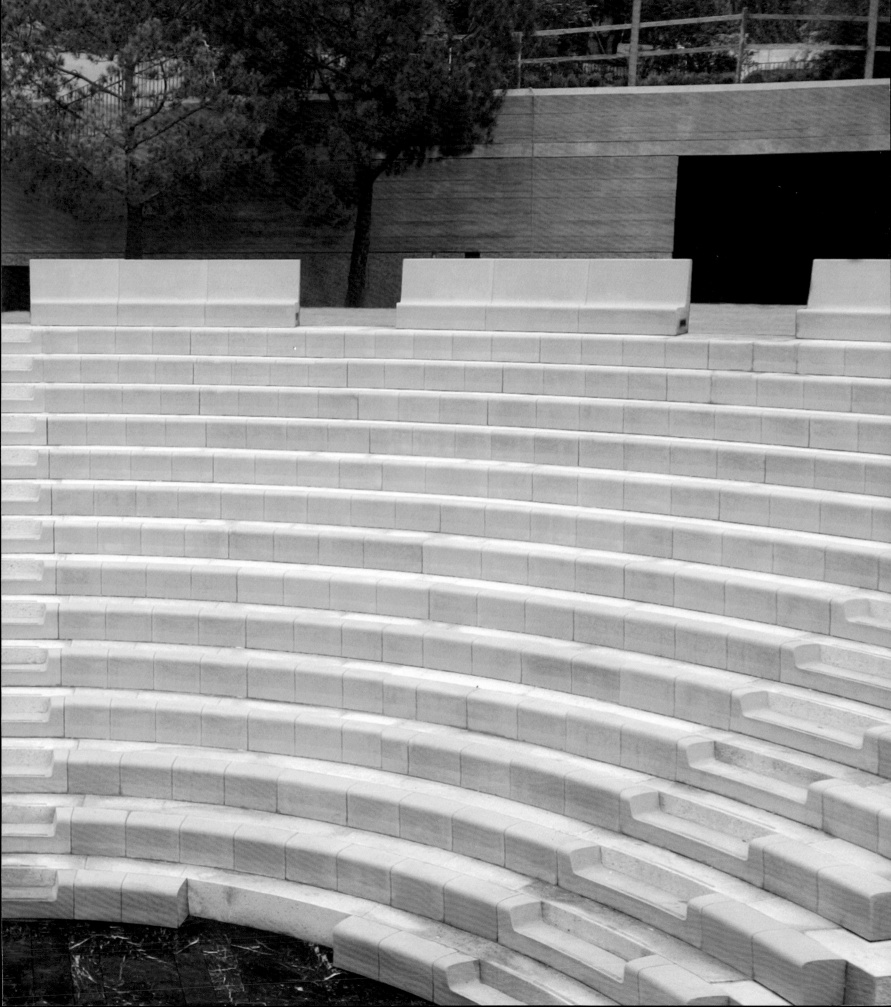

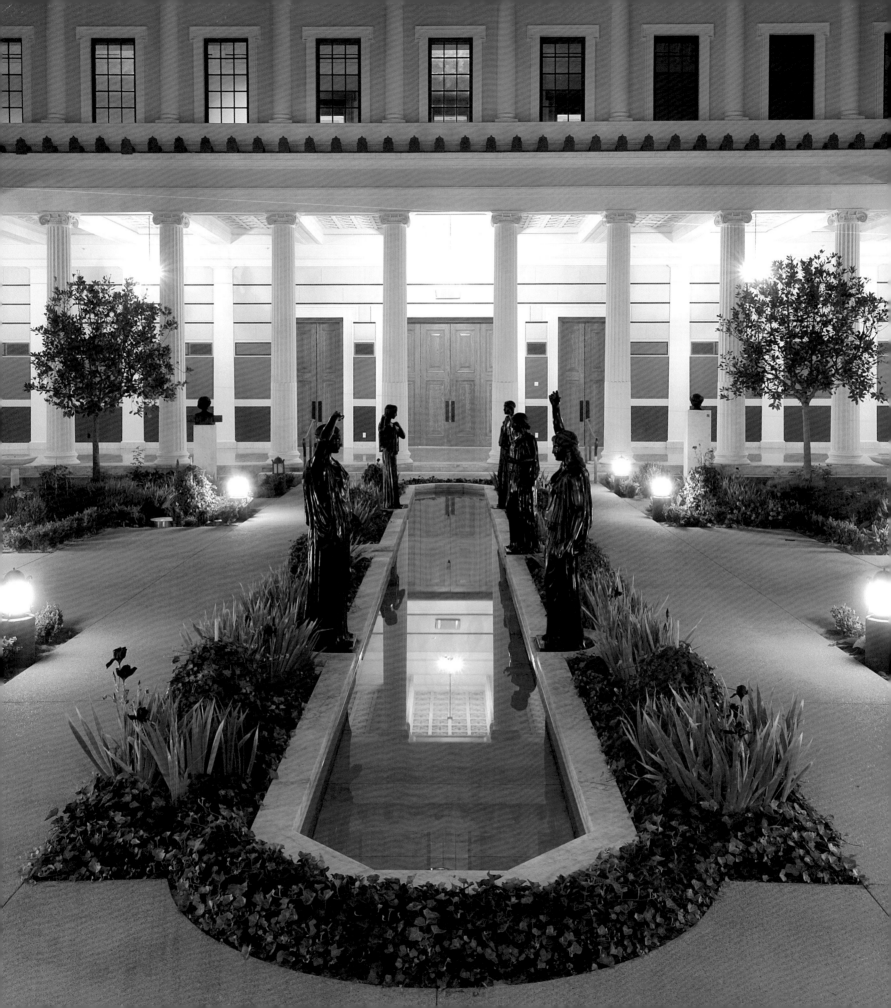

Acknowledgments

The realization of a project of this scope and complexity required the dedication and contributions of literally hundreds of people, and while it is impossible to thank each individually, we would like to express our gratitude to a special group of colleagues who were particularly instrumental in both the conception and completion of this undertaking.

From the Getty side, Harold Williams, the first President of the Getty Trust, and the current President and Chief Executive Officer, Barry Munitz, have been unwavering in their commitment to the Villa Master Plan from the beginning. The Villa's first Director, Stephen Garrett, who had overseen the original construction of the building for Mr. Getty, was equally enthusiastic and provided valuable information about the development of the first plans and important advice about the renovations. Former Vice President Stephen Rountree, former Getty Research Institute Director Salvatore Settis, former Getty Conservation Institute Director Miguel Angel Corzo, and former Getty Museum Director John Walsh were intimately involved in the selection of the architects, and Rountree and Walsh later took executive responsibility for the Villa planning even as they were finishing the construction of the larger Getty Center.

Rountree appointed Curt Williams, Head of Getty Facilities, as his deputy for the first four years of design development. Williams worked together with the members of the small Villa team until his departure in 2000 to head the building program of the University of Southern California. His associate and replacement, Corbin Smith, assumed direction of the Villa Project team halfway through the development of the Master Plan. Smith managed to keep everyone focused on the essentials of budget and schedule in the most positive way. Firm when necessary but sensitive to the aesthetic demands of such an undertaking, he was an indispensable part of this project's successful completion.

Another key player was Karol Wight, Associate Curator of Antiquities, who served as Marion True's deputy and backup throughout the eleven years of meetings and kept meticulous minutes recording all key discussions and decisions. Not only her records but also her thoughtful advice and intelligent observations have been essential in the preparation of this book. Merritt Price, Manager of the Museum's Exhibition Design Department, and his associate Ann Marshall were critical to the creation of the Museum gallery interiors and installation plans, working with the architects and curators to incorporate all of the lessons learned during the study trips to northern and southern Europe.

Guy Wheatley, Villa Transition Manager, organized and administered the intricate schedule for the move of collections, equipment, and staff and the completion of all aspects of the installation. Mark Greenberg, Jeffrey Cohen, Elizabeth Chapin Kahn, and Anita Keys of Getty Publications were all essential to the preparation and realization of this book. Greenberg's skillful editing brought a unity to the authors' different voices; Kahn discovered exciting, unpublished images in the Getty and USC archives; Cohen designed the handsome yet ingeniously flexible layout; and Keys managed the impossible task of completing all aspects of the publication of a still-incomplete project. Richard Ross provided, as he has for the entire project, incomparable images of every aspect of the Villa.

For the project itself, special mention must be made of two remarkable individuals, both of whom worked on the creation of the original Villa. Garth Benton, the talented muralist who painted the Outer Peristyle frescoes in 1972–74, returned to create new compositions for the wall that is now pierced by a small elevator on the north side of this garden. Denis Kurutz, our beloved landscape architect, who designed the original gardens for the Villa, worked with us for ten years on the plans for the new gardens and outdoor spaces. His death in 2003 was unexpected, but his young associate, Matt Randolph, together with Amy Korn, understood Kurutz's vision and very ably completed the project.

From the side of Machado and Silvetti Associates, among the many who contributed their imagination and technical expertise to the conception and building of the new Getty Villa, Peter Lofgren was the associate-in-charge during the competition and master planning phase of the project. For the sketchbook competition he was joined by Doug Dolezal, Monica Ponce de Leon, and Nader Tehrani. Together, during this critical phase when resources at the firm were scarce, they provided the energy and enthusiasm to complete the sketchbook successfully.

The arrival of Tim Love a year later was a major turning point in the process of expanding and reorganizing Machado and Silvetti's Getty team and the project itself — tasks in which he excelled. Acting as project director until 2002, he brought with him two new associates, Mimi Love and Conrad Ello, whose leadership and professionalism made it possible for the office to achieve the level of competence and delivery that a project of such complexity required. Special thanks are due to Kelly Wilson for his inspiring pencil sketches that helped visualize and convey the unique spirit of this project.

We all owe special recognition to the indefatigable commitment of Bradley Johnson, whose early role as Machado and Silvetti's Job Captain in Boston, and that of Field Team Leader in Los Angeles assured the successful interpretation of our design ideas and intentions by the general contractor, Morley Construction Company, and by our associates, Langdon Wilson Architecture Planning during the design phases and SPF: architects during construction. Among these latter groups special acknowledgment is due to Reginald Jackson, William Boehle, and Ed Doyle of Morley; Richard Sholl, Niall Kelly, and Douglas Gardner of Langdon Wilson; and Jeffrey Stenfors and Zoltan Pali of SPF: architects.

Finally, we would like to thank the many people listed below—at the Getty, at Machado and Silvetti, and at UCLA—without whose unique contributions the Villa could not have been reimagined and redesigned.

MARION TRUE
LOS ANGELES, JUNE 2005

JORGE SILVETTI
BOSTON, JUNE 2005

J. PAUL GETTY TRUST

Barry Munitz, *President
and Chief Executive Officer*
Jill Murphy, *Chief of Staff*

ACCOUNTING
Russ Shirvanian, *Assistant
Manager*

AUDIO VISUAL
Stephen Bennett, *Manager*
Stepheny Dirden

COMMUNICATIONS
Pamela Johnson, *Vice President
Communications
and Corporate Relations*
Tracy Gilbert
John Giurini
Kelly King
Megan Kissinger
Christopher Muniz
Heather Williamson

DIGITAL POLICY AND
INITIATIVES
Kenneth Hamma, *Executive
Director*

FACILITIES
Dorothy Osaki

FINANCE AND ADMINISTRATION
Bradley Wells, *Vice President
of Finance and Administration*
David Bigley
Steve Crabb
Steve Juarez
Merilee McAuliffe
Antoine Rose
Robin Weissberger

GENERAL COUNSEL
Peter Erichsen, *Vice President,
General Counsel, and Secretary*
Pamela Braunstein
Lori Fox

GROUNDS AND GARDENS
Richard Naranjo, *Manager,
Villa Grounds and Gardens*
Michael DeHart
Juan Romero

SECURITY ADMINISTRATION
Robert Combs, *Director of
Security*
Greg Gelberg
LJ Hartman
Vince Sarish
Bruce Segler

TELECOMMUNICATION SERVICES
Brian Brown, *Senior Technician*
Maurice Kerr

VILLA ENGINEERING
Oren Gray, *Manager*
John Donohoe

VILLA PERSONNEL AND
ADMINISTRATIVE SERVICES
Guy Wheatley,
Villa Transition Manager
Maria Mapes

VILLA PROGRAM COORDINATION
Lisa Guzzetta, *Project Specialist*

VILLA RENOVATION
Corbin Smith, *Head, Villa
Project Team*
Paula Cabot
Georgina Evans
Cheryl Freeman
Emily Tani
Barbara Waller-Wing
Kay Wilson
Trish Wolfe

J. PAUL GETTY MUSEUM

William Griswold,
Acting Director

ANTIQUITIES
Marion True, *Curator*
Jens Daehner
Peter Evans
Janet Grossman
Mary Louise Hart
Kenneth Lapatin
Toby Schreiber (volunteer)
Carrie Tovar
Karol Wight
Noel Wu

ANTIQUITIES CONSERVATION
AND MOUNTMAKING
Jerry Podany, *Conservator*
David Armendariz
BJ Farrar
Susan Lansing Maish
McKenzie Lowry
Jeff Maish
Adrienne Pamp
Stephanie Prabulos
Erik Risser
Eduardo Sanchez
Marie Svoboda

EDUCATION
Peggy Fogelman,
Assistant Director
Rainer Mack, *Head,
Villa Education*
Joan Alexander
Veronica Alvarez
Jennifer Calef
Elizabeth Escamilla
Guy Fish
Stephanie Lile
Viviane Meerbergen
Ann Steinsapir

EXHIBITION DESIGN
Merritt Price, *Manager*
Malek Chalabi
Patrick Frederickson
Davina Henderson
Reid Hoffman
Michael Lira
Ann Marshall
Tim McNeil
Silvina Niepomniszcze
Leon Rodriguez
Erica Schmidbauer
Mary Beth Trautwein
Nicole Trudeau
Julian Wulfart (intern)
Debi van Zyl

EXHIBITIONS
Quincy Houghton, *Assistant
Director*
Liz Andres, *Villa Exihibition
Coordinator*
Adrienne Davies
Ralph Flores
Laurel Kishi

GETTY PUBLICATIONS
Christopher Hudson, *Publisher*
ReBecca Bogner
Monica Case
Jeffrey Cohen
Catherine Comeau
Jim Drobka
Benedicte Gilman
Mark Greenberg
Kurt Hauser
Elizabeth Kahn
Anita Keys
Patrick Pardo
Kimberly Riback
Stephen Romio
Karen Shields
Sahar Tchaitchian

IMAGING SERVICES
Stanley R. Smith, *Manager*
Ellen Rosenbery
Jack Ross
Micheal Smith
Rebecca Vera-Martinez
Gerard Vuilleumier

INTERACTIVE PROGRAMS AND
COLLECTIONS INFORMATION
Alison Glazier, *Media Projects
    Specialist*
Steve Gemmel
Steve Konick
Rael Lewis
Ann Maertens
Christine Schuchart

PREPARATIONS
Bruce Metro, *Manager*
Marcus Adams
Al Aguilar
Todd Feldman
Richard Hards (on contract
    from Cooke's Crating)
Justin Lowman
Kevin Marshall
Tracy Witt

REGISTRAR
Sally Hibbard, *Chief Registrar*
Jacqueline Cabrera
Carole Campbell
Cherie Chen
Julia Flinker
Joyce Lee
Nancy Russell

RETAIL AND MERCHANDISING
Susan Deland, *Head*
Darcy Estes Pinelo

VISITOR SERVICES
Thomas Hook, *Manager*
Sandy Regan

**GETTY CONSERVATION
INSTITUTE**

Timothy P. Whalen, *Director*
Kathleen Dardes
Kathleen Gaines
Cecily Grzywacz
Mary Hardy
Kristin Kelly

GETTY RESEARCH INSTITUTE

Thomas Crow, *Director*
Susan Allen
Barbara Anderson
David Brafman
David Farneth
Gail Feigenbaum
Kathryn Girard
Ian Johnston
John Kiffe
Claire Lyons
Roberta Panzanelli
Melissa Piper
Marcia Reed
Charles Salas
Wim de Wit

GETTY FOUNDATION

Deborah Marrow, *Director*
Christina Olsen

FORMER GETTY STAFF

Erica Avrami
    (Conservation Institute)
Evelyn Bassel (Museum)
Sara Bujanda (intern)
Rogerio Carvalheiro (Villa Project)
Miguel Angel Corzo
    (Getty Conservation Institute)
Maria Dion (Villa Project)
Maya Elston
    (Antiquities Conservation)
Nevra Erturk (intern)

Vivian Flor-Escurra (Villa Project)
Gary Gibson (Villa Project)
Deborah Gribbon (Museum)
Jane Hamatani (Museum)
Kharon Hathaway (Villa Project)
James Hirschfeld (volunteer)
Marit Jentoft-Nilsen †
    (Antiquities Curatorial)
Chris Kendall (volunteer)
Cathy Klose (Trust)
Andrea Leonard (Museum)
Rea Lomas (Villa Project)
Gisele Lubsen (volunteer)
Emi Nam (intern)
John K. Papadopoulos
    (Antiquities Curatorial)
Charles Passela † (Museum)
Ann Pautnaude
    (Antiquities Curatorial)
Thomas Reese
    (Getty Research Institute)
Stephen Rountree (Trust)
Salvatore Settis
    (Getty Research Institute)
Robert Sieger
    (Antiquities Conservation)
Hy Tiano (Villa Project)
John Walsh (Museum)
Barbara Whitney (Museum)
Curt Williams (Trust)
Harold Williams (Trust)
Cari Winterich (volunteer)
Ellen Wirth (Museum)
Soojung Yoo (intern)

**MACHADO AND SILVETTI
ASSOCIATES, INC.**

Jorge Silvetti, *Principal-in-Charge*
Rodolfo Machado, *Consulting
    Principal*

SKETCHBOOK TEAM
Douglas Dolezal
Devin Hong
Christopher Keane

Peter Lofgren
Monica Ponce de Leon
Nader Tehrani

MASTER PLAN TEAM
Peter Lofgren, *Associate-in-Charge*
Tim Love, *Associate-in-Charge*
Hani Asfour
Stephen Atkinson
Conrad Ello
Mimi Love
Nader Tehrani
Russell Walker

PROJECT TEAM
Tim Love, *Project Director*
Conrad Ello, *Associate-in-Charge
    of New Construction*
Mimi Love, *Associate-in-Charge
    of Renovations*
Bradley Johnson, *Job Captain &
    Field Team Leader*
Dario Albanese
George Arnold
Jennifer Beningfield
Brett Bentson
Modesto Bigas-Valedon
Nathan Bishop
Greg Canaras
Brian Cavanaugh
Philip Chen
Pamela Choi
John Clegg
Maria De Las Mercedes Cornejo
Andrew Cruse
Christian Dagg
Signe Dinsdale
Maksim Drivin
Timothy Dumbleton
Markus Elkatsha
Rami el Samahy
Joshua Fenollosa
Jeremy Ficca
Aaron Follett
Juan Frigerio
Christopher Genter

Steven Gerrard
Kristen Giannattasio
James Gresalfi
Christopher Grimley
Andrew Hamblin
Natasha Harper
Steve Hoard
Sarah Holmes
Derek Johnson
Miks Karklins
Ben Karty
Seiee Kim
Peter Kleiner
Andrew Ku
Michael LeBlanc
Stephen Lee
Joseph Liechty
Matthew Littell
Samantha Lukacs
Sebastian Martellotto
Bruce Miller
Mimi Moncier
Kayoko Ohtsuki
Matthew Oudens
Mark Pasnik
Nick Papaefthimiou
Carie Penebad
Justin Pijak
Steven Poon
Jonathan Ramsey
Gary Rohrbacher
Susanne Schindler
Elena Serio
Jay Smith
Ted Touloukian
Ricardo Vargas
Rodrigo Vidal
Ethan Yungerman
Augustus Wendell

Special thanks to Kelly Wilson
for his inspiring pencil sketches
that helped visualize and convey
the unique spirit of this project.

**UNIVERSITY OF CALIFORNIA,
LOS ANGELES**

David Scott

**UNIVERSITY OF SOUTHERN
CALIFORNIA**

Claude Zachary

**MORLEY CONSTRUCTION
COMPANY**
GENERAL CONTRACTORS

Reginal Jackson, *Project Executive*
Ed Doyle, *Project Superintendent*
Tod Howard, *Senior Project
    Manager*
Mike Stone, *Project Manager*
Gordon Bradley, *Superintendent,
    Museum*
Lance Dixon, *Superintendent,
    West Campus*
Mike Klocki, *Superintendent,
    West Campus*
Jeff Rauls, *Superintendent,
    Ranch House*
Larry Sevilla, *Superintendent,
    North Campus*
Steve Wiegman, *Superintendent,
    South Parking*
Bill Boehle, *Architectural Finishes
    Coordinator*
Gabe Menkes, *Document
    Controller*
Veronica Willenbring, *MEP
    Coordinator*

PROJECT TEAM
Tony Carrasco
Christine Chan
Mark Cherogatti
Anna Ching
Bob Dampf
Jeremy Dominik
Gene Eagle

Brian Fritz
Jeff Funderburk
Jaime Garcia
Tim Giles
Kevin Hartzell
Cynthia Hughes-Doyle
Jessica Hupf
Ryan Hupf
Jason Kahle
Don Kahn
Ernest King
Sam Kong
Amy La Mere
Roger Loomis
Julie Masciale
John McGlynn
Brenda McGrew
Garrett Miller
Jeff Moe
Mike Rohrer
John Schmidt
Jeff Simonson
Jordan Smigielski
Edward So
Sam Sun
Courtney Taylor
Paul Vasquez
Carl Vizcarra
Tracy Warren
Caryn Wilson

SPF:ARCHITECTS
EXECUTIVE ARCHITECTS

Judit Fekete, *Principal*
Zoltan Pali, *Principal*
Jeffrey Stenfors, *Principal*

PROJECT TEAM
Don Barbaree
Joann Costello
David Dorn
Bea Egeto
Michelle Ewers
Joe Fedorowich
Wendi Gilbert

Nora Gordon
Jacquie Hernandez
Bronia Hernikova
Alec Johnson
Blaise Kim
Karl Lee
Frank Lopez
Siddhartha Majumdar
Jun Nagase
Giancarlo Renella
Lori Selna
Dan Seng
Shweta Sinha
Dan Spanton
Greg Smith
Greg Stutheit
Damon Surfas
Jeffrey Temple
Drew Wilson

LAM PARTNERS, INC
LIGHTING

Jennifer Pieszak
Paul Zaferiou

**DENIS L. KURUTZ A.S.L.A.
& ASSOCIATES**
LANDSCAPE ARCHITECTS

Denis Kurutz †

KORNRANDOLF
LANDSCAPE ARCHITECTS

Amy Korn
Matt Randolph

GLASBAU HAHN, GmBH
EXHIBITION FURNITURE

† Deceased

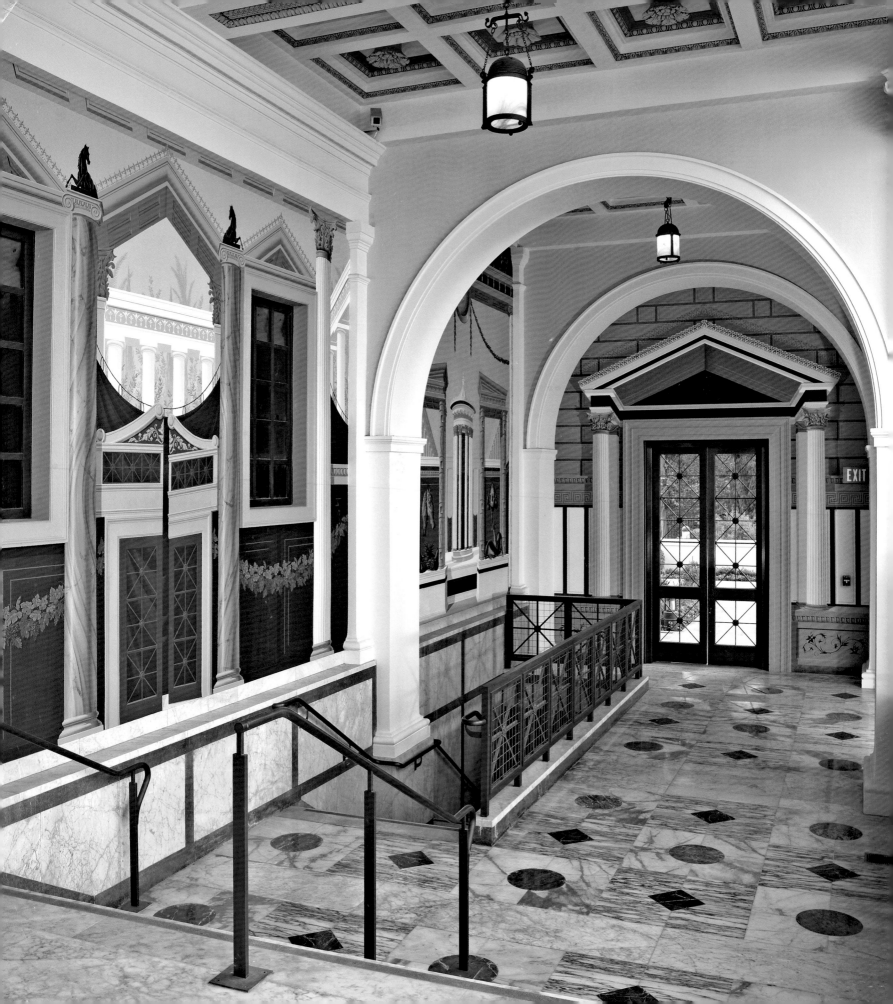

Illustration Credits

Unless otherwise noted, references are to figure numbers

AV	Photograph by Alexander Vertikoff
GRI:IA	The Getty Research Institute, Institutional Archives of the J. Paul Getty Trust
GRI:SC	The Getty Research Institute, Special Collections
JPGM: ADP (ER, GV)	J. Paul Getty Museum, Architectural Details project (Photograph by Ellen Rosenbery and Gerard Vuilleumier)
JPGM: ADP (JR)	J. Paul Getty Museum, Architectural Details project (Photograph by Jack Ross)
JPGM: LA	J. Paul Getty Museum at the Getty Center (Los Angeles)
JPGM: M	J. Paul Getty Museum at the Getty Villa (Malibu)
JS	Photograph by Julius Schulman
MCC	Morley Construction Company
MSA	Machado and Silvetti Associates
MT	Photograph by Marion True
RR	© Richard Ross (Principal photographer for the Getty Villa Project)
USC	University of Southern California, Los Angeles Specialized Libraries and Archival Collections

PAGE ii–iii. RR
PAGE vi. RR
PAGE viii. RR
PAGE x. RR

INTRODUCTION

PAGE xiii. (left) MT
PAGE xiii. (top right) Huntington Art Gallery
PAGE xiii. (bottom right) Postcard Booth Historical Photograph Archives, San Diego Historical Society

PAGE xv. MSA
PAGE xvi. MT
PAGE xvii. JPGM: LA Imaging Services
PAGE xix. Sonia Halliday Photographs

PAGE xxii–xxiv. RR

PART I: TRUE

1. GRI: IA BUI (10001)
2. GRI: IA BUI (10001)
3. Double Desk; By Bernard II van Risenburgh (b. after 1696–ca. 1766; master before 1730); French (Paris), ca. 1750; oak and mahogany veneered with tulipwood, kingwood, and *bois satiné*; gilt-bronze mounts; 107.8 × 158.7 × 84.7 cm (3 ft 6½ in × 5 ft 2½ in. × 2 ft 9¾ in); JPGM: LA 70.DA.87
4. The *Elgin Kore*; Greek, ca. 475 B.C.; marble; H: 71 cm (28 in); JPGM: M 70.AA.114
5. *James Christie*, 1778; Thomas Gainsborough (English, 1727–1788); oil on canvas; 126 × 102 cm (49⅝ × 40⅛ in); JPGM: LA 70.PA.16
6. *Saint Bartholomew*, 1661; Rembrandt van Rijn (Dutch, 1606–1669); oil on canvas;

86.5 × 75.5 cm (34⅛ × 29¾ in); JPGM: LA 71.PA.15
7. GRI: IA BUI (10001)
8. GRI: IA BUI (10001)
9. GRI: IA BUI (10001)
10. The Lansdowne Herakles; Roman (Tivoli), ca. A.D. 125; marble; H: 193.5 cm (76⅛ in); JPGM: M 70.AA.109
11. USC
12. GRI: IA BUI (10001)
13. Statue of Venus (the "Mazarin Venus"); Roman, 2nd c. A.D.; marble; H: 184 cm (72⁷⁄₁₆ in.) JPGM: M 54.AA.4
14. Music Stand; Paris, ca. 1770–1775; attributed to Martin Carlin; oak veneered with tulipwood, amaranth, holly, and fruitwood, incised with colored mastics; gilt-bronze mounts; maximum H: 148.6 cm (4 ft 10½ in); w: 50.2 cm (1 ft 7¾ in); D: 36.8 cm (1 ft 2½ in); JPGM: LA 55.DA.4
15. GRI: IA BUI (10001)
16. GRI: IA BUI (10001)
17. GRI: IA BUI (10001) Drawing: E. Genter
18. GRI: IA BUI (10001) Drawing: E. Genter
19. GRI: IA BUI (10001) Drawing: E. Genter
20. RR
21. Museo Archaeologico, Naples. Photo: Sandra Sider

22. GRI: IA 870517
23. USC
24. © Scala/Art Resource, New York
25. MT
26. MT
27. Courtesy Stephen Garrett
28. RR
29. Alfredo e Pio Foglia, Naples
30. RR
31. GRI: IA 870517
32. GRI: IA 870517 Drawing: E. Genter
33. GRI: IA 870517 Drawing: E. Genter
34. GRI: IA 870517
35. GRI: IA 870517
36. National Geographic Society. Photo: O. Louis Mazzantenta
37. GRI: IA 870517
38. GRI: IA 870517
39. GRI: IA 870517
40. GRI: IA 870517
41. RR
42. RR
43. RR
44. RR
45. GRI: IA BUI (10001) Photo: JS
46. GRI: IA BUI (10001) Photo: JS
47. GRI: IA BUI (10001) Photo: JS
48. AV
49. GRI: IA BUI (10001)
50. GRI: IA BUI (10001)
51. GRI: IA BUI (10001)
52. RR
53. RR
54. GRI: IA 870517 Drawing: E. Genter
55. GRI: IA BUI (10001)
56. GRI: IA BUI (10001)
57. RR
58. JS
59. GRI: IA BUI (10001)
60. GRI: IA 870517 Drawing: E. Genter
61. JPGM: LA Imaging Services
62. JS
63. JPGM: M
64. Statue of Aphrodite-Hygieia with Eros; Roman ca. A.D. 200; marble; H: 175 cm, W: 53 cm, D: 35 cm (H: 68⅞ W: 20⅞ D: 13¾ in); JPGM: M 71.AA.338
65. RR
66. RR
67. JS
68. GRI: IA 870517
69. GRI: IA BUI (10001) Photo: JS
70. JS
71. JS
72. RR
73. JPGM: ADP (ER, GV)
74. JPGM: ADP (JR)
75. GRI: IA BUI (10001) Photo: JS
76. J. Paul Getty Trust, Communications
77. MT
78. JPGM: M
79. RR
80. The Hope Hygieia; Roman copy after a Greek original sometimes attributed to Skopas, Greece, 4th c. B.C.; 2nd c. A.D.; marble; 190.5 × 63.5 × 45.72 cm (75 × 25 × 18 in.). Los Angeles County Museum of Art 50.33.23
81. Scarab; Etruscan; later 5th c. B.C.; carnelian; H: 0.7 cm W: 1.5 cm D: 1.1 cm (H: 14 in. W: 9⁄16 in. D: 7⁄16 in.) JPGM: M 81.AN.76.133
82. Attic Black-Figured Neck-Amphora; name-vase of the Bareiss Painter; Greek (Athens), 530–520 B.C.; terracotta; H: 32.8 cm (12⅞ in); DIAM: (body): 21.9 cm (8⅝ in); JPGM: M 86.AE.85
83, 84. JPGM: M
85. Attic Red-Figured Kylix, Type B; attributed to the Brygos Painter; Greek (Athens), ca. 490 B.C.; terracotta; H: 11.2 cm (4⅜ in); DIAM: 31.4 cm (12¼ in); JPGM: M 86.AE.286
86. Statuette of a Harpist; early Cycladic (Cyclades), ca. 2500 B.C.; marble; H: 35.8 cm (14⅛ in); D: 28 cm (11 in); W: 9.5 cm (3¾ in); JPGM: M 85.AA.103
87. Sculptural Group of Two Griffins Attacking a Fallen Doe; Greek (South Italy), 325–300 B.C.; marble with polychromy; H: 95 cm (37⅜ in); W: 148 cm (58¼ in); JPGM: M 85.AA.106
88. Female Figure of the Late Spedos Type; name-piece of the Steiner Master; early Cycladic (Cyclades), 2500–2400 B.C.; Marble; H: 59.9 cm (23⅝ in); JPGM: M 88.AA.80
89. Jerry Thompson
90. Statuette of a Seated Lion; Greek (Lakonia), ca. 550 B.C.; bronze; H: 9.3 cm (3¾ in), W: 5 cm (2 in); L: 13.3 cm (5¼ in); JPGM: M 96.AB.76
91. Lebes; Greek, 50–1 B.C.; bronze with silver inlays; H: 58 cm (22⅞ in); JPGM: M 96.AC.51
92. Two-handled Cup; Roman, A.D. 1–100; Silver; H: 12.5 cm (4⅞ in), DIAM: 16.3 cm (6⅜ in); JPGM: M 96.AM.57
93. Counterclockwise from left: Mold-blown head flask (Roman, 2nd c. A.D.) JPGM: M 2003.326; gold-band flask (Roman, late 1st c. B.C.–early 1st c. A.D.) JPGM: M 2003.230; gold-band pyxis (Roman, late 1st century B.C.–early 1st c. A.D.) JPGM: M 2003.231; agate glass pyxis with lid (Roman, 1st c. A.D.) JPGM: M 2003.256; faceted one-handled jug (Roman, late 1st-early second century A.D.) JPGM: M 2003.346; mosaic bowl (late Hellenistic-early Roman 1st c. B.C.) JPGM: M 2003.24; vessel with 13 handles (Roman, 3rd-4th c. A.D.) JPGM: M 2003.398. Tallest 19.4 cm
94. Tom Bonner
95. RR
96. JS
97. GRI: IA BUI (10001)
98. JS
99. MT
100. JS
101. MT
102. Actors left to right: Hope Alexander-Willis, Jon Matthews, Robert Machray, Larry Randolph. Photo: Craig Schwartz
103. AV
104. RR
105. GRI: IA 2004.IA.6
106. GRI: IA 2004.IA.6
107. GRI: IA 2004.IA.6
108. GRI: IA BUI (10001)
109. RR
110. MT
111. GRI: IA 2004.IA.6.
112. GRI: IA 2004.IA.6
113. MSA
114. MSA
115. MSA
116. MSA
117. MSA
118. RR
119. JS

120. GRI: IA 2004.1A.6
121. GRI: IA 2004.1A.6
122. RR
123. MSA
124. RR
125. RR
126. RR
127. GRI: IA 2004.1A.6
128. GRI: IA 2004.1A.6
129. MCC
130. JPGM: ADP (ER, GV)
131. RR
132. RR
133. RR
134. RR
135. RR
136. RR
PAGE 94–95. RR
PAGE 96. MSA

PART II: SILVETTI

137. GRI: SC
138. JPGM: ADP (ER, GV)
139. RR
140. MSA
141. RR
142. Jeffrey Cohen
143. GRI: IA 2004.1A.6
144. GRI: IA 2004.1A.6
145. MSA
146. GRI: IA 2004.1A.6
147. GRI: IA 2004.1A.6
148. GRI: IA 2004.1A.6
149. GRI: IA 2004.1A.6
150. GRI: IA 2004.1A.6
151. GRI: IA BUI (10001)
152. MSA
153. GRI: IA BUI (10001)
     Drawing: Dave Wilkins
154. GRI: IA 2004.1A.6
155. MSA
156. GRI: IA 2004.1A.6
157. MSA
158. MSA
159. GRI: IA 2004.1A.6

160. MSA
161. GRI: IA 2004.1A.6
162. GRI: IA 2004.1A.6
163. GRI: IA 2004.1A.6
164. MSA
165. MSA
166. MSA
167. GRI: IA 2004.1A.6
168. GRI: IA 2004.1A.6
169. GRI: IA 2004.1A.6
170. GRI: IA 2004.1A.6
171. MSA
172. GRI: IA 2004.1A.6
173. GRI: IA 2004.1A.6
174. GRI: IA 2004.1A.6
175. MSA
176. GRI: IA 2004.1A.6
177. MSA
178. GRI: IA 2004.1A.6
179. MSA
180. RR
181. MSA
182. MSA
183. MSA
184. JPGM: M
185. GRI: SC
186. MSA
187. Marina Berlozerskaya
188. GRI: IA 2004.1A.6
189. GRI: IA 2004.1A.6
190. GRI: IA 2004.1A.6
191. GRI: IA 2004.1A.6
192. GRI: IA 2004.1A.6
193. GRI: IA 2004.1A.6
194. MSA
195. MSA
196. GRI: IA 2004.1A.6
197. MSA
198. RR
199. GRI: IA 2004.1A.6
200. MSA
201. GRI: IA 2004.1A.6
202. GRI: IA 2004.1A.6
203. MSA
204. RR
205. MSA
206. MSA

207. MSA
208. MSA
209. MSA
210–211. RR
212. RR
213. RR
214. MSA
215. MSA
216. MSA
217. MSA
218. MSA
219. MSA
220. MSA
221. RR
222. B. J. Archer, Antony Vidler.
     *Follies: Architecture for the
     Late-Twentieth Century
     Landscape*, NY: Rizzoli, 1983
223. GRI: IA 2004.1A.6
224. RR
225. MSA
226. RR
227. GRI: IA 2004.1A.6
228. RR
229. GRI: IA 2004.1A.6
230. Jeffrey Cohen
231. GRI: IA 2004.1A.6
232. GRI: IA 2003.1A.6
233. MSA
234. Carnegie Museum of Art,
     Pittsburgh
235. RR
236. RR
237. MSA
238. RR
239. RR
240. RR
241. RR
242. MSA
243. MSA
244. JPGM: ADP (ER, GV)
245. MSA
246. MSA
247. MSA
248. JPGM: ADP (ER, GV)
249. MSA
250. MSA

251. JPGM: ADP (ER, GV)
252. RR
253. MSA
254. MSA
255. GRI: IA 2004.1A.6
256. GRI: IA 2004.1A.6
257. GRI: IA 2004.1A.6
258. MSA
259. RR
260. RR
261. RR
262. RR
263. JPGM: ADP (ER, GV)
264. JPGM: ADP (ER, GV)
265. RR
266. RR
267. RR
268. MSA
269. MSA
270. GRI: IA 2004.1A.6
271. RR
272. MSA
273. GRI: IA 2004.1A.6
274. RR
275. MSA
276. MSA
277. MSA
278. RR
279. RR
280. RR
281. MSA
282. MSA
283. MCC
284. GRI: IA 2004.1A.6
285. JS
286. RR
287. MSA
288. RR
PAGE 210–213. RR
PAGE 218. RR
PAGE 222. RR

COVER. RR

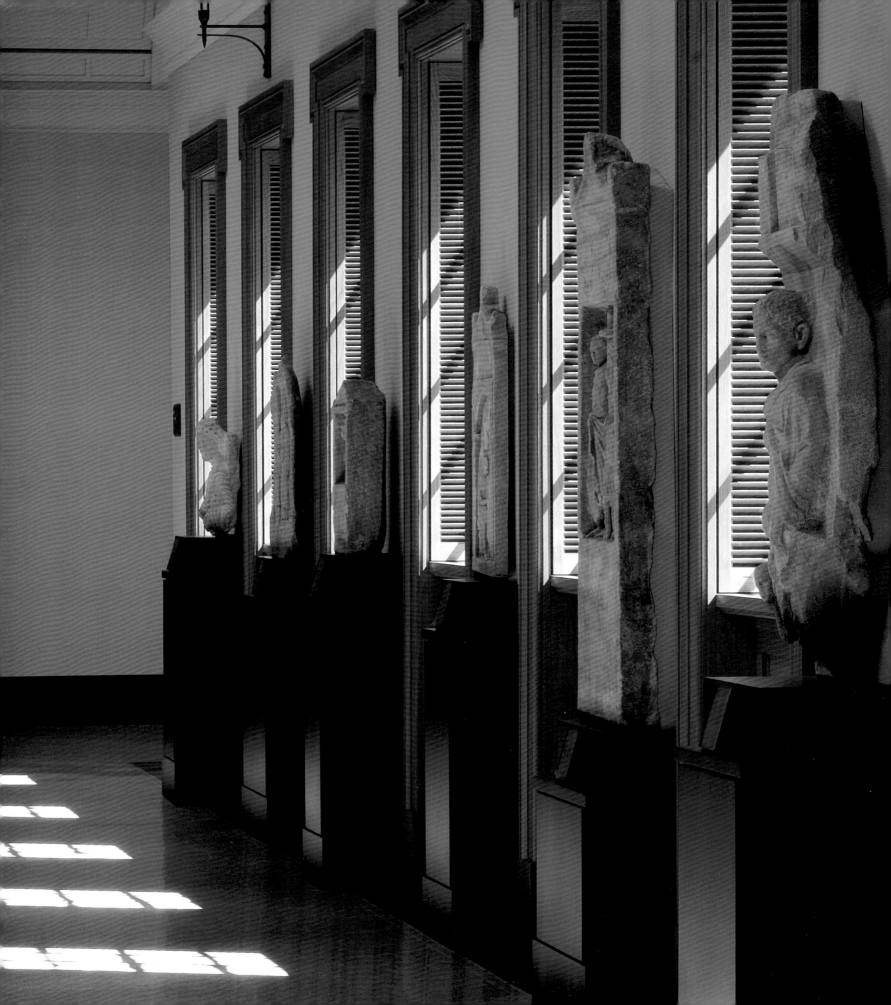

Index

Note: Page numbers in *italics* indicate photographs

acanthus plant, 34, 45
accessibility: of entire site, to pub-lic, 66, 121, 122; for disabled, 59, 60
acquisitions: of antiquities and furniture, 6, 9; of Bareiss vase collection, 51, 52; of bronze and marble sculpture, 52, 53; of decorative arts, 9; of Fleischman collection of ancient art, 52, 54, 55; of gem and cameo collec-tion, 51; of Greek and Roman examples of the minor arts, 37, 40; of Oppenländer glass collec-tion, 55, 55; of Steiner collection of Cycladic objects, 52, 53
Adam, Robert, 37
aerial photographs: of Cañon de Sentimiento, 2, 106; of Getty Center, 56; looking south to the sea, 67; of proposed site, 24; during renovation, 199; of site during renovation, 94, 95; of site prior to renovation, 72; of surrounding residential neighborhoods, 25
aesthetics, issues in, 157–59, 157, 158
Ajax, cup depicting suicide of, 52
alae, 18
Alcubierre, Roque Joaquín de, 13
Almodovar, Pedro, *Talk to Her*, 159
Altes Museum (Berlin), 78, 190

amarillo triana: and symbolic symmetries, 196, 197; use of, in East Stair, 177, 177
The Ambassadors (Holbein), 159
amenities: and addition of Garden Tea Room, 40, 42, 43; and cre-ation of Entry Pavilion, 75; lack of, prior to renovation, 59–60, 75; modification of villa to include, 27; visitor services in entry sequence, 150, 151
amphora, 52
anchoring system, 65, 89, 90
Antikenmuseum und Sammlung Ludwig (Basel), 78
Antikensammlung (Munich), 78
Antiquities Conservation, 57, 68
antiquity, presentation of, 130. *See also* history
Apelles, *Calumny*, xix
Apollo Belvedere, xvi, 15
archaeological excavation: as design conceit, 75–76, 76, 132–36, 161; in Herculaneum, 133, 134; Museum as artifact in, 170, 170
architect, selection of, 69–71, 70, 99, 101–5
architectural moldings, 26
architectural precedents, xii–xvi, xix, 204
architecture: classical, xviii, 155; confrontational juxtapositions in, 173–74; eclecticism of Cali-fornia sensibility in, xiii–xiv;

French Mediterranean, xvi; as "functional" art, 159; Hellenistic model of, xvi; language analogy in, 133, 135; museum design in, xi; Palladian, 10, 11; podium as device in, 148, 148; postmodern, xviii; "representing" construc-tion, as expressive device in, 156; Spanish colonial, xv, 10, 10; "The San Diego Look," xii; use of orthogonal grid in, 126
archives, 196–97
Arrival Balcony, 162, 168
Art History Information Program (later Getty Information Institute), 49
art market, 49
artifact, Museum as. *See under* archaeological excavation
artificial lighting. *See also* lighting: issues regarding, on upper level, 40, 41, 50, 192; vs natural, 190, 190, 192
art-support system, 65, 87, 87, 93
The Atrium, 33; ancient inspira-tions for, 18, 19, 21, 27, 61, 63; axial view of museum seen from, 82, 83; *compluvium* in, 61, 62, 194, 194, 195, 196, 196; with *compluvium* open, 195; elevation drawings for, 22; *impluvium* in, 62, 82, 194, 194, 195; inspiration for mosaic pat-terns in, 27, 28; need for natural lighting in, 18, 61, 62; prior to

renovation, 194; relation of, to main staircase, 174, 175; the-atrical productions presented in, 66
attachment points, 89, 90, 93
Auditorium, 111–12; model of, as freestanding structure, 138; model of, in present location, 138; perspective study of, 139; placement of, 138–39, 143
axial orientation: in alignment of stairway with Inner Peristyle, 174, 175, 176; of Entry Pavilion, 196, 196; of Outdoor Theater, 115, 126–27, 127; produced by *impluvium* system, 196, 196; as seen from Atrium, 82, 83, 83; west-east, of Museum, 176

Baldeweg, Juan Navarro, 69, 70
Bareiss, Molly, 51–52, 52
Bareiss, Walter, 51–52, 52
Bareiss Painter, 52
Baroque Paintings Gallery, 192
Basilica, 22, 33, 34, 37
Bavaria, xvi
Beaux Arts style: Frank Lloyd Wright on, xiv; of Huntington Art Gallery, xiv; in upper level galleries, 40, 41
behind-the-scene access, 73, 121, 122
Benton, Garth, 33, 33, 42, 43

Berlin Painter, 51

Beyond Beauty (Getty Center), 57

Bilbao Guggenheim, xi

Blackburn, Earleen, 57

Blackburn, Ralph, 57

Blackburn residence, 57

Board of Trustees. *See also* Trust: approval of twenty-year Master Plan by, 74; decision of, to phase renovation, 74, 77, 117–18; programmatic development by, 48–49; proposal to, of "reversible" entry-sequence solution, 124–26; recommendations of, concerning Master Plan, 127; at unveiling of Phase I model, *142*

Boehle, William, 214

bookstore, *122*, *142*, 143

Borges, Jorge Luis, "Pierre Menard, Author of Don Quixote," xvii, xxi

Boucher, François, 4

Bramlett, Norris, 4, 6, 10

bronzes: in Basilica, 37; creation of, in the two peristyles, *42*, *43*; Etruscan statuette of Tinia, 9; Hellenistic *lebes*, with relief protome of a satyr and inlaid with silver, *54*, 55; of maidens, in Inner Peristyle, *64*; replication of, from Villa dei Papiri, 30, *32*; of a seated lion, *54*, 55; in Tea Room fountains, 43

Brygos Painter, 51, *52*

building teams, 129, 173

busts: of emperor Hadrian, *16*; of empress Agrippina, 4; of empress Sabina, 4; of Julia Titi, 9; *Portrait Head of a Balding Man*, 52

Cafe: in "hub" of public activities, *116*, 117; in Phase I of Master Plan, 77, *143*; prior to renovation

114; staff, 147, *149*; view of, in entry sequence, *123*

Cafe Stair, *197*

California Coastal Commission, 81

Calumny (Apelles), xix

cameo collection, 51, *51*

camper lot, 59, 104, 119, *119*, 122, *122–23*

Cañon de Sentimiento. *See also* topographical conditions: access of visitors to, 66; aerial view of, with Ranch House, *2*; aerial view of, with sketch of Villa superimposed, *24*; history of ownership of, 3; topographical conditions of, 106, 108, 112, *112*

Canova, Antonio, xiv

carbonization, at Herculaneum, 13–14, *14*, 37, *40*

cardboard studies, *120*

Carlin, Martin, 3, 8, 9

Carnegie Museum (Pittsburgh), *171*

Casa di Cei (Pompeii), *21*

Cassina (Plautus), 66

casts, of classical architecture elements, 170, *171*

ceilings: decoration of, ancient inspirations for, *23*, 30, *31*, 33–34; in gallery lighting solution, 90; vaulted, 34, 79, *80*

centaur, *36*

center of gravity, of site organization, *112*, 113, 117, *118*, 126, *126*

Charles III, 13

Chester Beatty Collection, 9

Chiurazzi, Gennaro, xvi

Chiurazzi foundry, xvi, xvii, 30, 43, *64*

Christie's (London), 16

Churriguera, José Benito de, xii

Churrigueresque style, xiii, xiv

circulation, of visitors: at East Stair, 176, *176*; in siting of programmatic elements, 112–13, *118*

classicism: in Master Plan for Getty Center, 155; use of, in postmodernist vocabulary, xviii

climate control, 59, 65, 83

Colegiata de Santa María la Mayor (Ronda), xiv

Collector's Choice (Le Vane), 3, 16

color schemes: experiments in choice of, 85, *85*, *86*, *88*; for exterior walls, 183, *186*, *187*; and selection of wall colors, 183, *186*, *184–87*; use of coputer simulations in experimentation with, *84*; and use of Roman palette, 132

columns: of Corinthian colonnade, *30*; decorative elements on, *100*; of Doric colonnade, 23, *31*, *44*; Ionic capitals of Inner Peristyle, *26*; between Room of Colored Marbles and Basilica, 37; on West Porch, 43

commercialism, in presentation of history, 101, *101*, 103

Complexity and Contradiction in Architecture (Venturi), xviii

compluvium: after renovation, *195*, *196*; in introduction of natural light to the Atrium, 61, *62*; prior to renovation, *194*

computer access, 89, *90*

computer simulations, *84*

computer technology, 49, 89, *90*

concerts, 66, *66*

Conservation Court, 146–47, *149*. *See also* Monkey Court

conservation laboratories, 57, 68; assignment of, to Getty Conservation Institute, 113; design of state-of-the-art, 146; issues concerning, in renovation planning, 65–66; use of, in master's program, 77; view of, in entry sequence, *123*

construction: aerial views of, *2*, *94*, 95, *199*; legal issues delaying, 81, *197*–98; Morley Construction

Company role in, 150–51, *197*, 214; "representing," as expressive device, 156

Cook Collection, 5

Corinthian colonnade, *30*

Cortines, Ramon C., 77

Corzo, Miguel Angel, 69

cost, of renovation, 74, 111

courtyards, *148*

Cressant, Charles, 3, 9

Crouching Aphrodite, 6

cubicula, 50

Cycladic period: acquisition of Steiner collection of objects from, 52, 53; statuette of a harpist, 53; three large female figures of the folded-arm type, *53*

The Death of Dido (attributed to Peter Paul Rubens), 4, *6*

Decorative Arts Galleries, *190*

decorative elements, *100*

DeHart, Michael, 78

Der Rosenkavalier (Strauss), 159

design elements: color schemes for, 85, *85*, *86*, *88*, 183, *186*, *184–87*; computer simulations of, *84*; foam-core model of, *85*; natural lighting as, 130, 132

design process: development of vocabulary in, 130, 133, 135; first formalization in, 110–11; study trips in support of, 78–79, *78–80*, 129–32, *131*, *183*

Diana and Her Nymphs on the Hunt (attributed to workshop of Peter Paul Rubens), 9

dining. *See also* Cafe: in Garden Tea Room, 40, *42*, 43; in restaurant, 161; for staff, 147

Disney, 101

display cases, *88*, *90*, *91*, 188, *188*

display space, 50. *See also* galleries

dissonance, as an artistic tactic, 159

Dolezal, Doug, 214

Don Quixote (Cervantes), xvii–xviii
Doric colonnade, *23, 31, 44*
Douris, 51
Doyle, Ed, 214
drop-off area, 152, *152, 153*

earthquakes: damage to Getty
   Center by, 73–74; and installation of artwork, 65, 89, *90*, 178;
   need for protection from, 78, 85
East Garden, 43, *46*, 82
East Road, 59
East Stair: axial orientation of,
   174, *175, 176*; bronze *torchères*
   on, *189*; design elements of, 177,
   177; handrails on, 177, *177*;
   placement of, 174–77, *175, 176*
eclecticism, xiii
educational programs, 49. *See also*
   master's program on the
   conservation of ethnographic
   and archaeological materials
electrical system, 89–90, *90*, 178
elevation drawings: of the
   Atrium, *22*; showing climb
   from parking to Ranch House,
   122–23; showing original
   location for Outdoor Theater,
   114–15; of south vestibule, *35*;
   of strata wall, *155*; for Temple
   of Herakles, *38*; and two-
   dimensional representation of
   Villa dei Papiri, 18, *22*
Elgin Kore, 4, *4*
Ello, Conrad, 78, 129, 214
Emmet Wemple and Associates, 43
endowment, 48–49
entrance, 50, 74–75, *75, 172*. *See
   also* entry sequence
Entrance Porch, 73
entrance vestibule, 33, *35*
Entry Pavilion, 75, *77*; antecedents
   for, in Machado and Silvetti
   Associate's *Taberna Ancipitis
   Formae—Architectorum
   Machadus Silvettusque Mirabile

Inventio,* 159, *160*; axial orientation of, 196, *196*; cardboard
   study models of alternative
   designs for, *120*; in creation of a
   sense of expectation, 159, 161,
   162–65; enlargement of, in final
   entry solution, 151, *151*; as point
   of orientation, *119*, 121; in relation to strata wall, *141*, 141–42;
   in "reversible" entry-sequence
   solution, 124–26, *124, 125*; as
   vertical threshold, 159, *162–65*;
   visitor services in, *150*, 151
entry sequence. *See also* entrance:
   addition of raised walkway
   to, 75–76, *76*; in ancient Roman
   villa, 59, *60*; for behind-the-
   scene access, 73; in conceptual
   conceit of Museum as artifact,
   75–76, 132–36, 161, 170, *170*;
   Entry Pavilion's role in, 159,
   161, *162–65*; the final, definitive
   solution to, *150*, 151, *151*;
   impact of relocation of theater
   on, 117; inadequacy of, in original design, 27, 50; panoramic
   view created by, *168*; as
   priority of renovation, 59–60;
   "reversible," *124*, 124–26, *125*;
   role of West Porch in, 121, *121*;
   site plans for, *104*; topographical levels in, 122, *122–23*, 124;
   visitor arrival path in, *116*
Epicureanism, 13
euripus, 18
excavation: as design conceit,
   75–76, *76*, 132–36, 161, 170,
   170; in Herculaneum, *133, 134*;
   of Villa dei Papiri, *12*, 13–14,
   128, 134
Exhibition Design Department,
   183
exhibition furniture, *86, 88, 90, 90*
exhibitions. *See* special exhibitions

fire road, 58, 59
First Congregational Church
   (Riverside), xiv
Fleischman, Barbara, 52, *54*, 55
Fleischman, Lawrence, 52, *54*, 55
floors: ancient inspirations for, 34,
   36, 37, *38*, 79, 178, *178*; in
   Basilica, *37*; color and pattern
   selection for, 86, 87, *88, 89*;
   gallery numbers as decoration
   in, *188*; in Men and Heroes
   Gallery, *178*; in organization of
   installation of collection, 79, 87,
   88, 91; patterns for, in Museum
   Level 1 plan, *180*; patterns for,
   in Museum Level 2 plan, *181*;
   in Temple of Herakles, *38, 39*;
   use of terrazzo in, *30*, 178, *178*;
   in Women and Children Gallery,
   179
*Follies: Architecture for the Late-
   Twentieth-Century Landscape*
   (Leo Castelli Gallery), 159, *160*
food services, 147. *See also* dining
Fori Imperiali (Rome), 78
form and function, issues in, xx,
   108
Forum Baths (Pompeii), 34
Founders Room, 99
fountains: in East Garden, 43,
   46, 82, 83; in Monkey Court
   (Ranch House), *5, 6, 68, 113*;
   nymphaeum, in front of
   Garden Tea Room, *42*, 43
Fredericksen, Burton, 22
freight elevator, 66, 149, *149*
Frel, Jiří, 16, 37
French School of Archaeology, xvi
frescoes: garden, 43, *43*; of
   Polygnotus (Delphi), xix
frieze, of sea nymphs, above Tea
   Room *nymphaeum*, 43
funerary lions, 9
funerary monuments, 40
funicular, 73, *110*, 111
furniture: *bureau plat* by Charles
   Cressent, 3, 9; carbonized, at

Herculaneum, 37, *40*; commode
   by Gilles Joubert, 9; double
   desk by Bernard II van
   Risenburgh, 3, *4*; music stand
   attributed to Martin Carlin, *8,
   9*; replica, controversy on use
   of, 37; replica intarsia bed, *40*;
   rolltop desk by Bernard
   Molitor, 3; Sèvres mounted
   secrétaire by Adam Weisweiler,
   3; Sèvres mounted *secrétaire*
   by Martin Carlin, 3

Gainsborough, Thomas: and
   *Portrait of Anne, Countess of
   Chesterfield*, 9; and *Portrait of
   James Christie*, 4, *5*
galleries: access from, to Inner
   Peristyle, 81, 83; after renovation, 91; of ancient sculpture, 7;
   color schemes for, 85, *85, 86,
   88*, 183, *184, 185, 186*; computer
   simulations of, *84*; crowded
   condition of, prior to renovation, 50; floor color and pattern
   choice in, 86, 87, *88, 89, 178–81*;
   iconographic installation of,
   83, 85; lack of natural light in,
   50; of old master paintings, 9;
   original design scheme for, 40
gallery numbers, *188*
garages. *See also* parking: arched
   facade of, *30*; pedestrian
   connection from, to drop-off
   area, *153*; proposals for, during
   renovation planning, 73, *104*;
   staircase leading from, 50;
   subterranean, 111, 146
Garden Tea Room. *See* Tea Room
Gardener's House of
   Charlottenhof (Potsdam), 204
gardens: ancient inspirations for,
   78; East Garden, 43, *46, 82*;
   Herb Garden, 43, *47, 76*, 104,
   122, 161; historical accuracy of,
   43; in Inner Peristyle, 43;

Italian stone pines in, 104, *105*; landscaping of, 43; in Outer Peristyle, 43, *44*, *45*; peristyle, 18, *20*, *29*; on western slope, *114–15*, 115, 125, *166*

Gardner, Douglas, 71, 214

Garrett, Stephen, 10, *18*, 213

Gärtner, Friedrich von, xv, 204

Gasq, Jean-Paul-Baptiste, xvi

Gehry, Frank, xi

gem collection, 51

Genter, Edward, xii, 27

Getty, J. Paul, 7; death of, 48; on dislike of contemporary-style museums, 10; early art collections of, 3–4; envy of, for William Randolph Hearst, 16–17; focus of collections of, xv; at his villa in Palo, *15*; interest in antiquity of, 14–15; and *A Journey to Corinth*, xvii, 16; on reasons for building the Getty Villa, 17; on the tedium of being an art collector, 6

Getty Center for Education in the Arts (later Getty Education Institute), 49

Getty Center for the History of Art and the Humanities (now Getty Research Institute), 49, 68, 111, 113, 196–97

Getty Center (Los Angeles), xi; aerial view of, *56*; design and building of, 57; earthquake damage to, 73–74; impact of opening of, on Master Plan, 145; model of, *49*; opening exhibition at, 57; Scholars program at, 68; use of travertine stone in, 76, *154*, 155–56

Getty Conservation Institute: architectural identity of, in first Master Plan, 111; assignment of conservation laboratories to, 113; creation of master's program in conservation of ethnographic and archaeologi-

cal materials, 68, 74, 77; establishment of, 49

Getty Education Institute, 49

Getty Foundation, 49

Getty Grant Program (now Getty Foundation), 49

Getty Information Institute, 49

Getty Museum (Ranch House), *6*. *See also* Ranch House; acquisition of antiquities and furniture for, 6, 8; creation and early operations of, 5; decision to build new structure for, 9–10; designs for extension of, *10*, *11*; rendering of proposed museum building, *109*

Getty Museum (Villa): architectural precedents for, xii–xvi, xix, 204; architectural sources for, 129–32; conceptualization of, as an archaeological artifact, 75–76, 132–36, 161, 170, *170*; early conceptions of, 10, *10–11*; form and function in, xx, 108; historical accuracy of, prior to renovation, 173; as "ideal" model of a Roman house, 174; opening day, 48, *48*; as "philological" reconstruction, xix; reviews of, xviii, 48; selection of Villa dei Papiri as model for, xvii; as "space resource" for Trust, 145

"The Getty Museum Rises in Splendor" (Seldis), 17

Getty Ranch, 3

Getty Trust, xii. *See also* Board of Trustees; creation of, 5; and decision to expand programs, 49; and decision to select new museum site, 49; legal suit filed against, 81; resentment of art world toward, 49; status of, upon death of J. Paul Getty, 48–49; Villa as "space resource" for, 145

Glasbau Hahn (Frankfurt), *91*

glass collection, 55, *55*

glassmaking techniques, 55

Glyptothek (Munich), 78, *78*

Goethe, Johann Wolfgang von, 13

Goodhue, Bertram, xii

grant programs, 49

grave markers, 40

Grey, Elmer, xiv

Gribbon, Deborah, 69; *The J. Paul Getty Museum and Its Collections*, 5, 6, 155

groundskeeper's barn, 73

guest cottages, 57

Hadrian, portrait bust of, *16*

Hadrian's Villa (Tivoli), 16–17, *17*, 70, 78, 204

Handbook of the J. Paul Getty Museum (Malibu, 1986), 10

handrails, 177, *177*

Hearst, William Randolph, xii, 16–17

Hearst Castle (San Simeon), xii, xix; eclectic aesthetic of, xiii–xv; outdoor swimming pool at, 16–17, *17*

Herakles, statue of, 3, 5, 7. *See also* Temple of Herakles; as heroic ideal, 15; history of, 15–16; in *A Journey from Corinth* (Getty), 16; purchase of, by J. Paul Getty, 16

Herb Garden, 43, *47*, 76, 104, 122, 161

Herculaneum, 76; carbonized furniture found in, 37, 40; excavation of, 13, *133*, *134*

historical truth, in context and architecture, xvii

history: commercialism, in presentation of, 101, *101*, 103; referential treatment of, in design process, 159; replicas, in presentation of, 101, *101*, 103, 130; variety of presentations of, 130

Hodgetts + Fung Design Associates, 69

Holbein, Hans, *The Ambassadors*, 159

Homer, *The Odyssey*, 66

Hope Collection, 51

Hôtel Salé, 79

House of the Cryptoporticus (Pompeii), 34

House of Diomedes (Pompeii), 27, 34

House of Livia (Rome), *33*, 43, *43*

House of Loreius Tibertinus (Pompeii), *42*, 43

House of Menander (Pompeii), 34

House of the Deer (Herculaneum), 33

House of the Dioskouri (Pompeii), xv, 78

House of the Faun (Pompeii), 27, *27*, *28*

House of the Fruit Orchard (Pompeii), 34, 43

House of the Great Fountain (Pompeii), 43, *46*, 83

House of the Griffins (the Palatine), 33

House of the Relief of Orestes (Pompeii), *23*, 33, 34

House of the Samnites (Herculaneum), 22, 27, *63*

House of the Skeleton (Herculaneum), 43

household shrine, 37

Hunt, Myron, xiv

Huntington, Henry E., xiv–xv

Huntington Art Gallery (San Marino), xii, *xiii*, xiv, xix

Huxtable, Ada Louise, 69

Hygieia, statue of, 51, *51*

iconographic installation, 83, 85

Imperial Villa (Oplontis), *20*, 78

impluvium, 82, 194, *194*

information desk, 60, *150*

information terminals, 89, *90*

Inner Peristyle. *See also* peristyle gardens, Outer Peristyle: access of galleries to, *83;* addition of East Stair to, 174, *176;* color mock-ups for, *186;* gardens in, 43; Ionic capitals of, *26;* natural light in the galleries surrounding, *191;* painted decoration of, 30, 33, *33;* prior to renovation, *64;* theatrical productions presented in, 66, *66;* view into, from southwest corner of roof, *61*

installation: and mounting of artwork, 85, 87, *87, 90;* planning for, 83–91; thematic, 83, 85; use of anchoring system in, 65; use of attachment points in, 89, *90, 93*

Internal Revenue Service, 49

Ionic capitals, *26*

Israel, Callas, Chu, Shortridge Design Associates, 69

Israel, Frank, 69, *70*

The J. Paul Getty Museum and Its Collections (Walsh and Gribbon), 5, 6, 155

Jackson, Reginald, 214

Jashemski, Wilhelmina, 43

Jaulmes, Gustave-Louis, xvi

Johnson, Bradley, 157, 214

Josse Collection, 3

Joubert, Gilles, 9

A Journey from Corinth (Getty), xvii, 16

Julius Caesar, 14

Kallmann McKinnell & Wood Architects, 69

kantharos, depicting Odysseus in the Underworld, *54, 55*

Karbowsky, Adrien, xvi

Kelly, Niall, 71, 214

kitchen garden, 43, *47*

Kurutz, Denis, 43, 78, 214

Lacy, Bill, 69

landscape architecture, 43

Langdon Wilson Architecture Planning, xv, 214; in design of Getty Villa, 27; designs for extension of the Getty Museum, 10, *10, 11;* elevation and floor design of, of south vestibule, *35;* as executive architects of renovation project, 71, 108

language analogy, 108, 133, 201. *See also* vocabulary

Lansdowne Athlete, 51

Lansdowne Collection, 3, 5, 7, 15, 51

Lansdowne House (London), 37

lararium, 37

laurel wreath, *26*

Le Vane, Ethel, *Collector's Choice,* 3, 16

lebes, decorated with the relief protome of a satyr and inlaid with silver, *54, 55*

legal issues, 81, 197–98

Leo Castelli Gallery, 159, *160*

lighting. *See also* natural lighting: artificial vs natural, 190, *190, 192;* bronze *torchères,* on East Stair, *189;* goals for, in renovation, 60–61, *61;* issues concerning, on upper level, 40, 50; solutions for, in ceiling design, 90, *92*

loading dock, 66, 108, *143, 149*

Lofgren, Peter, 78, 115, 214

Los Angeles County Museum of Art, 51, *51*

Los Liones Drive, 74

Louvre (Paris), 79

Love, Mimi, 78, *88, 89,* 129, 214

Love, Tim, 78, 115, 129, 214

Ludwig I of Bavaria, xv, 204

MacDonald, William, 69; presentation of, on the eruption of Mt. Vesuvius and its aftermath, 99

Machado, Rodolfo, xii, *107;* and creation of archaeological conceit for Master Plan, 75–76, 132–36; selection of, as renovation architect, 71; on study trip, *183*

Machado and Silvetti Associates, 69; changes to, upon receipt of Getty commission, 107; in competition for selection of site-planning architect, 99, 101–5; competition sketchbooks of, *102, 103;* creating of renovation teams at, 129, 173; residence designed by, 103, *103;* "signature" architecture of, 174; and *Taberna Ancipitis Formae—Architectorum Machadus Silvettusque Mirabile Inventio,* 159, *160*

main staircase, 174–77, *175, 176, 177*

Maison Grecque (Cap-Ferrat), xv–xvi

Maiuri, Amedeo, 37

Marquez, Francisco, 3

Marshall, Ann, 213

Master Plan: approval of, by Board of Trustees, 127; creation of archaeological conceit for, 75–76, 132–36; early site plan for, *118;* final site plan for, *147;* initial conclusions of, 111–12; model for, 77; phasing of, 74, 77, 117–18; reestablishment of single phase in, 145–46; twenty-year, reservations concerning, 74

Master Plan, Phase I, 74; creation of Entry Pavilion in, 119, *119,* 121, 124, *124;* inclusion of programmatic elements in, 142, *143;* model of, 77; "reversible" entry-sequence solution in, *124,* 124–26; site plans for, *118, 143;* unveiling of model of, 142

Master Plan, Phase II, 124–26, *125*

master's program on the conservation of ethnographic and archaeological materials, 68, 74, 77

Mattei Collection, 9

Mazarin Venus, 5, 6, *8,* 9

medicinal plants, 43, *47*

Meier, Richard, xi, 56; modernist vocabulary used by, at Getty Center, 155

Men and Heroes Gallery, *178, 182*

Mies van der Rohe, xviii

mock-ups: color, for Inner Peristyle, *186;* full-scale, of Outdoor Theater steps and seats, *156, 157;* of room's corner, in test of design elements, *86,* 183

models: of alternative designs for Entry Court, *120;* of Auditorium, *138;* of gallery design elements, 85; of Phase I of Master Plan, 77; showing new buildings surrounding Theater Plaza, *126*

modernism, xviii, 99

Molitor, Bernard, 3

Moneo, Rafael, 150; and "The Solitude of Buildings," 201–2

Monkey Court (now Conservation Court): position of, in North Campus, 146; view of fountain in, 5, 6, 68, *113*

Morgan, Julia, xii

Morley Construction Company, 150–51, 197, 214

mosaic: ancient, in gallery floor, 37; in floor of Temple of Herakles, 34, *38, 39;* in fountain of East Garden, *46;* in gallery floors, 87, *88, 89;* as glassmaking technique, 55, *55;* of sea nymphs, above Tea Room *nymphaeum,* 43; tumbling-

blocks pattern, at House of the Faun (Pompeii), 27, *28*
mounting, of artwork, 85, 87, *87, 90*
Mt. Vesuvius, 10, *98*, 99
Munitz, Barry, 77, 213
murals: ancient inspiration for, 30, *33*, 33–34; in Garden Tea Room, *42*, 43; in House of Livia, *43*
Musée de l'Institut du Monde Arabe (Paris), 79
Musée Picasso (Paris), 79
Museo di Capodimonte (Naples), 78
museum design: in contemporary architecture, xi; and creation of social space, 194; modern context in evolution of, xi; as reflection of the character of the collection, xiv–xv; "thematization" in, 101, *101*, 103
Museum Management Program (now Getty Leadership Institute), 49
Museum of the Agora (Athens), xix
museum store, 77, 139–41
music stand, *8*, *9*

Naranjo, Richard, 78
National Archaeological Museum (Naples), 14, 78
National Gallery (London), 9
natural lighting. *See also* lighting: in East Stair, 177, *177*; environmental considerations in using, 50; in gallery surrounding Inner Peristyle, *191*; importance of, in display of antiquities, 190; lack of, on upper floor, 40; as priority of renovation, 60–61, *61*, *92*; skylight as source of, *92*, *192*, *193*; use of, as design element, 130, 132; vs artificial lighting, 190, *190*, *192*

neighbors: houses of, in relation to villa site, 24, 25, *143*; legal battles with, 81, 197–98; privacy concerns of, 66; reestablishment of single phase as goodwill gesture towards, 145–46
neoclassicism, xiii
Neuerburg, Norman, xii, xix, 22, 108; in design of Getty Villa, 27, 30, 33–34, 40, 50, *63*; elevation drawings of, for Getty Villa, *22*; and replication of ancient furniture, 37
Normand, Alfred Nicolas, 204
North Campus, 142–43, *147*; emergence of, as nonpublic area, 146–50; Monkey Court's position in, 146; site model for, *148*; staff cafe as "hinge" of, 147
north facade, *11*
Ny Carlsberg Glyptotek (Copenhagen), 78, 79, *183*
nymphaeum, 42, 43, 83

objet trouvé, xxi
Odysseus in the Underworld, *kantharos* depicting, *54*, 55
Office Court, *149*
office space, 48, 55, 57, 77, 146
Onesimos, 51
Oppenländer, Erwin, 55, *55*
orthogonal grid, 126
Our Lady of the Angels Cathedral (Los Angeles), 150, 197
Outdoor Theater, 77; addition of, in renovation, 66; ancient inspiration for, 78, 79, *80*; centrality of, in renovation project, 197–98; under construction, *96*, *144*; as described in competition sketchbook, *111*; design scheme for, *76*; in entry sequence, 117, *123*, 161; full-scale stair and seat mock-up of, *156*; as "hinge" of site organization, 196, 198; proposal of original site for, 73,

111; in relation to strata wall, *140*, 141–42; relocation of, 113–15, *114–15*; "rotated grid" in placement of, 126–27, *127*; sculptural form in, 157–59, *157*, *158*; as seen from Arrival Balcony, *168*, *169*
Outer Peristyle. *See also* Inner Peristyle; peristyle gardens: acanthus plants in, *45*; cast laurel wreath, *26*; Doric colonnade in, *23*; gardens in, 43, *44*, *45*; open colonnade of, 30; painted decoration of, 30, 33, *33*; perspective down west side of, *31*; reflecting pool in, 30, *32*

Pacific Coast Highway, 74, 75, 104
painted decoration: ancient inspirations for, 30, 33–34, *33–34*; in Garden Tea Room, *42*; in House of Livia, *43*
Paintings Conservation laboratory, 77
Palazzo Altemps (Rome), 78
Palazzo Ruspoli (Rome), 78
Pali, Zoltan, 214
Palladian architecture, 10, *11*
Pantheon (Rome), 79
papyrus rolls, 13–14, *14*
Parker, Claude I., 3
parking, 27. *See also* garages; expansion of available space for, 65; impact of twenty-year Master Plan on creation of, 74; as part of entry sequence, 59–60, 73; and proposal for a camper-lot garage, 104
A Passion for Antiquities: Ancient Art from the Collection of Barbara and Lawrence Fleischman (Getty Villa), 61
pathway. *See* walkway, raised
paving, pseudo-Roman, 26, 59
pedestals, *86*, *88*, *90*, 91
The Penitent Magdalene (Titian), 4

Pergamon Museum (Berlin), 78
peristyle gardens. *See also* Inner Peristyle; Outer Peristyle: in Imperial Villa in Oplontis, 20; in Villa dei Papiri, 18; in the Villa San Marco, 29
peristyle house (Delos), xvi
Philodemos of Gadara, 13–14, 16
"Pierre Menard, Author of Don Quixote" (Borges), xvii, xxi
Piso Caesoninus, Lucius Calpurnius, 14, 16
Planning Commission, 197
Plautus, *Cassina*, 66
Pliny the Younger, 204
podium: as architectural device, 148, *148*; creation of, by subterranean garage, 146; in creation of a service court, 149
poetic estrangement, tradition of, 159
The Pompejanum (Aschaffenburg), xv, xvi, xix, 78, *184*, 204
Ponce de Leon, Monica, 214
Pontremoli, Emmanuel, xvi
Poppaea, 20
porte cochere, 152, *153*
Portrait Head of a Balding Man, 52
Portrait of Anne, Countess of Chesterfield (Gainsborough), 9
Portrait of James Christie (Gainsborough), 4, 5
Portrait of Marten Looten (Rembrandt), 4
Posillipo (Bay of Naples), 14
postmodernism, xviii
Price, Merritt, 78, 213
Prince Napoleon's Pompeian House (Paris), 204
programmatic elements: assignment of buildings for, 113; in design of entry sequence, 122, 124; establishment of, in research and education, 49; in formalization of design process, 110–11; site plans addressing, *110*

Psiax, 51
public drop-off area, 152, *153*
public services. *See* amenities

Ranch House, xv, xvi, xx.
 See also Getty Museum (Ranch
 House); aerial view of, *2*;
 assignment of, to Research
 Institute, 113; conversion of, to
 office space, 48, 55, 57; crowded
 conditions in, *9*; decision to
 save, in renovation, 71, 73;
 gallery of ancient sculpture in,
 7; gallery of old master paintings in, *9*; use of, as J. Paul
 Getty Museum, xii, 5, *6*; view
 of, in entry sequence, *123*;
 view of south side of, *3*; view of
 the Monkey Fountain courtyard of, *6, 68, 113*
Rathaus, xiii
Raurica, Augusta, 204
red-figured vases, 51
Reese, Thomas, 69
reflecting pool, *x*, 30, *32, 175*
Reinach, Théodore, xvi, xviii,
 78–79, 204
Rembrandt: and *Portrait of Marten
 Looten*, 4; and *St. Bartholomew*,
 5, 9
renovation project: archive of
 plans concerning, 196–97;
 assignment of existing buildings during, 113; competition
 for selection of site-planning
 architect, 69–71, *70*, 99, 101–5;
 conjectures concerning, 170–
 71; cost prohibitions on, 74;
 creation of Master Plan for,
 71–77; creation of twenty-year
 Master Plan for, 74; legal issues
 stemming from, 81, 197–98;
 limitations of site in, 112–13;
 model for Phase I of, 77;
 need for, after transfer of non-
 antiquities, 49–51; Planning

Commission approval for, 197;
 reconversion to single-phase
 plan in, 77; reinterpretation of
 building as artifact in, 75–76,
 132–136, 161, 170, *170*; reorganization of site for behind-the-
 scene access, 73, *121*, 122; study
 trips in support of, 78–79, *78–
 80*, 129–30, *131*, 132, 183, *183,
 184*
reproductions/replicas: of art-
 works, 60; confusion created by
 use of, 60; controversy on use
 of, in museums, 37; and dangers
 of "thematization," 101, *101*,
 103; in presentation of history,
 101, *101*, 103, 130
research programs: and creation
 of Villa Scholars program,
 66, 68; support of Trust for, 49
restaurant, 161
restrooms, 60, 75, *150*
"reversible" entry sequence, 124–
 26, *124, 125*
reviews, xviii, 48
Reyes, Ysidro, 3
rhyta, 40
Richard Meier & Partners
 Architects, 57
Risenburgh, Bernard II van, 3, *4*
roads: fire road, 58, 59; Pacific
 Coast Highway, 74, 75, 104;
 pseudo-Roman, *26, 59*
Robert F. Wagner, Jr., Park
 (Manhattan), 107
Rockefeller, John D., xix
Roman First Style wall painting,
 33
Roman House (Basel), 204
Roman Second Style wall painting, 33, *33*
Romano, Giulio, xiv
Room of Colored Marbles: ancient
 sources for, 34, *34*; inspiration
 for floor of, *23*, 34; sculpture of
 young centaur in, *36*
"rotated grid," 126–27, *127*

Rountree, Stephen, *49*, 69, 71, 213
Royal Palace (Caserta), 78
Royal-Athena Gallery, 37, *40*
Rubens, Peter Paul, xiv, 4, *6*, 9

"The San Diego Look," xii
San Simeon. *See* Hearst Castle
 (San Simeon)
Sansovino, xiv
scarab, Etruscan, with kneeling
 archer, *51*
Schinkel, Karl Friedrich, 204
scholars program, 49, 66, 68
Scully Hall (Princeton
 University), 107
sculptural form, in Outdoor
 Theater, 157–59, *157, 158*
sculpture. *See also* statues:
 Cycladic female idols of the
 folded-arm type, *53*; Cycladic
 seated harpist, *53*; table
 support, with two griffins
 attacking a stag, *53*
sea level, 122, *122–23*, 124
security desk, 60
Seldis, H., "The Getty Museum
 Rises in Splendor," 17
service areas, 148, 149, *149*
Service Court, *149*
service tunnel, 108, *150*
Settis, Salvatore, 69
Sholl, Richard, 71, 214
Silvetti, Jorge, xii, *107*; on centrality of Outdoor Theater to renovation project, 197–98; on con-
 troversiality of sculptural form,
 157–59, *157, 158*; and creation
 of archaeological conceit for
 Master Plan, 75–76, 132–36; on
 news of legal breakthroughs,
 198; selection of, as renovation
 architect, 71; sketches of
 Outdoor Theater's steps by, *156*;
 on study trip, *183*
site organization, center of gravity
 in, *112*, 113, 117, *118*, 126, *126*

site plans: for entry sequence, *104*;
 in formalization of programmatic needs, *110*; for Master
 Plan Phase I, *118, 143, 147*; for
 North Campus, *148*; for theater
 plaza, *126*; of Villa dei Papiri, *15*
Siza, Alvaro, 69, *70*
sketchbooks, in selection of site-
 planning architect, 70, 70–71,
 102, 103
skylight gallery, 61, 92, 192–93,
 200
slot lighting, 90
Smith, Corbin, 71, 213
South Balcony, *166, 167*
south facade, *11, 153*
south vestibule, 33, *35*
special exhibitions: creation of
 suite of galleries for, 61, 64–65;
 inappropriateness of ground
 level for, 83; and *A Passion
 for Antiquities: Ancient Art from
 the Collection of Barbara
 and Lawrence Fleischman*, 61
SPF: architects, 197, 214
St. Bartholomew (Rembrandt), 5, 9
St. Louis World's Fair, xvi
Staatliche Kunsthalle (Karlsruhe),
 78
staff: office space for, 48, 55, 57,
 77, 146; parking for, 74, 77
staff cafe, 147
staircases: Cafe Stair, *197*; East
 Stair, 174–77, *175, 176, 177*;
 inadequacy of, in entry
 sequence, 50, 60; lighting in,
 189; at north end of garage, *50*;
 symbolic symmetry in, 196, *197*
statues. *See also* sculpture: of
 Crouching Aphrodite, *6*; of
 the Elgin Kore, *4*; of Faustina,
 5; of goddess Hygieia, *51*; of
 Herakles, 3, 7; of Leda, 3;
 of the Mazarin Venus, 5, 6, *8*;
 of Venus-Hygieia, 37, 40, *40*; of
 a woman as Cybele, 9; of young
 centaur, *36*

Steiner, Marianne, 52

Steiner, Paul, 52

Stenfors, Jeffrey, 214

Stoa of Attalos, reconstruction of (Athens), xix, *xix*

strata wall: disengagement of Theater and Entry Pavilion from, *140*, *141*, 141–42; early sketches of, *137*; elevation drawing of, *155*; inspiration for, at ancient sites, 130, *133*, *134*; materials found in, 76, *154*,155–57, *155*; as unifying "language" of Villa, 133, *134*, 135, 136–38, 141

Strauss, Richard, *Der Rosenkavalier,* 159

study trips: in creation of a common vocabulary, 78–79, *78–80,* *131*; goals of, 129–30; in selection of wall colors, 183, *183*, *184*

Sutton Place, 9

symbolic symmetries, 196, *196*

Taberna Ancipitis Formae— Architectorum Machadus Silvettusque Mirabile Inventio (Machado and Silvetti Associates), 159, *160*

tablinum, 18, *34*, 60

Talk to Her (Almodóvar), 159

Taplin, Oliver, *The Wanderings of Odysseus,* 66

tax considerations, 4, 49

Tea Room, *42*; concerns regarding, in renovation planning, *114,* 115; design elements of, 40, 43; fountains of, *42*, 43; painted decoration in, *42*, 43

technology: in collection and diffusion of knowledge, 49; in transformation of design process, 129

Tehrani, Nader, 214

Temple of Athena Alea (Aegina), *78*

Temple of Herakles, 33. *See also* Herakles, statue of; ground plan for, *38*; inspiration for dome of, 79; mosaic floor in, 34, *38, 39*

terrazzo stone, 178, *178*

textiles, 4, *9*

"The Solitude of Buildings" (Moneo), 201–2

Theater. *See* Outdoor Theater

theater, classical, 113–14, *114*, 115

theater (Autun), *114*

Theater Plaza: as center of gravity, *112*, 117, *118*, *126*; as hub of activity, *116*, 117; resolution of crowding in, 138–41, *139*; site model for, *126*

theater (Pompeii), 78, *80*

theatrical productions, 66, *66*

thematic installation, 83, 85

"thematization," 101, *101*, 103, 170, 203

Theseus Painter, 40

Thorvaldsen, Bertel, xiv

Thorvaldsens Museum (Copenhagen), 78, 79, *80*, *184*

threshold: Atrium as, 196, *196*; Entry Pavilion as, 159, *162–65*; symbolic symmetries of, 196, *197*

Tiano, Hy, 71

Tier, Carole, 10

Titian, *The Penitent Magdalene*, 4

topographical conditions. *See also* Cañon de Sentimiento: in adoption of horizontal terraces as organizational principle, 136; of Cañon de Sentimiento, *106*; in creation of a center of gravity for site, *112*, 112–13; in creation of entry sequence, 122, *122–23*; and the necessity of "listening" to the site, 108, 201; in placement of Outdoor Theater, 127, *127*

traffic patterns, 74–75

travertine stone: at Getty Center, *154*; as link between Villa and Getty Center, 76; in strata wall, *154*; as symbol of the Getty, 155–56

True, Marion, 69, 71, 78, 186, 188

tunnels, 108, 150

University California, Los Angeles, 68, 77

upper level: access to, prior to renovation, 65; Beaux Arts architecture of, 40, *41*; inspiration for vaulted corridor on, 79, *80*; lighting issues on, 40, *41*, 50; and need for context with lower level, 50, 51, 60, 173

vase collection: acquisition of Bareiss collection, 51, 52; amphora, by Bareiss Painter, 52; black-figured *pelike*, 40; cup, depicting the suicide of Ajax, 52; red-figured, 52, *53*

Venetian (Las Vegas), *101*

Venturi, Robert, *Complexity and Contradiction in Architecture,* xviii

Venus-Hygieia, statue of, 37, 40, *40*

vessels: in Bareiss Collection, 51, 52; bronze *lebes* decorated with the relief protome of a satyr and inlaid with silver, *54*, 55; *bucchero*, 40; drinking cup, depicting the suicide of Ajax, 52; Egyptian *krateriskos*, 55; glass, 55, *55*; wine cup, silver, depicting Odysseus in the Underworld, *54*, 55

Vesuvius, 10, *98*, *99*

villa, ancient Roman: atrium in, *19*, *21*; entry sequence in, 59, 60; gardens in, *20*; Hellenistic model as archetype for, xvi;

Pliny the Younger on, 204; rarity of second floors in, 174–76; as reflection of aristocratic aesthetic, xvi; study of, by design team, 78–79, *78*, 129–32, *131*; typical layout in, 18

Villa dei Papiri (Herculaneum): challenges in adapting to museum function, 18, 22; elevation reconstruction of, 18, 22; excavated section of, *12*, *128*, *134*; ground plan of, by Karl Weber, *15*; history of excavation and mapping of, 13–14; layout of, 18; marble pavement found in, 34; papyrus rolls found in, 13–14, *14*; "reconstruction" of, as Getty Villa, xii, xvii, 10; sketch of, superimposed on photo of Cañon de Sentimiento, *24*

Villa Floridiana (Naples), 78

Villa Kerylos (Cap-Ferrat), xvi, xix, 78, *78*, 79, 204

Villa Les Cèdres, 79

villa marittima, 18, 49

Villa of P. Fannius Synistor (Boscoreale), *33*, 33

Villa of the Mysteries (Pompeii), *34*

Villa Pignatelli (Naples), 78

Villa Rothschild (Cap-Ferrat), 79

Villa San Marco (Stabiae), *19*, *29*, *34*, 43

villa suburbana, 59

viridarium, 18, 43

visitor services. *See also* amenities: in expansion of Entry Pavilion, 151; site plan showing, *150*

Visitor Services building, *123*

Vitruvius, 59, 60

vocabulary: of confrontational juxtaposition, 173–74; creating a common, for display, 78–79; in design process, 130, 133, 135; language analogy in, 108, 133, 201

walkway, raised: in conceptuali-
    zation of Entry Pavilion, *104*,
    122, *164*; in exposition of villa,
    161; role of, in archaeological
    conceit, 75–76, *76*, *77*, 159, 161
wall, concrete, *105*
wall colors: exterior, 183, *186, 187*;
    selection of, 183, 186, *184–87*
wall paintings, 33, *33*, 34, *34. See
    also* painted decoration
wall treatments, 76, 85, *85*, *86*
Walsh, John, 69, 71, 78, 213;
    *The J. Paul Getty Museum and
    Its Collections*, 5, 6, 155; role of,

in preservation of Ranch
    House, 73
The Wanderings of Odysseus
    (Taplin), 66
Weber, Karl, xviii, 13; mapping of
    Villa dei Papiri by, 14, *15*, 18, 22
Weisweiler, Adam, 3
West Porch, *42*; adaptation of,
    as Tea Room seating area, 43;
    ease of movement to, 83;
    in entry sequence, 121, *121*
Weyden, Rogier van der, xiv
Wheatley, Guy, 213
Whitney, Barbara, 69, 78

Wight, Karol, 71, 78, 213
Williams, Curt, 71, 213
Williams, Harold, 49, *49*, 69, 73,
    77, 113, 213
Wilson, G., 6, 10
Wilson, Kelly, 214
Winckelmann, Johann Joachim,
    13
windows: covering of, on upper
    level, 40; design of, 188, *188*; in
    dome of Temple of Herakles,
    50; in establishing reference
    points, 194, *194*; in introduction
    of natural light, 60–61, *61*; in

lack of context between upper
    and lower levels, 50; in upper
    level, 40, 50, *61*, 194, *194*
Women and Children Gallery,
    179,193
Wright, Frank Lloyd, xiv

zoning, 81

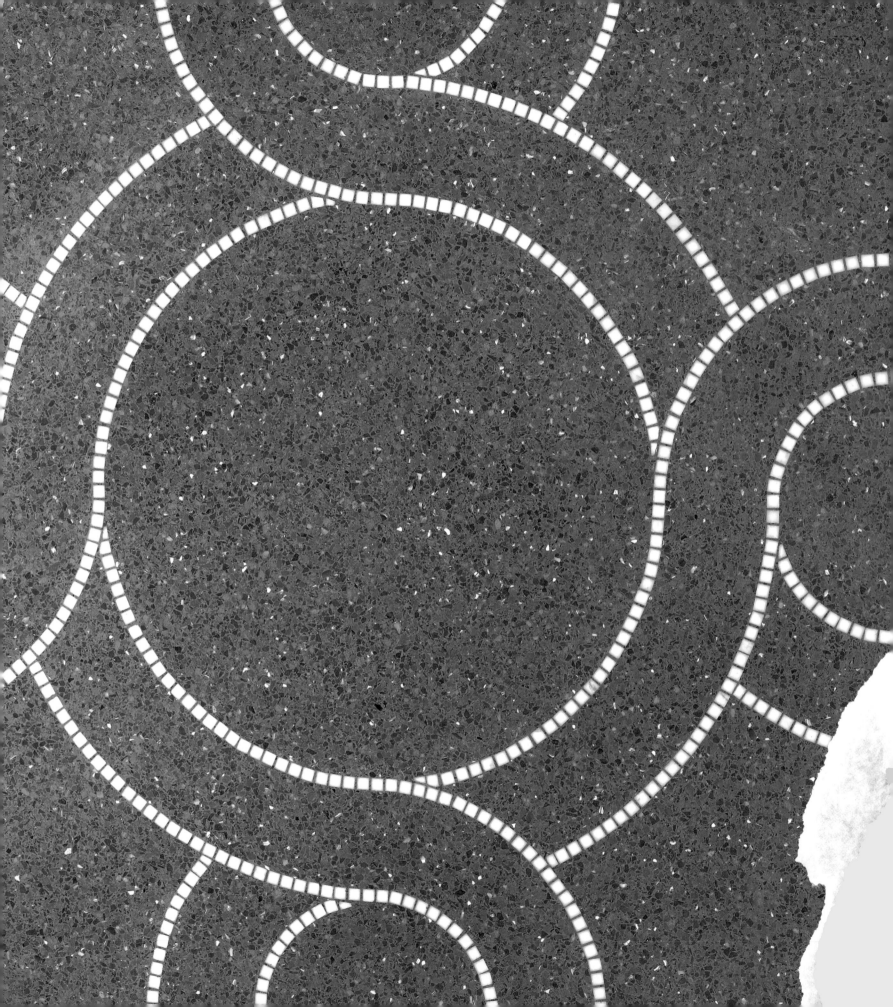